# *Baedeker's*
# MEDITERRANEAN
# ISLANDS

A SPECTRUM BOOK
**PRENTICE-HALL,** Inc., Englewood Cliffs, New Jersey 07632

**Cover picture:** Mazzarò, near Taormina, on the east coast of Sicily

136 color photographs
35 maps and plans
1 large folding map

Text:
Monika I. Baumgarten
Dr Gerhard Eckert
Armin Ganser
Dr Otto Gärtner
Dr Udo Moll
Dr Hans K. Weiler

Editorial work:
Baedeker Stuttgart
English Language: Alec Court

Cartography:
Ingenieurbüro für Kartographie
Huber & Oberländer, Munich
Georg Schiffner, Lahr

Design and layout:
HF Ottmann, Leonberg

Conception and general direction:
Dr Peter Baumgarten, Baedeker Stuttgart

English translation:
James Hogarth

© Baedekers Autoführer-Verlag GmbH,
   Ostfildern-Kemnat bei Stuttgart
   Original German edition

© The Automobile Association 57273
   United Kingdom and Ireland

© Jarrold & Sons Ltd
   English language edition worldwide

Licensed user:
Mairs Geographischer Verlag GmbH & Co.,
Ostfildern-Kemnat bei Stuttgart

Reproductions:
Gölz Repro-Service GmbH,
Ludwigsburg

The name *Baedeker* is a registered trademark

In a time of rapid change it is difficult to ensure that all the information given is entirely accurate and up to date, and the possibility of error can never be entirely eliminated. Although the publishers can accept no responsibility for inaccuracies and omissions, they are always grateful for corrections and suggestions for improvement.

Printed in Great Britain by Jarrold & Sons Ltd, Norwich

0-13-056862-7P

## Source of Illustrations

L. Ander, Munich (pp. 16, 33, 46, 61, 77, 78, 93, 97, 100, 101, 110, 111, 116; 123 (two); 124, 143, 148, 158, 216).
Anthony-Verlag, Starnberg (pp. 15; 44, foot; 80, top right; 162, right).
Assimakopouli, Athens (pp. 38, 43).
E. Bayer, Mainz (pp. 85, top; 72, top; 73, 214).
Bavaria-Verlag, Gauting (pp. 14, top; 14, foot; 19, right; 42; 69 (two); 70, top; 70, bottom; 80, bottom; 128, 133, 134, 161; 162, left; 182, 201; 217, bottom).
R. Braun, Karlsruhe (pp. 12–13, 218).
Cyprus Tourist Office, Frankfurt am Main (pp. 79, 81).
Delta, Athens (pp. 66, 67, 167).
French Government Tourist Office, Frankfurt am Main (p. 58 (two)).
D. Grathwohl, Stuttgart (p. 44, top).
Greek National Tourist Organisation, Athens and Frankfurt am Main (pp. 16, foot; 72, left; 90 (two); 95, 107, 108, 114, 147).
Hannibal (Tryfides), Athens (p. 85, foot).
Internationales Bildarchiv Horst von Irmer, Munich (p. 126).
Italian State Tourist Office, Rome and Frankfurt am Main (pp. 11, 41, 50, 89, 104, 120, 121, 149, 170; 172 (two); 176, 177, 179, 181, 190, 194).
E. Kock, Munich (pp. 86, 87).
E. Mahr, Munich (p. 184).
Bildagentur Mauritius, Mittenwald (cover picture; pp. 18, left; 37, 48, 105, 128, 169, 192; 217, top).
Olympic (Decopoulos), Athens (pp. 20, 55; 56, foot; 64, 65; 68, left; 84, 144, 145, 153, 163; 167, top; 186, right; 207).
Spanish National Tourist Office (p. 141).
Spyropoulos, Athens (pp. 21, top; 94, 162; 186, left).
Yugoslav National Tourist Office, Munich (p. 112).
Zentrale Farbbild Agentur GmbH (ZEFA), Düsseldorf (pp. 17; 18, right; 56, top; 60; 68, right; 80, left; 102, 103, 135, 174; 218, top right).

# How to use this Guide

The Mediterranean islands and some of their principal towns are described in alphabetical order. The names of other places referred to under these general headings can be found in the Index.

Following the tradition established by Karl Baedeker in 1844, sights of particular interest and hotels of particular quality are distinguished by either one or two asterisks.

In the list of hotels, etc., b. = beds, r. = rooms, SP = outdoor swimming pool and SB = indoor swimming bath. Only a selection of hotels can be given: no reflection is implied, therefore, on establishments not included.

The symbol ⓘ at the beginning of an entry or on a town plan indicates the local tourist office or other organization from which further information can be obtained. The post-horn symbol on a town plan indicates a post office.

This guidebook forms part of a completely new series of the world-famous Baedeker Guides to Europe.

Each volume is the result of long and careful preparation and, true to the traditions of Baedeker, is designed in every respect to meet the needs and expectations of the modern traveller.

The name of Baedeker has long been identified in the field of guidebooks with reliable, comprehensive and up-to-date information, prepared by expert writers who work from detailed, first-hand knowledge of the country concerned. Following a tradition that goes back over 150 years to the date when Karl Baedeker published the first of his handbooks for travellers, these guides have been planned to give the tourist all the essential information about the country and its inhabitants: where to go, how to get there and what to see. Baedeker's account of a country was always based on his personal observation and experience during his travels in that country. This tradition of writing a guidebook in the field rather than at an office desk has been maintained by Baedeker ever since.

Lavishly illustrated with superb colour photographs and numerous specially drawn maps and street plans of the major towns, the new Baedeker Guides concentrate on making available to the modern traveller all the information he needs in a format that is both attractive and easy to follow. For every place that appears in the gazetteer, the principal features of architectural, artistic and historic interest are described, as are its main areas of scenic beauty. Selected hotels and restaurants are also included. Features of exceptional merit are indicated by either one or two asterisks.

A special section at the end of each book contains practical information, details of leisure activities and useful addresses. The separate road map will prove an invaluable aid to planning your route and your travel within the country.

4          **Contents**

# Introduction to the Mediterranean Islands

**Cyprus**
**The French Islands**
**The Greek Islands**
**The Italian Islands**
**Malta**
**The Spanish Islands**
**The Tunisian Islands**
**The Yugoslav Islands**

Palaiokastrítsa, Corfu

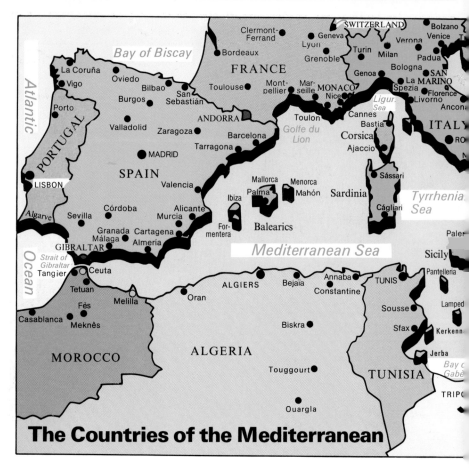

**The Countries of the Mediterranean**

From time immemorial the countries and islands of the Mediterranean, so generously endowed by nature, have drawn the peoples of other lands, and there are still few greater delights for the traveler than to discover the infinite variety and beauty of this sea – its coasts and inlets, its islands, its straits and channels, its ports and harbors, its towns with their picturesque old streets and bazaars, its ruins and monuments of the past, so abundant in this region where from the earliest times down to the present day the peoples and cultures of Europe, Asia and Africa have come into contact with one another and have left the indelible marks of their presence.

Everywhere in the Mediterranean visitors will experience not only the manifold charms of the scenery, the climate and the vegetation but also the interest and fascination of a region of ancient culture. There are few parts of the world where our knowledge of the past reaches so far back as in the Mediterranean area, a focal point of culture which exerted a decisive influence on the development of mankind during three millennia of prehistory and the Early Historical period and, directly or indirectly, in subsequent centuries. The relative nearness to one another of the shores of this sea, the many islands and the regular air currents, remaining constant for months at a time, mitigated men's natural fear of the sea and promoted the development of seafaring which liberated the peoples of the Mediterranean World from their confinement to the mainland.

It was in the Mediterranean countries, particularly in Greece and Italy, that those weapons of the mind were forged which – later sharpened and perfected in central and western Europe – have conquered the whole world. The Mediterranean was a great school for geographers and seafarers – Herodotus and Eratosthenes, Strabo and Ptolemy, Hanno and Pytheas, Toscanelli, Columbus, Amerigo Vespucci and Gabotto (Cabot) – the last of whom added a New World to the old one and established lasting contacts between

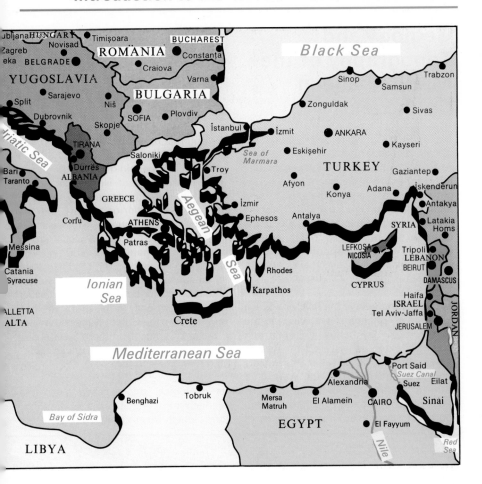

Europe and the rich cultures on the southern and eastern fringes of Asia. Italian seamen taught the skills of seafaring to the Spaniards and Portuguese, and directed the eyes of Frenchmen and many Englishmen across the Atlantic Ocean, which then began to play a major part in the cultural development of mankind.

The Romans recognized at an early stage that the position they had established on land could be maintained only if they controlled the sea. Favoured by Italy's central situation, they conquered the whole Mediterranean region and gave it a political and geographical unity which still finds expression in the name it has borne since Late Roman times (*Mare Mediterraneum*, the "sea in the middle of the land").

The advance of continental peoples to the coasts of the Mediterranean – the Germans and Slavs in the north, the Arabs and Turks in the south and east – destroyed this unity, and the discovery of the great seaways over the Atlantic deprived the

Mediterranean of its leading position. It was to recover its importance as a channel of world trade only with the opening of the Suez Canal in 1869.

*The Mediterranean* has a total area of some 1,160,000 sq. miles/3,000,000 sq. km and an average depth of 4760 ft/ 1450 m. Connected to it are a number of other seas – the *Adriatic*, the *Aegean*, the *Sea of Marmara* and the *Black Sea*. In the Adriatic, the northern Aegean, the Gulf of Gabès and the Strait of Gibraltar there is a tidal movement at the spring tides of over 20 inches/0·5 m; elsewhere the Mediterranean has no tide worth speaking of.

Although the Mediterranean region belongs in geographical terms to three different continents it is an area of distinctive and unified character, bounded on the north by a wall of mountains and even more sharply marked off on the south by a belt of desert. This unity is created by the mutual interplay of its climate, its vegetation and the sea, with variations produced by the varied topography of the land areas.

# Geology and Topography of the Mediterranean Countries

In terms of geological structure the Mediterranean region is part of the fault zone which encircles the earth, separating the northern and southern parts of the globe. In those areas where faults and folding have occurred, particularly on the edges of the continents, the interior of the earth has not yet settled into stability, as is shown by frequent earthquakes and recurrent volcanic activity (Bay of Naples, Mount Etna in Sicily, Dalmatian coast).

The Mediterranean is the relic of a much larger inter-continental sea which in the Mesozoic era lay between Europe and Africa and extended eastward into Asia. In this sea were deposited sediments (mainly limestone and clays) which were later pressed together by the lateral thrust of older rocks and forced upward to form land and mountains. Thus two-thirds of

Italy and four-fifths of Sicily consist of rocks formed on the sea bottom during the Tertiary period and sometimes even later.

The main part of the Mediterranean lies within this geologically recent trough, some 930 miles/1500 km wide, formed by the upthrust of the surrounding land and bounded on the north by the mountains of southern Europe and on the south by the great desert table of North Africa. It is broken up into the large north-western basin, the Adriatic/Ionian Sea and the Aegean with its scatter of Greek islands. Its coasts are much indented, and a profusion of peninsulas and islands, straits and inlets, give the Mediterranean its characteristic pattern. The greater regularity of the coastline in the smaller south-eastern part, to the south of a line running from the Gulf of Gabès by way of Crete and Cyprus to northern Syria, is due to a collapse of the North African tableland lying close to the coast.

Its geological origins have given the Mediterranean region a topographical form which distinguishes it from the

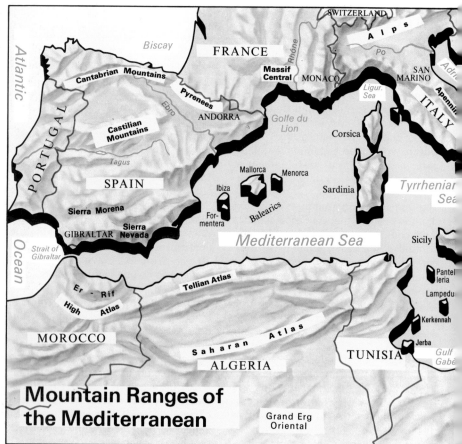

**Mountain Ranges of the Mediterranean**

Vesuvius, seen from the port of Naples

surrounding areas in important respects, notably in the intimate penetration of the sea into the land mass – more deeply here than at any other point in the inhabited regions of the earth. The distinctive nature of the surface topography and the other natural conditions which depend on this is also clearly evident when it is considered as a territory for human settlement.

In the structure of the Mediterranean area three older sections of the earth's crust are of particular importance – in the west the *Iberian Block* (Meseta), which was probably linked with the similarly structured Atlas Mountains of Morocco, in the middle the *Tyrrhenian Block* and in the east the *South-East European and Anatolian Block*. All three are built up from rocks

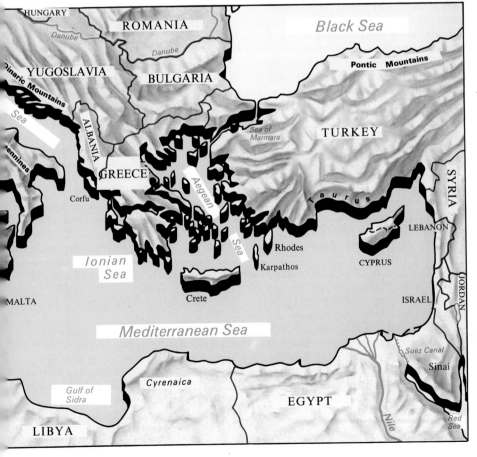

The Oasis of Zarzis on the Tunisian coast

of the Pre-Cambrian and Palaeozoic eras. Their strata were upfolded to form mountains, then eroded down to the basement rock, part of which was in turn overlaid by new beds formed from rock debris. Later these "rump blocks", originally uniformly flat, were broken up by crustal movements. In the Iberian Meseta and the Atlas foreland they have preserved their original form, while in the Tyrrhenian Massif, south-eastern Europe and Asia Minor they have been incorporated in later folded mountains and reshaped.

Against these older formations, deeply anchored in the earth's crust, were thrust the young folded mountains of the Tertiary period. Thus on the north side of the Iberian Block there rear steeply up from the Biscayan Collapse Basin the **Pyrenees** or *Pyrenean-Cantabrian Mountains* (reaching a height of 11,365 ft/3464 m in the Pico de Aneto), the eastern end of which is separated from the Meseta by the Ebro Collapse Basin; while abutting it on the south are the **Andalusian Mountains**, with Europe's highest peak outside the Alps, Mulhacén (11,421 ft/3481 m), lying only 22 miles/35 km from the Mediterranean in the Sierra Nevada. Like the Pyrenees, the Andalusian Mountains come immediately up against the Meseta for only part of their length, in the north-east, while to the south-east the fault zone

of the Guadalquivir Basin (Lower Andalusia) – the counterpart to the Ebro Basin in the north – thrusts its way between younger mountains and the old rump block.

Like the Pyrenees, too, which have a much-indented coast at their eastern end around Port-Vendres, near the French-Spanish frontier, the Andalusian Mountains are broken up by transverse faults, which at the eastern end have led to the separation of the Balearics from the mainland. – Of much greater importance is the *Strait of Gibraltar* fault zone, which separates Europe from Africa. A submarine ridge lying at an average depth of only 655 ft/200 m (maximum depth 1050 ft/320 m) runs for a distance of 27 miles/44 km from Cape Trafalgar to Cape Spartel in Morocco, separating the Alborán Collapse Basin to the east from the Andalusian Basin to the west, the Mediterranean from the Atlantic.

Thus the Iberian Meseta is bounded on both north and south by high mountains, with coastal strips at either end which offer little encouragement to traffic. It is cut off from Europe by the Pyrenees, from Africa by the Andalusian Mountains. To the east, between the Pyrenees and Cabo Nao, it falls down to a tectonically formed coast and to the sea. Its main slope,

however, is westward toward the Atlantic, which here has transgressed into the lower part of the river valleys of Galicia and Portugal, creating Lisbon's magnificent harbor at the mouth of the Tagus (Tajo, Tejo) and such major ports, farther north, as Porto (Oporto), Vigo, La Coruña and El Ferrol. – The plain of Lower Andalusia, the Guadalquivir Basin, also opens on to the Atlantic, occupying the fault zone between the Iberian rump block and the folded mountains of Andalusia. On this stretch of coast are the principal Spanish ports for traffic to and from Africa and Central and South America – Cádiz with its island harbor, Huelva at the mouth of the Guadalquivir, and Seville, 54 miles/ 87 km from its mouth but accessible by seagoing vessels at high tide.

In north-western Africa the Andalusian system of folded mountains has its counterparts in the **Rif Mountains** of Morocco and the **Tellian Atlas** of Algeria, which run south and then turn east, with ranges of hills separated by depressions striking out toward the coast at acute angles and falling steeply down to the sea. The whole of the north coast of Morocco, Algeria and Tunisia, in spite of numerous inlets gouged out by the sea and fault clefts, is a real barrier coast, on which it is difficult to establish even artificial harbors like that of Algiers. This enhances the importance of the *Gulf of Tunis* at its eastern end, reaching into the longitudinal trough between the Tellian Atlas and the Saharan Atlas; into this flow the Tunisian rivers, in particular the Medjerda coming from the west, and from it radiate the roads into the interior. Accordingly, like Lower Andalusia, this part of the country is accessible for human settlement and traffic; and from the foundation of Utica (11th c. B.C.) and the "new town" of Carthage, predecessor of present-day Tunis, this area was a focal point of communications and trade, and of great political importance in virtue of its location on the Sicilian Channel. From here the Carthaginians, the Vandals and the Moors ruled Sicily and Sardinia; and nearby Bizerta (Bizerte, Binzert) became one of the principal ports of Tunisia.

The *Sicilian Channel*, which links the western and eastern basins of the Mediterranean and separates the Atlas Mountains from the Apennines, is, like the Strait of Messina, the result of a transverse fault, which the sea has enlarged to a width of some 95 miles/150 km. – The **Maltese Islands**, a former tableland of tectonic origin, much dissected by faults, are in process of rapid erosion by the sea. The little island of *Pantelleria*, which rises to a height of 2743 ft/836 m in the 3300 ft/1000 m deep central part of

Natural arch on the island of Gozo (Malta)

a height of almost 6560 ft/2000 m above sea-level in the Aspromonte Range, separates the very young **Tyrrhenian Sea**, over 12,000 ft/3700 m deep, from the **Ionian Sea**, the deepest trough (14,440 ft/4400 m) in the Mediterranean. The curving line of the **Apennines** is no doubt influenced by the old tectonic land mass known as Tyrrhenis, which has been fragmented by crustal movements beginning in the Mesozoic, reaching their peak in the Late Tertiary and still continuing today; its remnants (eastern Corsica, Elba, Tuscany, Calabria, Sicily) were involved in the Apenninic folding movement. Western **Corsica** and most of **Sardinia**, on the other hand, are regarded as continuations of the Alps. Here, too, vigorously active volcanoes came into being along the fault lines, particularly between Cosenza and Palermo. In an arc running parallel to the steeply scarped coasts of Calabria and Sicily are the volcanoes of the *Lipari Islands* (Stromboli) and Ustica. To the north of these, on the inner side of the Apennines, are Vesuvius, Monte Epomeo, the Pontine Islands and the Alban Hills near Rome; to the south, on the outer side of the Apennines, Mount Etna on **Sicily**. At the end of the Tertiary period the Apenninic

the channel, is of volcanic origin. Volcanic activity is characteristic of such transverse faults occurring at points where young folded mountain ranges change direction sharply.

The land bridge from the southern edge of the Mediterranean fault zone, in the latitude of Cap Bon in Tunisia, to its northern edge is formed by Italy. Like a ridge in the earth's crust over 20,000 ft/6000 m high, Italy's semi-insular southernmost tip, Calabria, which rises to

Coastal scenery, Scopello, to the west of Palermo (Sicily)

Rocky coast near Bonifacio (Corsica)

Almost the whole of the NORTH-WESTERN BASIN of the Mediterranean is fringed by geologically young folded mountain ranges descending to the sea in picturesque cliffs. Only in the north-west, on either side of the Pyrenees, is it bounded by tectonically formed coasts. In this area it is accessible from the Iberian mountains by way of the Ebro and Jucar valleys, but the easiest approach routes are from Aquitaine by the Col de Naurouze and down the Rhône Valley. Thus the culture of the Mediterranean area was able to reach western and central Europe at an early period from Narbonne and Marseilles by way of southern France. Along the coast of southern France, however, there are also great gaps in the protective wall of mountains which, like the karstic area around Trieste and the Bosporus, allow heavy masses of cold air to penetrate into the warm Mediterranean region and move the northern boundary of Mediterranean vegetation farther to the south.

region underwent an upthrust, as a consequence of which the mountains developed into their present uniformity.

Of the channels which had linked the Tyrrhenian and Ionian troughs by way of southern Italy there then remained only the *Strait of Messina*, and even this was reduced to a width of 3500 yds/3200 m and to a depth at its northern end of only 335 ft/102 m. The violence of the upthrust is demonstrated by the marine deposits which cover the terraces of the Aspromonte Range in Calabria to a height of up to 3940 ft/1200 m above present sea-level. That the crustal movements have continued into recent times is shown by the variations in level that have been recorded during the historical period in the *Bay of Naples* and at other places. In this connection it is interesting also to note some comparable evidence from **Capri**: in prehistoric times, when the famous Blue Grotto was gouged out of the rock by the sea, the cave is believed to have been some 60 ft/18 m above sea-level, and to have still been 20 ft/6 m above the sea in the time of the Emperor Tiberius, when the flight of steps which is now partly under water was cut.

The open face of Italy is toward the west. On this side are its picturesque bays, its islands and its main cultural centers – Rome, Florence and the other cities of Tuscany, Genoa, Naples, Palermo. But it also has close connections with the south-eastern Mediterranean Basin through the port of Venice, long an important channel for trade with central and northern Europe, and the southern ports of Brindisi, Taranto, Messina and Syracuse.

The northern edge of the SOUTH-EASTERN BASIN of the Mediterranean (Cape Tainaron in the Peloponnese, the south coast of Asia Minor) lies below the 36th degree of latitude, as does the southern edge of the north-western basin. Off this south-eastern basin, less favored in other respects than the north-western one, open two arms, the **Adriatic Sea** and the **Aegean Sea**, pointing north-westward toward central Europe and south-eastward toward the Suez Canal and the Red Sea. The Aegean borders the **Balkan Peninsula**, which extends eastward to the Black Sea. In the western half of the peninsula are Yugoslavia, Albania and Greece, in the eastern half Bulgaria and the European part of Turkey. The Balkan Peninsula is a rump territory of older rocks formed by tectonic action into geologically recent mountains, with extensive basins between the mountains. The most fragmented part of this region is the island world of the Aegean, with the Cyclades, the Sporades, the large islands off Asia Minor and the narrow arms of the sea which separate them. Here, too, the much-fragmented and altered older formations are flanked by a younger folded system, the *Dinaric and Hellenic Mountains*, which extend in a broad belt around the southern coasts of the peninsula but close it off from the Adriatic. Containing a high proportion of limestones, these mountains rank with the

Brela: holiday pleasures on the Dalmatian coast

Syrian hills among the areas in the Mediterranean most affected by karstic action.

Just as the Balearics form part of the Andalusian folding system and Sicily and some neighboring islands belong to the Apennines, so the western belt of much- folded mountains in the Balkan Peninsula breaks down into a fringe of peninsulas and islands. Thus came into being a country which contributed so much to Western culture, the sea-girt mountainous land of Greece. The folded ranges of Greek mountains turn eastward – as can be seen with particular clarity in **Crete** –

Aghios Nikólaos, Crete

Petra tou Romaiou, on the south-west coast of Cyprus

to link up with the *Taurus* of Asia Minor. Thus the Balkan Peninsula and Asia Minor are the two piers of a bridge which carried traffic from the ancient cultural centers of Mesopotamia and Syria into Europe and which still points the way for the great transcontinental routes between Europe and western Asia.

The south-eastern basin of the Mediterranean, to the south of Malta, Crete and **Cyprus**, lies within the area of the extensive *Saharan and Arabian Tableland*, which includes the whole of North Africa, apart from the Atlas regions, together with the Levant. The basin was created by a collapse on the edge of this tabular area. In contrast to the much-indented coastline of most of the Mediterranean, the coast in this area is fairly regular; it lacks harbors and offshore islands, and has no large rivers apart from the Nile, which draws its water from the Abyssinian Highlands beyond the desertic tableland and from the tropics with their abundance of rain. Alexandria has almost the only natural harbor on this stretch of coast, the distinctive character of which is formed not only by the religion and language of its inhabitants but also by the very nature of the country.

This part of the Mediterranean – or at any rate the **Levantine Basin**, to the east of the narrower part of the sea between Crete and Barqah (Africa) – is geologically young. The Barqah uplands (ancient *Cyrenaica*), which rise to an average height of 1640 ft/500 m, consist of marine deposits of the Late Tertiary period. The *Nile Delta*, originally an inlet of the Mediterranean which for a time was

linked with the Red Sea, may have come into being as late as the Glacial period.

Beyond the Red Sea the desert areas of North Africa are continued in the deserts of the Arabian Peninsula; to the north is the Syrian Desert. Along the western edge of this desert tableland runs the fault line at the south end of the great Syrian Rift Valley, continuing down the Gulf of Aqaba into the Red Sea, the Erythraean Rift Valley, which came into being at about the same time. On either side of these long narrow troughs, in places reaching a depth of almost 2625 ft/800 m below the level of the Mediterranean, strips of the earth's crust little wider than the rifts were thrust up to a considerable height. In spite of heavy erosion these still reach a height of over 9850 ft/3000 m in the **Lebanon** and **Antilebanon** mountains. Against the great mountain wall of Lebanon the sea winds, heavily laden with moisture, discharge their load in the form of rain, so that the coastal strip, here 9–12 miles/15–20 km wide, is covered with lush subtropical vegetation.

To the north-east of the Greek Archipelago the **Black Sea** reaches farther into the land mass of Europe. Like the Caspian, it is a remnant of the Sarmatian Sea of the Tertiary period. It was first linked with the Mediterranean by the tectonic collapses of the Glacial period and by subsidences which led to the Bosporus Valley being drowned by the sea.

# Climate

The climate of the Mediterranean region is characterized by **hot, dry summers** and **mild, wet winters**. In the late spring there is usually a sharp rise in air pressure over northern Europe; and the belt of high pressure then moves south, finally reaching the Mediterranean. As a result there is a sudden cessation of rainfall in that area in June. The Pyrenees and the Alps act as barriers preventing the flow of Arctic cold air into the Mediterranean region, while in the south the Atlas Mountains shut off the Western Mediterranean against the hot winds from the interior of Africa. – Under the influence of solar radiation the surface temperature of the sea rises in summer to 68–86 °F/20–30 °C. Average air temperatures in July range between 72 °F/22 °C in the Western Mediterranean (Barcelona 72·7 °F/22·6 °C, Genoa 75·4 °F/24·1 °C) and 81 °F/27 °C in the Eastern Mediterranean (Alexandria 79 °F/26 °C, Athens 81 °F/27 °C). – Cool winds blowing off the sea make a stay on the coast agreeable even in the heat of summer. Farther away from the coast of southern Europe and nearer the North African coast the summer drought period increases steadily in length: at Tripoli (Libya) it lasts for seven months, at Alexandria for eight or nine, while in central Italy it falls to two months, on the Riviera to one.

From the fall onward the climate of the Mediterranean region is influenced by areas of low pressure over the Atlantic. Rain now begins to fall, more heavily in the Western than in the Eastern Mediterranean. The average air temperature in winter ranges between 46 °F/8 °C in the Aegean and 61 °F/16 °C off the Egyptian coast. – During the winter months there may be severe storms, as well as cold winds from the north (the mistral in the Lower Rhône Valley, the bora on the Dalmatian coast) and hot winds from the south (the sirocco). The surface temperature of the Mediterranean is relatively high even in winter, ranging in the coldest month (February) between 45 °F/ 7 °C and 63 °F/17 °C; and as a result the winds which blow off the sea at this time of year warm up the air over the land. In general winter temperatures in the Mediterranean area, in places sheltered from the wind and to an increasing degree from south-east to north-west, are up to 14 °F/8 °C higher than in other countries in the same latitudes.

Beach near Calvi (Corsica)

The climate of the coastal regions is influenced not only by solar radiation and rainfall but also by the temperature patterns of the Mediterranean itself. The submarine ridge in the Strait of Gibraltar prevents the cold water from the deeper levels of the Atlantic from entering the Mediterranean Basin: only the warmer upper current is allowed in, and this can be traced along the whole length of North Africa and up to the Syrian coast. Other currents branch off in a northward direction in the Levantine-Aegean, Adriatic and north-western basins, flowing counter-clockwise. Water also flows into the Mediterranean from the Black Sea by way of the Bosporus, the Sea of Marmara and the Dardanelles. Apart from the water brought in by rivers (in the south mainly the Nile) the Mediterranean receives little fresh water. Since the rate of evaporation during the period of drought is very high (annual average 51 inches/1·3 m) the water of the Mediterranean has an above-average salt content, reaching 3·9% in the warmest parts (in the oceans about 2·7%).

The mild weather which prevails throughout the year in the Mediterranean region influences both the architecture of the coastal areas and the way of life of the population. Since sunshine and warmth suit most people's constitution, large numbers of holiday resorts have grown up on the coasts of the Mediterranean, and the islands have also become very popular holiday places.

**Summer weather in the Mediterranean:** see map in the Practical Information section.

# Plants of the Mediterranean

The Mediterranean countries have none of the dense forests found in more temperate latitudes, and in many areas there is only a sparse covering of vegetation. As a result of the low rainfall in the summer months (Naples 2·7 in./69 mm, Athens 1·4 in./36 mm, Algiers 0·9 in./ 24 mm, Malta 0·2 in./6 mm) many Mediterranean plants have developed leathery leaves and other features which prevent the water they contain from evaporating too quickly in the strong sunshine. Often, too, the leaves of these plants have a thin coating of wax. Plants of this type are know as "xerophytes" (drought-lovers). Some plants also have provision for storing water (e.g. thick fleshy roots); these plants are known as "succulents". *Cacti* and bulbous and tuberous plants can also store water for long periods. *Agaves* and *prickly pears*, now thought of as typically Mediterranean plants, are in fact introductions from America which have reverted to the wild. In the gardens of the Mediterranean, particularly in Italy, on

Agaves on Corsica

the French Riviera and in Algeria, plants from all over the world can be found.

A species particularly characteristic of the Mediterranean region is the **olive tree** (*Olea europea*), and the area within which it grows coincides broadly with the zone of Mediterranean vegetation. Since the olive tree yields olive oil, a product of great economic importance, it is intensively cultivated in many Mediterranean countries, particularly in Spain and the Atlas regions. The olives, which change color from green to blackish blue as they ripen, need a long period of dry weather in summer to reach full ripeness. The harvest begins in November and continues until March. In some Mediterranean countries long-established traditional methods of extracting the oil are still practiced alongside modern factory methods.

Huerta, Valencia

Olive trees, Andalusia

The **mulberry tree** (*Morus alba, Morus nigra*) came to the Mediterranean area from East Asia. The black mulberry is now cultivated for the sake of the berries; formerly it was grown primarily for its leaves, which were used to feed silkworms. – In the lowland regions of the Mediterranean evergreen plants, shrubs and trees flourish. In wooded areas the *holm oak* predominates, but the *laurel*, the *cork oak* and various pines also occur. Prominent among the pines is the **stone pine** (*Pinus pinea*), which prefers coastal areas. The umbrella-shaped crowns of this pine are a characteristic feature of the Italian landscape. The cones of the pine were used by the Romans as a decorative motif, particularly in architecture. In the Eastern Mediterranean the stone pine gives place to the **Aleppo pine** (*Pinus*

*halepensis*). Other trees characteristic of the Eastern Mediterranean are *cedars* (particularly in Lebanon) and *cypresses*.

More commonly found than trees, however, are bushes and shrubs, which form an almost impenetrable scrub, the **macchia** (French *maquis*), or the more open **garrigue** (Greek *frygana*). In these areas are found mastic trees, myrtles, strawberry trees, brooms, tree heaths, liana-like climbing plants and the resinous and aromatic cistus, which is covered in spring with large flowers resembling wild roses. Here, too, occurs the dwarf fan palm, the only species of palm native to the Mediterranean.

In sharp contrast to the areas with a sparse growth of natural vegetation are the cultivated areas, mostly with artificial irrigation, in the basins near the coasts and along the coastal strip, such as the *huerta* of Valencia and the *terra di lavoro* around Naples. In these areas, in gardens and orchards, are grown **citrus fruits** (oranges, lemons, mandarines, etc.), *pomegranates, figs, dates* and *almonds*, together with *olives* and **vines**. The grapes are mainly used to make wine, but some are dried to produce currants and raisins. – Different crops are grown at different levels; at the lower levels vegetables and grain. The predominant types of grain are *wheat* and *maize*; rice is less commonly grown. The vegetables grown include particularly tomatoes, artichokes and paprika. – Mediterranean plants are also grown on the North African coast in the Western Mediterranean; but dates ripen best in the oases of North Africa.

In the Eastern Mediterranean, particularly along the North African coast, the vegetation is very sparse indeed as a result of the still greater aridity of this region. In the Nile Delta there are large cotton plantations: the conditions here are excellent for the growing of cotton, which requires plenty of water and at least 200 frost-free days.

In addition to wild plants and plants grown to provide food large numbers of **ornamental plants** grow in the Mediterranean area, many of them cultivated in parks and gardens – camellias, climbing roses, narcissi, hyacinths, carnations, orchids, magnolias and bougainvilleas, an introduction from South America which produces showy red bracts in spring.

# Marine Life

Visitors sailing in the Mediterranean will occasionally observe **dolphins** accompanying the boat; and Greek and Roman legends tell of dolphins rescuing men in peril on the sea. The dolphin is a marine mammal which orientates itself by a form of echo-sounding. Two species are found in the Mediterranean – the smaller *common dolphin* (*Delphinus delphis*), up to $6\frac{1}{2}$ ft/2 m long, and the *bottle-nosed dolphin* (*Tursiops truncatus*), which may reach a length of 10 ft/3 m. In captivity dolphins are quick to learn, and can be seen performing their tricks in many "dolphinaria".

The largest group of marine creatures in the Mediterranean consists of the **fishes**, of which there are some 450 different species. There are also numerous species of seaweed, gastropods, crustaceans, bivalves, sea-urchins, starfishes, sponges and corals with their intricately ramified tree-like structure. Sea water teems with countless tiny organisms, drifting plants and animals, forming the *plankton* which is the staple food of larger sea creatures.

In the sea and along its coasts there are a variety of different biospheres or habitats. The most important of these in the Mediterranean are the rocky coasts, the flat coasts, the open sea and the sea bottom.

In the rocky coastal areas a distinction must be made between the zone above sea-level which is washed by the sea only at certain times and the underwater zone. The rocks themselves are often undermined by *piddocks* (a mollusc). In the marginal area between the sea and the land live *periwinkles*, sizeable crabs including the *ghost crab, limpets, barnacles* and *sea woodlice*. In the underwater zone *mussels* and *oysters* are found. *Sponges*, often very colourful, cling to the underwater rocks like cushions of moss. Some marine animals in this zone look like plants, for example the *sea anemones*. They have long tentacles with which they catch small swimming creatures such as shrimps, and countless stinging cells with which they paralyze and kill their prey. In this zone, too, live *eels* and *morays*.

The marine creatures of the flat coasts are adapted in a great variety of ways to living in sand. Many of them hide in the sand, with only a small part of their body remaining visible. The *sand fleas* which are usually present in great numbers are easily overlooked, being of the same color as the sand. In the case of some of the **molluscs**, including the heart cockle and the Venus shell, only the tip of the breathing-tube emerges from the sand; and yet under the surface of the sand they are so numerous that in places they form a regular pavement of shells.

From the economic point of view the open sea is the most important of the zones, since this is the area in which fish can be caught. In the waters of the Mediterranean **sardines** and **anchovies** are common, together with **mackerel, tuna**, *sunfish* and **cuttlefish**. The swarms of sardines and anchovies are caught in a kind of large seine-net thrown out from the boat, the bottom of which is gradually pulled tighter so that the fish can find no way out. Tuna are caught with ring-nets.

The open sea is also the home of **sharks**, which can be dangerous to man. Most of

Dolphin fresco, Knossos (Crete)

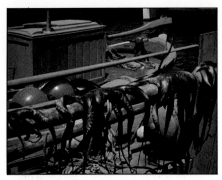
Cuttlefish, Greece

*hound, greater weever, ray,* various *flat fishes, gurnard* and *barbel,* together with *invertebrates* including sea-cucumbers, tunicates, starfish, spider crabs, hermit crabs living in borrowed shells, prawns and crayfish.

The various fishes differ considerably from one another in appearance. Some have the normal fish shape, but others are flat fish, and there are also such curious creatures as the *sea-horse* (*Hippocampus*). And even greater than the variety of form is the variety of color and markings. The color is produced by special color cells (chromatophores) in the skin, and in many species the effect of the coloring is still further enhanced by the relief pattern of the scales.

them are carnivorous, but are usually content with small sea creatures; the shark is, however, a predator, equipped with large jaws and pointed teeth for tearing its prey. The predatory reaction is often triggered off by movement on the part of a potential prey: thus a man swimming with vigorous strokes will attract a shark's attention to himself. Sharks are not so common in the Mediterranean as in tropical waters, but they are frequently found along the main shipping routes, coming quite close to the coast.

The numbers and types of marine creatures found on the sea bottom depend on the depth of the water; but so long as some light reaches the bottom a variety of creatures adapted to life in this zone will be found. Among the fish commonly found on the bottom are the *smooth-*

# History of the Mediterranean

From the earliest times the Mediterranean region has occupied a position of predominant importance in the history of mankind. This resulted from the fact that countries inhabited by very different peoples were brought into contact with one another across a sea which was relatively easy to traverse, long before modern methods of transport led to a further shrinking of distances. An inland sea which offers favorable conditions for seafaring enables different peoples to establish relations with one another at an early stage in their development; and the closer the association between the habitable land and the sea which affords a means of communication, the greater the influence of the sea on the peoples concerned. The Mediterranean offers the best example of this.

The situation of the Mediterranean between the three continents of the Old World, with their inexhaustible reservoir of population of the most varied ethnic origin, led at a very early period to the establishment of active interrelationships which played a major part in the development of culture. A constant succession of new forces came to the fore, giving rise to an incessant process of interaction and interchange such as occurred in no other region of the earth. The links between the various Mediterranean countries which in spite of all conflicts and rivalries have

Fish ready for the market, Martigues (France)

persisted down to the present day, the reaching out from each continent to the others, the fragmentation of the land into islands and peninsulas, the broad similarity of climate, vegetation and soils: all these factors combined to create in the peoples of the Mediterranean a recurrent urge to expand over the whole region.

At the same time the intricately indented conformation of the Mediterranean coasts was a factor tending toward segregation and isolation and giving rise to a separatism which set limits to the urge toward unification. This interplay between amalgamation and separation is the special characteristic of the Mediterranean region. The constant alternation between conflict and reconciliation and the constant succession of new peoples and cultures gave this region the extraordinary importance it enjoys in the history of the Ancient World, and thus in the whole history of mankind.

PREHISTORY. – It must be admitted that the Mediterranean region is no longer the undisputed source of all human history which, together with the area between the Nile and the Tigris, it represented not so long ago. Historians and archeologists have now discovered cultural interconnections which have to some extent deprived the Mediterranean of its absolute supremacy; and the old tag "ex Oriente lux" ("out of the East comes light") is now contradicted by the rival view that in the earliest periods the broad movement of culture was from west to east. But even if it is true that history did not begin in the ancient East and then move to the west and north by way of Asia Minor, Greece and Italy, liberating the peoples of Europe from their historical limbo by bringing them Mediterranean culture, this does not by any means diminish the incomparable importance of the Mediterranean area in the history of the world. In the light of modern research its significance as the collecting basin for the various cultural currents which developed at a very early period in the surrounding regions of Europe, Asia and Africa remains unchallenged. It is now necessary, however, to accept that there were a number of different cultural foci, and that during prehistoric times the western and southern centres of development extended their influence over the sea at an earlier stage than those in the east. These cultures, which produced the cave-paintings of southern France, north-eastern Spain and North Africa, the *nuraghi* (tower dwellings) of Sardinia, the *talayots* (round towers) of the Balearics and the great temples of Malta and built their megalithic chamber tombs all over the area between the Bay of Biscay and the Red Sea, advanced eastward and reached their peak in the island world of the Aegean, where Western and Eastern influences met and mingled.

EARLY HISTORICAL PERIOD. – The **Crete** of the legendary King Minos with its splendid palace culture (2nd millennium B.C.) marks the high point of pre-Indo-European culture in the Mediterranean. The Cretans were also the first seafaring people known to us, whose trade – though not their political and military power – extended westward to the Strait of Gibraltar and northward as far as the Baltic. During this period, too, *Babylon* and *Egypt* achieved positions of great historical importance; but their cultural achievements did not reach out beyond the valleys of their rivers, and only in the intellectual field did they exert any lasting influence on neighboring countries.

From the second quarter of the 2nd millennium B.C. life in the Mediterranean World underwent far-reaching changes. The peoples of central and northern Europe pressed into the countries to the south and over the course of many centuries dispossessed the existing occupants and settled in the Balkan, Appeninic and Pyrenean peninsulas, some of them moving farther east into western Asia; they were unable, however, to gain a foothold in Africa. During the first wave of incomers the Greeks of the Mycenaean period were able for a time to maintain the heritage of the declining culture of Crete; but when further hordes came down from the north the springs of development dried up, and southern Europe sank for many generations into historical obscurity.

These were the centuries during which the **Phoenicians** established their dominance in the Mediterranean. The influence of this trading people extended from their coastal cities in Syria along the coasts of Europe and Africa and their offshore islands to the Atlantic Ocean, and the many trading-posts they established amounted to a kind of colonial empire.

## The Odyssey

The shores of the Mediterranean and its innumerable islands and islets were already densely populated in prehistoric times. This was the end point of the migrations of many different peoples, whose origins are often lost in obscurity. These new peoples brought with them a great variety of cultural, social and religious characteristics. They soon learned the craft of seafaring, which led them to distant and unknown shores. As early as the 2nd millennium B.C. the Greeks, vying with the Phoenicians in their skill as seafarers, ventured on hazardous voyages as far afield as Spain, founded trading-posts and colonies all along the coasts of the Mediterranean and carried on an extensive trade with other peoples.

In the course of their voyages the seafarers encountered cultures unknown to them, always strange and sometimes menacing and mysterious. When they returned home they recounted their experiences and impressions in seamen's yarns – tales of incredible adventures which were then handed on from generation to generation by word of mouth.

The most famous work of this kind is Homer's "Odyssey", a heroic epic in flowing and artistically wrought hexameters. It relates the adventures of the wily *Odysseus*, King of Ithaca, who took part in the Trojan War and devised the stratagem of the wooden horse. On his voyage home after the end of the war he was detained by the nymph Calypso on the island of Ogygia; then, released by Calypso after seven years at the behest of the gods, he built himself a boat and continued his voyage, but was caught in a fearful storm and cast ashore on the island of Scheria in the land of the Phaeacians. There he was hospitably received by King Alcinous (Alkinoos) and his daughter Nausicaa, to whom he related the dangers and adventures he had undergone, including his encounters with the one-eyed Cyclops Polyphemus and the enchantress Circe, his journey to the realm of the dead, his escape from the Sirens and the sea-monsters Scylla and Charybdis, the loss of all his companions as a punishment for killing the sun god's oxen and finally his seven years with Calypso. Alcinous then gave him a boat to take him back to Ithaca, where he killed the insolent suitors of his wife Penelope and restored order in his kingdom.

Homer's "Odyssey" probably represents a collection of seamen's tales by a number of different authors of the Mycenaean period (1300 B.C.), interwoven with the social circumstances and mythological conceptions of the 7th and 6th c. and skilfully fitted together by Homer. This is suggested by the stylistic differences and imbalances between different parts of the poem.

Repeated attempts have been made over the centuries to follow the course of Odysseus's wanderings and to identify his various ports of call. For this purpose both geographical similarities and archeological evidence have been called into play. Thus the little island of **Gavdos** off the south coast of Crete has been thought to be Calypso's island of Ogygia. **Corfu** (*Kérkyra*) was already held in Antiquity to be the island of Scheria, in the land of the Phaeacians, and the little offshore islet of *Pontikonísi* (Mouse Island) was seen as Odysseus's boat, turned to stone by Poseidon. Strabo identified the sea-monsters **Scylla** and **Charybdis** as two violent whirlpools on either side of the Strait of Messina. The German archeologist Wilhelm Dörpfeld believed the island of **Lefkás** to be Odysseus's kingdom of **Ithaca**, basing himself on topographical parallels between present-day Lefkás and Ithaca as described by Homer; the excavations he carried out there, however, proved inconclusive.

Ithaca, legendary home of Odysseus

The far-flung commercial domination of the Phoenicians, however, did not lead to any major spread of Eastern influence in the Mediterranean. After the Phoenician interlude Indo-European peoples asserted their leadership, and only in **Carthage** was there established in the 8th c. B.C., in the territory of the nomadic Berber tribes of North Africa, an outpost of Oriental power and culture which was later to achieve a position of international importance.

ANTIQUITY. – The Mediterranean region played a pre-eminent part in the development of mankind, for here were evolved the fundamental ideas on which human life and human society are still based. The **Greeks**, emerging in the 8th and 7th c. B.C. from a preliminary Archaic phase, developed into a people of thinkers and artists who laid the foundations of European intellectual life. On the shores of ancient Hellas the fertile Greek intelligence asserted itself at this early stage in human history, and following the establishment of Greek colonies around the Mediterranean became the directing force of a "Greater Greece" which took in not only the lands bordering the Aegean but also southern Italy, Sicily and the eastern regions of North Africa and even extended as far west as the Iberian Peninsula.

The **Etruscans** established themselves for a time as a considerable sea power, but from about 500 B.C. were gradually driven back; but the Greeks were unable to expel the Carthaginians, now rising into a major Power, from their European possessions. – The westward advance of Persian power was halted in the Persian Wars of the 5th c., which briefly brought the Greek peoples together in a united effort. The 4th c. saw the rise of the kingdom of *Macedon*, which amalgamated the fragmented territories and city states of ancient Greece and under Alexander the Great carried Greek culture into Asia, where it mingled with Oriental elements.

When the thrust of Hellenism faltered in the east it found in Rome an heir to continue its work in the west. In contrast to the Greek cities, Rome ceased at an early stage to be a mere city state, expanded into the Italian regions and beyond the bounds of Italy, and became a great State and finally a World Empire. An incomparable skill in the art of government and a fierce drive for power brought this disciplined people of the Tiber Valley to greatness and made them masters over the other peoples of the Mediterranean. The Roman Republic overthrew Carthage in the three Punic Wars and established a foothold in the Greek and Oriental World; then from the 1st c. B.C. onward the Romans brought the whole of the Mediterranean region into a unified State, the Roman Empire. At the same time this simple peasant people assimilated the superior culture of the Greeks and by their victories in the west, south and east made themselves its savior. The Latin civilization which was now imposed on the conquered peoples became the intermediary in diffusing the spirit of Hellenism.

To this cultural and political unity was then added a religious unity, binding the Mediterranean World into one great community and bringing the development of the Ancient World to a close. The Roman Empire with its Greek culture now became a Christian world empire, and the culture of Europe was fertilized by the Judaeo-Arab World with the idea of **Christianity**. State, culture and religion were denationalized and given a universal validity.

But Rome's creative force was now exhausted, and the Roman unified State, in which there was no room for any sense of nationality, fell to pieces. Imperial Rome was succeeded by ecclesiastical Rome, which set out on the task of winning over the peoples of the European continent to the culture of the Mediterranean by peaceful rather than by warlike means.

There now remained, however, only ruins to be passed on to the young peoples of the north, for the foundations of the older world had collapsed in an immense process of political, economic, social and intellectual disintegration. With the fall of the Ancient World unity gave place to separation; the division of the Empire into two in A.D. 395 was an early pointer in this direction. Western Europe, built up on Latin and Romance foundations, grew apart from eastern Europe and the Near East, where Hellenic and Oriental characteristics remained predominant, while at first North Africa was divided between a western and an eastern half linked with these two different cultures. Large areas broke away from these territorial groupings and began to strike out on their own; and the incursion of the Nordic peoples into the Mediterranean area merely set the seal on a development which was already under way.

THE GREAT MIGRATIONS (4th–8th c.). – In the turmoil of the great migrations the territory of the Ancient World took on a totally different aspect. The masses of barbarians pressing down from the north were drawn into the dying struggles of the Roman Empire, and poured in successive waves into the depopulated lands of the Mediterranean which now lay wide open to their passage. Prominent in this drive southward were a variety of **Northern Tribes** – *Visigoths* and *Ostrogoths*, *Vandals*, the *Suevi* and finally the *Lombards*. Although they failed to establish themselves in the south, finding an early grave rather than the new home they were looking for, they left a profound mark on the area. The loosely knit States they founded in Italy and the Iberian Peninsula initiated a fruitful mingling of races and created in the prevailing chaos – in which the new Roman Empire of **Byzantium** for a time established a unified State taking in almost the whole of the Mediterranean World – the focal points around which a new world of national States could develop.

During the conflicts of these centuries the Italian and Spanish nations gradually came into being, while in the territory of the *Franks*, which reached into the Mediterranean World in the coastal regions between the Pyrenees and the Alps and for a time even extended into Italy, the French nation was being formed. – In the east the **Slavs**, advancing from the Danube, succeeded in establishing themselves on the Balkan Peninsula. In this area the *Albanians* and *Greeks* were now joined by *Croats*, *Serbs* and *Bulgars*, creating an extraordinary mixture of peoples. Politically the Balkans now led a life of their own, marked by many vicissitudes, but culturally they were wholly under the influence of Byzantium, which broke away from the ecclesiastical authority of Rome and developed an independent culture of its own.

It thus seemed that the Mediterranean World had finally lost all unity; but now a new universal movement originating in Asia turned the trend of development back in that direction. **Islam**, a monotheistic religion like Christianity, stemmed from the same Oriental cultural soil as Christianity, now wholly Westernized, and sought to establish its validity as an expression of a renascent Oriental spirit. During the 7th c. the conquering armies of Islam advanced eastward, northward and westward, making the same claims to universality as the Christian Faith. Western Asia as far as the Taurus and the Indus was conquered and Arabized in a series of rapid campaigns. The old Roman and Christian culture of North Africa was now also destroyed; the **Arabs**, constantly reinforced, mingled with the Hamitic *Berbers* and occupied the whole area from the Gulf of Sidra to the Atlantic Ocean. Muslim armies also pressed far into the heart of Europe, seeking to subjugate the peoples of the west with fire and sword. Their advance was halted at Poitiers in 732 by the military power of the new Frankish kingdom, but Spain and Sicily remained in their hands. In the cultural field the Arabs established a dominance lasting several centuries, and their economic and intellectual activity made them the teachers of Christian Europe.

MIDDLE AGES. – The Mediterranean region was now divided into three cultural

and political spheres of influence – the *Germanic and Roman West*, the leadership of which, after the fall of the Frankish Empire, passed in 962 to the Holy Roman Empire, at first dominant over the Pope and later accepting his separate authority; the *Greek and Slav East*, which for a time was united under Byzantine rule, and the *Oriental territories*. It seemed at first that a state of peaceful coexistence would develop; but then came the **Crusades** – a form of Western counterblast to the Islamic advance – and the temperature rose again. The knightly armies of the West embarked on the sacred task of liberating Christ's tomb from the hands of the infidels; and in the same spirit of Christian enthusiasm the Reconquista was launched in Spain in the 11th c., marking the start of four centuries of conflict which won back the land of the Cid from the Moors. At the same time the *Normans* in southern Italy bent all their efforts towards wresting from Arab control the channel between Sicily and Tunis.

Only in the western and central Mediterranean did Christian forces achieve their aim. The ambitious attempts to bring the Oriental territories back under European influence and establish a new ethnic and cultural unity throughout the whole Mediterranean region foundered on the increasingly marked differences between the various parts of the region. The collapse of the old medieval idea of a unified Christian community was most strikingly shown by the self-centered policies of the rising Italian maritime cities – in particular **Venice**, which now established itself as Queen of the Adriatic. In 1204 Venice brought about the conquest of Constantinople by the Crusaders; but, like the Crusader States in the Holy Land, the Latin Empire of Constantinople soon collapsed (1261), and the Greek Empire was able to hold on to its much-reduced territory for another two centuries. Repeated attempts to restore the unity of the Greek and Roman Churches were no more successful than the effort to re-establish political unity.

RENAISSANCE. – After the ebb of the Crusading spirit the Mediterranean area returned to its former state. One result of this period of turmoil, however, was that Europe and the culture of Western Christendom gained military, economic and intellectual predominance over the Greek and Islamic cultures, both now in decline, and enjoyed a vigorous upsurge, based on the abandonment of the old ideals of the medieval Church in favour of a purely secular approach and on the rediscovered heritage of Antiquity. During the Renaissance, which brought mankind into the modern world, the Mediterranean again became the scene of imperishable cultural achievements of the highest quality. But at the same time the Renaissance saw the renewed emergence of individual national States.

The two great universal powers of medieval Christendom, the Empire and the Papacy, which had finally destroyed themselves in their contest for supremacy, were now compelled to give place to a series of smaller Powers centered on cities, while the Pope himself became a Renaissance prince as ruler of the *Papal States*. The spirit of ancient Greece was revived on the soil of Italy, and *Venice* and *Genoa* now played similar roles to those of Athens, Corinth and Syracuse in earlier days. They possessed powerful colonial empires in the Levant, and as commercial Powers with command of the sea exercised a kind of economic tutelage over the declining Islamic World. They were followed later by the cities of *Provence* and *Catalonia* in the west and the Dalmatian commercial republic of *Ragusa* (now Dubrovnik) in the east. Over and above all these smaller units, however, the distinctive characteristics of the newly emerging nations now began to find expression, taking visible form in the establishment of large national States. This process reached its conclusion in Spain and France before the end of the Middle Ages, while Italy, seat of the universal power of the Church, was still embroiled in local particularism and finally fell under foreign rule for several centuries.

Then once again the threat from the East welded the Europeans together, when from the late 14th c. onward the **Turks**, who had given up their nomadic life in Central Asia and settled in Asia Minor, began to spread over the whole of the Eastern Mediterranean. The Slav peoples of the Balkan Peninsula were subjugated, and in 1453 Constantinople was taken and destroyed. The Near East and North Africa became part of the Ottoman Empire, and it was only with great difficulty and effort that the peoples of Central Europe were able to halt the Turkish advance at the very gates of the West – at the First Siege of Vienna in 1529. The new

Christian Empire of the *Habsburgs*, which brought together the power of Austria and Spain, held large territories in Italy and for a time also incorporated considerable areas in the Germanic Principalities and in North Africa, became, in alliance with the now stronger Papacy of the Counter-Reformation, the savior of European Christian culture.

This was all happening at a time when the peoples of western and northern Europe, learning from the experience gained by the seamen of the Mediterranean, were setting out across the oceans and finding in tropical and subtropical countries fresh scope for expanding their trade and their political influence (discovery of America in 1492). The Mediterranean now became an inland sea, and the interruption of the old trade routes in the Levant accelerated the process. In consequence the Mediterranean region for a time lost its importance on the world stage, and the Germanic and Latin peoples of the north took over the cultural and political leadership of Europe. The political and economic existence of the people of the Mediterranean now became involved in, and subordinate to, that of Europe as a whole; and in this respect the old maritime city states were no exception.

16th–18th CENTURIES. – In this new development two factors went hand in hand and paved the way for a change. In the first place there was the collapse of the Turkish Empire: the question which now preoccupied the peoples of Europe was no longer the defence of their countries from the dreaded enemy of Christendom but rather the partition of the Ottoman Empire. On the other hand the consolidation of the large national States of northern Europe continued to make steady progress, and as their interests extended across the oceans the Mediterranean, too, became the object of their political and economic rivalries and the scene of their military encounters. And again and again the temporary predominance of one particular State gave rise to a striving for universal rule: after the empires of Charles V and Philip II of Spain came the great colonial empire of Louis XIV of France.

From the end of the 16th c. the *Dutch* and the *British*, the leading sea powers of the day, established firm footholds in the Mediterranean. France could do no more than maintain its position, on the basis of its traditional friendship with the Turks; and Britain, already mistress of the oceans, gained control of the Mediterranean from the Strait of Gibraltar to Alexandria and Constantinople. – Of lesser weight in the Mediterranean was the Danubian State of *Austria*, which since its victory over the Turks had become the heir of Venice and from its base at Trieste was competing for trade in Levantine waters. Even the little State of Savoy, later to bring about the unification of Italy, now raised its head. From the north-east, too, Peter the Great's new Slav State of *Russia* thrust into the Mediterranean on a broad front, practically controlling the development of the eastern part of the region during the 18th and the first half of the 19th c. and always cherishing the ambition to occupy the place vacated by Turkey.

Europe and European interests had thus become the determining factors in the history of the Mediterranean. Given the impotence of the Ottoman Empire, the Near East could now play only a passive role. **North Africa** intervened actively in developments, but its actions were obstructive and destructive rather than helpful. In this area, particularly in the Turkish tributary States of *Algiers*, *Tunis* and *Tripoli*, a flourishing trade in piracy had developed in the 16th c., and the divisions and conflicts between the European States allowed the pirates almost unrestricted scope. Even the great maritime Powers were obliged to ensure freedom of navigation for their ships by the payment of an annual tribute to these *Barbary corsairs*. The rulers of these loosely organized pirate States finally took advantage of the decline of the Ottoman Empire to become totally independent. On the Muslim as well as the Christian side this was a period of splitting up and fragmentation.

**19th CENTURY**. – To **Napoleon**, a Corsican and a "son of the Mediterranean", the idea of a unified Mediterranean region under the leadership of France came naturally, and in his plans for universal domination the Mediterranean was an element of central importance. He was unable, however, to realize his ambitions, and in the Wars of Liberation of 1808–15 the principle of the national State was victorious over Napoleon and the strivings of Revolutionary France.

Continually increasing in force, it has remained the determining factor of historical development down to the present day.

The desire of subject nations to achieve freedom and independence was the force behind the two great burning questions in the history of southern Europe, the Eastern Question and the Italian Question. After the restoration of the old order by the Congress of Vienna in 1815 two passionate *liberation movements* developed in the Italian and Balkan peninsulas. In the east, where the Ottoman Empire was increasingly powerless and a newly strengthened *Egypt* sought for a time to take its place as ruler of the Muslim World, the oppressed Christian peoples rose against their alien rulers and gained their freedom, with the European Great Powers playing a helping and regulating part. Between the Greek Rebellion and the Russo-Turkish Wars of the 1820s to the 1850s during which the Eastern Question became an acute danger for Europe, one after another of the European possessions of the Ottoman Empire broke free. But in spite of all its successes Russia was repeatedly prevented by the intervention of the other Powers from gaining control of the Bosporus. The Congress of Berlin in 1878 marked the end of a first phase in this development. There were now the independent States of *Greece*, *Romania*, *Serbia*, *Bulgaria* and *Montenegro* in the Balkans. After Russia's latest victory Turkey would have lost its last territory in Europe, in line with Russian wishes, had not the Great Powers – each of them unwilling to concede possession of Constantinople to any of the others – extended a protective hand over the Sultan.

During these decades **Italy** became a unified national State, and after an interruption of several hundred years the peninsula in the Central Mediterranean, belonging to both the western and the eastern basin, which had afforded the Romans such a well-placed base for the establishment of their Empire, recovered its national independence. The new State was established in the face of opposition both from the Habsburg monarchy and from the Papacy, which was reluctant to give up its secular possessions. Now expelled from Italy, Austria turned its eyes to the south-east and became a Balkan power by the occupation of Bosnia and Hercegovina.

During this period all activity in the Mediterranean region emanated from Europe. In the discussion of all matters concerning the political, economic and cultural life of this area the Islamic World still played a merely passive role. A further decisive step in this direction was taken by the involvement of North Africa in the historical development of the region. The activities and machinations of the Barbary States led France to intervene, and in 1830 part of North Africa became a French colonial possession – a final gift of the Bourbon kings to France. This marked the beginning, after a long pause, of a period of European expansion. The French example was followed by the new Kingdom of Italy, which crossed the Sicilian Channel, long the means of passage between the two continents, and occupied what is now Tunisia and Libya. The two Latin nations thus became involved in a contest for possession of North Africa.

A new factor of the greatest importance was the completion in 1869 of the *Suez Canal*, which gave the Mediterranean a wholly new character. Whereas it had previously been connected with the oceans of the world only by the Strait of Gibraltar, the piercing of the Isthmus of Suez made it an essential element in the world's seaways and one of the most important areas of sea in the world. The direct route from Europe to southern and eastern Asia, the importance of which was steadily increasing, was now very considerably shortened, and new commercial routes were opened up. Along with them were reopened the routes which had once been followed by Cretan, Phoenician, Greek, Arab and Italian merchants. The Mediterranean region once again began to play an active part in world history – a part reaching out far beyond its geographical bounds. This was a situation in which the peoples of the Mediterranean were offered the prospect of rapid development, but one in which they were tempted to enlarge their ambitions. The colonial expansion in which the European Powers became involved at this time was calculated to accelerate still further the pace of this development.

In these decades the Mediterranean acquired a wholly new importance for **Britain**. Undisputed mistress of the seas since the defeat of Napoleon and already in possession of *Gibraltar* (acquired 1704) and *Malta* (1800), it was now presented by the new political and economic conditions in the Mediterranean with an opportunity to strengthen its strategic and commercial position. It acquired the Suez Canal Co. (1869), established important bases along the Canal and – having acquired *Cyprus* at the time of the Congress of Berlin – soon afterwards gained possession of *Egypt* and with it undisputed control of the Suez Canal.

IMPERIALISM. – The British occupation of Egypt is commonly held to mark the beginning of the modern striving for world dominance. A parallel step was taken at the same time by **France**, which already held *Algiers* and in 1881 occupied *Tunis*, which the Italians had come to regard as their future colony. What now followed, reaching its peak in the First World War, was a competition between the European Great Powers for possession of the remaining independent Muslim countries and their desirable resources. The two great systems of alliances whose irreconcilable differences led to the outbreak of war in 1914 involved the Mediterranean in their imperialist activities: indeed they were almost more concerned with Mediterranean than with continental questions. Their main preoccupation was with the East and with North Africa, and Morocco, Tripolitania, Arabia, Syria and Mesopotamia were the territories which engaged the attention of European diplomacy. – In the Balkans a further complication was presented by the idea of the national State, as represented by the now independent countries of that region, which gave rise to an urge to complete, at the expense of Turkey and the Austro-Hungarian multi-national State, the process of development which had been left unfinished.

For decades the Powers, conscious of the danger of unleashing a world conflagration, kept matters within diplomatic channels; but the establishment of a French protectorate over **Morocco**, accompanied by similar action by Spain, led others to follow this example. Italy, which had joined the German-Austrian Alliance after the French occupation of Tunis but had later sought a *rapprochement* with France, occupied *Tripolitania* (1911), its claim to which had been recognized by the Entente Powers; and its war with Turkey gave the signal for further developments in eastern Europe. The Balkan peoples, incited by Russia, took to arms to assert their national claims against the Sultan; and although they then fell into dispute over the sharing of the spoils and were compelled to accept the establishment of *Albania* as a separate buffer State (1912), Turkey – whose only remaining territory in Europe consisted of Istanbul and its immediate surroundings – now seemed ripe for partition into European spheres of interest, more particularly since there was a nationalist movement in the Arab countries between the Taurus and the Indian Ocean, fostered by the Entente Powers, which seemed to threaten the Turkish presence in Asia.

**20th CENTURY.** – The **First World War** had basically arisen out of conflicts in the Mediterranean area, and was thus largely a struggle for dominance in the Mediterranean. The secret imperialist treaties which the Entente Powers had concluded among themselves and with Italy, which had joined the alliance, were all directed against Turkey and the Danube monarchy, and with the defeat of Germany and its allies they had every prospect of being put into effect. The collapse of Russia before the Allied victory, however, put a very different complexion on the situation at the end of the war. Austria-Hungary had disappeared from the map, and the Balkans and the East lay wholly at the mercy of the victors; but the creation of *Yugoslavia* and the consolidation of *Turkey* as a modern national State, together with the emergence of various *Arab national States* with a greater or lesser degree of independence, had effects which brought out sharp differences of view between the victorious Powers and turned the development of the Mediterranean region in new directions.

While in the west there were at first no major changes, since Spain had kept out of the war and was content to keep a firm hold on its zone of influence in northern Morocco, in the central Mediterranean *Italy*, now a Fascist State, felt that its sacrifices had not been adequately rewarded and put forward claims which amounted to a program for the establishment of a Mediterranean empire modeled on that of ancient Rome. It established a "protectorate" over Albania at the expense of Yugoslavia, and through a series of treaties of friendship with the other Balkan States, with Turkey and finally with the Soviet Union built up a strong position in the Eastern Mediterranean which was given additional support by the new Italian colonial possessions off the coast of Asia Minor (Dodecanese). In 1928 Italy gained a share in the administration of the internationalized town of *Tangier* on the Strait of Gibraltar. It concluded a Concordat with the Papacy and thus won valuable assistance in its conflicts with France. Britain's position in the Mediterranean was also directly affected. But bounds were set to Italy's political, economic and cultural hegemony in the Eastern Mediterranean by the concern of the smaller nations in the area for their independence. – In 1922, after violent disturbances directed against colonial rule, Britain was compelled to grant **Egypt** independence, though it still remained influential in the region.

In pursuing their imperialist policies the European Great Powers had very similar aims, though these might differ in many respects. Everywhere, however, Muslim national resistance to alien rule grew steadily stronger, and although the Turks, the Arabs, the Egyptians and the Berbers all went their separate ways the idea of *Pan-Islam* had already emerged.

The Italian involvement in the Spanish Civil War finally made unmistakably clear how firmly Mussolini was resolved to extend Italian influence throughout the whole Mediterranean World. Thanks to massive support from Fascist Italy and Nazi Germany (where Hitler had come to power in 1933) General Franco's Falange Party was able in 1939, after three years of bloody warfare, to put an end to the young Spanish Republic.

With Italy's entry into the **Second World War** in 1940 the Mediterranean once again became the scene of bitter fighting. Italy's drive for expansion on the European continent, to which Albania had fallen victim in 1939, led it to march into Greece in October 1940. But Mussolini's Greek adventure proved a fiasco, and Germany was compelled to go to the aid of its ally. In April 1941 Hitler launched a campaign against Greece and Yugoslavia. A military coup in the latter country threatened the position of the Axis Powers, and within a short time both countries were occupied. Crete was also taken by German troops.

In September 1940 Italian forces advanced on Egypt from Cyrenaica, but were defeated and driven back by General Wavell, and Cyrenaica fell into British hands. The Germans then intervened with Rommel's Africa Corps, and British forces were compelled in February 1941 to retreat. In June 1942 Tobruk, still held by Britain, was hard pressed, but Rommel's supply difficulties prevented him from winning a decisive victory. A British counter-attack then recovered Cyrenaica, and with the landing of Allied troops in Morocco and Algeria the Africa Corps was faced with a war on two fronts. In October 1942 General Montgomery's Eighth Army inflicted a crushing defeat on Rommel's forces, and it was clear that for the Axis Powers the war in North Africa was lost. In 1943 they evacuated Tripolitania, and after the war, in 1947, Italy finally renounced its claims to this territory. In 1952 it became independent, at first as a monarchy under King Idris; then in 1969 Lieutenant Muammar el-Gaddafi led a bloodless coup and established the Islamic Socialist Republic of **Libya**.

During the Second World War two other independent Arab States were established. In 1941 **Syria** and **Lebanon**, which at the beginning of the war were under French Mandate, declared their independence and were recognized by the Allies as Independent States in 1946.

SINCE THE SECOND WORLD WAR.
– With the defeat of Italy and Germany Italy's dominance in the Mediterranean area was destroyed and its influence permanently weakened. The immediate post-war years saw a reshaped Mediterranean World with newly formed States in the Levant and North Africa. In addition to Syria, Lebanon and Libya there was now also **Israel**, the emergence of which radically altered the political constellations of the Eastern Mediterranean. Israel declared its independence in 1948 after the expiry of the British Mandate in Palestine, and even before the status of the country could be settled by international agreements the Jewish population of the former Mandated Territory had asserted their independence by military action against the troops of the Arab League and the Palestinian population.

New shifts of power favoring the two Super Powers, the United States and the Soviet Union, now occurred, and the position of Britain and France in the Mediterranean was further weakened. In 1956 France granted independence to **Morocco**, and soon afterwards to **Tunisia**. The transition to independence did not go so easily in **Algeria**, which was fully integrated in France and ranked as a French *département*. There was much violence by the Algerian population against the French, which the French Army sought to repress by violent means. After years of unrest, long diplomatic exchanges and a coup by the army against the Fourth Republic, General de Gaulle finally recognized Algeria's independence in 1962.

Meanwhile, in Europe, the Mediterranean countries which had been involved in the war were concerned to return to normal as rapidly as possible and to come to terms with the shifts in power resulting from the war. Faced with domestic political and economic as well as international problems, France and Italy were ready to admit that the only prospect of a solution lay in the establishment of systems of alliances transcending national boundaries. In 1949 both States became members of NATO (although France withdrew from direct military cooperation with NATO in 1966), in 1951 they joined the European Coal and Steel Community and in 1957 the European Community.

**Spain**, which under the Franco régime had long been isolated, gained admittance to international organizations such as the United Nations and OECD only toward the end of the 1950s, and its opening-up was a gradual process. The end of the Franco era in the early 1970s was marked by separatist movements, particularly in the Basque country, and by increasing political unrest, but also by the first moves toward reform, though these bore fruit only after Franco's death under the freely elected Suárez Government, with Spain again a monarchy under King Juan Carlos I. In 1982 the Socialist Felipe González became Prime Minister.

**Yugoslavia** became at the end of 1945 a non-aligned Federal People's Republic, in which the former partisan leader Marshal Tito succeeded in uniting the country's different ethnic groups in a national Slav form of Socialism. – After a period of internal political turmoil **Greece** became a monarchy again, and in 1953 a member

Gibraltar

of NATO. A *coup d'état* in 1967 was followed by some years of military dictatorship. After the abolition of the monarchy in 1973 and the fall of the dictatorship soon afterward Greece finally became a democratic republic in 1974. A Socialist government came to power in 1981.

**Turkey**, which had been relatively unscathed by the Second World War, sought after the war to develop cooperation with the United States and became a member of NATO. During the 1970s, however, economic difficulties, domestic political controversies, terrorism by both the right and the left and conflicts with Greece – a fellow member of NATO – over the Aegean and Cyprus brought on a grave crisis. With international help the country has begun to recover from this crisis, but it will need further assistance to enable it to return to normal.

**Cyprus**, a British possession since 1878, became an independent republic in 1960 under the presidency of Archbishop Makarios, who had been leader of the independence movement as "Ethnarch" since 1950. In 1974 it was the scene of a rising by Greek officers seeking union with Greece, and this gave Turkey a pretext for occupying the nothern half of the island. In 1975 the occupied zone was unilaterally declared a Turkish Cypriot Federal State by the Turkish Government in Ankara.

The British colony of **Gibraltar**, acquired in 1704, became in 1969 an independent State within the British Commonwealth. Spanish claims to the territory – a majority of the population of which have expressed the desire to remain British – continue to be a cause of friction between Britain and Spain. The other British colony in the Mediterranean, **Malta**, became independent in 1964 and was declared a republic in 1974.

During the post-war period, however, the main political problems in the Mediterranean region have been centered on the **Middle East** (as what used to be called the Near East has become known since the last war). In recent decades this area – thanks to a situation of high strategic importance on the access routes to the Red Sea and the oilfields of the Arab countries, to the religious and ethnic conflicts between Jews and Arabs, to the Palestinian problem and the acts of violence by Palestinian irregular forces to which it gives rise – has lurched from one crisis to another and enjoyed no real peace. The armed conflict between Jews and Arabs which had accompanied the establishment of Israel broke out again in 1956. In October of that year British and French forces launched an attack on the Suez Canal Zone and Israeli troops occupied the Sinai Peninsula and the Gaza Strip, but were compelled by United Nations action, initiated by the Great Powers, to withdraw from the occupied territory.

The Eastern Mediterranean now increasingly fell into dependence on the Great Powers, which sought to increase their influence in the area by supporting one or other of the contending parties. The Soviet Union supported Egypt and Syria, while the United States gave massive assistance to **Israel**. In 1967 the *Six Day War* brought a further Israeli occupation of Sinai. In spite of Egypt's devastating defeat in this war military action continued for another three years, with increased activity by the Palestine underground army against Israel. In 1973 the Egyptians and Syrians took the initiative in attacking Israel, in what became known as the *Yom Kippur War*, but failed to achieve any decisive breakthrough. A phase of increased diplomatic activity led in 1974 to an agreement between Israel and Egypt on the disengagement of their forces. Then, after Egypt under President Sadat was once again opened up to Western influence and Sadat had paid a historic visit to Jerusalem, President Carter of the United States was instrumental in bringing about the Camp David Agreements of 1978, which led in 1979 to the signature of a peace treaty between Israel and Egypt and a year later to the establishment of diplomatic relations between the two countries. By the end of 1982 Israel had returned the occupied territory in Sinai to Egypt. The Palestinian problem, however, remained unresolved.

Under President Sadat **Egypt** had largely isolated itself from the other Arab countries by its cautious Middle East policy. Colonel Gaddafi of Libya, one of the leading figures in the Arab front against Israel, is a particularly virulent opponent of the Camp David Agreements. Under Hosni Mubarak, who became President after Sadat's assassination in 1981, Egypt is now seeking a *rapprochement* with the Arab League.

The crisis in Lebanon has also contributed to the turmoil in the Eastern Mediterranean. In this country situated at the meeting-place between the Christian and Muslim worlds there have been repeated outbreaks of armed conflict with all the characteristics of a civil war, and in the 1970s, after the Lebanese Government began to take a stronger line against Israel, a real and bloody civil war broke out between right-wing Falangists and left-wing Muslims and Palestinians. By 1975 the unity of the country had fallen apart, and in 1976 Syria felt compelled to intervene, while Israel made repeated military incursions into Lebanon.

In the spring of 1982 the conflict took a graver turn. In an operation code-named "Peace in Galilee" strong Israeli forces advanced into Lebanon, while the Israeli Government called for the withdrawal from the country of all members of the PLO (Palestine Liberation Organization). Pushing northward to Beirut, the Israelis bottled up in the western part of the city a considerable force of armed Palestinians and prominent PLO leaders. The United Nations Security Council passed a Resolution calling on Israel to put an end to hostilities. Thereafter, following the evacuation of the PLO chief Yassir Arafat at the end of August, most of his troops left the country. In May 1983 Israel and Lebanon signed an agreement on the withdrawal of Israeli troops, but Syria and the PLO refused to adhere to this agreement.

The situation in the European countries of the Mediterranean World in the early 1980s is characterized by the effort to achieve an international equilibrium between the two great blocs in east and west and an accommodation with the countries of the Third World: by the quest for a distinctive European identity and for greater European influence on international policy; by the struggle to establish European unity, in spite of the inevitable setbacks; and by the search for means of overcoming the present world-wide energy crisis with all the problems to which it gives rise. The complexities of the situation which confronts them have led the European countries to draw closer together. Greece has joined the European Community, while Spain and Portugal are both seeking entry and Spain has become a member of NATO.

The world has grown smaller, and as a result crisis situations in distant lands, well away from the Mediterranean, have their repercussions in Europe and in the Mediterranean region, where important traffic routes meet, where there is a permanent United States and Soviet naval presence and where some of the leading members of NATO are based. Today as in distant prehistoric times the Mediterranean lies at the center of world events; it is one of the great political and cultural focal points, destined to play a central part

Sunset near Caesarea (Israel)

in the history of nations, on a stage reaching far beyond the bounds of the Mediterranean itself.

## Cultural Landscapes of the Mediterranean

As a result of the fragmentation of the Mediterranean region into a multitude of separate countries, peninsulas, isthmuses and islands and the further subdivision of the land area into geographical units of very different character the people of the Mediterranean countries, adapting to the particular conditions in which they live, show a corresponding variety.

With the expansion of the Roman Empire and its unifying culture the Romance languages descended from Latin established themselves in the north-western part of the region and have maintained their position to this day. It is surprising how well the territories of the Portuguese, Spanish, Catalan, Provençal, French and Italian languages match the geographical divisions of the area. In the eastern part of the Mediterranean region only Romanian

belongs to the Romance language group. – Like the Romance languages, the languages of the southern Slavs (Slovenes, Croats, Serbs, Macedonians, Bulgarians), the Albanians and the Greeks belong to the Indo-European language family. The Greeks and Albanians represent early waves, the southern Slavs a later wave of the peoples who penetrated into the Balkan Peninsula from the north, as the Italic peoples swept into Italy and the Celts into the Iberian Peninsula.

The second great family of peoples in the Mediterranean region consists of the Hamito-Semites in the Middle East and North Africa. The older Hamitic stratum, once unmixed, is represented by the Copts of Egypt and the larger group of Berbers in North Africa. During the period of expansion of the Caliphate the Arabs spread over the whole of the Middle Eastern tablelands, Egypt and large areas of North Africa, where they mingled with the Berbers. The Arabic language is divided into Northern Arabic and Southern Arabic; and when Islam spread from the Arabian Peninsula to Asia and Africa in the 7th c. A.D. Northern Arabic became predominant. The spoken language differs considerably from country to country. Five main groups have developed in the course of time: Peninsular Arabic, Iraqi, the Arabic of Syria and Palestine, Egyptian Arabic and Maghrebine Arabic. These dialects differ considerably from one another, so that the inhabitants of different Arab countries frequently have great difficulty in understanding one another; and this gives the written language (which is common to all) a particular importance.

The Turkish spoken in Turkey is the most westerly member of the Turco-Tatar language family. For centuries it was written in the Arabic script, until in 1928 the Latin alphabet, with some diacritic marks, was introduced by Kemal Atatürk. – Since 1948 the official language of Israel has been modern Hebrew (Ivrit).

The various cultural regions of the Mediterranean area correspond with the areas of diffusion of the religions which are vital elements in the different cultures. Christianity as the main faith of the population is confined to southern Europe, with the Dinaric Mountains forming the boundary between the western territory of the Roman Catholic Church and the eastern territory of the Greek Orthodox Faith. It is found only in small pockets in Syria, Lebanon, Egypt and the Atlas countries, within the Islamic zone which takes in all the Mediterranean countries along the coasts of North Africa and the Middle East. There are also outposts of Islam in the Christian territory of southeastern Europe, in Thrace, Bulgaria, Macedonia, Albania, Bosnia and Hercegovina.

This distribution of the Christian and Islamic faiths has left its mark on the landscape and townscape of the various countries. The territory of Islam coincides with the region of towns with narrow irregular lanes, houses with window grilles (removed in areas which later became Christian) and balconies, bazaars and mosques. In the steppes of Africa and the Middle East Islam extends into the main territories inhabited by nomadic tribes. – The Roman Catholic area is distinguished by its imposing churches and monastic houses from the Greek Orthodox area, where the churches tend to be inconspicuous but the monasteries occupy a special position, often being built in striking situations selected for their remoteness or defensive strength (monastic republic of Athos, monasteries of Meteora, Megaspilaion).

The Mediterranean countries attract huge numbers of vacationers every year with their variety of historic and artistic treasures and their warm sunny weather; and accordingly the tourist trade now makes a major contribution to the economy of the various countries. The coastal regions appeal particularly both to the inhabitants of the countries concerned and to visitors; and one consequence of this is that considerable quantities of sewage and other effluents flow into the sea. In addition much pollution is created by large-scale industrial development around ports and other towns. The effects of the pollution of the sea are aggravated by the fact that there is relatively little exchange of water between the Mediterranean and the Atlantic. Fortunately some Mediterranean States are conscious of the dangers of water pollution and are taking steps to deal with it.

One other unfortunate effect of the growth of tourism has been the excessive and ill-judged building development designed to cater for increased numbers of visitors which has disfigured the Mediterranean coasts in so many places.

# Mediterranean Islands from A to Z

Marina Grande, Capri

# Aegina
## (Aíyina)

Greece
Nomos: Attica.
Area: 32 sq. miles/83 sq. km. – Population: 9550.
Telephone code: 0297.

ⓘ Tourist Police,
Vasiléos Yeoryíou 11;
tel. 2 23 91.

HOTELS. – AEGINA TOWN: *Aegina Maris*, II, 310 b.; *Moondy Bay*, II, 144 b.; *Danae*, II, 100 b.; *Nausikaa Bungalows*, II, 66 b.; *Klonos*, III, 84 b.; *Pharos*, III, 72 b.; *Avra*, III, 57 b.; *Brown*, III, 48 b.; *Areti*, III, 39 b.

AGHIA MARÍNA: *Apollo*, II, 203 b.; *Argo*, II, 116 b.; *Pantelaros*, III, 106 b.; *Galinie*, III, 67 b.; *Kyriakakis*, III, 57 b.; *Karyatides*, III, 56 b.; *Marina*, III, 56 b.; *Akti*, III, 44 b.; *Magda*, III, 40 b.; *Aphaea*, III, 32 b.; *Blue Horizon*, III, 28 b.; *Nuremberg*, III, 24 b.; *Ammudia*, III, 26 b.; *Kalliopi*, III, 25 b.; *Aegli*, III, 14 b.

MÉSAGROS (near Aghia Marína, altitude 260 ft/80 m): *Poseidon*, III, 48 b. – SOUVÁLA AND VÁTA: *Ephi*, III, 59 b.; *Saronikos*, IV, 33 b.; *Xeni*, III, 14 b.

ISLAND OF ANGÍSTRI: *Keryphalia*, III, 16 b.

TRANSPORTATION. – Frequent boat services from Piraeus to Aegina town and Aghia Marína. – Bus from quay at Aegina to Temple of Aphaia and Aghia Marína on the E coast, Pérdika in the S and Vayía on the N coast. – Boat trips to the island of Angístri and to Epídavros (Epidaurus).

*Aegina, an island in the Saronic Gulf within easy reach of Athens, is a popular resort with both Athenians and foreigners. It combines the charms of its agreeable setting of fields, macchia and forests with its great tourist attraction, the Temple of Aphaia, extensive beaches and facilities for all kinds of water sports.

HISTORY. – The earliest settlement of the island dates back to the 4th millennium B.C., and by 2500 B.C. there was a fortified trading-post on the W coast carrying on trade between the mainland, the Cyclades and Crete. Dorian immigrants who arrived about 1000 B.C. continued this tradition, and by the 7th c. the island's trading connections reached as far afield as Egypt and Spain. About 650 B.C. Aegina minted the first coins in Europe. In the 5th c. there was increasing conflict with Aegina's near neighbor, Athens, which in 459 B.C. compelled the island to surrender and destroyed its economic power. – In 1826 Aegina became the seat of the first Greek Government, headed by Kapodistrias.

The island's capital **Aegina** (pop. 6100), with its Neo-Classical buildings, recalls the later period in its history. The most notable features of the town are its beautifully shaped harbor and the dazzling white Church of Aghios Nikólaos dedicated to St Nicholas, the patron saint of sailors. On the site of the ancient city on the N side of the town (new excavations in progress) stood a Temple of Apollo; a single marble pillar to the left of the harbor is the only relic still standing. Most of the temple stones were used in the construction of the harbor. In a museum near the Mitrópolis Church can be seen finds from the temples of Apollo and Aphaia as well as pottery from the 3rd millennium onwards.

Temple of Aphaia, Aegina

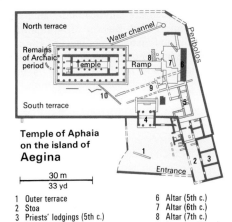

**Temple of Aphaia
on the island of
Aegina**

30 m
33 yd

1 Outer terrace
2 Stoa
3 Priests' lodgings (5th c.)
4 Propylon (5th c.)
5 Priests' lodgings (7th c.)

6 Altar (5th c.)
7 Altar (6th c.)
8 Altar (7th c.)
9 Propylon (6th c.)
10 Peribolos (7th c.)

The road to the Temple of Aphaia passes the old medieval capital of the island, which was abandoned about 1800, *Palaiokhóra* (5 miles/8 km). Scattered about among the ruins are more than 20 whitewashed churches and chapels, mostly dating from the 13th and 14th c., some of them containing frescoes.

The *Temple of Aphaia stands in a commanding situation above the E coast, 7½ miles/12 km from the town. It is usually crowded in the daytime and is best visited in the evening when the setting sun makes it look as if it were built of golden-rose stone. The marble figures from the pediments were acquired by King Ludwig I of Bavaria at the beginning of the 19th c. and are now in Munich. German excavations in 1901 brought to light a dedicatory inscription to the goddess of fertility from an earlier temple of about 580 B.C. which preceded the present one (erected about 510). In the later temple the old goddess Aphaia was probably joined by Athena.

The **sacred precinct** is entered on the S side. Passing the *propylon*, with *priests' lodgings* adjoining it on the right, we come to the main complex, which consists of the temple itself, the altar to the E of the temple and the ramp linking the two. The **Doric temple**, "the most polished building of the Late Archaic period" (G ruben), is built of limestone, which was originally faced with fine stucco. The *pediment figures*, depicting the Trojan War, and the roof were of marble. Well preserved and extensively restored, the temple is of imposing effect. The *cella*, with three aisles separated by rows of columns in two tiers, is surrounded by a colonnade (6×12 columns). The cult image stood between the second-last pair of columns in the cella. At the W end of the temple, where further excavations are in progress, the foundations of the building can be seen.

In clear weather the view from the temple extends to the Acropolis in Athens.

From the temple it is only a short distance on foot (25 minutes) or by car to the bay of **Aghia Marína**, where a much-frequented little resort has grown up in the last 20 years or so. Many boats do not put in at Aegina town but anchor off Aghia Marína, providing a shorter way to reach the temple.

Also worth a visit are the Hill of *Profítis Ilías* or *Óros* (1719 ft/524 m), on the summit of which there was a Sanctuary of Zeus Hellanios (bus to Marathón on the W coast); the Convent (nunnery) of *Panayía Khrysoleóndissa*; and the *Ómorfi Ekklisía* (Beautiful Church), between Aegina and Palaiokhóra, which dates from 1289 (frescoes).

**Other islands in the Saronic Gulf and the Gulf of Argolis: see Argo-Saronic Islands. – *Hydra: see p. 94.**

# Aeolian Islands
## See Lipari Islands

# Agrigento

Italy
Region: Sicily. – Province: Agrigento.
Altitude: 1070 ft/326 m. – Population: 52,000.
Post code: I-02100. – Telephone code: 0922.
Ⓘ **AA,**
   Piazzale Roma 5;
   tel: 2 04 54.
   **EPT,**
   Viale della Vittoria 255;
   tel. 2 69 26.
   **ACI,**
   Via San Vito 25;
   tel. 2 65 01.
   **TCI,**
   *Viaggi Akratur,*
   Via Cicerone 1;
   tel. 2 59 49.

HOTELS. – *Jolly dei Templi* (3 miles/5 km SE on SS 115, Villaggio Mosè), I, 292 b., SP; *Villa Athena* (in the temple area), I, 56 b., SP; *Akrabello* (4 miles/6 km SE, at Parco Angeli), II, 247 b., SP; *Della Valle*, Via dei Templi 94, II, 164 b.; *Belvedere*, Via San Vito 20, III, 63 b.

**Agrigento, one of the most beautifully situated towns in Sicily, halfway along the S coast, is one of the island's principal tourist attractions with its magnificent ruined ** temples. The skyline of the town itself, however, has been drastically altered by the tall blocks of modern**

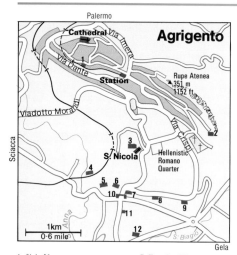

1 Civic Museum
2 Temple of Ceres and Proserpine
3 National Archeological Museum
4 Temple of Vulcan
5 Temple of Castor and Pollux
6 Temple of Zeus
7 Temple of Hercules
8 Temple of Concord
9 Temple of Juno Lacinia
10 Porta Aurea
11 Tomb of Theron
12 Temple of Aesculapius

**flats, particularly on the S side of the old town.**

HISTORY. – Agrigento was founded in 582 B.C., under the name of *Akragas*, by settlers from the Greek colony of Gela, 50 miles/80 km SE. Magnificently situated on a ridge between the rivers *Akragas* (now known as San Biagio) and *Hypsas* (Santa Anna), it was celebrated by Pindar as "the fairest city of mortal men". On the N side of the hill, now occupied by the modern town, was the acropolis, and the ancient city lay to the S of this on land sloping down gradually toward the sea, in the area now marked by the remains of its walls and temples. The town was mostly ruled by tyrants. Akragas rose to wealth and power, at first by war and later by trade with Carthage, and some of its citizens lived in princely state. It reached its peak of prosperity as a free State under the leadership of *Empedokles* (who died about 424 B.C.), but soon afterward, in 406 B.C., succumbed to the Carthaginians. The town was plundered, its art treasures carried off to Carthage and its temples burned. – As the Roman *Agrigentum* (from 210 B.C.) the town was a place of no consequence. – In A.D. 828 it was taken by the Saracens and grew to rival Palermo. In 1086 the Norman ruler *Roger I* established a bishopric here which developed during the Middle Ages into the richest in Sicily. Until 1927 the town was known by its Saracenic name of *Girgenti*. It is famous as the home of Pirandello.

SIGHTS. – At the NW corner of the old town, a huddle of narrow winding streets, stands the **Cathedral** (*Duomo*), built on the foundations of a Temple of Jupiter of the 6th c. B.C. It was begun in the 11th c., enlarged in the 13th and 14th c. and largely rebuilt in the 16th–17th c. A landslip in 1966 caused considerable damage, now mostly made good. At the end of the N aisle is the *Cappella de Marinis*, with the Tomb of Gaspare de Marinis (1492). Beyond the Gothic doorway to the right of the choir is a silver

shrine (1639) containing the remains of St Gerlando, first Bishop of Agrigento. From the unfinished campanile (14th c.) there are fine *views. Beside the staircase on the W side of the cathedral is the *Diocesan Museum.*

To the S of the old town, in the Piazza Pirandello, is the Civic Museum (*Museo Civico*) (medieval and modern art, pictures by Sicilian artists).

The principal street of the town is the busy *Via Atenea*, which runs E from the Piazza del Municipio to the Piazzale Roma. 1 mile/1·5 km farther E, in a private garden, rises the **Rupe Atenea** (Rock of Athena; 1152 ft/351 m), from which there are extensive views.

The temples are reached by following the signposted *Passeggiata Archeologica*, which runs SE along Via Crispi from Piazza Marconi (railway station), immediately S of the Piazzale Roma. – In ¾ mile/1 km a road goes off on the left to the *cemetery*, at the SE corner of which are remains of the Greek town walls. From here it is 550 yds/500 m E on the stony ancient road to the *Temple of Ceres and Proserpine* (*Tempio di Demetra*), standing on high ground; originally built about 470 B.C., it was converted by the Normans into the little *Church of San Biagio* (Chiesa di S. Biagio). To the E, below the terrace, is a cave sanctuary of Demeter (about 650 B.C.).

Soon afterward another road branches off Via Crispi on the left to the Temple of Juno Lacinia and the road to Gela (SS 115). In another 550 yds/500 m a recently excavated section of the *Greco-Roman city* (4th c. B.C. to 5th c. A.D.; fine wall-paintings and mosaic pavements) is passed on the left, and 330 yds/300 m beyond this, on the right, we come to the **National Archeological Museum** (*Museo Archeologico Nazionale*), with prehistoric material, ancient sarcophagi, vases, coins and architectural fragments; particularly fine is a marble statue of an *ephebe (about 490 B.C.). Immediately S of the museum is the little Gothic *Church of San Nicola* (13th c.; fine doorway), which contains an ancient marble *sarcophagus carved with scenes from the story of Phaedra and Hippolytus. Close to the church, to the W, are the so-called *Oratory of Phalaris* and an almost square *cella*, the tomb of a Roman matron (1st c. B.C.).

¾ mile/1 km beyond San Nicola the road reaches the entrance to the enclosed **Temple Area** (freely accessible at all times). To the right can be seen the Temple of Zeus; to the left, near the S wall of the ancient city, is the so-called **Temple of Hercules** (*Tempio di Ércole*, 6th c. B.C.), with eight columns on the S side (out of the original 38) which were re-erected in 1923.

From the Temple of Hercules a new road leads E past the *Villa Aurea* (offices of the Temple Area administration; periodic exhibitions) to the magnificent Doric **\*\*Temple of Concord** (Tempio della Concordia; 5th c. B.C.; converted into a church in the Middle Ages), with all its 34 columns still standing; it ranks with the Theseion in Athens as the best-preserved temple surviving from Antiquity.

Temple of Castor and Pollux, Agrigento

Some 770 yds/700 m farther E, magnificently situated above a steep escarpment at the SE corner of the ancient city, near the road to Gela, stands the so-called **\*\*Temple of Juno Lacinia** (second half of 5th c. B.C.), a classic example of the Doric style. The temple, actually dedicated to Hera, has 25 complete columns standing and nine others partly re-erected.

Between the temples of Hercules and Zeus is the *Porta Aurea* or harbor gate, through which passes the road to *Porto Empédocle* (6 miles/10 km SW; pop. 20,000) and the ancient port, which lay due S at the mouth of the River San Biagio. Outside the Porta Aurea we come to the so-called **Tomb of Theron** (*Tomba di Terone*), the remains of a tower-like Roman mausoleum.

NW of the Porta Aurea are the ruins of the unfinished **Temple of Zeus** (*Tempio di Giove Olimpico*; 5th c. B.C.), the largest ancient Greek temple, 371 ft/113 m long (Temple G at Selinunte 364 ft/111 m; Artemision, Ephesus, 358 ft/109 m; Parthenon, Athens, 230 ft/70 m). The entablature was probably supported by the huge Telamones or Atlas figures whose remains were found on the site; one of them, restored (lying on the ground), measures 25 ft/7·75 m ("il Gigante").

W of the Temple of Zeus is the **Temple of Castor and Pollux** (*Tempio di Castore e Polluce*) or Temple of the Dioscuri, four columns of which have been re-erected and a little way N the *Sanctuary of the Chthonic Divinities* (Santuario delle Divinità Ctonie; 6th c. B.C.), a unique cult place dedicated to the divinities of the Underworld (probably Demeter and Persephone). The remains of 12 altars and eight small temples in the form of treasuries have been excavated.

Farther to the NW, beyond the railway, are remains of the so-called *Temple of Vulcan* (about 470 B.C.), from which there is a view of the main range of temples.

# Ajaccio
## See under Corsica

# Alonnisos
## See under Sporades

# Amorgos
## See under Cyclades

# Andros
## (Ándhros)

Greece
Nomos: Cyclades.
Area: 147 sq. miles/380 sq. km. – Population: 10,450.

HOTELS. – ANDROS TOWN: *Paradisos* II, 76 b.; *Xenia*, II, 44 b.; *Aegli*, III, 27 b. – APIKIA: *Helena*, III, 27 b. – BATSI:

Lykion (pension), II, 28 b.; Chrysi Akti, III, 118 b. –
GÁVRION: Aphrodite, II, 43 b. – KÓRTHION: Korthion, III,
27 b.

ON TÍNOS: Tinos Beach, I, 339 b.; Theoxenia, II, 59 b.;
Tinion, II, 47 b.; Asteria, III, 92 b.; Delphinia, III, 73 b.;
Meltemi, III, 77 b.

BATHING BEACHES. – Batsí, Gávrion, etc.

TRANSPORTATION. – Boat connections with Rafína
(on the E coast of Attica, 15 miles/24 km from Athens)
and Tínos. – Island buses: Ándros–Gávrion,
Ándros–Apikiá, etc.

**Ándros is the most northerly of the
Cyclades, lying only 7 miles/11 km
from Euboea and 1300 yds/1200 m
from Tínos. Characteristic features
of the landscape are the many large
*dovecots (also found on Tínos).**

The chief town, **Ándros** (pop. 2450), lies
half-way down the E coast. In the newer
part of the town is the *Zoodókhos Piyí
Church*, with a carved iconostasis of
1717. From the oldest part of the town a
bridge leads to the ruins of the medieval
*Castle*.

From Ándros (commonly known as
*Khóra*) a road runs S to the second port on
the E coast, **Órmos**, and the little village
of *Kórthion*, situated amid lemon groves.
NW of Ándros is *Apikiá*, with a mineral
spring, and beyond this the *Aghios
Nikólaos Monastery*.

A road runs from Ándros to the W coast, by way of
*Mesariá* (3 miles/5 km; church of 1158) and
*Palaiópolis* (7 miles/11 km), on the site of the ancient
capital of the island, to the little ports of **Batsí**
(5 miles/8 km) and **Gávrion** (5 miles/8 km).

SE of Ándros and separated from it by a
very narrow strait, lies the island of **Tínos**
or **Tenos** (area 75 sq. miles/194 sq. km;
pop. 8200). The chief town, **Tínos** (pop.
2900), on the S coast is a place of
pilgrimage. From the harbor a broad
processional avenue leads up through the
town to the gleaming white complex, built
from 1822 onward, using stone from the
Sanctuary of Poseidon, of the Monastery
and *Pilgrimage Church of Panayía Evan-
gelístria or Tiniótissa* where each year on
August 15 the Feast of the Holy Virgin
takes place. Within the church, under a
stone canopy, is the wonder-working
icon of the Mother of God, spangled with
pearls and precious stones and surrounded by large numbers of pictures and
offerings from those who believe that its
miracles have worked for them. On the
lower floor of the building are a room

commemorating those who were killed in
the Italian attack on the Greek cruiser
"Elli" in 1940 and an impressive little
chapel (to the left).

The small *Archeological Museum some distance
below the church contains finds from the Sanctuary of
Poseidon and Amphitrite, including architectural
elements (in the courtyard) and, on the upper
floor, large pottery vessels, among them a *pithos
(large storage jar) with relief decoration depicting
the birth of Athena from the head of a winged Zeus
(7th c. B.C.).

2½ miles/4 km NW of Tínos at **Kiónia** the
foundations of the Hellenistic Sanctuary
of Poseidon have been excavated (propylaia, Doric colonnade, court containing an
altar, Doric temple).

From Tínos a road runs NW across the
island to **Istérnia** (14 miles/22 km;
church with ceramic-faced dome), the
island's largest and most picturesque
village of **Pýrgos** (art school) and its
harbor at **Pánormos** (18 miles/29 km).
At Xinara a road goes off on the right to
*Loutrá*, one of the island's most charming
villages.

8 miles/13 km N of Tínos (bus to
Falatádos) stands the large *Convent of
Kekhrovoúni*, founded in the 12th c. and
at present occupied by some 70 nuns. In
addition to a number of interesting icons
visitors are shown the quarters occupied
by Pelagia, the nun who found the
wonder-working icon in 1822. From the
convent there are fine *views of the harbor
of Tínos and *Mount Exóbourgo* (1749 ft/
533 m), site of the island's chief town in
medieval times, with the ruins of Santa
Elena, built by the Venetians, where a
huge stone cross has been erected.

Dovecots, Tínos

Characteristic of Tínos are the handsome Venetian *dovecots which are encountered all over the island.

# Argo-Saronic Islands
## (Nísi Argosaronikoú)

**Greece**
Nomos: Attica.

HOTELS. – ON MÉTHANA: *Pigae*, II, 47 b.; *Saronis* II, 44 b.; *Ghionis*, III, 100 b.; *Methanien*, III, 57 b.; *American*, III, 49 b.; *Dima*, III, 38 b. – ON PÓROS: *Sirene*, II, 228 b.; *Poros*, II, 146 b.; *Chrysi Avgi*, II, 145 b.; *Neon Aegli*, II, 132 b.; *Latsi*, II, 54 b.; *Saron*, II, 46 b. – ON SALAMÍS: *Selinia*, III, 92 b.; *Gabriel*, III, 40 b.

This name is now applied to a number of islands within easy reach of Athens, from Salamís by way of Aegina to Póros, Hýdra and Spétsai.

Salamís can be reached from Athens by the ferry from Pérama. Connections with the other islands (hydrofoils as well as ordinary boats) are provided by the Argosaronikos service from Piraeus, which also serves the peninsulas of Méthana and Ermióni on the E coast of the Peloponnese.

**Méthana**, linked with the Peloponnese only by a narrow strip of land, is a spa (sulfur springs) recommended for the treatment of rheumatism, arthritis, gynaecological conditions and skin diseases.

Póros Sferia, the ancient *Kalavria*, is a very small island, separated from the NE coast of the Peloponnese by a strait only 275 yds/250 m wide now crossed by a bridge. The quiet bay to the W of the town is like an inland lake; and indeed the channels at the E and W ends are passable only by small boats. – The town of **Póros** has a

Póros

strikingly beautiful setting. The old Arsenal built by Kapodistrias now houses a naval training school, of which the cruiser "Averof", moored in the bay, forms part. A road runs past the naval school to the *Panayía Monastery (2½ miles/4 km), which has a richly gilded iconostasis. From here a footpath ascends (1 hour) to the Sanctuary of Poseidon on the Paláti Plateau. There are only scanty remains of the temple (6th c. B.C.), but the climb is worthwhile for the sake of the view. – From the temple it is another 45 minutes' walk through a pine forest to the N coast with its beautiful bays.

Just off the coast of Attica lies the island of **Salamís** the largest and most populated of the Saronic group, shutting off the Bay of Eleusis (Elefsis), which can be entered only through two narrow channels. The famous naval Battle of Salamís (480 B.C.) took place in the more easterly of these channels.

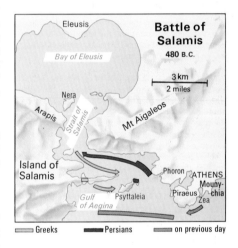

This limestone island, with hills rising to 1326 ft/404 m and a deeply indented gulf on the W side, has little arable land. It is now involved in the rapid growth of the Athens region. – The ferry from Pérama passes through the waters in which the battle was fought, where Xerxes watched from a throne set up on the mainland. 2 miles/3 km W of the landing-stage at Paloukiá, at the head of the deep bay on the W side of the island, is the chief town, **Salamís** (locally called Koulouri, pop. 12,000), with the Church of Panayía tou Katharoú. 4 miles/6 km W of the town is the *Faneroméni Monastery* (the Apparitions of the Virgins), founded in 1661, in the building of which material from an ancient sanctuary was used. The church has frescoes of 1735. – The road continues to the NW tip of the island, where the ferry from Néa Péramos puts in.

*Aegina: see p. 38. – *Hýdra and *Spétsai: see Hydra.

# Astypalaia
## See under Cyclades

# Balearics/Islas Baleares

Spain
Region and province: Balearics.
Area: 2195 sq. miles/5684 sq. km. –
Population: 640,000. Capital: Palma de Mallorca.

DISTANCES from mainland: Palma de Mallorca to *Barcelona* 132 miles/245 km; to *Valencia* 140 miles/259 km; to *Algiers* 172 miles/319 km; to *Marseilles* 287 miles/532 km; to *Genoa* 439 miles/823 km.

BOAT SERVICES. – Car ferry services between the islands and between the Spanish mainland (Barcelona, Valencia, Alicante) and the islands; also regular connections with France (Sète, Marseilles); regular service between Palma and Cabrera.

LANGUAGE. – As in the rest of Spain, the official language and the language of business is Castilian Spanish (*castellano*). The everyday languages of the inhabitants, however, are Majorcan (*mallorquí*), Minorcan (*menorquí*) and Ibizan (*ibizenco*) – all closely related dialects of **Catalan** (*català*), a Romance language spoken in NE Spain (Catalonia) which is markedly different from Castilian and shows Provençal influence in its vocabulary.

**The group of islands known as the Balearics, lying off the SE coast of Spain in the Western Mediterranean, between latitude 38° and 40° N and between longitude 1° and 4° E, consists of the \*\*Balearics proper (Spanish Islas Baleares), with the two main islands of Majorca (Mallorca; area 1413 sq. miles/3660 sq. km) and Minorca (Menorca; 270 sq. miles/700 sq. km). together with Ibiza (Ibizan Eivissa; 221 sq. miles/572 sq. km) and Formentera (39 sq. miles/100 sq. km), which are also known as the Pityusas or Pitiusas, as well as some 150 small islands, including Cabrera (S of Majorca; $6\frac{1}{2}$ sq. miles/17 sq. km), and a variety of rocky islets, some of them serving military or naval purposes, some totally deserted. Together these islands form the Spanish province of the Balearics, the capital of which is**

Majorcan windmill

**Palma de Mallorca. (The "ll" in Spanish is pronounced as a "y".)**

HISTORY. – The original inhabitants of the Balearics were Iberians, who were famous for their skill with the sling. In the 3rd c. B.C. the islands were taken by the Carthaginians, and in 123 B.C. by the Romans. The Roman Consul, Q. Caecilius Metellus, who acquired the agnomen "Balearicus" after his conquest of the islands, founded *Palma* (the "palm" of victory) and *Pollentia* ("power"). Later the islands were held successively by the Vandals, Visigoths, Byzantines, Franks and Moors (798). In 1229 King Jaime I of Aragon ("el Conquistador") conquered Majorca and bestowed it on a younger son as an independent kingdom. In the 14th c., however, it was reunited with Aragon. From 1708 to 1782 and from 1798 to 1802 Minorca was held by Britain, with a brief interlude under French control after a naval battle in 1756. – Features of great archeological interest are the Bronze Age (about 1200 B.C.) *talayots* (round towers which are believed to have been built as chieftains' houses and later served as watch-towers), *taulas* (T-shaped stone structures) and *navetas* (boat-shaped megalithic tombs).

See also \*\***Majorca** (with *Cabrera*), *Minorca, \*Ibiza and **Formentera**.

Cala d'Or, Majorca

# Bastia
## See under Corsica

# Bonifacio
## See under Corsica

# Brač

Yugoslavia
Republic: Croatia (Hrvatska).
Area: 152 sq. miles/394 sq. km. –
Population: 12,500. Telephone code: 058.

(i) Turističko Biro,
YU-58420 **Bol;**
tel. 8 06 04.
**Turističko Društvo,**
YU-58426 **Sumartin;**
tel. 8 05 11.
**Turističko Biro,**
YU-58400 **Supetar;**
tel. 63 12 60.

HOTELS. – BOL: *Elaphusa*, I, 368 b., with annexe *Pavillons*, II, 426 b.; *Borak*, II, 326 b.; *Bjela Kuća*, with annexes *Martinica* and *Tamaris*, II, 204 b.; *Kaštil*, II, 72 b. – SUPETAR: *Kaktus*, I, 245 b.; *Complex Palma*, II, 592 b.; *Tamaris*, II, 50 b. – POSTIRA: *Vrilo*, II, 42 b.; *Park*, III, 42 b., with annexes *Tamaris* and *Agava*, II, 80 b.

CAMP SITES. – *Supetar*, at Supetar; also site at Bol.

EVENTS. – "Masquerades", with donkey-races, at Supetar (July and August); song contests at Bol in summer.

BATHING BEACHES. – The beach at *Supetar* begins near the harbor and extends past the hotel and bungalow complex, with plenty of shade. It is well cared for and kept clean, but tends to be crowded. The other coastal resorts do not have good beaches.

CAR FERRIES. – From Split to Supetar, Postira, Pučišća, Povlja and Luka; from Makarska to Sumartin; hydrofoils.

**Brač** (25 miles/40 km long, 3–7½ miles/ 5–12 km wide), the largest of the Yugoslav Adriatic islands after Krk, is separated from the mainland by the Brač Channel (Brački Kanal) and from the island of Hvar by the Hvar Channel (Hvarski Kanal). With its attractive resorts, mostly situated in beautiful bays, Brač is a good place to choose for a long, leisurely (and not too expensive) holiday.

HISTORY. – The island was already occupied in Neolithic times. The earliest inhabitants in the Historical period were Illyrians. Later, surrounded by Greek colonies, the Illyrians traded with the Greeks but resisted Greek attempts to settle on the island. In the reign of Diocletian the Romans began to work the limestone quarries at Škrip. After a period under Byzantine rule Brač was occupied by a Slav tribe, the

Neretljani, in the 9th c. Later it became part of the Croatian kingdom. When pirate raids became frequent many of the inhabitants left the coastal settlements and moved into the interior of the island. At the beginning of the 13th c. Brač came under the control of the mainland town of Omiš, but in 1240 it passed to Split. Then followed a period under the rule of the Hungaro-Croatian monarchy, after which the island was annexed by Venice and remained in Venetian hands until 1797, when it passed to Austria. Apart from a brief period of French rule in 1807–15 it remained part of the Austro-Hungarian monarchy until 1918.

During the Second World War the Partisans on Brač fought against the Italian and later the German occupying forces. By 1944 Tito had gained the upper hand, and Brač became a base for Partisan vessels.

The semicircular harbor of **Supetar**, the administrative center of the island which is connected by ferry with Split on the mainland, is surrounded by brightly painted buildings dating from the period of the Austro-Hungarian monarchy. The tourists' part of the town lies E of the harbor in a setting of parkland and meadows. A surprising feature at the end of the long beach is the cemetery, with the Mausoleum of the Petrinović family, who emigrated from Brač to Chile and made a fortune from the mining of saltpeter. The mausoleum, with Oriental and Byzantine architectural features, was designed by Toma Rosandić (1879–1958). This unusual cemetery contains other tombs and works of sculpture commemorating wealthy inhabitants of Brač.

A narrow and winding road runs E along the coast to **Spliska**, in a bay fringed by beautiful pine woods. Stone from the nearby quarries at Škrip was once shipped from here. In the *Roman quarry of Rasoha*, ½ mile/800 m from Spliska, is a figure of Hercules carved from the rock – the finest piece of Roman sculpture on the island. The 16th c. Parish Church near the harbor has a graceful slender tower. A minor road runs inland to the quarries.

The next place along the coast road is **Postira**, birthplace of the great Croatian writer Vladimir Nazor (1876–1949). From the large harbor a steep street leads up to the center of the town. Below the parish church is a picturesque square surrounded by handsome house fronts and doorways. The church, with defensive loopholes in its walls, contains 18th c. Stations of the Cross. Still higher up, on Mount Glavica, are the primitive old houses of the peasants and herdsmen. The farm buildings are often constructed of

Zlatni Rat beach, near Bol (island of Brač)

undressed stone without the use of mortar; in front of them are ovens, wine-presses and old querns. – Returning to the harbor, we see at the head of the bay the *Castle* of the Lazanić family. Adjoining it is a mansion with a Renaissance gable, on the S side of which are many religious inscriptions.

**Pučišća**, a fishing village at the head of a bay reaching far inland, was once strongly fortified. The Parish Church contains a fine wooden altar dedicated to St Anthony – one of the most beautiful on the island – with an Altar-piece of St Roch painted by Palma Giovane, a pupil of Titian, and a carved group with a figure of St Jerome, the island's patron saint. Accommodation is readily available in villagers' houses.

**Selca**, the most southerly place on the island, is another characteristic local village, its houses demonstrating the skill of its stonemasons. Croatian national aspirations and Pan-Slav ideas have found expression here in the establishment of a Croatian Association dedicated to maintaining the local way of life and culture. The monument to Tolstoy in the village was erected by the association.

**Sumartin**, the most easterly and most recently established village on Brač, had until recently no motor road connecting it with the rest of the island. The monastery here has a number of fine pictures of the Venetian School.

**Bol**, huddled on a narrow coastal strip between the hills and the sea is now the principal tourists resort on the island after Supetar. Features of interest include a 17th c. mansion on the seafront, partly Renaissance and partly Baroque; the Church of Our Lady of Mount Carmel (Crkva Gospe od Karmela); a large Dominican monastery; and a gallery of contemporary art. The museum in the monastery contains prehistoric material found in caves, a collection of coins, material recovered by underwater archeologists and a collection of incunabula and parchments.

Near Bol, reached by a steep climb from the sandy Bay of Blaca, is a **hermitage** which in the 16th c. served as a refuge for Glagolithic priests (see under Krk). The hermitage remained in occupation until 1973, the last hermit being a well-known astronomer who had the largest telescope in the country and an extensive library. Visitors are shown the monks' cells, the observatory, a collection of old watches and clocks, weapons, etc. – Another excursion from Bol is to the summit of **Vidova Gora** (St Vitus's Hill; 2553 ft/ 778 m), the highest point on the island, which affords magnificent views.

From Bol a road runs via *Nerežišće*, exactly in the center of the island, to its oldest settlement, **Škrip**. Hundreds of Roman slaves once worked in the quarries here. Many objects illustrating the village's long history have been found at different levels in the soil, and these are to be brought together in a local museum in the Radojković Tower. – Among notable buildings in which the beautiful white limestones of Škrip have been used are

Diocletian's Palace in Split, the Reichstag in Berlin and the Parliament Building in Vienna.

To the W of Brač is the island of **Šolta** (area 20 sq. miles/52 sq. km; pop. 3000; car ferry from Split), separated from the mainland by the Split Channel (Splitski Kanal). Although a popular place for excursions from the mainland, it has not yet been developed for mass tourism and has still only one asphalted road (from the port of Rogač, where the ferry puts in, to the chief place on the island, Grohote). – At **Grohote**, the largest village on the island, lying a little way inland, are the remains of Roman buildings with mosaic-paintings. Beside the Parish Church are the foundations of an Early Christian Basilica (6th c.). The church itself has an altar-piece by the Flemish painter Pieter de Coster. There is also a 17th c. watch-tower in the village. In the fields outside the village stands a little Gothic church dedicated to St Michael (Sv. Mihovil), with beautiful wall-paintings.

**Maslinica**, situated in the middle cove of a group of three at the N end of the island, has a fortified Baroque castle, now converted into a hotel. – On Gradina Hill, at the little port of **Rogač**, is a ruined castle in which, according to tradition, the Illyrian Queen Teuta sought refuge when fleeing from the Romans.

# Brioni/Brijuni Islands

Yugoslavia
Republic: Croatia (Hrvatska).
Altitude: 0–165 ft/0–50 m. – No permanent inhabitants.

**This group of islands (closed to visitors; landing from boats prohibited) lies off the Dalmatian coast some 15 miles/25 km NW of Pula. It consists of the two principal islands of Veli Brijun (area 2·7 sq. miles/6·9 sq. km) and Mali Brijun together with a number of smaller islands. Veli Brijun in particular has luxuriant vegetation.**

At the end of the 19th c. the islands were bought by a Merano industrialist with the idea of developing them for the tourist trade which was then beginning to increase. Lavishly equipped with every amenity, Veli Brijun became an exclusive resort frequented by the nobility and financial aristocracy of Europe. Between the wars the glory began to depart, and during the Second World War the islands suffered frequent bombardment and looting. After the war Brioni became the summer residence of President Tito (1892–1980), the island was closed to the public and the hotels were converted into Government guest-houses for the accommodation of official visitors.

# Cabrera
## See under Majorca

# Cagliari
## See under Sardinia

# Calvi
## See under Corsica

# Capri

Italy
Region: Campania. – Province: Napoli (Naples).
Area: 4 sq. miles/10·5 sq. km. – Population: 12,000.
Post code: I-80073. – Telephone code: 081.
(i) **AA,**
Piazza Umberto I;
tel. 8 37 06 86.
**CIT,**
Via Vittorio Emanuele 25;
tel. 8 37 04 66.

HOTELS. – *Quisisana & Grande Hotel, L, 229 b., SP; Tiberio Palace, I, 172 b.; La Palma, I, 143 b.; Regina Cristina, I, 107 b., SP; Luna, I, 94 b., SP; Residence Punta Tragara, I, 77 b., SP; La Scalinatella, I, 57 b.; Calypso, I, 14 b.; La Residenza, II, 146 b., SP; La Pineta, II, 83 b., SP; La Floridiana, II, 62 b.; Semiramis, II, 61 b.; Gatto Bianco, II, 56 b.; Pagano Vittoria, III, 110 b.; Villa Pina, III, 88 b., SP.

IN MARINA GRANDE: Excelsior Parco, II, 53 b.; Maresca, III, 48 b.

BOAT SERVICES. – Regular service several times daily from Naples in 1 hour 20 minutes (taking car not worth while: use prohibited in summer); also hydrofoil service (30 minutes). – Also services from Sorrento, Positano, Amalfi and Ischia.

**The island of ** Capri, lying off the tip of the Sorrento Peninsula on the S side of the Bay of Naples, is one of**

The Faraglioni, Capri

the most beautiful and most visited of the islands in the Tyrrhenian Sea. In Roman times, when it was known as Caprae, it was a favorite resort of the Emperors Augustus and Tiberius.

The island, 4 miles/6 km long and $\frac{3}{4}$–$1\frac{1}{2}$ miles/1–2·5 km wide, has rugged limestone crags rising to a height of 1933 ft/ 589 m. The only places of any size are the picturesque little towns of Capri and Anacapri. The island has a rich vegetation of some 800 species, including the acanthus, whose leaves form the characteristic ornament of Corinthian capitals.

THE ISLAND. – The regular boats land their passengers in the picturesque little port of *Marina Grande*, on the N coast of the island. From here a funicular (5 minutes), a stepped footpath (30 minutes) and a road (2 miles/3 km) lead up to the town of **Capri** (alt. 453 ft/138 m; pop. 8000), the island's capital, situated on a saddle between the hills of *Il Capo* to the E, *Monte Solaro* to the W, *San Michele* to the NE and *Castiglione* (ruined castle) to the SW. The central feature of the town is the little Piazza Umberto I ("the Piazza" for short), at the top of the funicular from Marina Grande. From here it is a 5-minute walk past the steps leading up to the Church of Santo Stéfano (1683) and along the main shopping street to the *Certosa* (founded 1371, restored 1933), a former Carthusian monastery, with the Church of San Giácomo (Gothic doorway; 12th c. frescoes) and two cloisters (access to *viewpoint). – From the Hotel

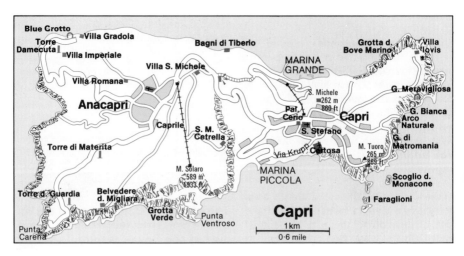

Quisisana, half-way along the road to the Certosa, it is a 15-minute walk to the terrace on *Punta Tragara, the SE promontory of the island, which commands a picturesque view of the S coast and the three stacks known as the *Faraglioni.

From the town of Capri a very attractive footpath, the Via Tiberio (45 minutes), runs NE to the promontory of Il Capo. Immediately beyond a gateway can be seen the rock known as the Salto di Tiberio (974 ft/297 m), from which legend has it that the tyrannical Emperor Tiberius had his victims thrown into the sea (*view). To the right are the substructures of an ancient lighthouse and beyond this the extensive remains of the *Villa di Tiberio or Villa Iovis, rising in terraces to the top of the hill, in which Tiberius is said to have lived from A.D. 27 until his death in 37. On the adjoining promontory is the Chapel of Santa Maria di Soccorso, with a conspicuous statue of the Virgin; magnificent *views. – From the Villa di Tiberio a footpath to the right leads in 15 minutes to the *Arco Naturale, a natural archway in the rock (*view), from which steps lead down to the Grotta di Matromania, perhaps a sanctuary of the nymphs. From the cave a *footpath (45 minutes) runs along above the sea, with views of the Scoglio del Monacone, a rocky islet, and the *Faraglioni, and so back to the *Punta Tragara.

SW of Capri is the little harbor of Marina Piccola, reached by a wide footpath, the *Via Krupp, laid out by the German industrialist Friedrich Krupp. The path begins W of the Certosa and runs below the beautiful Parco Augusto (*terrace affording fine views) and round the steep-sided Castiglione Hill to join (15 minutes) the road from Capri, on which it is another 10 minutes' walk to the harbor.

Anacapri, in the W of the island, is reached either by a beautiful *road (2 miles/ 3·5 km; bus service) which winds its way up the rocky slope from the town of Capri or by an ancient flight of 960 steps which leads up from Marina Grande to the viewpoint of *Capodimonte, 10 minutes' walk E of the town. Above the viewpoint is the Castello di Barbarossa, the ruins of a castle destroyed by the corsair Khaireddin Barbarossa in 1544. On the slopes of Capodimonte stands the conspicuous Villa San Michele, once the home of the Swedish doctor and writer Axel Munthe (1857–1949). – *Anacapri (alt. 938 ft/286 m), a little town of almost Oriental aspect, straggles over the plateau, surrounded by vineyards. The Church of San Michele has a fine majolica pavement (1761). In the piazza is the town's principal church, Santa Sofia. – Half an hour's walk SW of the town is the viewpoint of Migliara, 985 ft/300 m above the sea.

From Anacapri a chair-lift (12 minutes) and a footpath (1 hour) lead up to the top of Monte Solaro (1933 ft/589 m; restaurant), to the SE, the highest point on the island, from which on clear days there are superb **views extending as far as the Abruzzi.

2 miles/3 km NW of Anacapri, in the steep cliffs on the N coast of the island, is one of Capri's principal tourist attractions, the **Blue Grotto (Grotta Azzurra), which can be reached either by boat from Marina Grande or by the Via Pagliaro (2 miles/ 3 km) from Anacapri. This, the most celebrated of Capri's caves, was gouged out of the rock in prehistoric times by the constant battering of the sea, and as a result of the sinking of the land is now half filled with water. The entrance, only 5 ft 9 in/1·75 m high, can be negotiated only by small boats when the sea is calm. The cave is 175 ft/54 m long, 100 ft/30 m wide and 50 ft/15 m high, with 52 ft/16 m depth of water. When the sun is shining it is filled with an extraordinary blue light (at its best between 11 a.m. and 1 p.m.).

Another very attractive excursion is a *boat trip around the island (1$\frac{1}{2}$–2 hours by motor-boat, 3–4 hours by rowing-boat), which allows visitors to see the other caves on the coast of Capri. The finest of these are the Grotta Bianca and the Grotta Meravigliosa above it (on the E coast, near the Arco Naturale), the Grotta Verde at the foot of Monte Solaro, the Grotta Rossa and the green Grotta del Brillante.

# Catania

Italy
Region: Sicily. – Province: Catania.
Altitude: 0–125 ft/0–38 m. – Population: 400,000.
Post code: I–95100. – Telephone code: 095.

ⓘ EPT,
Largo Paesiello 5;
tel. 31 77 20.
Information Offices at station and Fontana Rossa Airport, 2$\frac{1}{2}$ miles/4 km S.
ACI,
Via Etnea 28;
tel. 31 78 90.

HOTELS. – Excelsior, Piazza G. Verga, I, 240 b.; Central Palace, Via Etnea 218, I, 200 b.; Jolly Trinacria, Piazza Trento 13, I, 199 b.; Costa, Via Etnea 551, II, 304 b.; Nettuno, Viale Ruggero di Lauria 121–123, II, 99 b. – Motel Agip, 2$\frac{1}{2}$ miles/4 km S on SS 114, III, 87 b. – Two CAMP SITES.

EVENTS. – Feast of St Agatha (February 3–5), with processions; Agricultural Show (February).

Catania, capital of its province, the see of an archbishop and a university town, lies half-way down the flat eastern coast of Sicily, to the SE of Mount Etna. It is Sicily's second largest town (after Palermo) and one of the most important ports in

**Italy, shipping the produce of the wide and fertile Piana di Catania, the principal grain-growing region in Sicily.**

Catania is a city of imposing modern aspect, having been almost completely rebuilt, with long straight streets, after a devastating earthquake in 1963 and many subsequent smaller eruptions. Its prosperity is demonstrated by its handsome Baroque churches and large aristocratic mansions, frequently rebuilt after earthquake damage. It is a convenient base for touring by rail, boat or car.

HISTORY. – *Katana* was founded about 729 B.C. by Greek settlers from Naxos, and was one of the first places on the island to be taken by the Romans (263 B.C.). Under Roman rule it grew into one of the largest towns in Sicily; but during the early medieval period it declined into insignificance, recovering its prosperity only in the 14th c. under Aragonese rule. The 1693 earthquake, which affected the whole of Sicily, was particularly destructive in Catania.

SIGHTS. – The central feature of the town is the beautiful *Piazza del Duomo*, in the center of which is a fountain with an ancient figure of an *elephant* carved from lava and supporting an Egyptian obelisk of granite. On the E side of the square rises the 18th c. **Cathedral** (choir apses and E wall of transept 13th c.). In the interior (second pillar on right) is the Tomb of the composer Vincenzo Bellini (1801–35), a native of Catania. To the right, in front of the choir (beautiful choir-stalls), is the Chapel of St Agatha, with the tomb of the Spanish Viceroy, Acuña (d. 1494). – Across the street from the cathedral, to the N, stands the *Abbey of Sant'Agata*, with a Baroque church. – SE of the Piazza del Duomo, beyond the railway viaduct, lies the **harbor**.

550 yds/500 m SW of the Piazza del Duomo, in Piazza Federico di Suevia, we come to the **Castello Ursino**, lying close to the sea, which was built for Frederick II about 1240 and later, in the 14th c., became the residence of the kings of Aragon. Thereafter it served as a prison and as barracks, and since 1934 has housed the *Museo Civico*, with the fine municipal collection.

From the SW corner of the Piazza del Duomo the busy Via Garibaldi runs past the Piazza Mazzini, surrounded by 32 ancient columns, to the *Porta Garibaldi* (1768). To the N, in Via Vittorio Emanuele II, a wide street 2 miles/3 km long, the Piazza San Francesco opens out; here stands the *Bellini Museum*, in the house in which the composer was born. Immediately to the W (entrance in the Via Teatro Greco) is the **Ancient Theater** (*Teatro Romano*), on Greek foundations; most of it is now underground. On its W side can be seen the *Odeon*, a small and well-preserved Roman theater which was used for rehearsals and musical competitions.

Roman theater, Catania

In Via Crociferi, which runs N from the Piazza San Francesco, are two churches with Baroque façades, *San Benedetto* and the *Jesuit Church* (on the left). – 550 yds/500 m W, in Piazza Dante, is the former Benedictine **Monastery of San Nicolò** (founded 1518, rebuilt 1735), used from 1866 as a barracks and a school. The church, with an unfinished façade, is a massive Baroque structure, the largest in Sicily. From the lantern of the dome

Catania

Pal. di Giustizia
Villa Bellini
Via Androne
Via Etnea
Piazza Carlo Alberto
450 m
495 yd
Via Plebiscito
Via Maddalena
Corso Sicilia
Piazza della Repubblica
C. Martini
Station
Via Antonino di Sangiuliano
Bus Station
S. Niccolò
Via Vittorio
Emanuele II
Adrano
Via Garibaldi
Duomo
Via Dusmet
Marine Station
Via Naumachia
Castello Ursino
Via Plebiscito
Porto Vecchio
Ferries
Siracusa

1 Sant' Agata
2 Town Hall
3 University
4 Collegiate Church
5 Bellini Museum
6 Ancient Theatre
7 Observatory
8 San Benedetto
9 Amphitheater
10 San Carcere

(internal height 203 ft/62 m) there are extensive* views. There are also fine views from the *Observatory* which adjoins the church on the NW.

From the Piazza del Duomo **Via Etnea**, the town's wide principal street, runs N for 2 miles/3 km, interrupted by a series of spacious squares, with a prospect of Etna in the background. Immediately on the left we come to the *Town Hall*. Beyond this, in the Piazza dell'Università, is the **University** (founded 1444), in a handsome building erected in 1818, and farther on the *Collegiate Church*, with a fine Baroque façade (1768). The next square is the palm-shaded Piazza Stesícoro, with a *monument to Bellini*. On the left side of the square are the remains of a Roman **amphitheater**, demolished during the reign of Theodoric in order to provide material for building the town walls; only the N end is visible. The amphitheater originally measured 138 yds/126 m by 116 yds/106 m; its unusually large arena (77 yds/70 m by 55 yds/50 m) was second only to the Colosseum in Rome (94 yds/86 m by 59 yds/54 m). A little way to the W is the *Church of San Cárcere* (13th c. doorway). – Farther along Via Etnea, on the left, is the main entrance to the **Villa Bellini**, an attractive public garden (pleasant views from the terrace).

Along the N side of the Villa Bellini extends the tree-lined Viale Regina Margherita, which with its eastward continuation the Viale XX Settembre and the wide Corso Italia (beginning at the beautiful Piazza Verga, in which are the modern Law Courts) forms the main traffic artery of the northern part of the city. At its eastern end the Piazza Europa looks down on to the sea and from here a magnificent *coast road* (several outlook terraces) leads N to the suburban district of OGNINA, with the little *Porto d'Ulisse* in a sheltered bay.

**Ascent of Etna**. – To the N of Catania rises Mount **Etna** (10,913 ft/3326 m), in the Sicilian dialect called Mongibello, Europe's largest active volcano and after the Alpine peaks the highest mountain in Italy. It has the form of a truncated cone with an almost circular base 25 miles/40 km in diameter and 90 miles/145 km in circumference. The upper slopes have only a meager cover of vegetation, since the porous rock allows water to sink down rapidly to lower levels, where it encoun-

ters an impervious bed of rock and emerges in many places as springs which water the fertile lower slopes. Oranges and lemons are grown up to about 1650 ft/500 m above sea-level, olives and vines to 4250 ft/1300 m. Above this, reaching to about 6900 ft/2100 m, are forest trees and macchia, sometimes with recent lava flows cutting through them. The summit region, up to the snow-line, is a dull black wasteland which glistens in the sun. The volcanic vents, more than 260 in number, are mostly on the flanks of the mountain, in groups and rows. Major activity occurs at intervals of 4 to 12 years; the most recent occasion was in 1978. Anyone desiring to ascend Etna should first of all check with the CIT for there have been many small quakes since 1978 and many areas are blocked and even dangerous. It is possible occasionally to take a flight around the area which is a truly remarkable experience.

The little town of **Nicolosi** (alt. 2290 ft/698 m; pop. 3500), on the S side of Etna, is the starting-point of the ascent to the subsidiary craters of *Monti Rossi* (3110 ft/948 m; $\frac{3}{4}$–1 hour; view), the walls of which show clear volcanic stratification. At the foot of the Monti Rossi, to the NW, is a lava cave, the *Grotta delle Palombe*. – From Nicolosi the road runs first NW and then N, passing between lava flows, and in 10$\frac{1}{2}$ miles/17 km reaches the turning (on the left; $\frac{3}{4}$ mile/1 km) to the *Grande Albergo Etna* (III, 50 b.) and in another $\frac{3}{4}$ mile/1 km to the *Casa Cantoniera* (roadmen's depot, 1881), which now houses the vulcanological and meteorological station of Catania University. Near this is the *Rifugio-Albergo G. Sapienza* (IV, 110 b.), with a restaurant. Opposite the Rifugio is the lower station of a cableway which formerly went up to an observatory at 9656 ft/2943 m, destroyed in 1971. The cableway is now threatened by further eruptions of lava and runs up to only just over 8500 ft/2600 m. The **crater**, at some 10,800 ft/3300 m, is constantly changing its form as a result of further eruptions. On a clear day the **view can extend as far as Malta, 130 miles/210 km away; the effect is particularly impressive at sunrise. – SE of the former observatory is the beginning of the **Valle del Bove** (Ox Valley), a black and desolate chasm 3 miles/5 km wide surrounded on three sides by rock walls 2000–4000 ft/600–1200 m high. Geologically, it is a collapse valley enlarged by an explosive eruption into a gigantic gorge. The stratification of lava, tuffs and conglomerates is clearly visible. Experienced climbers can walk down (with a guide) through the Valle del Bove to *Zafferana Etnea* (alt. 1970 ft/600 m; Albergo Primavera dell'Etna, II, 100 b.; Albergo del Bosco, III, 130 b.); the descent takes 5 hours.

ROUND ETNA. – An attractive drive of 89 miles/ 144 km, starting from Catania (also possible by rail). The road runs via *Misterbianco* (alt. 699 ft/213 m; pop. 15,000) and **Paternò** (919 ft/280 m), with a castle built by Roger I in 1073 (rebuilt in the 14th c.; well-preserved interior), to **Adrano** (1850 ft/564 m; pop. 32,000), beautifully situated on a lava plateau, with an 11th c. Norman castle and the Convent of Santa Lucia (founded 1157). – 6 miles/9 km SW of Adrano, on a steep hill above the Simeto Valley, with a magnificent view of Etna, is **Centuripe** (alt. 2382 ft/ 726 m; pop. 10,000), formerly *Centorbi*, with the so-called Castello di Corradino (1st c. B.C.). The Archeological Museum contains material from the ancient Siculan town of *Centuripae*, which rose to importance in the Late Hellenistic and Roman periods and was destroyed by Frederick II in 1233 (interesting Hellenistic and Roman house, Contrada Panneria, with paintings of 2nd–1st c. B.C.). – From Adrano the road continues via **Bronte** (alt. 2602 ft/793 m; pop. 22,000), **Maletto** (3084 ft/940 m; old castle), **Randazzo** and *Linguaglossa* (1723 ft/525 m; pop. 8000) to *Fiumefreddo* (203 ft/62 m). Then back to Catania on the motorway (A 18) or SS 114.

# Chios
## (Khíos)

Greece
Nomos: Chíos.
Area: 331 sq. miles/858 sq. km. – Population: 75,000.
Altitude: 0–4255 ft/0–1297 m.
Telephone code: 0271 (Chíos), 0272 (Kardámyla).
(i) **Tourist Police,**
   Neorion 35,
   **Chíos;**
   tel. 2 65 55.
   **Olympic Airways,**
   Prokymaia,
   **Chíos;**
   tel. 2 45 15.

HOTELS. – CHÍOS TOWN: *Chandris Chíos*, II, 294 b., SP; *Xenia*, II, 50 b.; *Kyma*, III, 82 b. – Holiday apartments in renovated patrician houses in the little town of *Mésta*.

AIR SERVICES. – Airport 3 miles/5 km SW of Chíos town. – Regular flights Athens–Chíos once or twice daily (55 minutes), including flights by helicopter.

BOAT SERVICES. – Frequent service from Athens (Piraeus in winter; daily in summer); cars carried; 10 hours. Weekly service from Saloniki (17 hours). – Local services to Sámos, Mytilíni and Psará.

ROAD TRAVEL – There are motor roads to the principal towns and villages on the island. – CAR RENTAL: in Chíos town. – Several BUS ROUTES to the larger places.

BATHING BEACHES. – *Bellavista*, at Chíos town, and *Vrontádes*, N of the town (both pebbles); *Kontári* and *Karfás*, S of Chíos town; S of *Empórion*; *Pasa Limani* and *Límnia*, on W coast; *Kardámyla*, to the N.

**The large island of Chíos lies just off the Peninsula of Çeşme in Turkey, which forms the S side of the Gulf of Smyrna, and at the narrowest point in the gulf is only 5 miles/8 km from the Turkish mainland. The island is traversed from N to S by a range of limestone mountains rising to 4255 ft/1297 m. Small boats ply twice weekly from the port of Chíos to Kuşadasi, the port of Ephesus, in Turkey.**

The rugged limestone massif rises to its greatest height in the northern part of the island, descending to the sea, particularly on the E side, in impressive cliffs. The population of the island is concentrated in the fertile southern part, where the lentisk tree (*Pistacia lentiscus* L.) is grown for the sake of its aromatic resin (mastic), which was already being exported in ancient times and made a major contribution to the prosperity of the island. Mastic is used on Chíos to make *mastikha*, a sweetish-sharp liqueur, and an over-sweet confection. Apart from agriculture the Chians' main sources of income are commerce and shipping: something like a third of the Greek merchant fleet is based in Chíos.

HISTORY. – The earliest evidence of human occupation on Chíos, recovered by excavation, dates back to the 4th millennium B.C. – In the 8th c. B.C. Ionian Greeks settled on the island and made it one of the wealthiest and most important members of the league of Ionian cities which was established about 700 B.C. In the 6th c. there was an important school of sculptors on the island. – Chíos was conquered by Cyrus the Great of Persia about 545 B.C. During the Ionian Rebellion it took part in the Battle of Lade (494 B.C.), contributing the largest number of ships (100) to the Greek fleet. In 477 Chíos became an independent member of the First Attic Maritime League. In 412 B.C. it broke away from Athens and in 394 from Sparta, having suffered severely under Spartan rule. In 377 it briefly became a member of the Second Attic Maritime League. It gained its independence in 85 B.C. – In A.D. 1204 the island passed to the Venetians, in 1346 to the Giustiniani family of Genoa and in 1566 to the Turks. – Throughout their history the Chians were renowned as seafarers and merchants. They took part in the Greek War of Independence in the 19th c., and the island was the scene of bloody massacres in 1822. In November 1912, during the Balkan War, a Greek squadron appeared off Chíos and captured it from the Turks after a brief resistance. Chíos claims to have been the birthplace of Homer.

The island's capital and principal harbor, **Chíos** (pop. 25,000), occupies approximately the same site as the ancient city, half-way down the E coast. Its houses extend in a semicircle around the harbor bay, which is dominated on the N by the ruined medieval *Kastro* or Citadel (13th–16th c.). Of the ancient city no trace remains. Archeological Museum, in a former mosque; Folk Museum.

3 miles/5 km N of Chíos town, at the fishing village of *Vrontádes*, is the **Daskalópetra** (Teacher's Stone), also known as the "School of Homer". This is a massive block of dressed stone with the remains of an altar, probably a *Shrine of Cybele*. – 6 miles/9 km farther N, above *Langáda Bay*, are remains of the Delphinion, a fortress which played a part in the Peloponnesian War. – Another 6 miles/9 km N is the little town of *Kardámyla*, with its sheltered harbor at *Mármaro*.

25 miles/40 km NW of Chíos town lies the little fortified town of **Vólyssos**, alleged to be Homer's birthplace. A short distance W is the port of *Límnia* (boats to Psará).

7½ miles/12 km W of Chíos town, in a lonely hill setting, the **Convent of Néa Moní** (1042–54) has important Byzantine * mosaics (scenes from the life of Christ) which suffered severe damage in an earthquake in 1881.

5 miles/8 km SW of Chíos town is the Byzantine Church of the *Panayíatis Krínis* (Mother of God at the Fountain), with

frescoes. – 15 miles/25 km SW of Chíos, in the mastic-growing region (now partly given over to fruit-growing), is the picturesque little town of **Pyrgí**, where the house fronts are decorated with characteristic geometric patterns in sgraffito. In the main square stands the Church of the Aghii Apostoli (13th c.), with 18th c. frescoes. – 2 miles/3 km farther S can be seen the site of the ancient port of **Phanai**, where there are remains of a Temple of Apollo (6th c. B.C.) with a Basilica of the 6th c. A.D. built over it. – 2 miles/3 km SE of Pyrgí, at *Emporíon*, are the remains of an acropolis which was fortified at four different periods (from Neolithic to Hellenistic) and of a Temple of Athena (6th c. B.C.). – From Pyrgí a road runs W via the little medieval town of *Ólympos* (4½ miles/ 7 km) to *Mésta* (2½ miles/4 km), with a Byzantine church.

7 miles/11 km S of Chíos town is the **Monastery of Aghios Minás**, now a memorial to the victims of the 1822 Massacres.

To the N of the island of Chíos, at the N end of the Chíos Strait, are the **Oinoussai Islands** (formerly known as the *Spalmatori Islands*), an archipelago extending from SE to NW. The principal island is *Oinoussai* (nautical school), to the E of which are the islets of Pasas, Gavathion and Vaton together with many isolated rocks. – To the SW of Chíos, off Elata Bay, are the little islands of *Pelagonisos, Aghios Yeoryios* and *Aghios Stéfanos*, with the remains of Hellenistic watch-towers.

**Chios**     **Nea Moni**

## ICONOGRAPHY

1 Symeon Stylites
2 Stylite, Isaiah, Jeremiah
3 Daniel, Ezechiel, Symeon Stylites
4 Daniel Stylites
5 Washing of the Feet
6 Before the Washing of the Feet, Entry into Jerusalem
7 Stephen the Yr, Ephraim, Arsenius, Nicetas, Antony, Maximus, John Calybites
8 Joachim, Anna, Stephen, Panteleimon, Theodore Stratelates, Bacchus, Orestes, Mardarius, Eugenius, Auxentius, Eustratius, Sergius, Mary
9 John Studites, Theodosius, Euthymius, Menas,

Pachomius, Sabbas, John Climacus
10 Pentecost
11 Gethsemane, Betrayal
12 Pantocrator
13 Nativity, Presentation in Temple, Baptism, Transfiguration, Crucifixion, Descent from Cross, Descent into Hell, Annunciation, Cherubim, John the Theologian, Andrew, Luke, Bartholomew, Seraphim, Philip, Mark, Matthew, Angels, Pantocrator
14 Archangel Michael
15 Mother of God Orans
16 Archangel Gabriel

# Corfu/Kerkyra
## *(Kérkira)*

Greece
Nomos: Kérkyra (Corfu).
Area: 229 sq. miles/593 sq. km. – Population: 89,600.
Telephone code: 0661.
(i) **Tourist Police,**
Odós Arseníou 31,
**Kérkyra;**
tel. 3 02 65.
**Olympic Airways,**
Kapodistriou 20,
**Kérkyra;**
tel. 3 86 94.

HOTELS. – KÉRKYRA: * *Corfu Palace*, L, 195 b., SP; *Cavalieri*, I, 91 b.; *King Alkinoos*, II, 102 b.; *Olympic*, II, 90 b.; *Astron*, II, 63 b.; *Ionion*, III, 144 b.; *Atlantis*, III, 112 b.; *Arcadion*, III, 95 b.; *Bretagne*, III, 65 b.; *Hermes*, III, 62 b.; *Calypso*, III, 34 b.; *Dalia*, III, 32 b. – SUBURBS OF ANEMÓMYLOS AND KANÓNI: * *Corfu Hilton*, L, 515 b., SP; *Artiti*, I, 312 b., SP; *Corfu Divani Palace*, I, 306 b., SP; *Marina*, II, 192 b.; *Arion*, II, 199 b.; *Royal*, III, 218 b.; *Salvos*, III, 176 b. – YOUTH HOSTEL.

S OF KÉRKYRA: ALYKÉS (2 miles/3 km): *Kerkyra Golf*, I, 444 b., SP. – PÉRAMA (4½ miles/7 km): *Alexandros*, I, 138 b.; *Aeolos Beach*, II, 451 b., SP; *Oasis*, II, 122 b.; *Akti*, II, 117 b.; *Aegli*, III, 71 b. – GASTOÚRI (6 miles/ 10 km); *Frini*, III, 34 b.; *Argo*, III, 28 b.; *Achillion*, III, 27 b. – BENÍTSES (8 miles/12·5 km): *Potomaki*, II, 288 b., SP; *Benitses Inn*, III, 44 b. – MORAITIKÁ (12¼ miles/ 20 km): *Miramare Beach*, L, 285 b.; *Delphinia*, I, 151 b.; *Mesoyi Beach*, II, 1528 b., SP; *Sea Bird*, III, 31 b. – MESÓYI (14 miles/22 km): *Rossis*, III, 57 b.; *Roulis*, III, 30 b. – KOUSPÁDHES (20 miles/33 km): *Boukari*, III, 20 b.

N OF KÉRKYRA. – KONTOKÁLI (4 miles/6 km): *Kontokali Palace*, I, 467 b. – GOUVIÁ (5 miles/8 km): *Astir Palace Corfu*, L, 590 b., SP; *Corcyra Beach*, I, 487 b., SP; *Galaxias*, III, 67 b. – DAFNÍLA (7 miles/11 km): *Eva Palace*, L, 323 b., SP; *Robinson Club*, I, 481 b. – DASIÁ (7½ miles/12 km): *Castello*, L, 132 b.; *Chandris Corfu*, I, 558 b., SP; *Chandris Dasia*, I, 467 b., SP; *Elaea Beach*, I, 366 b.; *Dasia*, III, 102 b. – YPSOS (9 miles/14 km): *Ypsos Beach*, II, 114 b.; *Mega*, III, 61 b. – NISÁKI (14 miles/22 km): *Nisaki Beach*, I, 444 b.

W COAST (FROM N TO S). – ARÍLLAS (28 miles/45 km): *Marina*, III, 32 b.; *Arilla Beach*, III, 30 b. – PALAIOKA- STRITSA (12½–15 miles/20–25 km): *Akrotiri Beach*, I, 238 b., SP; *Paleokastritsa*, II, 267 b., SP; *Oceanis*, II, 123 b.; *Xenia Pavilion*, II, 14 b.; *Odysseus*, III, 64 b. – LIAPÁDES (14 miles/22 km): *Golden Beach*, III, 34 b. – ERMÓNES (9 miles/14 km): *Ermones Beach*, I, 504 b., SP. – GLYFÁDA (10 miles/16 km): *Grand Hotel Glyphada Beach*, I, 417 b., SP. – AYIOS GÓRDIOS, (10 miles/16 km): *Ayios Gordios*, I, 388 b., SP; *Alonakia*, II, 30 b.; *Chrysses Folies*, III, 40 b. – ANÓ PAVLIÁNA (12 miles/19 km): *Iliovassilevma*, IV, 16 b.

CAMP SITES. – Kontokáli, Dasiá, Ýpsos, Pyrgí.

TRANSPORTATION. – Air services from Athens and London; boat services from Venice, Ancona, Brindisi and Piraeus; ferry services from Igoumenitsa and Patras.

*Corfu (Kérkyra), the most northerly of the Ionian Islands and their administrative center, offers a varied range of attractions to visitors – its mild climate, its pleasant scenery and its many excellent beaches – and is well equipped with tourist facilities and amenities.

HISTORY. – Corfu is identified as the Homeric Scheria, the land of the Phaeacians and their king Alkinoos. – The oldest traces of human settlement on the island point to the presence of farming peoples who may have come from Italy. Corfu was colonized by Corinth in 734 B.C., but developed into a powerful State which became a danger to the mother city. A naval victory by the Corinthians over the Corcyraeans in the Sybota Islands (probably around the mouth of the River Kalamas, now silted up) in 432 B.C. was a major factor in the outbreak of the Peloponnesian War. In 229 B.C. the island was captured by Rome, and when the Roman Empire was split into two in A.D. 395 Corfu fell to Byzantium. – From 1386 to 1797 it was held by Venice. Thereafter it briefly belonged to France, and in 1815 it was assigned to Britain along with the other Ionian Islands. In 1864 it was returned to Greece. – In the course of its eventful history the island was frequently devastated and plundered, so that it has preserved few relics of ancient or medieval times.

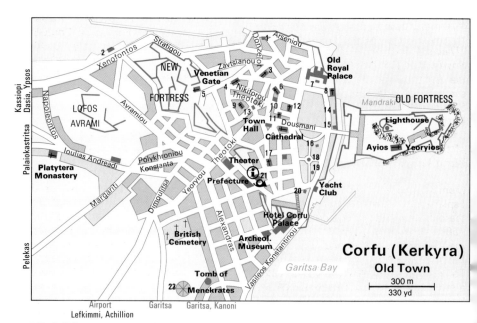

Corfu (Kerkyra)
Old Town
300 m
330 yd

1  Tourist Police
2  Yacht Supply Station
3  Mitropolis (Cathedral)
4  Ayios Antonios
5  Panayia Tenedou
6  Ayios Spyridon

7  Statue of Adam
8  Panayia Mandrakina
9  Ayii Peteres
10 Ionian Bank
11 Ayios Ioannis
12 Panayia ton Xenon

13 National Bank of Greece
14 Guilford statue
15 Schulenburg statue
16 Enosis Monument
17 Anglican church
18 Bandstand

19 Maitland Rotunda
20 Douglas Obelisk
21 EOT, Post Office
22 Prison

The island's capital, **Kerkyra** or *Corfu Town* (pop. 27,900) occupies the site of ancient Korkyra, founded by settlers from Corinth in 734 B.C. The modern town, though mostly Italian in style, displays a combination of Greek, Venetian and British features. – Starting from the harbor, we pass the New Fortress (1576–89) and enter the old town, the most notable buildings in which are the Venetian

A glimpse of St Spyridon's Church, Kérkyra

*Theater* (1663–93) and the *Church of St Spyridon*. In the sacristy of the church, to the right of the chancel, is a *silver sarcophagus containing the relics of St Spyridon, Archbishop of Cyprus in the 4th c. His remains were taken to Constantinople and brought to Corfu after the fall of that city; since then he has been the island's patron saint.

From the church we continue to the Esplanade, an area of gardens between the old town and the *Old Fortress* (built 1386, strengthened 1500). From here there are fine *views extending to Mount Pantokrátor and the mainland of Greece. To the left of the entrance to the fortress is a monument to Count Matthias von der Schulenburg, who defended the island against the Turks in 1716. Venice did him the rare honor of erecting a monument to him during his lifetime, and on his death granted him the further distinction of burial in the Arsenal in Venice.

Along the W side of the Esplanade are colonnaded houses dating from the period of British rule. Another reminder of that period is a small round temple in Neo-Classical style in the gardens to the S. On the N side of the Esplanade is the former residence of the British Governor, erected in 1816, which later (from 1846) became the Royal Palace and now houses the *Museum of Asiatic Art*, with the large collection of Japanese and Chinese art assembled by Ambassador Manos and the collection of Ambassador Chadzivasiliou (450 items from India, Tibet, Nepal, Thailand, Korea and Japan). – The *Archeological Museum* is in King Constantine Street.

The finest exhibit in the Archeological Museum is the monumental *Gorgo Pediment (56 ft long/17 m) from the W front of a Temple of Artemis of about 600 B.C. The central figure in this is the Gorgon Medusa, represented as mistress of the beasts and accompanied by her childred Pegasos and Chrysaor. Other items of interest are Gorgon antefixes (ornamental tiles), statuettes of Artemis found near the temple, portrait heads of the historian Thucydides and the dramatist Menander, and an Archaic lioness from the Tomb of Menekrates (about 600 B.C.). 220 yds/200 m beyond the museum, on the road out of town, a side road on the right leads to the Tomb of Menekrates, the circular substructure of which is preserved.

The seafront promenade runs S through the suburb of Garitsa and past the former royal summer residence, Mon Repos (in which the Duke of Edinburgh was born), to the Peninsula of Palaiópolis. Opposite the park gate stands Palaiópolis Church, on the site of an ancient temple. To the right is a road leading to the site of the Temple of Artemis discovered in 1911.

At the end of the peninsula (3 miles/ 4·5 km) is **Kanóni**, a tree-shaded terrace affording a magnificent *view of the bay, a scene of Classical beauty; in recent years increasing numbers of cafés and restaurants have been established here. Immediately in front are two small islets: on the nearer one, which is linked with the mainland by a causeway, stands the little **Monastery of Vlakhernai**; to the rear, reached by boat, is **Pontikonísi** (Mouse Island), with a large clump of trees. Pontikonísi is claimed to be the Phaeacian ship which took Odysseus back from Scheria to Ithaca and was turned to stone by Poseidon. The scenery of Kanóni and its situation near the ancient city have led some to suppose that the meeting between Odysseus and Nausicaa took place here; another candidate is Palaiokastrítsa.

The Vlakhernai Monastery and Mouse Island, Corfu

NORTH OF THE ISLAND. – The road runs N from Kérkyra and comes to the **Platytéra Monastery** on the outskirts of the town, which contains the Tomb of Kapodistrias, first President of Greece, who was murdered at Nauplia in 1831. The road then continues up the E coast and after passing through the resorts of **Kontokáli** and **Gouviá** (5 miles/8 km) reaches a fork, where one road continues along the coast to **Kassiópi** (23 miles/37 km), at the N end of the island, while the other cuts across to **Palaiokastrítsa** (15 miles/25 km) on the NW coast. Some archeologists believe this to be the site of the city and palace of the Phaeacian King Alkinoos. There is excellent bathing on the local beaches. Near here are the *Palaiokastrítsa Monastery*, situated on a promontory, and the *Castle of Angelókastro* (alt. 1079 ft/329 m). Half-way up to the castle is a parking place with a small restaurant which affords the finest *views of Palaiokastrítsa and the surrounding area. – The best return route to Kérkyra is by way of **Glyfáda** and the crag of *Pélekas* (*view).

SOUTH OF THE ISLAND. – A favorite outing from Kérkyra is to the *Villa Akhillion** (Achilleion; 6 miles/10 km), built for the Empress Elisabeth of Austria in 1890, acquired by Kaiser Wilhelm II in 1907 and now occupied by a gaming casino. The road to **Mesóyi** (9 miles/15 km) passes several beaches and then leaves the coast, reaching the sea again at **Kávos** (29 miles/47 km), at the southernmost tip of the island.

Corfu is one of the few places in Greece where wild strawberries can be found. Georgian houses and two cricket clubs are relics of the British occupation.

# Corsica/Corse

France
Region: Corse (Corsica).
Départements: Corse du Sud, Haute-Corse.
Area: 3368 sq. miles/8722 sq. km. – Population: 290,000.

ⓘ **Comité Régional au Tourisme,**
38 Cours Napoléon,
F-20178 **Ajaccio;**
tel. (95) 21 55 31–32.

HOTELS. – AJACCIO: *Castel Vecchio*, II, 105 r., SP; *Fesch*, II, 77 r.; *Albion*, II, 64 r.; *Impérial*, II, 60 r.; *Des Etrangers*, II, 46 r.; *Des Mouettes*, II, 31 r. – *Iles Sanguinaires*, II, 60 r., SP, *Dolce Vita*, II, 34 r., SP, *Cala di Sole*, II, 31 r., SP, *Eden Roc*, II, 30 r., SP, all on the road to La Parata. – *Campo dell'Oro*, I, 140 r., SP, 4½ miles/7 km SE at the airport. – *Sofitel*, L, 100 r., SP, 11 miles/17 km SE at Porticcio. – CAMP SITE, 7½ miles/12 km E.

PROPRIANO: *Arena Bianca*, II, 100 r.; *Roc e Mare*, II, 60 r.; *Du Valcino*, II, 54 r.; *Miramar*, II, 30 r., SP; *Ollandini*, III, 55 r.; two CAMP SITES. – OLMETO: *Marinca*, II, 60 r.; *Abartello*, IV, 32 r.; CAMP SITE. – SARTÈNE: *Les Roches*, III, 76 r. – BONIFACIO: *Solemare*, II, 47 r.; *La Caravelle*, II, 21 r. – PORTO-VECCHIO: *Cala Rossa*, II, 63 r.; *Cala Verde*, II, 40 r.; *Ziglione*, II, 32 r.; *Robinson Naturist Club La Chiappa* (9 miles/15 km E), 650 b. – SOLENZARA: *Maquis et Mer*, II, 35 r.; *Tourisme*, III, 25 r. – PORTO: *Méditerranée*, II, 40 r., SP; *Kalliste*, II, 33 r.; *Le Vaita*, II, 30 r.; *Corsica*, III, 35 r. – CALVI: *Grand Hôtel*, I, 60 r.; *Palm Beach*, I, 152 r.; *La Revellata*, II, 45 r.; *St-Erasme*, II, 31 r.; *Kalliste*, II, 24 r. – ILLE-ROUSSE: *Napoléon Bonaparte*, I, 100 r., SP; *La Pietra*, II, 40 r.

BASTIA: *Ile de Beauté*, II, 57 r.; *Ostella*, II, 30 r.; *Posta Vecchia*, III, 25 r.; *De l'Univers*, IV, 50 r.

Glyfáda beach, Corfu

*Corsica (in French, Corse), France's largest island and the fourth largest in the Mediterranean, lies nearer Italy than the French mainland. It is 114 miles/183 km long by up to 52 miles/84 km wide, giving it an area of 3368 sq. miles/8722 sq. km and a coastline of some 620 miles/1000 km. It is a mountainous island, reaching its highest point in Monte Cinto (8914 ft/2717 m). The population is about 290,000, with an average density of only 86 to the square mile (33 to the square kilometre). The capital of the region, which is divided into two *départements*, is Ajaccio.

The island, which has been christened the "island of light" and the "island of beauty", offers its visitors a great variety of scenery and occupation, combining subtropical vegetation with scope for climbing and even skiing in the hills of the interior, as well as a whole range of sandy beaches on the coasts. The luxuriant growth of vegetation – forest, maquis, olive trees, orange groves, vineyards and an abundance of flowers – led Napoleon, a native of the island, to say: "I would recognize Corsica with my eyes closed from its perfume alone." Even today, when approaching by sea, one can smell the fragrance of the maquis.

CLIMATE. – The nature of its topography gives the island a wide range of climatic variations. Visitors tend to think in the first place of its hot dry Mediterranean summer and its rainy autumn; but in addition the winter temperatures in its coastal regions, averaging 57 °F/14 °C, are distinctly higher than on the Côte d'Azur, the climate of which is most nearly comparable. At the height of summer, in spite of Corsica's insular situation, it can be very hot (average 77 °F/ 25 °C). The best time for a visit, therefore, is in May, June or September. Spring comes to the S coast as early as the end of February or the beginning of March. In the mountains the climate is considerably harsher, and the pattern of snowfall and snow-melt is similar to that of the Alps. At the height of summer, however, the cooler climate of the mountainous regions in the interior can be very agreeable.

HISTORY. – The original inhabitants of Corsica were a mixture of Iberians and Ligurians. In 564 B.C. Phocaeans settled on the E side of the island, followed by Etruscans and Carthaginians. The Romans landed on Corsica in 259 B.C. and had considerable difficulty in subduing the inhabitants. The fall of the Western Roman Empire was followed by the arrival successively of Vandals, Ostrogoths, Byzantines, Franks and Saracens, so that the island was always falling into the hands of new masters. In 1070 Pisa annexed Corsica, but lost it in 1284 to Genoa, which pursued a harsh policy of repression and exploitation. There were various risings against the oppressors, during one of which the Corsican freedom fighter Sampiero di Bastelica was murdered by the Genoese (1527); but

until the 18th c. these had no success. At last, in 1735, the Corsicans succeeded in breaking free from Genoa, and a German adventurer called Theodor von Neuhof became King. In 1746 Corsica declared its independence, and Pasquale Paoli (1725–1807) showed himself a skilled and successful politician. But although the Genoese had been worsted they still held out in Bastia, and in 1768 they ceded the island to France. There was some resistance, but the cession went through, and in the following year Napoleon Bonaparte was born in Ajaccio. Nevertheless the conflict between the Corsicans, the French (particularly during the Revolution) and the British, to whom the Corsicans had appealed for aid, continued until 1796, when Napoleon made "his" island finally part of France. During the Second World War Corsica was occupied by Italian and German forces until 1943. – In recent years there has been an increasingly active separatist movement in Corsica; and under legislation passed in February 1982 the island is to be granted internal self-government.

## Car Ferries to Corsica

### From France

| | |
|---|---|
| Marseilles–Bastia | daily |
| Nice–Ajaccio | daily |
| Nice–Bastia | daily |
| Nice–Calvi | daily |
| Nice–Ile Rousse | daily |
| Nice–Propriano | several times weekly |
| Toulon–Bastia | several times weekly |

These services are run by the **SNCM** line. Agent in Britain: P & O Normandy Ferries, Arundel Towers, Portland Terrace, Southampton SO9 4AE, tel. (0703) 34141.

### From Italy

| | |
|---|---|
| Genoa–Bastia | several times weekly |
| La Spezia–Bastia | several times weekly |
| Livorno–Bastia | several times weekly |
| Piombino–Bastia | several times weekly |
| San Remo–Bastia | several times weekly |
| San Remo–Calvi | several times weekly |

These services are mostly run by **Corsica Ferries**.

There are also services between Bonifacio (Corsica) and Santa Teresa Gallura (Sardinia).

TRANSPORTATION. – Corsica can be reached either by air or by sea. – *Air services*: by Air France from Paris, Marseilles and Nice to Ajaccio and Bastia; by Air Inter from Paris, Marseilles and Nice to Ajaccio, Bastia and Calvi. The services from Marseilles and Nice to Calvi operate throughout the year. – There are *boat services* from both France and Italy. The shortest crossing is from Livorno in Italy to Bastia (4 hours); from Genoa it is about the same. The crossing from the French ports of Marseilles, Toulon and Nice to Ajaccio, Bastia or Calvi takes between 6¼ and 11½ hours. – *Car ferries*: see box.

# Ajaccio

The Corsican capital, Ajaccio (pronounced Azhaksió in French, Ayácho in Italian; pop. 50,000) lies half-way down the W coast of the island in the beautiful Gulf of Ajaccio, surrounded by mountains which have a covering of snow right into summer. The town was founded by the Genoese in 1492, and in 1811 Napoleon made it the capital of the island in place of Bastia. As Corsica's second largest port Ajaccio handles a substantial part of the traffic to the island. In addition to its situation its attractions include a mild climate (average winter temperature 52·3 °F/11·3 °C) and a fine sandy beach near by.

Statue of Napoleon, Ajaccio

SIGHTS. – The *Maison Bonaparte in Rue St-Charles, Napoleon's birthplace, dates from the early 17th c. Napoleon was born here on August 15 1769, but the present interior arrangement and furnishings date from the end of the 18th c. There is also a *Musée Napoléonien* in the Town Hall, mainly containing material on the history of the Napoleonic period. Other evidence of the continuing importance of Napoleon in Ajaccio is provided by a statue of the Emperor, a group showing Napoleon with his four brothers, a statue of the First Consul and the collection of material in the *Palais Fesch*. The town's main street is called the Cours Napoléon. The *Cathedral*, in the Venetian Renaissance style of the second half of the 16th c., also contains mementoes of Napoleon. The *Citadel* in the old town (not open to the public) dates from the same period as the cathedral.

The harbor, Ajaccio

SURROUNDINGS of Ajaccio. – 2¼ miles/4 km W is **Monte Salario** (1020 ft/311 m). – 7½ miles/12 km W is *Cap de la Parata.

CIRCUIT OF THE ISLAND. – From Ajaccio the route runs S to **Olmeto** (pop. 1300), set amid olive groves under the ruined *Castello della Rocca*, and **Propriano** (pop. 2800), a seaside resort and spa with a beautiful beach near the town. – Then on to **Sartène** (pop. 5500), in the Sartenais district, with a picturesque *old town of medieval aspect whose narrow streets are entered under the arch of the Town Hall. The *Sartenais* contains much unspoiled country typical of southern Corsica. – The road continues S to **Bonifacio** (pop. 2640), a picturesque little fortified town in a magnificent **situation on a limestone peninsula 1650 yds/1500 m long with cliffs rising sheer from the sea to a height of 210 ft/ 64 m. It faces Sardinia, only 7 miles away across the strait called the Bouches de Bonifacio. It is worth taking time to explore the town, with its old houses flanking medieval lanes. The Citadel can be visited by arrangement. The most notable of the churches is Ste-Marie-Majeure (originally 12th c. but several times rebuilt), with a 15th c. tower. St-Dominique (13th–14th c.) is one of the finest Gothic churches on the island; it contains interesting groups of figures which are carried in procession.

From Bonifacio the road runs N to **Porto-Vecchio** (pop. 7000), on the gulf of the same name, a center of the cork trade. It still preserves parts of its old walls and a 16th c. Genoese citadel. In the vicinity are beaches of fine sand. – Then through the *Forêt de l'Ospedale* (oaks, pines) to **Zonza** (alt. 2572 ft/784 m; pop. 1030), set amid chestnut trees. From here a road runs NE over the **Col de Bavella** (4078 ft/1243 m) to **Solenzara**, with remains of a Roman road (a feature unique in Corsica), from which the coast road continues N to **Ghisonaccia** (pop. 1020); Genoese watch-tower, the Torre di Vignale.

From Zonza the route goes W and then N through the interior of the island to **Zicavo** (pop. 1240), a popular summer resort, from which *Mont l'Incudine* (7008 ft/2136 m) can be climbed (with guide and mule); from the summit there are magnificent views over Corsica. – **Vivario** (alt. 2034 ft/620 m), in a very beautiful *situation; handsome bridge

over the Vecchio, fountain with a figure of Diana the Huntress. – Through the ***Forêt de Vizzavona** (the village of Vizzavona being a popular summer resort) and over the Col de Vizzavona (3809 ft/1161 m) to **Corte** (pop. 6000), roughly in the center of the island. Above the town, on a rocky ridge, stands the 15th c. Citadel. Corte has played an important part in the history of Corsica: from 1755 to 1769 it was the island's capital, with a university which continued in existence until 1790. The Citadel is occupied by the Foreign Legion and is not open to the public. The Palais National is of interest for its associations with Pasquale Paoli, the champion of Corsican independence, and for an instructive museum devoted to the history of the island. The 17th c. Church of the Annunciation has a free-standing Baroque bell-tower. – From Corte a detour can be made to the ***Gorges de la Restonica**, below *Monte Rotondo* (8613 ft/ 2625 m).

Beyond Corte, at *Francardo*, turn W and continue via *Calacuccia*, below the island's highest peak, ***Monte Cinto** (8882 ft/2707 m), and the ***Forêt de Valdo-Niello** with its laricio pines; then over the *Col de Vergio* (4803 ft/1464 m) to **Porto** (pop. 350), a popular resort, with the bathing station of *Marine de Porto* on the bay of the same name. – Above the bay, between Porto and *Piana*, are the curious rock formations known as the **Calanche**, granite pinnacles eroded into bizarre forms resembling fabulous animals. Similar formations are to be seen on the road which continues N over the *Col de la Croix* (892 ft/272 m) and *Col de Palmarella* (1227 ft/374 m) and through the lonely *Balagne Déserte*, with the ruins of a silver-mine, to **Calvi** (pop. 3600), the Corsican port situated nearest to France. During the period of Genoese rule Calvi was the principal place on the island, and from this period dates the fortress-like upper town. The town was completely destroyed in 1794 by a British naval expedition commanded by Nelson. There is an attractive palm-fringed promenade along the harbor, and near this stands the Church of Santa Maria, originally founded in the 4th c. but rebuilt in the 14th. In the upper town is the Cathedral of St-Jean-Baptiste, originally built in the 13th c., destroyed in 1533 and soon afterwards rebuilt; it contains a celebrated Crucifix and other fine pieces of carving. The house in Rue Colombo which claims to be Columbus's birthplace (the Maison Colomb) is probably not authentic: there are other alleged birthplaces of the great discoverer in Italy and Spain. The situation and appearance of Calvi are striking, and in the Gulf of Calvi a flat sandy beach $2\frac{1}{2}$ miles/4 km long attracts so many visitors to this holiday resort with its many hotels.

Beyond Calvi the road runs E through the fertile Balagne area (or alternatively on the shorter coastal route via *Algajola*) to *Belgodere* (pop. 530), in a picturesque *situation on the slopes of a hill, with a 13th c. castle. – Then on to **Ile-Rousse** (pop. 2500), which is not an island, as its name suggests; the name comes from the red rocks of La Pietra. Like Calvi, this is a very popular resort, though on a more modest level, with no luxury hotels. It was founded in 1758 by Pasquale Paoli, on the site of an earlier Roman settlement, as a counterpart to Calvi. The climate has the reputation of being particularly mild. – Then, into the hills and over the *Col de Lavezzo* (1024 ft/312 m) to **St-Florent** (pop. 830), charmingly situated on the gulf of the same name, with an old castle. Near by are the remains of medieval *Nebbio*, with the Romanesque Cathedral of Santa Maria dell'Assunta (12th c.), built of limestone. – To the E of St-Florent is Bastia.

**Bastia** (pop. 52,000), Corsica's largest town and principal port, grew out of a small fishing village and takes its name from a bastion built by the Genoese in 1380. As the residence of the Genoese Governor and from 1570 of the Bishop, it became the island's capital, but in 1811 was deprived of that status by Napoleon in favor of his own birthplace, Ajaccio.

The town is made up of a number of different parts – the old fishing village, the Terra Vecchia; the Terra Nuova around the Citadel which stands above the Old Harbor; the original settlement of Bastia; and the modern housing area of St-Joseph.

The building of the Citadel, until 1766 the palace of the Genoese Governor, was begun in 1378 and completed about 1530 with the construction of the tower at the entrance. The interior courtyard is surrounded by two-story galleries. Here, too, are the Church of Ste-Marie (begun about 1495, completed at the beginning of the

17th c.) and the Chapel of Sainte-Croix, built in 1547 to house a miraculous Crucifix (Christ des Miracles) which was recovered from the sea by fishermen in 1428. Also in the Citadel are the interesting Corsican Ethnographical Museum and a military museum.

The old town is a fascinating labyrinth of narrow lanes with houses up to nine storys high. Here there are more churches and chapels, including the former Cathedral (17th c.). – N of Place St-Nicolas (marble statue of Napoleon), which dominates the town, is the excellent New Harbor.

Coastal scenery, Cap Corse

The tour of Corsica can be completed by a trip around the Peninsula of *Cap Corse, the northernmost tip of the island, a circuit of 80 miles/130 km (starting either from Bastia or St-Florent) through beautiful and typically Corsican scenery. Along the peninsula runs the *Serra* Range, reaching heights of up to 4282 ft/1305 m, while on the W side fertile valleys run down to the coast, offering favorable conditions for the growing of vines, olives and fruit, which are cultivated on a considerable scale. For much of the way the road is narrow, with poor visibility, and plenty of time should, therefore, be allowed for the trip. The principal places on the route are the following:

**Nonza** (pop. 200), with an old defensive tower, in a magnificent *situation E of *Monte Stello* (4282 ft/1305 m).

**Canari**, with two medieval churches; large asbestos workings.

**Pino** (pop. 1000), in a picturesque *situation, with a former Franciscan friary (1486). The Torre de Seneca on the Col Ste-Lucie, 3 miles/5 km away, is said to have been the philosopher's prison in the years A.D. 43–49.

**Centuri** (pop. 600) is an attractive place, consisting of a number of different settlements between the road and the river. There are several churches. From the mill at Mattei, on the road to the **Col de la Serra* (1188 ft/362 m) there are extensive views.

**Rogliano**, with the fishing village of *Macinaggio* (pop. 500), is made up of a number of separate hamlets. Napoleon landed here in 1793. Old Genoese watchtowers. From the Franciscan friary at Vignale (now in ruins) and from Cagnano Christianity spread out over Corsica.

**Erbalunga** has old patrician houses. Interesting Good Friday processions here and in the surrounding area.

Near **Brando** (pop. 1000) is a stalactitic cave from which there are fine views. At Castello is a charming Romanesque Church of Notre-Dame des Neiges (13th–14th c.).

# Costa Smeralda
## See under Sardinia

# Cres

Yugoslavia
Republic: Croatia (Hrvatska).
Area: 156 sq. miles/404 sq. km. – Population: 4000.
Telephone code: 051.
ⓘ **Turističko Društvo Cres,**
YU-51557 **Cres;**
tel. 82 08 33.
**Turističko Društvo Osor-Nerezine,**
YU-51554 **Osor-Nerezine**
(on the island of Mali Lošinj);
tel. (051) 86 50 07.
*Punta Križa:* apply to Osor-Nerezine office.

HOTELS. – CRES TOWN: Kimen, II, 385 b. – OSOR AND PUNTA KRIŽA: accommodation in private houses only.

CAMP SITES. – CRES: *Kovačine*, 550 yds/500 m from Kimen Hotel. – OSOR: *Adria, Bijar.* – PUNTA KRIŽA: *Baldarin* (naturist site).

BATHING BEACHES. The Cres town beach is not particularly good, and bathers usually take a boat to the other side of the bay, where there is also a large naturist beach. The largest naturist center on Cres, the Baldarin camp site, with plenty of shade, is right at the S end of the island.

EVENTS. – Concerts in the cathedral square, Osor, in summer.

CAR FERRIES. – The shortest connection with the mainland (frequent crossings) is between Brestova, on the coast road from Opatija to Pula, and Porozina on Cres. An alternative route, with less frequent services, is from Rijeka to Porozina (runs only during the season). Cres is connected to Mali Lošinj by a bridge.

**Cres (pronounced Tsress) is the largest of the Yugoslav Adriatic islands after Krk, measuring 42 miles/68 km from N to S but only 8 miles/13 km from E to W. It is an island of bare hills and plateaux, criss-crossed by low walls built to protect crops from the wind. At some points there are small patches of woodland, but much of the island is covered with impenetrable macchia. The highest part of the island is in the N, rising to 2133 ft/ 650 m in Mount Sis; from there the land falls gradually away to the large valley basin around the bay in which the town of Cres lies.**

The old port of **Cres** is a picturesque little place, with towers and narrow lanes, gateways, staircases and secluded inner courtyards which recall the period of Venetian rule. Of the town's once massive fortifications, a circuit of walls and towers enclosing a pentagonal area around the harbor, on a line now marked by the road encircling the town, there survive the *Bragadina Gate* (1581) and the *Marcella*

The town of Cres

*Gate* (1588), with coats of arms and the Lion of St Mark to commemorate the Venetian governors after whom they are named. In the market square is the *Municipal Loggia* (15th–16th c.) in which the citizens used to assemble. Close by, in the line of buildings fronting the harbor, is the *Clock-Tower*, which gives access to the Parish Church of *St Mary of the Snows*. Its cathedral status is reflected in the elaborately decorated Renaissance doorway, with capitals depicting dolphins and fruit, symbolizing the sea and the land, the town's two sources of subsistence.

Going along the side of the cathedral, we come to *St Isidore's Church*, the most ancient in the town, with the oldest bell on the island, cast in the 14th c. The church has a fine Romanesque apse with an elaborate frieze of round-headed arches.

Other notable buildings are the old *Town Hall*, with the municipal coat of arms under the balcony; the former *Bishop's Palace*; and a number of *patrician houses*, some renovated but others in a rather dilapidated condition. The *Franciscan friary* has a fine church, the carved wooden choir-stalls (15th c.) being particularly notable; the three dolphins are the heraldic emblem of one of the Venetian governors. Farther out is the *Benedictine convent*, in which the few remaining nuns rent rooms to vacationers. The *Municipal Museum*, in an old patrician house which belonged to the Petris family, contains material illustrating the history of the two islands together with objects salvaged from a merchant ship wrecked off Cape Pernat.

THE ISLAND. – A visitor approaching **Osor** (pop. 100), at the S end of the island on the way to Lošinj (see p. 122), is likely to take it for a sleepy little village of no particular consequence. A walk around it, however, will reveal evidence of the time when it was a flourishing town of some 30,000 inhabitants. In the center of the village stands the 15th c. Cathedral; the little square in front of it, flanked by the Bishop's Palace and old burghers' houses, has excellent acoustics and is used for concerts and serenades in summer. The cathedral, in Early Renaissance style (1464–98), contains the Shrine of St Gaudentius, Bishop of Osor, who is credited with banishing all venomous snakes from the islands of Cres and Lošinj. The massive separate tower dates from the

17th c. – The town walls and towers now visible date from the 15th c., when Osor had already shrunk from its former extent.

The largest place on the island after Cres is **Martinšćica**, in a bay on the W coast. The little Church of St Jerome, belonging to a monastery which is still occupied, contains a notable altar-piece.

There are regular boat trips from Cres town across the bay to the little village of **Valun**, huddled under conspicuous steep cliffs, with attractive beaches of light-colored pebbles on either side. The simple Parish Church of St Mary has in its sacristy the Valun Stone (Valunska ploča), which ranks with a similar stone from the island of Krk as the oldest Croatian text in Yugoslavia. It is particularly notable as being bilingual: the upper part has an inscription in Glagolitic (Old Slav) script, while on the lower part is the Latin equivalent.

From Valun a mule-track runs inland to **Lake Vrana**, the green waters of which lie 223 ft/68 m above sea-level, while the bottom of the lake is up to 52 ft/16 m below sea-level, giving it a maximum depth of 275 ft/84 m. It is believed that the lake draws its abundance of water, which supplied both Cres and Lošinj, from the mainland through a system of underground caverns.

It is well worth while making the trip to the only place of any consequence on the E coast of the island, **Beli**. At the highest point on the road which leads up into the hills from the ferry landing-stage at Porozina (fine views of Plavnik and Krk) a narrow side road branches off, heading for the N end of the island. The main road, skirting macchia and deciduous woodland, comes in 4 miles/6 km to Beli, on a hill high above the sea. There was a fortified settlement here in prehistoric times. Commandingly placed on top of the hill are the parish church and market square. There are Glagolitic inscriptions on a stone in the left-hand wall of a side chapel and on a tombstone set into the floor of the church. (On the Glagolitic script, see under Krk). – From here a steep path runs down to the landing-stage.

The most northerly place on the island is the old-world little village of **Dragoze-tići**, perched 985 ft/300 m above the sea, with low houses, vine arbors, vaulted rooms and cisterns.

# Crete
## (Kríti)

Greece
Nomoi: Iráklion, Chaniá, Réthymnon, Lasíthi.
Area: 3189 sq. miles/8259 sq. km. –
Altitude: 0–8058 ft/0–2456 m. Population: 460,000.
Telephone codes: Iráklion 081, Chaniá 0821,
Réthymnon 0831, Ághios Nikólaos 0841.

ⓘ **EOT,**
Xanthoudidoú 1,
**Iráklion;**
tel. 28 20 96.
**Tourist Police,**
Vas. Konstantinou,
**Iráklion;**
tel. 28 31 90.
**Olympic Airways,**
Platía Eleftherías,
**Iráklion;**
tel. 22 51 71.
**EOT,**
Akti Tombási 6,
**Khaniá;**
tel. 2 64 26.
**Tourist Police,**
Karaiskáki 23,
**Chaniá;**
tel. 2 44 77.
**Tourist Police,**
Vas. Yeoryíou B 52,
**Réthymnon;**
tel. 2 81 56.
**Tourist Police,**
Omirou 7,
**Aghios Nikólaos;**
tel. 2 23 21.

HOTELS. – IRÁKLION: *Arina Sand* (1¼ miles/2 km), I,
452 b., SP; *Atlantis*, I, 296 b., SP; *Astoria*, I, 273 b., SP;
*Galaxy*, I, 264 b., SP; *Knossos Beach* (hotel and
bungalows), Khani Kokkini, I, 207 b., SP; *Xenia*, I,
156 b., SP; *Mediterranean*, II, 105 b.; *Esperia*, II, 92 b.;
*Kastro*, II, 63 b.; *Cosmopolit*, II, 69 b.; *Petra*, II, 59 b.;
*El Greco*, III, 165 b.; *Olympic*, III, 135 b.; *Castello*, III,
124 b.; *Daedalos*, III, 115 b.; *Lato*, III, 99 b.; *Apollon*,
III, 92 b.; *Athinaikon*, III, 77 b.; *Domenico*, III, 73 b.;
*Heracleion*, III, 72 b.; *Selena*, III, 52 b.; *Park*, III, 51 b.;
*Poseidon*, III, 49 b.; *Alex*, III, 47 b.; *Knossos*, III, 46 b.;
*Mirabello*, III, 43 b.; *Akti*, Khani Kokkini, III, 36 b.;
*Robinson Club Lyttos Beach*, 320 r.; YOUTH
HOSTEL. – CAMP SITE.

PHAISTÓS: *Xenia Pavilion*, IV. 11 b. – MÁTALA: *Matala
Bay*, III, 104 b.; *Bamboo Sands*, III, 19 b. – KASTÉLLI
KISÁMOU: *Kisamos*, III, 30 b. ; *Castle* (Kastron), III,
21 b. – CHANIA: *Kydon*, I, 195 b.; *Porto Veneziano*, II,
120 b.; *Samaria*, III, 110 b.; *Xenia*, III, 88 b.; *Lissos*, II,
68 b.; *Doma*, II, 56 b.; *Kriti*, III, 170 b.; *Canea*, III, 94 b.;
*Aperta Beach* (bungalows), III, 92 b.; *Lucia*, III, 72 b.;
*Diktynna*, III, 66 b.; *Kypros*, III, 36 b.; *Hellinis*, III, 28 b.;
*Plaza*, III, 17 b.; YOUTH HOSTEL. – ÓMALOS: *Xenia
Pavilion*, II, 7 b.

RÉTHYMNON: *Rithymna*, I, 947 b.; *El Greco* (hotel and
bungalows), I, 573 b.; *Brascos*, II, 151 b.; *Idaeon*, II,
133 b.; *Xenia*, II, 50 b.; *Minos*, III, 89 b.; *Valari*, III,
55 b.; *Ionia*, III, 32 b.; YOUTH HOSTEL; CAMP SITE.
– MÁLIA: *Kernos Beach*, I, 519 b., SP; *Sirens' Beach*, I,
422 b., SP; *Malia Beach*, III, 354 b., SP; *Grammatikaki*,
II, 91 b.; YOUTH HOSTEL.

AGHIOS NIKÓLAOS: *Minos Palace*, L, 276 b., SP;
*Mirabello Village* (hotel and bungalows), L, 251 b.,
SP; *Minos Beach*, L, 233 b.; *Mirabello*, I, 322 b., SP;
*Coral*, II, 323 b.; *Ariadni Beach*, II, 142 b.; *Apollon*, III,
111 b.; *Du Lac*, III, 74 b.; *Cronos*, III, 68 b.; *Acratos*, III,
60 b.; *Creta*, III, 50 b.; *Alkistis*, III, 45 b.; YOUTH
HOSTEL. – IERÁPETRA: *Petra Mare*, I, 409 b., SP; *Creta*,
II, 47 b.; *Lygia*, III, 29 b. – MOKHLOS: *Club Aldiana* (due
to open 1984). – SITÍA: *Sitian Beach*, I, 310 b., SP;
*Itanos*, III, 138 b.; *Vai*, III, 84 b.; *Crystal*, III, 75 b.; *Sitia*,
III, 70 b.

AIR SERVICES. – Airports at *Iráklion*, 3 miles/5 km E
of the town, and *Chaniá*, 10 miles/ 16 km E on the
Akrotíri Peninsula, at Stérnes. – Regular flights
Athens–Iráklion (40 minutes), Athens–Chaniá
(45 minutes), Iráklion–Rhodes (only in summer).

BOAT SERVICES. – Regular services between Athens
(Piraeus) and Iráklion and Chaniá (cars carried),
Kastélli, Aghios Nikólaos and Sitía several times daily
(10–14 hours); also local services to the islands of
Milos, Ios, Santorin and Rhodes. – Approaching
*Chaniá*, Cape Spátha (Psakon; at northern tip remains
of a Sanctuary of Diktynna) is seen on the right and the
Akrotíri (Kyamon) Peninsula on the left, with the wide
bay of Chaniá (often exposed to storms from the N)
opening up between them; in the background are the
Léfka Óri (White Mountains). Ships anchor at Chánia
in the open bay, larger vessels in Soúda Bay beyond
the Akrotíri Peninsula, the only good harbor on Crete.
– Approaching *Iráklion*, Cape Stávros, an important
landmark, is seen on the right and the bare island of
Día (wild goat reserve), a safe haven in a storm from
the N, on the left; straight ahead is Iráklion Bay,
bounded on the W by Cape Panalia.

WATER SPORTS. – Boat rental: agencies in Iráklion.
– Water-skiing schools: Boat Club, Chaniá, and Hotel
Elounda Beach, Elounda.

ROAD TRAVEL. – Car rental: the main firms are in
Iráklion. – Bus services between the main places on
the island.

**★★Crete, the largest Greek island and
the fourth largest in the Mediterranean, lies on the southern verge of
the Aegean some 60 miles/97 km SE
of the Peloponnese. It is the most
southerly outpost of Europe and one
of the main elements in the arc of
islands which links southern Greece
with Asia Minor.**

Famed both for its Minoan remains and for
the beauty of its scenery, Crete extends for
some 160 miles/260 km from E to W,
ranging in width between 7½ miles/12 km
and 35 miles/57 km. It is broken up by
three ranges of mountains, much affected
by karstic action: in the W the *Léfka Óri*
(White Mountains; 8045 ft/2452 m),
which are usually covered with snow, in
the central part of the island the Psilorítis
Mountains (Idi Oros, the classical Mount
Ida, 8058 ft/2456 m; rewarding climb),
which also have an abundance of snow,
and in the E the **Díkti** Range (7048 ft/
2148 m). These rugged and barren
mountains are the home of the Cretan wild

A Cretan in local costume

goat (*Capra aegagrus creticus*), the ancestral form of the domesticated goat. Agriculture is possible in these regions only in the karstic collapse depressions (poljes). Between the mountain ranges are fertile plains (Mesará; Omalós; Lasíthi, irrigated with the help of windmills) in which palms, olives, bananas, oranges and vines are grown. On the N coast are the towns of *Chaniá*, *Iráklion* and *Réthymnon*.

The climate is Mediterranean, with comparatively mild and rainy winters and absolutely dry and subtropically hot summers (lasting 6–7 months). The main source of income is agriculture, with the tourist trade now making an increasing contribution to the economy.

HISTORY. – The earliest traces of human settlement, probably by incomers from North Africa, date back to the 7th millennium B.C. – From the 3rd millennium onward there developed in Crete a pre-Greek Bronze Age culture which reached its peak about 2000–1600 B.C. and is known as the *Minoan culture*. The cultural and economic influence of the Minoan kingdom – the first Mediterranean sea power – extended as far afield as the Iberian Peninsula. Then about 1400 B.C. the Minoan civilization suddenly collapsed. The cause of the collapse is not known: one possibility is that the Cretan cities were destroyed by a catastrophic earthquake, perhaps associated with the explosion of

the volcanic island of Thera (Santorin: see p. 166). – Toward the end of the 12th c. B.C. *Dorian Greeks* conquered the greater part of the island. – In 66 B.C. Crete was taken by the *Romans*, who thus gained a base of major importance in the Mediterranean. When the Roman Empire was split into two in A.D. 395 Crete fell to *Byzantium*, and it remained in Byzantine hands until it was taken by the *Arabs* in 824. Between 961 and 1204 it was again part of the Byzantine Empire. Thereafter followed the long period of *Venetian* rule (1204–1669) – a period which saw long and bitter struggles by the Cretans to recover their independence but also brought the island a considerable cultural upsurge. The great painter and sculptor Domenikos Theotokopoulos, better known as *El Greco*, lived during this period (b. 1541 in the village of Fodele near Iráklion, d. 1614 in Toledo). – In 1669 Crete was captured by the *Turks*, who held it until 1898, when they were forced to leave by Greek and Western European military action. – After a period of independence Crete was incorporated in the kingdom of *Greece* on October 5 1912, thanks to the initiative of *Eleftherios Kyriakos Venizélos* (1864–1936), the Cretan-born lawyer and Liberal politican who later became Prime Minister of Greece. He was born in Chania, and his house and monument are still there. – In the spring of 1941 German airborne troops occupied the island, which was of great strategic importance because of its situation between southern Europe and Africa. German forces were evacuated from Crete in May 1945.

While the S coast of Crete generally falls steeply down to the sea, the N coast is flatter, with long beaches suitable for bathing. The northern coastal area is well served by good roads. Iráklion, the largest town in Crete, is the starting-point of a number of major routes.

# Iráklion

**Iráklion (pop. 85,000), situated halfway along the N coast of Crete, is the island's principal commercial port and its administrative center. In ancient times it was the port of Knossós, but under the Romans it declined; then in A.D. 824 it was captured by the Arabs and given a new lease of life under the name of Kandak. In 1204 it passed to Venice, who called it Candia; and from 1538 onward it was surrounded by a massive circuit of walls 3 miles/5 km long designed by the celebrated Italian military engineer Michele Sammicheli and became the capital of the island. After Crete was made part of Greece, in 1913, the town was given its present name, after the ancient Greek port of Herakleion.**

SIGHTS. – The principal feature of interest in Iráklion, and one of the great tourist

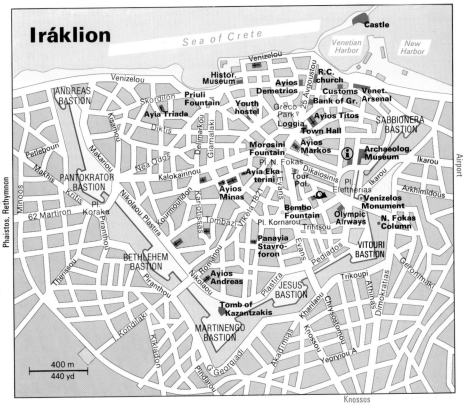

attractions of Crete, is the **Archeological Museum** (*Kretikon Mouseion*; in Platía Eleftherías or Liberty Square), which contains the magnificent finds from Knossós, Phaistós, Aghia Triáda and other sites on the island. Here it is possible to do no more than list some of the most important exhibits.

GROUND FLOOR. – SECTION ALPHA, Room I: Neolithic (5000–2600 B.C.) and Early Minoan period (2600–2000 B.C.): stone vessels from the island of *Mókhlos* (NE of Crete) and seals. – SECTION BETA, Rooms II and III: material of the Middle Minoan (Proto-Palatial) period (2000–1700 B.C.), in particular vases in Kamáres style (named after the village of Kamáres) from Knossós, Mália and Phaistós. – SECTION GAMMA, Rooms IV, V, VII and VIII: material of the Middle Minoan (Neo-Palatial) period (1700–1450 B.C.): libation vessels, inscribed tablets, statuettes, ivory gaming-board, jewelry. – SECTION DELTA, Room VI: jewelry and other valuable grave-goods of the Late Minoan (Post-Palatial) period (1400–1250 B.C.). – SECTION ETA, Room X: Late Minoan/Helladic material (1400–1100 B.C.). – SECTION THETA, Rooms XI and XII: Late Minoan/Geometric period (Dorian; 1100–650 B.C.) and later developments. SECTION IOTA, Room XIII: Minoan sarcophagi, etc., from Aghia Triáda, Tylissós and Gourniá. – SECTION NU, Room XIX: Archaic Greek period (7th–6th c.). – SECTION XI, Room XX: Greek and Roman sculpture (5th c. B.C. – A.D. 4th c).

FIRST FLOOR. – SECTION KAPPA, Rooms XIV (long hall) to XVI: **frescoes** and *reliefs* from Minoan palaces; a magnificent stone sarcophagus from Aghia Triáda. – SECTION LAMBDA, Room XVII: Giamalakis

Collection of Dorian sculpture (700–500 B.C.). – SECTION MU, Room XVIII: material of the Archaic and Roman periods (700 B.C.–A.D. 400).

NE of the old part of the town is the charming Venetian harbor, with a *castle*

Bull's-head rhyton from Knossós

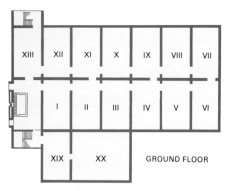

| | | | | | | | |
|---|---|---|---|---|---|---|---|
| XIII | XII | XI | X | IX | VIII | VII | |
| I | II | III | IV | V | VI | | |

| XIX | XX | GROUND FLOOR |
|---|---|---|

I     Neolithic and Pre-Palatial (2500–2000 B.C.)
II     Proto-Palatial: Knossós, Mália (2000–1700 B.C.)
III     Proto-Palatial: Phaistós (2000–1700 B.C.)
IV     Neo-Palatial: Knossós, Phaistós, Mália (1700–1450 B.C.)
V     Late Neo-Palatial: Knossós (1450–1400 B.C.)
VI     Neo-Palatial and Post-Palatial: Knossós, Phaistós (1400–1350 B.C.)
VII     Neo-Palatial: central Crete
VIII     Neo-Palatial: Káto Zákros (1700–1450 B.C.)
IX     Neo-Palatial: eastern Crete
X     Post-Palatial (1400–1100 B.C.)
XI     Sub-Minoan and Early Geometric (1100–800 B.C.)
XII     Late Geometric and Orientalising (800–650 B.C.)
XIII     Sarcophagi
XIX     Archaic period (7th–6th c. B.C.)
XX     Classical and late (5th c. B.C.–4th c. A.D.)

## Iraklion Archaeological Museum

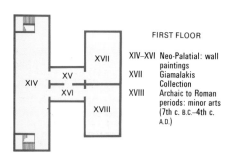

| | | FIRST FLOOR |
|---|---|---|
| | XVII | XIV–XVI Neo-Palatial: wall paintings |
| XIV | XV | XVII Giamalakis Collection |
| | XVI | XVIII Archaic to Roman periods: minor arts (7th c. B.C.–4th c. A.D.) |
| | XVIII | |

**Palace**, which was excavated and partly reconstructed by Sir Arthur Evans (1851–1941) from 1899 onwards.

This extensive complex of buildings laid out on four levels on the slopes of the Hill of Kefalá and originally of two and three storys, was several times destroyed, presumably by earthquakes, and subsequently rebuilt. The palace stood from about 2000 to 1400 B.C., and during this period three phases can be distinguished – the First Palace from 2000 to 1800, the Second Palace from 1800 to 1700 and the Third Palace from 1700 to 1400. The parts now visible belong mainly to the Third Palace, and broadly represent its condition in the 16th c. B.C. The complicated layout of the palace provided a basis for the belief that this was the legendary Labyrinth of King Minos, particularly in view of the frequent occurrence in the palace of the double axe (Greek *labrys*) which was the emblem of Minoan Crete.

Entering the palace from the West Court (on the left, the remains of a theater), we pass along the *Processional Corridor* (so-called from the frescoes with which it was decorated), through the *South Propylaia* and past numerous *store-rooms* containing pottery storage jars into the spacious *Central Court*, which may have been the scene of the contests with bulls depicted on finds from Knossós in the Archeological Museum in Iráklion. – On the W side of the court are the *Grand Staircase* and the *Throne Room*,

"Throne of Minos", Knossós

on the outer breakwater. – In Venizélos Square are the *Morosini Fountain* (1628), with 14th c. figures of lions, and the former *Church of St Mark* (1303), now a *museum of Byzantine painting*. Near the church, in August 25th Street, which runs N to the harbor, stands the old Venetian *Loggia* (1627), now the Town Hall. Close by, to the NE, is the *Church of St Titos*. – In St Catherine's Square are the 19th c. *Cathedral of St Menas* (Aghios Minás) and the little **Church of St Catherine** (Aghia Ekateríni; 16th c.), now a *museum of religious art*. – The *Historical Museum* in Kalokerinou Street contains examples of Cretan folk art and mementoes of the period of Turkish rule.

3 miles/5 km SE of Iráklion, near the village of *Makritíkhos*, is the site of **Knossós**, with the Minoan **Royal**

with a stone throne of about 2000 B.C.; on the E side *residential apartments* and *domestic offices*, with bathrooms and flushing lavatories. Adjoining the *Hall of Double Axes* are the *King's Apartments* and the *Queen's Apartments*. The many frescoes are copies; the originals are now in the museum in Iráklion. – Around the palace is the site of the ancient city of Knossós, which may have had a population as great as 100,000. Most of the site is still unexcavated, but the remains of a number of villas and of the "Little Palace" (220 yds/200 m NW) can be seen.

Some 25 miles/40 km SW of Knossós is the site of ancient **Gortys** (*Gortyn*), once the rival of Knossós and later capital of the Roman province of Creta-Cyrenaica. On the left of the road, surrounded by olive groves, are the foundations of a Temple of Apollo Pythios, a Roman palace with baths (2nd c. A.D.), a theater, an amphitheater and a circus (stadium) 410 yds/374 m long. 550 yds/500 m beyond this

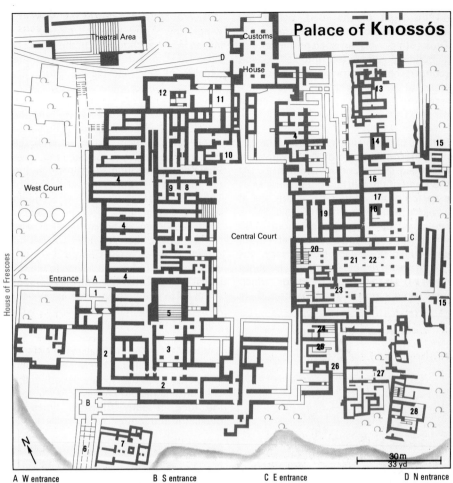

**Palace of Knossós**

Theatral Area

Customs House

West Court

House of Frescoes

Entrance    A

Central Court

N

30 m
33 yd

A  W entrance    B  S entrance    C  E entrance    D  N entrance

| | | | |
|---|---|---|---|
| 1 W Propylaia | 8 Throne-room | 15 Bastions | 22 King's Megaron |
| 2 Processional corridor | 9 Inner shrine | 16 Workshops | 23 Queen's Megaron |
| 3 S Propylaia | 10 Prison | 17 Potter's workshop | 24 Bathroom |
| 4 Store-rooms | 11 NW Portico | 18 Lapidary's workshop | 25 Shrine of Double Axes |
| 5 Grand Staircase | 12 Lustral basin | 19 Water channel | 26 Lustral basin |
| 6 Stepped Porch | 13 Pottery stores | 20 Grand staircase | 27 High altar |
| 7 S House | 14 Store-rooms with giant pithoi | 21 Hall of Double Axes | 28 SE House |

The Palace of Knossós

on the right of the road, below the acropolis, are the ruins of the *Basilica of St Titos* (6th c. A.D.), an ancient theater and a building, converted into an odeon (concert hall) in Roman times, on the walls of which is a long inscription recording the *Law Code of Gortys* (about 450 B.C.).

In the S of the island is the site of the city of **Phaistós**, founded by King Minos and destroyed in the 2nd millennium B.C. At the E end of the hill, laid out in terraces, is a *palace* of the same type as the one at Knossós. Built soon after 1650 B.C. on the site of an earlier palace of about 1800 which was destroyed a century later by an earthquake, this palace, like Knossós, was in turn destroyed by an earthquake about 1450 B.C. Of the palace buildings, which were laid out around a central court, there

survive only the remains of the W and N wings, the S and E wings having collapsed in the earthquake. On the W and N sides of the surviving structures are remains of the first palace. From the uppermost terrace there is a superb view.

1¼ miles/2 km W of Phaistós are the remains of the Minoan Summer Palace of *Aghia Triáda*, originally linked with the Phaistós palace by a paved road. Like Phaistós, it was originally constructed in the 16th c B.C., but after the earthquake of 1450 B.C. it was rebuilt and was occupied down to Dorian times. From the W side of the palace there is a magnificent view. Higher up is the Venetian Chapel of *Aghios Gheórgios* (St George; 14th c.), with frescoes. Below the palace to the NE parts of a Late Minoan settlement (14th–11th c. B.C.) have been excavated. At the foot of the hill is a necropolis, with a domed tomb (tholos).

6 miles/10 km SW of Phaistós is *Mátala*, the port of Phaistós in the Minoan period and of Gortys in the Roman period. In the cliffs around the bay are caves hewn from the rock in Early Christian times as dwellings and tombs.

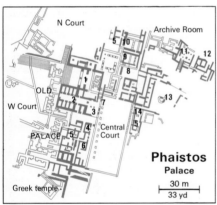

**Phaistos**
Palace

├─ 30 m ─┤
├─ 33 yd ─┤

1 Propylon
2 Store-rooms
3 Pillared hall
4 Alabaster benches
5 Lustral basin
6 Pillar crypt
7 Altar

8 Small court
9 Queen's Apartments
10 King's Apartments
11 Pillared hall
12 Potters' workshop
13 Furnace
14 Pillared room

Mátala Bay, on the S coast of Crete

On the N coast of the island, apart from Iráklion, there are a number of other towns and places of interest. Near the western end, in the Gulf of Kísamos, is **Kastélli Kisámou**, on the site of ancient *Kisamos*, with remains of a theater and a temple.

22 miles/35 km E of Kastélli Kisámou is **Chaniá** the former capital, the second largest town on the island, the economic center of western Crete and chief town of

The Phaistós Disc (Iráklion Museum)

the nomos of Chaniá. There was a settlement here in Minoan times.

The old town is surrounded by a 2 mile/3 km long circuit of 16th c. *walls*. On the N side of the town lies the *Venetian harbor* (lighthouse at end of breakwater), with *arsenals* of about 1500 (now boatsheds) and remains of the old *fortress*. The Gothic Church of St Francis now houses the *Archeological Museum* (material of the Dorian period). Other features of interest are the *Church of the Savior* (San Salvatore; 16th c.), the *Janissaries' Mosque* (1645), some handsome Venetian *patrician houses* and the large modern *Market Hall*. To the S of the old town are the *Historical Archives* (Odós I. Sfakianaki 20), with interesting manuscripts, documents, weapons and icons.

2½ miles/4 km SE of the old town is *Soúda Bay*, the largest and most sheltered natural harbor on the island (Chaniá's commercial harbor; naval base). – 10½ miles/17 km NE, on the Akrotíri Peninsula, is the *Monastery of Aghia Triáda* (1631), and 2½ miles/4 km N of this is the *Monastery of Gouvernéto* (16th c.), near which, on the coast, are the cave-dwelling and church of a hermit named John (Venetian doorway).

Samariá Gorge

26 miles/42 km S of Chaniá lies the village of *Omalós*, on the edge of the fertile Omalós Plateau. From here it is possible to walk down to the S coast through the impressive **Samariá Gorge** (Farángi Samariás), 11 miles/18 km long, up to 1000 ft/300 m deep and, at the Iron Gate (Sideroportes), only 6–10 ft/2–3 m wide. Here the Cretan wild goat (*kri-kri*) can still be found.

43 miles/70 km E of Chaniá is **Réthymnon**, the third largest town on the island and administrative center of the nomos of Réthymnon. It shows an attractive mingling of different cultures, with relics of both the Venetian and the Turkish periods. – The old part of the town contains many Venetian palazzos, Turkish houses with their latticed wooden balconies, a number of small mosques (18th c.) and the Venetian Citadel (Fortezza; 14th c., enlarged in 16th c.), with a mosque spanned by a massive dome. The 17th c. Loggia now houses the Municipal Museum.

Some 6 miles/10 km E of the town, in the *Piyí* area, is the largest olive grove in the Mediterranean area (1·5 million trees).

14 miles/23 km SE of Réthymnon are the ruins of the Early Byzantine *Monastery of Arkádi*, the scene of a heroic episode in 1866 when a party of Cretan insurgents were besieged in the monastery by Turkish troops and blew themselves up rather than surrender. – Some 20–25 miles/ 30–40 km SE, in the Amári area, are a number of typical Cretan villages, some of which have interesting old churches – in particular *Apostóli, Méronas, Yerakári, Vríses, Áno Méros* and *Fourfourás*, as well as the *Asomáton Monastery*.

Some 30 miles/50 km SE of Réthymnon, on the S coast, is **Aghia Galíni** (many hotels; water sports).

Aghia Galíni, on the S coast of Crete

48 miles/78 km E of Réthymnon we come to Iráklion, from which it is another 22 miles/35 km to **Mália**. Adjoining this little town on the N coast is the Minoan *Palace of Mália*, excavated by Chadzidakis in 1921 and later by French archeologists.

20 miles/30 km farther E is **Aghios Nikólaos**, magnificently situated on the slopes above the *Gulf of Mirabello*. A few years ago it was just a small fishing village, but is now chief town of the nomos of Lasíthi and a favorite tourist resort, with

Aghios Nikólaos, on the N coast

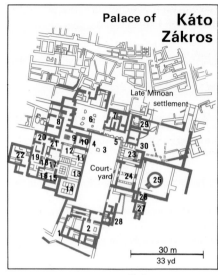

Palace of **Káto Zákros**

Late Minoan settlement

Court-yard

| | 30 m |
|---|---|
| | 33 yd |

| 1 | S entrance | 16 | Treasury |
|---|---|---|---|
| 2 | Workshops | 17 | Lustral basin |
| 3 | Square foundation (for altar?) | 18 | Shrine |
| 4 | Entrance to W wing | 19 | Archives |
| 5 | Pillared portico | 20–21 | Rooms in which bronze |
| 6 | Kitchen and dining-room | | ingots and elephants' |
| 7 | Room with kitchen utensils | | tusks were found |
| 8 | Store-rooms | 22 | Dyers' workshop |
| 9 | Room with tiled floor | 23 | Queen's Apartments |
| 10 | Vestibule | 24 | King's Apartments |
| 11 | Large pillared hall | 25 | Large circular basin |
| 12 | Light-well | 26 | Square fountain |
| 13 | Square room | 27 | Square basin |
| 14 | Banqueting room | 28 | Circular fountain |
| 15 | Workshop | 29 | Lustral basin |
| | | 30 | Entrance |

beautiful beaches and much of interest to see in the surrounding area. The harbor is linked with the small inland lake (fresh water) of *Voulisméni,* in which legend has it that the goddess Athena once bathed. Offshore is the island of *Aghii Pántes* (wild goat reserve).

45 miles/73 km E of Aghios Nikólaos is **Sitía,** a small port town (beach) dominated by a Venetian castle. – 29 miles/46 km SE of Sitía are the remains, excavated since 1962, of the Minoan Palace of *\*Káto Zákros,* surrounded by a settlement which existed between 1600 and 1450 B.C. and carried on trade with Egypt and North Africa.

12 miles/19 km SE of Aghios Nikólaos can be seen the site, only partly excavated, of *Gourniá,* which gives an excellent impression of a town of the Late Minoan period (1600–1400 B.C.), with its narrow paved lanes, small dwelling-houses and palace and sanctuary standing on higher ground.

22 miles/36 km S of Aghios Nikólaos, on the S coast, is **Ierápetra,** the most southerly town in Europe, in a fertile

Sitía

vegetable-growing area. It occupies the site of the ancient port of *Hierapydna.* Venetian fortress; small museum in Town Hall.

# Cyclades
## (Kikládhes)

Greece

HOTELS. – ON KÉA: *Kea Beach,* II, 150 b.; *I Tzia Mas,* II, 48 b.; *Ioulis,* II, 21 b.; *Charthea,* III, 67 b.

ON KÝTHNOS: *Posidonion,* III, 158 b.; *Xenia Anagenissis,* III, 93 b.

ON SÝROS: *Hermes,* II, 47 b., *Nissaki,* III, 78 b., *Europe,* III, 51 b., *Cycladion,* III, 29 b., all in Hermoúpolis. – *Olympia,* III, 78 b., *Finikas,* III, 26 b., both in Fínikas. – *Poseidonion,* III, 51 b., *Delagrazia,* II, 19 b., both in Posidonia. – *Alexandra,* III, 58 b., *Romantica,* III, 58 b., *Kamelo,* III, 45 b., *Ahladi,* III, 25 b., all in Váry.

ON SÉRIFOS: *Perseus,* II, 20 b.; *Serifos Beach,* III, 63 b.; *Maistrali,* III, 40 b.

ON SÍFNOS: *Apollonia,* II, 18 b., *Sofia,* III, 22 b., *Sifnos,* III, 19 b., *Anthousa,* III, 12 b., all in Apollonía. – *Artemon,* III, 54 b., in Artemón. – *Stavros,* III, 28 b., in Kamáres. – *Platys Yialos,* II, 38 b., in Platýs Yialós.

ON MÍLOS: *Venus Village*, II, 173 b.; *Adamas*, II, 22 b.; *Corali*, III, 31 b.

ON IOS: *Chrysi Akti*, II, 19 b.; *Armadoros*, III, 50 b.; *Corali*, III, 29 b.; *Fragakis*, III, 27 b.; *Flisvos*, III, 25 b.; *Philippou*, III, 22 b.

ON AMORGÓS: *Mike*, III, 19 b.

The *Cyclades are the many islands in the southern Aegean which lie between the Peloponnese and the Greek mainland in the W, Crete in the S and the islands off the Anatolian coast in the E. They are so named because to the ancient Greeks they lay in a circle (kyklos) around the little island of Délos, the birthplace of Apollo.

Geologically the islands are a continuation of the hills of Attica and Euboea (Evia). Two chains of islands can be distinguished: to the W, linking up with Attica, are the island of Kéa, Kýthnos, Sérifos, Sífnos, Kímolos, Mílos (Melos) and Folégandros; to the E, linked with Euboea, are Ándros, Tínos, Mýkonos, Délos and Rinía. Between these two chains is a central group of many islands, including Sýros, Páros, Náxos, Íos, Amorgós, Santorin, Anáfi and Astypálaia. Mílos and Santorin are of volcanic origin; the other islands are formed of crystalline rocks, schists and limestones.

HISTORY. – The Cyclades were of great importance in early days through their situation on the shipping routes between Greece and Asia Minor. In the 3rd millennium B.C. they developed the culture known as Cycladic. In the 2nd millennium Minoan and Mycenaean influence became predominant. After the Dorian migrations most of the islands were inhabited by Ionians, those to the S by Dorians. In the 7th c. B.C. the island of Naxos was dominant; in the 6th c. the Cyclades fell under Athenian control; in the Hellenistic period they formed the Nesiotic (Island) League. During the Byzantine period the islands were exposed to piratical raids by Arabs and others. After the fourth Crusade (1203–04) the Italian Duchy of the Archipelago or of Naxos was established. In 1566 the islands were occupied by the Turks. Finally in 1830 they became part of the kingdom of Greece.

Common to all these islands are their poor soil and the characteristic Cycladic architecture, derived from very early structural forms – cube-shaped whitewashed houses with flat roofs, churches built up from simple formal elements (the cube, the cylinder, barrel vaulting, spherical vaulting). The Cyclades are rich in evidence of 4500 years of history: to the 3rd millennium B.C. belong the Cycladic idols found on Náxos, to the 2nd millennium the excavated sites of Akrotíri (Santorin), Fylakopí (Mílos) and Aghia Iríni (Kéa), to the 1st millennium such sites as Délos, Thera and Mílos, to the Byzantine centuries the Ekatontapylianí Church on Páros, to the Frankish period in the Middle Ages many castles (Náxos, Amorgós, Anáfi, Folégandros, etc.). Nor should the fantastic scenery of

Santorin's volcanic caldera be forgotten. Several of the islands, in particular Mýkonos (see p. 144), are now popular and well-equipped holiday resorts.

**Ándros** and **Tínos**: see the entry for Ándros.

**Kéa** (area 52 sq. miles/134 sq. km; pop. 1650), lying close to the coast of Attica, was the birthplace of the poets Simonides and Bacchylides (6th–5th c. B.C.). – The boat puts in at *Korissiá* (locally known also as *Livádi*) on the NW coast, which has recently begun to attract tourists. – On the little peninsula of **Aghia Iríni**, opposite the fishing village of *Vourkári* (10 minutes' walk), is a *Bronze Age settlement (excavated by American archeologists from 1960 onward) which flourished between about 2000 and 1200 B.C.

Entering the excavation site by a modern staircase, near which is an ancient *fountain-house*, visitors can observe the various settlement levels, with walls standing to some height. The most notable features are the *walls of the oldest temple found in Greece; *House A*, a large building with cellars which may have served religious and administrative purposes; and the remains of a *tumulus tomb*. In the temple the altar, the doorway into the narrow cella and a bipartite adyton beyond the cella can be distinguished.

The chief place on the island, **Kéa**, on the site of ancient *Ioulis*, has a Venetian castle, now occupied by a hotel (views, extending over Attica). 1¼ miles/2 km NE is an Archaic *lion hewn from a rock face. 4 miles/6 km S of Kéa is the Monastery of **Aghia Triáda**, near which is an ancient tower.

**Kýthnos** (area 38 sq. miles/99 sq. km; pop. 1600) is a bare island lying S of Kéa. – The boats call at **Loutrá**, a small health resort on the E coast (recommended for rheumatism, arthritis and gynaecological conditions), from which there is a road to the chief place on the island, **Kýthnos** (3 miles/5 km S; alt. 525 ft/160 m; pop. 880; church of 1613) and **Dryopís** (4 miles/6 km farther; alt. 625 ft/190 m; pop. 1100), where there are many windmills. – On the W coast is the fishing village of **Meríkhas**, with a beach near by at *Nisí*. On a hill between the two bays on the W coast stood the ancient city of Kýthnos, of which there are some remains at Evraiókastro. At the NW tip of the island is the medieval castle known as *Tis Oraias to Kastro* (Castle of the Fair Lady).

**Sýros** (area 32 sq. miles/84 sq. km; pop. 18,600), centrally situated within the group, is the most important fishing and commercial center in the Cyclades. – **Ermoúpolis**, capital of the island and of the Cyclades as a whole, combines with **Anó Sýros**, 2½ miles/4 km inland, to present a striking and distinctive sight: the Neo-Classical town (with a museum in the Town Hall) rising above the harbor, to the rear the hill (345 ft/105 m) on which stands the principal Orthodox church, and to the left of this the Hill of Anó Sýros (591 ft/180 m) with its stepped lanes and the Roman Catholic cathedral on the summit. The boatyards and boathouses around the harbor bay are a reminder of the island's importance (not yet lost) in the shipping trade.

*\*Mýkonos* and *\*\*Délos*: see the entry for Mýkonos.

**Sérifos** (area 27½ sq. miles;/71 sq. km; pop. 1100) was of importance in ancient times as a source of iron ore. The port, **Livádi**, lies in a sandy bay below the chief place on the island, **Sérifos** or *Khóra* (2 miles/3 km; pop. 800), an unspoiled little Cycladic village with its trim lanes densely packed with houses, its chapels

On the island of Sérifos

and its tiny gardens. Two hours' walk away we come to the village of **Panayía**, with a *Church of the Panayía dating from 950, the oldest on the island. Near the village stands the *Monastery of the Taxiarchs* (Archangels), built in the 16th c. (18th c., frescoes, library).

**Sífnos** (area 28 sq. miles/73 sq. km; pop. 2100) has many sandy bays on its E and W coasts. From the island's port, **Kamáres**, on the W coast, a road traverses a verdant valley to the chief place, **Apollonía** (3 miles/5 km; pop. 940), in the fertile eastern half of the island, with a Folk Museum in the tree-shaded main square. Most of the settlements (and a great many

Church on the island of Sífnos

dovecots) are in this part. Among them are **Artemón**, immediately N of Apollonía – twin villages which preserve the names of the divine twins Apollo and Artemis – and **Kástro**, on the coast 3 miles/5 km E at the foot of a medieval castle.

Scattered about on the island are a number of Hellenistic watch-towers and numerous chapels, mostly of the 16th and 17th c. On Mount Profítis Ilías (2277 ft/694 m) is the **Profítis Ilías Monastery**; in Vathý Bay the *Church of the Taxiarchs*; and, in the beautiful southern part of the island, the *Monastery of Panayía tou Vounoú* (Mother of God on the Hill), from which there is a charming view of **Platýs Yialós**, the longest beach in the Cyclades (9 miles/15 km from Apollonía; tavernas, potter's workshop).

**Páros**: see p. 153.

**Náxos**: see p. 146.

**Mílos** (area 58 sq. miles/151 sq. km; pop. 4500), the most southerly of the western Cyclades, offers the attractions of archeological sites, beautiful scenery and good beaches. The island is almost divided into two by a gulf which cuts deep inland from the NW and contains the port of Adámas. The southern part, with the Hill of *Profítis Ilías* (2536 ft/773 m), is almost uninhabited. Unlike most of the other islands in the Cyclades, Mílos is of volcanic origin – a fact reflected in the bizarre rock formations and fantastic colorings to be seen when entering the gulf. Sulfur, quartzite, barytes and kaolin are worked on the island. – The port of **Adámas** (alt. 33 ft/10 m; pop. 750), on the N side of the gulf, is a very typical Cycladic village. 2½ miles/4 km NW the chief place on the island, **Mílos** or *Pláka* (alt. 656 ft/200 m; pop. 900; bus service), has an interesting little *museum. On the way up to the Venetian fortress which crowns the hill is the interesting Church of *Panayía Thalassítra.

¾ mile/1 km below Pláka is the village of **Trypití** (alt. 460 ft/140 m; pop. 700), from which a concrete road leads to Early Christian *Catacombs (2nd c.), with a Saint's tomb in the principal chamber and some 2000 tomb niches. The catacombs are unique in Greece.

From the concrete road a side road branches off on the right to the remains of the Dorian town of **Mílos**. A signpost marks the spot where the Aphrodite of Mílos (the Venus de Milo, now in the Louvre), a Hellenistic work of about 150 B.C., was found in 1820. To the right can be seen remains of the town walls and a tower. We then come to a small Roman theater, beautifully situated on the hillside overlooking the gulf.

E of Trypití, above the precipitous N coast, is the site of **Phylakope** (*Fylakopí*), with the foundations of houses of the 3rd and 2nd millennia and Mycenaean walls of about 1500 B.C. Beyond this is the pretty little port of **Apollónia** (7 miles/11 km; alt. 33 ft/10 m; pop. 140), which has a sandy beach.

SE of Adámas are **Zefaría** (4 miles/6 km; pop. 350) and the ruins of **Palaiokhóra**, founded in the 8th c. and abandoned in 1793.

Three smaller islands can be reached by boat – the rocky islet of **Antímilos** (area 3 sq. miles/8 sq. km; alt. 2100 ft/643 m), occupied only by wild goats, from Adámas, Kímolos and Polýaigos from Apollónia.

**Folégandros** (area 13 sq. miles/34 sq. km; pop. 7000) is situated off the beaten track of modern tourism. The little port of **Karavostásis** lies in the eastern part of the N coast. The chief place, **Folégandros**, is 2 miles/3 km away on a plateau; near by is a medieval castle.

**Síkinos** (area 16 sq. miles/41 sq. km; pop. 420) is a bare little island lying between Mílos and Ios. Visitors to the island are landed by small boats in Aloprónia Bay on the S coast (sandy beach). The only village on the island, **Síkinos** (2 miles/3 km from the landing-place), is a typical Cycladic settlement situated at an altitude of 920 ft/280 m

above the steeply scarped N coast; it has a medieval castle. 1½ hours' walk W of the village is the *Episkopí Chapel*, converted from an ancient mausoleum, which is also known as the Naós Apóllonos (Temple of Apollo).

**Ios** (area 42 sq. miles/108 sq. km; pop. 1300) is traditionally believed to have been the island on which Homer died. – The port of **Órmos Íou** (alt. 16 ft/5 m; pop. 110) lies in a sheltered bay on the W coast (sandy beach). As the boat approaches the harbor the eye is caught by the dazzlingly white Church of Aghia Iríni on the S side of the bay (10 minutes' walk

On the island of Íos

from the harbor). 1¼ miles/2 km away, on the hillside above the island's principal valley, is **Khóra** (alt. 330 ft/100 m; pop. 1100), on the site of an ancient settlement, with a row of typical windmills. A chapel overlooking the charming little village has an attractive terrace, above which, on the summit of the hill, is another chapel (view).

Excursions can be made to *Yialó Beach*, *Kálamos Monastery* and Plakotó Cave on the N coast. There are also possible boat trips to the sandy bays in the S and SW of the island and to the neighboring islands of Síkinos (see above), to the W, and Iráklion, to the N.

*Iráklion* (area 7 sq. miles/18 sq. km; pop. 150), together with *Kéros* (6 sq. miles/15 sq. km; pop. 8), *Káto* and *Anó Koufonísi* (5 sq. miles;/13 sq. km; pop. 250) and *Skhinoúsa* (4 sq. miles/10 sq. km; pop. 188), belongs to the **Erimonísia**, the group of "Lonely Islands" between Íos and Náxos.

**Amorgós** (area 47 sq. miles/121 sq. km; pop. 1800) is traversed by a ridge of hills which falls steeply down to the S. There were three ancient settlements on the much-indented NW coast, Now represented by the villages of *Arkesíni* (S), **Katápola** (middle), the island's main harbor, and *Aiviáli* (N).

The principal place on the island is **Amorgós** or *Khóra* (pop. 450), 2½ miles/ 4 km from Katápola (bus), with a castle which belonged to the dukes of Náxos. From here it is a 20-minute climb, on a track which is fairly steep in the final section, to the *Monastery of Panayía Khozoviótissa*, founded in 1088, where whitewashed buildings cling to the rock in a fantastic situation above the rugged coast. The chapel on the topmost level contains a miraculous icon and numerous silver lamps presented by worshipers. From the terrace in front of the chapel there are far-ranging views.

From Aiyiáli the hill of **Kríkelas** (2497 ft/ 761 m) can be climbed; extensive views from the top.

**Astypálaia** (area 37 sq. miles/96 sq. km; pop. 1500), the most south-easterly of the Cyclades, is associated for administrative purposes with the Dodecanese. The SW and NE ends of the island are linked by an isthmus 4½ miles/7 km long and only 110 yds/100 m across in places. On this isthmus is the chief place on the island, **Astypálaia** (pop. 1200), with many chapels and an imposingly situated Venetian castle. There are beaches on both sides of the isthmus.

**\*\*Santorin (Thera)**: see p. 166.

# Cyprus/ Kypros/ Kıbrıs

## Republic of Cyprus
*Kypriaki Dimokratia/ Cumhuriyeti Kıbrıs*

Nationality letters: CY.
Area: 3572 sq. miles/9251 sq. km
Capital: Nicosia (Lefkosia)/Lefkoşa (at present divided).
Population: 650,000.
Religion: In the N mainly Muslims, in the S Orthodox Greeks; Roman Catholic and small Jewish and Armenian minorities.
Language: Greek in S, Turkish in N; English as language of commerce and communications.
Currency: Cyprus pound (C£) of 1000 mils; in the N the Turkish pound (TL) of 100 kuruş.
Time: Eastern European Time (GMT+2 hours).
Travel documents: Passport.

**ⓘ Cyprus Tourism Organization,**
18 Th. Theodotou Street,
**Nicosia;**
tel. (021) 4 33 74.
**Tourist Information Bureaux in Cyprus:**
5 Princess de Tyras Street,
**Nicosia;**
tel. (021) 4 42 64.
15 Spyrou Araouzou Street,
**Limassol;**
tel. (051) 6 27 56.
Democratias Square,
**Larnaca;**
tel. (041) 5 43 22.
International Airport,
**Larnaca;**
tel. (041) 2 13 16.
3 Gladstone Street,
**Paphos;**
tel. (061) 3 28 41.
**Aghia Napa;**
tel. (046) 2 17 96.
**Platres;**
tel. (054) 2 13 16.
**Cyprus Tourist Office,**
213 Regent Street,
**London** W1R 8DA;
tel. (01) 734 9822.
**Cyprus Trade Centre,**
13 East 40th Street,
**New York,** NY 10016;
tel. (212) 686 6016.

DIPLOMATIC MISSIONS. – *United Kingdom*: High Commission, Alexander Pallis Street, P.O. Box 1978, Nicosia, tel. (021) 7 31 31–37, 4 87 41, 4 87 03, 4 83 78. – *United States*: Embassy, Therissos Street and Dositheos Street, Nicosia, tel. 6 51 51–55.

HOTELS. – NICOSIA: *Cyprus Hilton*, Archbishop Makarios Avenue, L, 466 b.; *Ledra*, Grivas Digenis Avenue, I, 206 b.; *Churchill*, 1 Achaeans Street, I, 108 b.; *Philoxenia*, Eylenja Avenue, I, 64 b.; *Kennedy*, 70 Regaena Street, II, 176 b.; *Cleopatra*, 8 Florina Street, II, 105 b.; *Asty*, 12 Prince Charles Street, II, 105 b.; *Catsellis Hill*, 11 Kasos Street, II, 80 b. – LIMASSOL: *Amathus Beach*, L, 524 b.; *Apollonia Beach*, L, 408 b.; *Churchill Limassol*, I, 292 b.; *Poseidonia Beach*, I, 268 b.; *Miramare*, I, 240 b.; *Curium Palace*, I, 112 b.; *Astir*, II, 145 b.; *Kanika Beach*, II, 133 b.; *Alasia*, II, 130 b.; *Pavemar*, II, 124 b.; several blocks of apartments. – LARNACA: *Palm Beach*, I, 376 b.; *Lordos Beach*, I, 360 b.; *Sun Hall*, I, 224 b.; *Karpasiana Beach*, I, 210 b.; *Four Lanterns*, II, 98 b. – AGHIA NAPA: *Grecian Bay*, L, 500 b.; *Nissi Beach*, II, 564 b.; *Nissi Beach No. 2*, II, 136 b.; *Mirabella* (apartments), Green Bungalows, 136 b. – PARALIMNI: *Sunrise Beach*, I, 280 b.; *Vrisiana Beach*, I, 234 b. – PAPHOS: *Paphos Beach*, I, 360 b.; *Dionysos*, II, 177 b.; *Aloe*, II, 160 b.; *Cynthiana Beach*, II, 118 b. – PLATRES: *Forest Park*, I, 164 b.; *Edelweiss*, III, 42 b. – KAKOPETRIA: *Makris*, II, 59 b. – PEDHOULAS: *Pinewood Valley*, II, 52 b.

FAMAGUSTA (Gazi Mağusa): *Golden Sands*, I, 896 b.; *Salamis Bay*, I, 720 b.; *Loiziana*, I, 340 b.; *Sandy Beach*, I, 288 b.; *Aspelia*, I, 284 b.; *Asterias*, I, 278 b. – KYRENIA (Girne): *Zephyros*, I, 400 b.; *Catsellis Dome*, 305 b.; *Castle Beach*, II, 292 b.; *Mare Monte*, II, 152 b.

YOUTH HOSTELS. – NICOSIA: 13 Prince Charles Street. – LIMASSOL: 120 Ankara Street. – PAPHOS: Eleftherios Venizélos Avenue. – IN THE TROODOS: former Olympos Hotel (summer only). – CAMPING: free, with permission of District Officer.

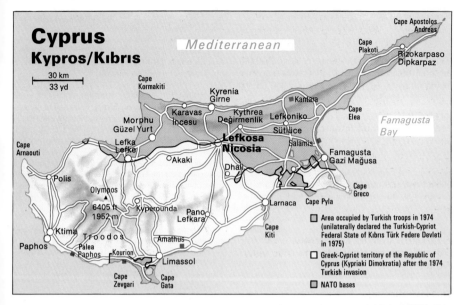

# Cyprus
## Kypros/Kıbrıs

Mediterranean

30 km
33 yd

Cape Apostolos Andreas
Cape Plakoti
Rizokarpaso Dipkarpaz
Cape Kormakiti
Kyrenia Girne
Kantara
Cape Elea
Famagusta Bay
Cape Arnaouti
Morphu Güzel Yurt
Karavas İncesu
Kythrea Değirmenlik
Lefkoniko
Cape Kormakiti
Lefka Lefke
**Lefkoşa Nicosia**
Sütlüce
Salamis
Akaki
Famagusta Gazi Mağusa
Dhali
Polis
Olympos
6405 ft 1952 m
Kyperounda
Pano Lefkara
Larnaca
Cape Greco
Cape Pyla
Ktima Tróodos
Amathus
Cape Kiti
Paphos
Palea Paphos
Kourion
Limassol
Cape Zevgari
Cape Gata

☐ Area occupied by Turkish troops in 1974 (unilaterally declared the Turkish-Cypriot Federal State of Kıbrıs Türk Federe Devleti in 1975)

☐ Greek-Cypriot territory of the Republic of Cyprus (Kypriaki Dimokratia) after the 1974 Turkish invasion

☐ NATO bases

CAR RENTAL. – NICOSIA: *Rent-a-Car*, Eleftherias Square, tel. (021) 7 34 55; *Astra Hire Cars*, Hilton Hotel and Charalambou Mouskou Street, tel. (021) 7 58 00/7 40 50; *Avis*, 2 Homer Avenue, tel. (021) 7 20 62; *Hertz*, Eleftherias Square, tel. (021) 7 77 83, and Grivas Digenis Avenue, tel. 6 34 13; etc. – LIMASSOL: *Avis*, Limassol–Nicosia road, tel. (051) 6 91 92; *Hertz*, Limassol–Nicosia road, tel. (051) 6 87 58; etc. – LARNACA: *Avis*, 43 Archbishop Makarios Avenue, tel. (041) 5 71 32, and at Airport; *Hertz*, 33F Archbishop Makarios Avenue, tel. (041) 5 51 45, and at Airport.

SHOPPING. – Good buys for visitors are needlework, Lefkara lace, woven and crochet-work rugs, pottery and copper articles.

EVENTS. – Carnival; Flower Festival; Wine Festival, Limassol.

RECREATION and SPORT. – Sailing, wind-surfing, water-skiing, motor-boats, pedalos, fishing; winter sports in Tróodos Mountains; walking; tennis.

**\*Cyprus, the third largest Mediterranean island (after Sardinia and Sicily), lies in the NE corner of the Mediterranean between latitude 34° 32' and 35° 42' N and between longitude 32° 16' and 34° 35' E, some 40 miles/64 km off the coast of Asia Minor and 70 miles/113 km from the Syrian coast, with a long spur reaching NE into the Gulf of Iskenderun.**

Although geologically associated with Asia, Cyprus is closely linked in history and culture with Europe and particularly with Greece. Its distinctive charm results from its geographical situation at the point where cultural influences from three continents meet, each of them having left their mark on the island over many thousand years of history. In addition the years of British occupation have in-troduced many features which will help the English-speaking visitor in particular to feel at home on the island. – Cyprus has thus a whole range of attractions to offer the vacationer – its variety of scenery, its art and architecture, its archeological sites, its lively and colorful folk traditions, its beautiful sandy beaches and its excellent hotels and other amenities for visitors.

The division of Cyprus into the Greek Cypriot southern part (the Republic of Cyprus) and the Turkish northern part entails restrictions on travel to and within the island. The southern part can be entered only at Larnaca Airport and the ports of Larnaca, Limassol and Paphos; entry to the Republic from the Turkish zone is not permitted. Visitors to the northern part must travel via Turkey, and must have no Greek Cypriot stamps in their passport. Visitors to the Republic can enter the Turkish sector through the checkpoint at the Ledra Palace Hotel, Nicosia; for a stay of longer than 24 hours advance application is necessary.

Traffic in Cyprus travels on the left.

GEOLOGY. – Geologically considered, Cyprus is a continuation of the folded mountain massif of Syria and Anatolia. Along the whole N coast of the island extends the Kerynis or Pentadaktylos (Five Fingers) Range, built up from Tertiary limestones and marls, with steep-sided hills rising to over 3300 ft/1000 m in the W and lower and gentler hills toward the E. The whole of the southern part of the island is occupied by the forest-covered Tróodos or Olympos range, a massif of volcanic origin (diabase and trachyte) which rises to 6405 ft/1952 m in Mount Tróodos or Olympos, Cyprus's highest peak. During the Tertiary era these two ranges were separate islands, which were later joined by an upthrust of the sea bottom and are now linked by the very fertile Mesaoria Plain. Recurring earth tremors show that this part of the earth's crust has not yet settled down.

**CLIMATE.** – Cyprus has a very healthy temperate Mediterranean climate. The summer months are hot and dry, with average temperatures of fully 82 °F/28 °C at Famagusta and 72 °F/22 °C in the mountain regions. The winters are mild, with high precipitation, which in the Tróodos Mountains falls in the form of snow between November and March–April, offering excellent facilities for winter sports from the end of January to March. Precipitation is highest in the mountain regions, particularly in the W (an average of up to 40 in./1000 mm a year in the Tróodos), falling toward the E, with the lowest figures in the plain (about 16 in./400 mm). There are 340 days of sunshine in the year. – The rivers, most of which rise in the Tróodos Mountains, have a flow of water only during the winter months.

**HISTORY.** – Cyprus has been settled by man since the Stone Age, and the island's copper (Latin *aes cyprium*) was already being worked in the Chalcolithic period. Here the Cretan/Mycenaean culture came into contact with influences from Asia Minor and Mesopotamia. After being successively controlled by Egyptians, Achaeans, Phoenicians and Persians Cyprus was occupied by *Rome* in 58 B.C.. After the collapse of the Western Roman Empire the island fell to the *Byzantines*; in 1191 it was conquered by Richard Cœur-de-Lion of England; and in 1489 it passed to *Venice*. In 1570–71 it was taken by the *Turks*, who were compelled in 1878 to cede it to *Britain*.

The resistance of the Greek population to British rule found expression in a rising in 1931 in favour of *enosis* (union with Greece); and even after Archbishop *Makarios* (1913–77) came to power as Ethnarch in 1950 guerrilla activity continued. In 1960 Cyprus became an independent republic within the British Commonwealth. – In 1974 an attempted coup by officers of the National Guard aimed at securing union with Greece led to the occupation of the northern half of the island by Turkish troops, and most of the Greeks living in that area sought refuge in the southern half. Since the unilateral proclamation of a Turkish-Cypriot Federal State in 1975 the boundary between northern and southern Cyprus along the "Attila line", which passes through the island's capital, Nicosia, has become practically impassable.

**POPULATION.** – Since the division of Cyprus into two parts its population structure has undergone a fundamental change. Of the 650,000 inhabitants some 80% are Greeks professing the Orthodox Faith, who occupy only 60% of the island's area, while the 18% of Turks (Muslims) have 40%. The vacuum created by the expulsion of the Greek population from northern Cyprus is being filled by the immigration of settlers from Anatolia, while there has been a considerable increase, over the past 10 years, in the emigration of Greeks from the overcrowded southern part of the island. In addition to Greeks and Turks there are small minorities of Armenians, Maronites and Jews. – Some 58% of the population live in rural areas and 42% in towns.

The six principal towns, all district capitals, are **Nicosia** (officially *Lefkosia*, Turkish *Lefkoşa*),

Limassol (*Lemesos*) in the S, **Famagusta** (*Ammokhostos*, Turkish *Mağusa*) in the E, *Larnaca* in the S, *Paphos* in the SW and Kyrenia (Turkish *Girne*) in the N. Some 100 sq. miles/260 sq. km of the island around *Dekelia* on the SE coast and *Akrotiri* at its southern tip are British sovereign base areas.

**ECONOMY.** – A major contribution is made to Cyprus's economy by *agriculture*. Fully half of its total area is under cultivation, in particular the very fertile Mesaoria Plain (wheat and barley in the E, citrus fruits, olives and almonds in the W) and the northern coastal areas with their large plantations of citrus fruits. Vineyards, fields of vegetables and orchards cover the lower slopes of the Tróodos Mountains and contribute most of the island's exports. The mild climate makes it possible, with the help of judicious irrigation, to harvest two or more crops a year.

Stock-farming has declined in favor of crop-farming, but sheep and poultry are still extensively reared. – Some 25% of the island's area is covered with coniferous forests, but in order to preserve the stock these are not worked. – Fishing is only of local importance.

Cyprus is well supplied with *minerals*, although the copper-mines of the Classical period are now almost worked out. The main export products are pyrites, asbestos, chromium, gypsum and umber. – *Industry* is still in process of development. Most of the firms are of small or medium size, usually family-owned. The main emphasis is on the processing of agricultural produce (foodstuffs industries, textiles). – The island's energy supply depends entirely on imported oil. – There is a fairly dense road network of some 3100 miles/5000 km. One relic of the British occupation is that vehicles travel on the left. – The tourist trade, which had been brought almost to a standstill by the tense political situation, has enjoyed a vigorous revival in the Greek part of the island during the last few years.

The capital of Cyprus, **Nicosia** (officially *Lefkosia*; Turkish *Lefkoşa*; pop. 120,000), the only large town in the interior of the island, grew up in the 7th c. A.D. on the site of ancient *Ledra*. It was selected as the administrative center of Cyprus when the coastal towns became increasingly unsafe as a result of continual raiding and plunder.

SIGHTS. – In the old center of Nicosia , a town of narrow lanes enclosed within a massive ring of Venetian walls, stands the Gothic *St John's Cathedral*, seat of the Greek Orthodox Archbishop of Cyprus. Immediately N of the cathedral is an interesting *Museum of Folk Art*; to the E is the Archbishop's Palace. In one of the buildings adjoining is an *Icon Museum*. – The bazaar of the old town is full of interest, with shops selling a variety of craft products. – To the SW, outside the town walls, is the very fine *Cyprus Museum*, with everyday objects and works of art ranging in date from the Neolithic period to Roman times (about 5800 B.C. to A.D. 300). – The modern town

**The coast of Cyprus near Episkopi**

Nicosia

outside the old walls is steadily expanding into the plain with its housing areas and commercial buildings. – In the Turkish-occupied part of Nicosia are the Gothic *St Sophia's Cathedral* (13th c.), in which the kings of Cyprus were crowned (now the Selimiye Mosque), and other medieval buildings.

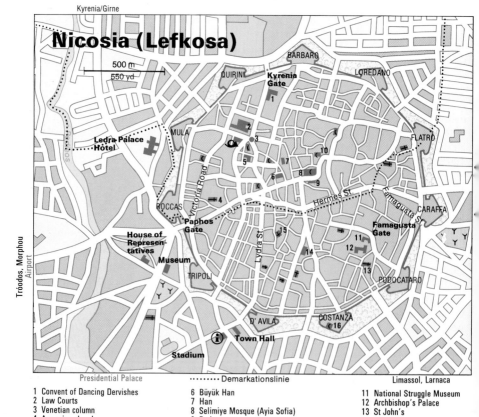

1 Convent of Dancing Dervishes
2 Law Courts
3 Venetian column
4 Armenian church
5 Evkaf Administration
6 Büyük Han
7 Han
8 Selimiye Mosque (Ayia Sofia)
9 Bedestan
10 Sultan Mahmut Mosque
11 National Struggle Museum
12 Archbishop's Palace
13 St John's
14 Theater
15 Phaneromeni Church
16 Baiaktar Mosque

**EXCURSIONS from Nicosia.** – Attractive trips can be made SW of the town into the Pitsilia Hills, the eastern foothills of the Tróodos Range, and into the Tróodos itself. Of particular interest are the *Tombs of Tamassos* and, farther SW, the *Monastery of Makheras*, situated on a windy hill commanding extensive views. Also well worth visiting are the Byzantine churches of *Peristerona, Perakhorio* (frescoes), *Lagoudera* and *Asinou*; the picturesque medieval villages of *Kakopetria, Galata, Moutoullas, Kalopanayiotis* (sulfur springs) and *Pedhoulas* (cherry blossom in April), which also have Byzantine churches; the *Mesapotamos Monastery*; and the **Kykko Monastery**, founded in 1100, with an icon said to have been painted by St Luke. On the nearby hill of *Throni* can be seen the grave of President Archbishop Makarios.

**Larnaca** (pop. 22,000), a quiet little town which has developed in recent years into a rising port with a modern marina, an airport and beautiful beaches on the SE coast of the island, occupies the site of the Mycenaean town of *Kition*, traditionally believed to have been founded by Noah's grandson, and later the birthplace of the Greek philosopher Zeno. In the old town is St Lazarus's Church, with the relics of the Saint. To the W lies the Salt Lake, the haunt of migrant flamingoes from December to March. On the W side of the lake is the Hala Sultan Tekke, a mosque built to house the tomb of the Prophet Moham-med's foster-mother. – 1¼ miles/2 km SW, in the village of *Kiti*, is the Church of the **Panayía Angeloktistos**, with beautiful Early Byzantine mosaics (6th c. (?)).

The village of **Lefkara**, W of Larnaca, is famous for its lace. It is said that Leonardo da Vinci bought lace here in 1481 for an altar-cloth in Milan Cathedral. – W of Larnaca, on a commanding hill, stands the **Stavrovouni Monastery** (Hill of the Cross, 2231 ft/680 m), founded in 327 by St Helena, mother of the Emperor Con-stantine. – A short distance NW is the village of *Kornos*, famed for its unglazed pottery in Archaic designs. – Some 10½ miles/17 km SW of Larnaca are the remains of the Neolithic settlement of *Khirokitia* (about 5800–5250 B.C.), with the foundations of walls, circular hut bases and tombs.

15 miles/25 km E of Larnaca is the fishing village and seaside resort of **Aghia Nápa** (*beach), surrounded by fertile planta-tions of vegetables and fruit, bizarre rock formations and windmills. In the center of the little town is the famous Monastery of Aghia Nápa (Byzantine/Venetian), one of the last buildings erected in Cyprus by the Venetians, with a rock-cut church. – In the surrounding area there are many attrac-tive villages, bays and sandy beaches, in particular *Paralimni* (gastronomic specialities), *Liopetri, Potamos tis Xylo-phagou, Protaras* and *Fig-Tree Bay*, with one of the best beaches on the island.

**Limassol** (*Lemesos*; pop. 80,000), Cyprus's second largest town, a center of industry and of the wine trade and an important exporting port, lies on the S coast of the island between the two ancient cities of Curium to the W and Amathus to the E. From 1291 Limassol was a base of the Templars and the Knights of St John, and here King Richard Cœur-de-Lion married Berengaria of Navarre. Among features of interest are the Castle, now housing the District Museum, the municipal park (minizoo) and the wine-making establishments. – 6 miles/10 km W, surrounded by rich orchards, stands the massive *Kolossi Castle*, built in 1210 by the Knights of St John. – 12½ miles/20 km W of Limassol are the remains of the ancient city of **Kou-rion**, where are baths (5th c. B.C.), fine

The site of ancient Kourion

pavement mosaics, the theater (A.D. 50–175; performances of music and drama – ancient dramatists, Shakespeare – in summer) and a Temple of Apollo. – To the SW, at *Episkopí*, is a small but interesting Archeological Museum. – Other features of interest within easy reach of Limassol are the citrus-fruit plantations and vineyards of *Phasouri*, the monasteries of *Tróoditissa* and *Omodos* (Stavros, the Holy Cross) and the picturesque villages of *Fini, Kilani, Platres, Prodromos* and *Tróodos* in the Tróodos Mountains.

**Paphos** (pop. 10,000), in Roman times the chief town of Cyprus and the landing-place for pilgrims visiting the Sanctuary of Aphrodite, consists of the old port of *Kato Paphos*, with defensive walls and a picturesque harbor originally constructed by Alexander the Great, and the modern town of *Ktima* 2 miles/3 km inland. Near the harbor are the excellently preserved * mosaic pavements of the Villa of Diony-

Paphos

sos, among the finest in the Mediterranean area. Above the harbor stands a Turkish fort (1592), built on the site of an earlier medieval castle. There are two interesting museums, the small Archeological Museum and the Byzantine Museum in the Bishop's Palace. – Outside the town are the so-called Tombs of the Kings, rock-cut tomb chambers with architectural embellishments.

9 miles/15 km SE of Paphos, at the village of *Kouklia* (Palea Paphos), are the remains of a Sanctuary of Aphrodite which was much venerated in ancient times. – 6 miles/9 km farther on we come to the *Petra tou Romaiou*, the legendary spot where Aphrodite is said to have emerged from the waves ("Odyssey", VIII, 362). – Other places of interest NE and N of Paphos are the monasteries of *Khrysoroyiatissa, Aghios Neophytos* and *Aghia Moni*, the *Valley of Cedars* and the *Fontana Amorosa* and *Baths of Aphrodite*, near *Polis* in *Khrysokhou Bay*, at the north-western tip of the island.

Kyrenia (Girne) in northern Cyprus

The principal port in the Turkish-occupied northern part of Cyprus is **Kyrenia** (*Kerinis*; Turkish *Girne*; pop. 4000), the ancient *Kerynia*, picturesquely situated on the flanks of the Pentadaktylos Range. Its remote and secluded situation gives it a particular charm. To the E of the harbor towers a massive castle (9th–16th c.).

The port of **Famagusta** (*Ammokhostos*: Turkish *Gazi Mağusa* or *Magosa*; pop. 50,000), also under Turkish occupation, lies in a bay on the E coast of Cyprus, at the eastern end of the fertile Mesaoria Plain. It grew up some 7 miles/11 km N of the ancient city of *Salamis*, which had a good natural harbor and was the main port of shipment for the island's much-sought-after copper. The city was destroyed by an earthquake in the 4th c. A.D. The remains of a large theater, a Temple of Zeus, a gymnasium, an aqueduct and the city's necropolis have been excavated. – The old town of Famagusta is enclosed by a mighty circuit of walls 56 ft/17 m high, originally built by the Lusignan rulers of

The beach at Famagusta (Mağusa)

Sunset at the birthplace of Aphrodite

Cyprus in the 13th c. and later strengthened by the Venetians. On the seaward side is a citadel with Othello's Tower, said to have been the scene of Shakespeare's tragedy. In the heart of the old town stands the Gothic St Nicholas's Cathedral (14th c.), now the Lala Mustafa Mosque. To the SW of this are the remains of the Palazzo del Provveditore, once the residence of the Venetian Governor. The Early Gothic Church of SS. Peter and Paul (14th c.), now the Sinan Pasha Mosque, and the Church of St George (1359) bear witness to the splendors of Famagusta in its heyday. There is an interesting Archeological Museum. – The **beaches around Famagusta are perhaps the finest on the island.

# Delos
## (Dhílos)

Greece
Nomos: Cyclades.
Area: 1·4 sq. miles/3·6 sq. km

HOTEL. – *Xenia*, II, 7 b.

TRANSPORTATION. – Boats from Mýkonos.

**Although it is one of the smallest of the Cyclades, and much the smallest of the group formed by Mýkonos, Delos and Riría, **Delos was a place of such importance in ancient times that the surrounding islands were known as the Cyclades, since it was thought that they lay in a circle (kyklos) around the island on which the god Apollo was born. The extensive area of remains is one of the most important archeological sites in Greece. Delos leaves an unforgettable impression on visitors,**

whether they see it in spring, when it is gay with an abundance of flowers, or in the fall, when the austere lines of this granite island are revealed in their nakedness.

HISTORY. – The myth relates that Leto, pursued by Hera, found refuge on a floating rocky island, which Poseidon then anchored to the sea bottom with pillars of granite. Here, under a palm, she bore to Zeus the twins Apollo and Artemis, attended by Arge and Opis, two maidens from the hyperborean regions of the north, which the god was required to visit annually in winter.

The cult of Apollo was introduced by Ionian Greeks about 1000 B.C., while the worship of Artemis can be traced back to the cult of the Great Goddess revered by the pre-Greek population. Toward the end of the 3rd millennium B.C. this earlier population established a settlement on the hill of Kýnthos (371 ft/113 m), followed in the 2nd millennium by another settlement in the area of the later sacred precinct. The oldest cult buildings (Sanctuary of Artemis, Tomb of the Hyperborean Maidens) date from Mycenean, if not from pre-Greek, times. From the 7th c. B.C. Delos was under the influence of the large neighboring island of Náxos, which promoted the development of the sanctuary. Later Athens won a predominant position, and in the 6th c. Peisistratos carried out a "purification" of the island, removing all the tombs (except that of the two Hyperborean Maidens) to the nearby island of Rheneia. In the 5th c. B.C. Delos became the headquarters of the Delian Confederacy, a maritime league headed by Athens; but in 454 the Athenians carried off the treasury of the league and deposited it on the Acropolis. A second purification of the island was carried out in 426–425 B.C., after which it was forbidden for anyone to be born or to die on Delos. In 314 B.C. Delos broke away from Athens to become independent, and thereafter enjoyed a period of great prosperity. In 166 B.C. the Romans declared Delos a free port, which promoted its development as a trading center – dealing, among other things, in slaves – and led to the growth of a considerable commercial town to the S of the sacred area. The end came after the island was plundered by Mithridates IX of Pontus in 88 B.C., followed by a further plundering in 69 B.C. Thereafter Delos was almost uninhabited, and when Pausanias visited it in the 2nd c A.D. he saw only the custodians of the deserted sanctuary. A fresh settlement was established in Christian times, but this had only a brief life.

THE SITE. – The tour of the site, taking in remains of various periods from the 2nd millennium B.C. to Roman times, begins on the W side of the island, in the area of the ancient harbor.

From the Agora of the Competaliasts (Freedmen) we follow a broad ceremonial way (to the left) which runs N to the entrance to the *Sacred Precinct. It is flanked by two stoas, the Stoa of Philip V of Macedon of about 210 B.C. and the South Stoa of about 180 B.C., beyond which are the remains of the South Agora. Climbing the three marble steps of the Propylon, worn by the feet of countless pilgrims, we enter the Hieron of Apollo, which extends northward to the Stoa of Antigonos and eastward to the Hellenistic wall beyond the Ship Hall (see below). Immediately adjoining the Propylon, to the right, is the House of the Naxians (beginning of the 6th c. B.C.), on the N side of which is the base (17 ft/5·10 m by 11 ft/3·50 m and 28 inches/70 cm high) of a marble statue of Apollo erected by the Naxians about 600 B.C. Part of the trunk and thighs of this colossal figure, originally some 30 ft/9 m high, can be seen to the NW of the precinct, which was bounded on the S and W by the Stoa of the Naxians. Here the excavators found a large building, almost square in plan, identified as the Keraton in which the old Horned Altar of Apollo once stood. Immediately adjoining to the N is the badly ruined Precinct of Artemis, which centered on a Temple of Artemis built in the 2nd c. B.C. on the site of an older 7th c. building.

In the center of the Sacred Precinct are three temples of Apollo, of which only the substructures remain. The oldest and smallest, the most northerly of the three, dates from the first half of the 6th c. B.C. It was built of porous limestone and housed a 26 ft/8 m high bronze statue of Apollo cast by Tektaios and Angelion of Aegina. The second temple, the most southerly, was the largest of the three and the only one to be surrounded by columns (6 × 13). It was begun in the 5th c. but apparently not completed until the 3rd. Between these two temples is the third and latest of the three, the Temple of the Athenians (after 426 B.C.). – To the N of the temples, set in a semicircle, are the treasuries, from which we continue to the so-called Prytaneion and farther E to a long building of the 3rd c. B.C. (30 ft/9 m by 220 ft/67 m) which is known as the Hall of the Bulls after its bull's-head capitals, or as the Ship Hall after a ship which was set up here in thanksgiving for a Macedonian naval victory.

We now proceed to the Sanctuary of Dionysos, on the E side of the Hieron of Apollo, in which are several marble phalluses. On one of the bases are carvings of scenes from the cult of Dionysos of about 300 B.C. From here we turn W along the Stoa of Antigonos, with bull's-head metopes on the entablature, which was built by King Antigonos Gonates of Macedon about 250 B.C.

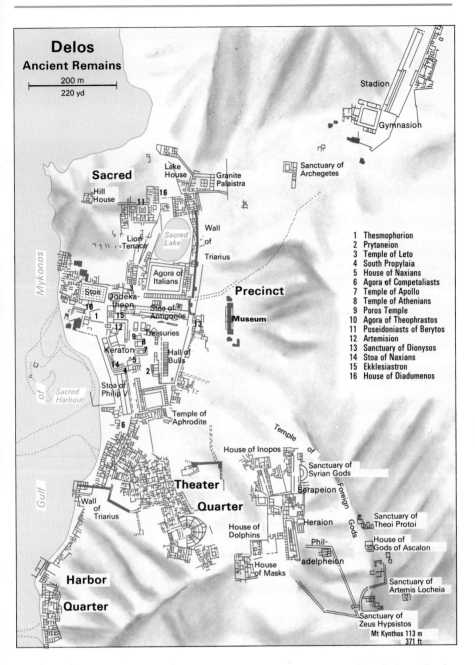

**Delos**
**Ancient Remains**

200 m
220 yd

Mykonos

Sacred
Hill House
Lake House
Granite Palaistra
16
11
Lion Terrace
Sacred Lake
Wall of Triarius
Agora of Italians
Stoa
10
1
Dodeka-theon
Stoa of Antigonos
15
12
Treasuries
9
Keraton
14
5
Hall of Bulls
4
2
Stoa of Philip
6

Gulf of

Sacred Harbour

Temple of Aphrodite

Stadion
Gymnasion
Sanctuary of Archegetes

Precinct

Museum

Temple of

House of Inopos
Sanctuary of Syrian Gods
Serapeion
Foreign Gods

Theater
Quarter

Wall of Triarius

House of Dolphins

Heraion

Phil-adelpheion

Sanctuary of Theoi Protoi
House of Gods of Ascalon

House of Masks

Harbor
Quarter

Sanctuary of Artemis Locheia

Sanctuary of Zeus Hypsistos
Mt Kynthos 113 m
371 ft

1  Thesmophorion
2  Prytaneion
3  Temple of Leto
4  South Propylaia
5  House of Naxians
6  Agora of Competaliasts
7  Temple of Apollo
8  Temple of Athenians
9  Poros Temple
10  Agora of Theophrastos
11  Poseidoniasts of Berytos
12  Artemision
13  Sanctuary of Dionysos
14  Stoa of Naxians
15  Ekklesiastron
16  House of Diadumenos

Rather less than half-way along this is a semicircular structure dating from Mycenaean times, the *Tomb of the Hyperborean Maidens* who attended Leto at the birth of the divine twins.

At the W end of the Stoa of Antigonos we leave the Hieron of Apollo, continue past the *Agora of Theophrastos* (126 B.C.) and a *hypostyle hall* (208 B.C.) on the left, and then pass the *Temple of the Twelve Gods* to reach the *Temple of Leto* (on the right of the path). This was built about 550 B.C. and preserves some courses of marble, with a bench running around the exterior,

on gneiss and granite foundations. To the right, E of the temple, is the *Agora of the Italians* (end of 2nd c. B.C.), the largest of a number of similar structures built to house foreign merchants. From here, passing between the Temple of Leto and a long granite building, we follow the processional way, flanked by a number of *lions in Naxian marble dating from the 7th c. B.C. – the earliest monumental figures of animals in Greek art. They look out over the Sacred Lake, filled in on account of the danger of malaria in 1925–26. In the area of the lake is a palm tree, recalling the palm under which Leto

Lion Terrace, Delos

gave birth to Apollo and Artemis. Other remains in the northern part of the site are the *Establishment of the Poseidoniasts of Berytus* (built for the accommodation of merchants from what is now Beirut), the *Granite Palaistra* and the *Lake Palaistra*. We now return to the Agora of the Italians and continue past the *Fountain of Minoa* (to which a flight of steps leads down) to the Museum.

The * **Museum** contains a fine collection of material from the site, although some of the finest items (e.g. the relief of Nikandre) are now in the National Archeological Museum in Athens.

To the NE of the museum are the *Gymnasion*, the *Stadion* and a *residential quarter* near the sea, with a synagogue.

The next part of our tour leads from the museum to Mount Kýnthos. We come first to the * **Terrace of the Syrian and Egyptian Gods** (2nd c. B.C.), with the **Sanctuary of Hadad and Atargatis**, which includes a small theater, and the *Sanctuary of Serapis and Isis* (façade of temple re-erected). Here, too, is a **Temple of Hera**, from which a flight of steps climbs the slopes of Mount **Kýnthos**. On the summit of the hill are remains of a 3rd c. *temple* dedicated to Zeus Kynthios and Athena Kynthia, who were worshiped here from the 7th c. B.C. From the hilltop there are extensive views. On the way down we can see, on the W side of the hill, a *grotto* roofed with massive stone slabs containing the base of a statue.

We now come to the site of the **ancient city of Delos**, which has been called the "Greek Pompeii". A typical example of a house of the Hellenistic period is the one known as the *House of the Dolphins*. The entrance leads into the peristyle, with the mosaic pavement which gives the house its name, and adjoining this are a large room and several smaller apartments, with a kitchen at the SE corner. Opposite it is the larger *House of the Masks*, the peristyle of which has been re-erected (masks and mosaics of Dionysos). The badly ruined *Theater*, with seating for some 5000 spectators, dates from the 3rd c. B.C. Behind the stage is a large cistern with nine chambers in which rainwater flowing down from the audi-torium was collected. There are a number of other notable buildings on the "Theater Road" which brings us back to the harbor, including (on the right) the *House of the Trident* and the *House of Dionysos*, both named after their mosaics, and (on the left) the *House of Cleopatra*, named after the statues of Kleopatra and her husband Dioskourides which were found here.

Immediately W of Delos is the island of **Rínia**, the ancient *Rheneia* (area 5 sq. miles/14 sq. km; pop. 45). A narrow isthmus, with a sandy beach, links the northern part of the island with its southern part, in which many ancient tombs, sarcophagi and funerary altars have been found.

# Djerba
See Jerba

# Dodecanese/
# Dodekanisa
*(Dhodhekanísa)*

Greece

Sými, in the Dodecanese

The Dodecanese (Twelve Islands) are the group of islands extending from Pátmos to Rhodes, together with the Kárpathos group and the island of Meyísti (Kastellorízo) which lie respectively SW and E of Rhodes.

Together with Sámos and its neighboring islands they form the Southern Sporades. The largest of these islands, with an area of 540 sq. miles/1398 sq. km, is **Rhodes** (see p. 158), which frequently played an important part in history. The islands were first regarded as a group when the Knights of St John moved from Cyprus to Rhodes in 1309; and until their further move to Malta in 1522 they were also known as the Knights of Rhodes. In modern times the name of Dodecanese has been applied to the group of islands which were ceded to Italy by Turkey in 1912 and at the end of the Second World War passed to Greece.

Ancient remains in the Dodecanese include the Asklepieion on **Kos** (see p. 113) and, on the island of Rhodes, the acropolises of Rhodes and Lindos and the city of Kameiros. Buildings recalling the Knights of St John can be seen on Rhodes, Kos, **Kálymos** (see p. 107) and **Sými** (see p. 188). There are important Christian remains on **Pátmos** (see p. 155), among them the Monastery of St John and the cave in which St John is reputed to have written the Book of Revelation.

The excellent climate and the infrastructure built up during the period of Italian occupation have promoted the development of some of the islands, in particular Rhodes, into major tourist centers.

# Dugi Otok

Yugoslavia
Republic: Croatia (Hrvatska).
Area: 48 sq. miles/124 sq. km. – Population: 6000.
Telephone code: 067.
ⓘ **Turističko Društvo,**
YU-57281 **Sali**;
tel. 8 79 33.
**Turističko Društvo,**
YU-57286 **Božava**
(in Božava Hotel);
tel. 8 63 08.

Fishermen on the island of Pátmos (Dodecanese)

HOTELS. – SALI: *Alga, Koralj, Perla* and *Sirena*, III, 96 b. – LUKA: *Luka*, with annexes, III, 126 b. – BOŽAVA: Lavanda, *II, 160 b.;* Palma, *II, 70 b., with annexes* Agava *and* Mirta Pavilions, *III, 126 b.*

BATHING BEACHES. – Almost the whole of the W coast of Dugi Otok is inaccessible, with cliffs rising sheer out of the sea to heights of 330 ft/100 m or more. The most attractive holiday resort is **Božava**, in a natural bay with a small pine wood. The bathing-places mostly have rock approaches, but there are also a few small shingle beaches. The rocky beach of the chalet hotel at **Sali** (10 minutes' walk from the village) is laid with concrete. There is also a shingle beach, and in the water the bottom is sandy. At **Luka** there is at present only one hotel. – Some parts of the coast of Dugi Otok are closed to divers (information from hotels in Božava).

FERRIES. – Daily services from Zadar to the island of Molat and Božava and from Zadar to Sali, Luka and the island of Iž. Cars not carried.

**Dugi Otok (Long Island) is 27 miles/ 44 km long and nowhere wider than 3 miles/5 km – at some points no more than 1 mile/1·5 km across. With an area of 48 sq. miles/124 sq. km, however, it is the largest island in the North Dalmatian Archipelago. The great attraction of Dugi Otok for visitors seeking a quiet and relaxing holiday has been the absence of cars; but with the construction of a new road between the port of Božava and**

**Sali it seems likely to lose this advantage.**

The island has no springs or surface watercourses, but in winter the karstic depressions of Malo Jezero, Velo Jezero and Dugo Polje fill up with fresh water, and the rainfall and ground-water are sufficient to allow vines, olives, vegetables and pines to flourish. The only accommodation for visitors is at Božava, Sali and Luka.

HISTORY. – the island was already occupied by man in prehistoric times; the earliest finds, near the village of Žman, date from the Neolithic period. The remains of Illyrian forts and burial mounds can be seen on some of the hills. Roman villas, settlements and tombs have been excavated, and on the *Proversa* Peninsula can be seen the foundations of a villa with its water-supply and drainage system; a mosaic pavement found here is now in the Zadar Museum. The island was settled by Slavs at an early stage, and there are remains of small churches, houses and tombs of the Early Croatian period, wholly or partly preserved. From the 10th c. onward the island belonged to religious houses or the municipality of Zadar. It first appears in the records, under the name of *Pizuh*, in a document of the Byzantine Emperor Constantine Porphyrogenitus (mid 10th c.); toward the end of the 10th and during the 11th c. it begins to appear in documents as *Insula Tilaga*.

THE ISLAND. – Apart from the remains of buildings and tombs which have already

Boats in Božava Harbor, Dugi Otok

been mentioned Dugi Otok has few relics of the past. In **Sali**, the largest place on the island and the main fishing center of the Kornati Islands (several fish-processing plants), there is a pleasant walk from the lower to the upper part of the village, ending at the cemetery, where an unusual form of burial, found nowhere else in the Adriatic islands, can be seen – stone vaults blasted out of the rock and closed with slabs of stone.

An interesting day trip from Sali by boat is to the impressive Cave of *Strašna Pećina*, with stalactites up to 40 in./1 m thick. A view of more than a hundred islands can be had by climbing the Hill of *Bručastac*.

# Elaphite Islands
# Koločep, Lopud, Šipan

Yugoslavia
Republic: Croatia (Hrvatska).
Area: 9 sq. miles/24 km. – Population: 1600.
Telephone code: 050.

(i) **Mjesna Zajednica,**
YU-52221 **Koločep;**
tel. 2 42 42.
**Mjesna Zajednica,**
YU-50222 **Lopud;**
tel. 8 70 30.
**Turističko Društvo,**
YU-50223 **Šipanska Luka;**
no telephone.

HOTELS. – ON KOLOČEP: *Koločep*, with annexes, II, 321 b. – ON LOPUD: *Lafodia*, II, 402 b.; *Dubrava-Pracat*, II, 203 b.; *Grand Hotel Lopud*, II, 200 b. – ON ŠIPAN: *Dubravka*, III, 49 b.

CAMP SITES. – ON KOLOČEP: sites for tents (no cars or caravans/trailers) at Gornje Čelo and Donje Čelo. – ON ŠIPAN: at Sudjurad.

TRANSPORTATION. – No car ferries. Boat services from Dubrovnik. No motor vehicles on Koločep or Lopud; on Šipan only buses.

**The Elaphite Islands lie NW of Dubrovnik 6 miles/10 km from the Dalmatian coast. There are seven islands altogether, but of these only Koločep, Lopud and Šipan are inhabited and have facilities for visitors. The islands' main attraction lies in their rich Mediterranean vegetation.**

HISTORY. – The islands are first mentioned, under the name of the Elaphites (Deer Islands), by Pliny the Elder. During the Roman period wealthy citizens of Ragusa built villas here, of which remains have been found. In the 15th c. the islands came under the control of Dubrovnik, and in 1457 Lopud and Koločep were given their own Rector (Governor). After a raid on Lopud and Koločep by the notorious pirate Ali Ulić in 1571 many watch-towers – still prominent land-marks – were built on the islands. With the abolition of the Republic of Dubrovnik in 1808 the islands became part of Napoleon's Illyrian Provinces. Since then they have shared the history of the Dalmatian coastal regions.

THE ISLANDS. – Koločep is the smallest of the islands, with an area of only 1 sq. mile/2·4 sq. km. It has rich subtropical vegetation, and the inhabitants live by farming, fishing and the tourist trade. **Donje Čelo** has a Parish Church containing fragments of Roman marble sculpture and remains of early medieval interlace ornament. Above the church is one of the watch-towers built as a protection against pirates. The road to *Gornje Čelo*, the other settlement on Koločep, passes the ruins of a considerable castle. Like the other islands in the group, Koločep has a large number of ruined or half-ruined churches and chapels.

The island of **Lopud** is the second largest in the group, with an area of 1·8 sq. miles/ 4·6 sq. km. Thanks to the island's springs of fresh water the vegetation is even more luxuriant, with palms, cypresses, oranges, lemons and other subtropical species. The township of **Lopud**, the only settlement on the island, was the residence of the Rector appointed by Ragusa, and the ruins of his house, commandingly situated on high ground, can still be seen. There is an interesting little pre-Romanesque church dedicated to Sv. Ilija (St Elias, Elijah), with wall-paintings. A particular attraction for visitors is the museum adjoining the presbytery, established by the local priest, who has systematically assembled here anything of historical interest left in abandoned houses or salvaged from ruined churches.

Lopud, on the island of the same name

**Šipan**, the largest of the islands with an area of $6\frac{1}{2}$ sq. miles/16·5 sq. km is the nearest island to Dubrovnik and is popular with visitors. Its highest point is *Velji Vrh* (797 ft/243 m). Olives, figs, grapes, carobs, almonds and pomegranates flourish here. In the principal settlement, **Šipanska Luka**, the Rector's Palace still bears witness to the splendors of the past; above the Gothic doorway is an inscription of 1450. The Parish Church contains a fine painting by the 15th c. Venetian artist Maestro Pantaleone, "The Virgin adoring the Infant Jesus". The footpath to the village of **Sudjurad**, $2\frac{1}{2}$ miles/4 km from Šipanska Luka, passes the former summer residence of the bishops of Ragusa (16th c.; partly restored). Sudjurad itself has a fortified castle of 1539 with a tower of 1577.

# Elba

Italy
Region: Tuscany. – Province: Livorno.
Area: 86 sq. miles/223 sq. km. – Population: 25,000.
Post code: I-57030. – Telephone code: 0565.

(i) **Ente per la Valorizzazione dell'Isola d'Elba,**
Calata Italia 26,
I-57037 **Portoferraio;**
tel. (0565) 9 26 71.

HOTELS. – PORTOFERRAIO: *Fabricia*, I, 119 b., SP; *Picchiaie Residence*, in Picchiaie, II, 192 b., SP; *Massimo*, II, 132 b.; *Garden*, in Schiopparello, II, 98 b.; *Adriana*, in Padulella, II, 60 b.; *Touring*, II, 51 b.; *Acquabona Golf*, in Acquabona, II, 45 b., SP; several CAMP SITES. – MARCIANA PROCCHIO: *Del Golfo*, I, 175 b., SP; *Désirée*, II, 133 b.; *Di Procchio*, II, 95 b.; *La Perla*, II, 94 b., SP; *Mona Lisa*, II, 65 b.; *Valle Verde*, II, 62 b.; *Brigantino*, II, 56 b.; *Fontalleccio*, II, 40 b. – MARCIANA MARINA: *La Primula*, I, 112 b., SP; *Gabbiano Azzurro*, II, 78 b., SP; *Marinella*, III, 112 b.; *La Conchiglia*, III, 82 b., SP. – RIO MARINA: *Ortano Mare*, II, 277 b., SP; *Rio*, II, 63 b.; *Cristallo*, in Cavo, III, 90 b. – PORTO AZZURRO: *Cala di Mola*, II, 229 b., SP; *Plaza*, II, 46 b.; *Residence Reale*, III, 88 b.; several CAMP SITES. – MARINA DI CAMPO: *Select*, II, 162 b.; *Club Hotel Marina 2*, II, 152 b.; SP; *Dei Coralli*, II, 120 b., SP; *Santa Catarina*, II, 78 b.; *Riva*, II, 77 b.; *Acquarius*, II, 58 b.; *La Barcarola*, II, 56 b.; *Meridiana*, II, 54 b.; *Barracuda*, III, 70 b.; several CAMP SITES. – CAPOLIVERI-NARENGO: *Elba International*, II, 513 b., SP.

BOAT SERVICES. – Regular service (cars carried) up to 20 times daily in summer from Piombino to Cavo ($\frac{3}{4}$ hour) or Portoferraio (1–1$\frac{1}{2}$ hours); twice daily to Rio Marina and Porto Azzurro; daily from Livorno to Portoferraio (2$\frac{1}{2}$–5$\frac{1}{4}$ hours). In summer also hydrofoil services several times daily from Piombino to Portoferraio (40 minutes) and to Cavo (20 minutes).

**The island of Elba, lying between the N Italian coast and the French island of Corsica, is the largest of the**

**Tuscan offshore islands (17 miles/ 27 km long, up to 11$\frac{1}{2}$ miles/18·5 km wide). It consists mainly of granite and porphyry, and has considerable deposits of high-quality iron ore (metal content 40–80%), particularly in the eastern part of the island.**

The possession of the iron-mines of Elba enabled the Etruscans to assert their dominance in Italy, and the mines were later worked by the Romans. Together with the tuna and anchovy fisheries and agriculture (fruit, wine), the working of iron is still one of the island's main sources of income. Elba's mild and equable climate, its great scenic beauty and the excellent conditions for underwater sport off its cliff-fringed coasts have attracted increasing numbers of visitors and residents to the island in recent years.

HISTORY. – Elba belonged to Pisa from 962 onward; then in 1290 it passed to Genoa, later to Lucca and in 1736 to Spain. After Napoleon's defeat in 1814 he was granted full sovereign rights over the island, and lived there from May 4, 1814 to February 26, 1815. Elba was returned to the Grand Duchy of Tuscany by the Congress of Vienna.

THE ISLAND. – The island's capital, **Portoferraio** (Iron Port; alt. 33 ft/10 m; pop. 11,000), lies on a promontory on the W side of the entrance to a wide bay on the N coast. In the main street, Via Garibaldi, is the Town Hall, and a little way NE, in Via Napoleone, is the Misericordia Church, in which a Mass is said for Napoleon's soul on May 5 every year; it contains a reproduction of his coffin and a bronze cast of his death-mask. On the highest-point in the town is the Piazza Napoleone (view). To the W is Forte Falcone (alt. 259 ft/79 m), to the E, above the lighthouse, Forte Stella (157 ft/48 m), both originally built in 1548 and strengthened by Napoleon. On the seaward side of the square is the simple Villa dei Molini, Napoleon's official residence, which contains his library and other relics.

4 miles/6 km SW of Portoferraio, set amid luxuriant vegetation on the slopes of the wooded *Monte San Martino* (1214 ft/ 370 m), is the **Villa Napoleone**, the Emperor's summer residence (closed on Tuesdays; fine views from terrace).

A road runs W from Portoferraio to the seaside resort of *Procchio*, in the wide bay of the same name, and the village of *Marciana Marina* (11 miles/18 km), another popular resort. – $2\frac{1}{2}$ miles/4 km inland is the Fort of *Poggio* (alt. 1178 ft/ 359 m), and $2\frac{1}{2}$ miles/4 km W of this is the village of *Marciana* (1230 ft/375 m), a summer resort surrounded by fine chestnut forests, with a ruined castle. – From here there is a cableway up **Monte Capanne** (3343 ft/1019 m), the island's highest peak (*view). – From Poggio there is an attractive walk up *Monte Perone* (2067 ft/630 m), to the SE (1 hour).

On the E coast are *Rio Marina* (pop. 2500), with large opencast ironworkings, and the little fishing port of **Porto Azzurro** (pop. 3000), picturesquely situated in a long inlet, which was fortified by the Spaniards in the 17th c. – On the lonely S coast is the popular seaside resort of **Marina di Campo**, finely situated in the Golfo di Campo.

Marina di Campo, Elba

# Etna
## See under Catania

# Euboea
*(Évvia)*

Greece
Nomos: Euboea.
Area: 1412 sq. miles/3658 sq. km. – Population: 163,000.
ⓘ **Tourist Police,**
Kótsou 2,
**Chalkís;**
tel. (0221) 2 46 62.
**Tourist Police,**
Okeanídon 3,
**Aidipsós** (summer only);
tel. (0226) 2 24 56.

HOTELS. – CHALKÍS: *Lucy*, I, 156 b.; *Hilda*, II, 223 b.; *Paliria*, II, 214 b.; *John's*, II, 98 b.; *Khara*, III, 73 b.; *Manica*, III, 48 b.; *Kentrikon*, III, 35 b. – NEAR TOWN: *St Minas Beach*, I, 148 b.

NORTH OF CHALKÍS. – NÉA ARTÁKI (5 miles/8 km): *Bel-Air*, II, 82 b.; *Angela*, III, 78 b.; *Telemachus*, III, 48 b. – AGHIA ANNA (48 miles/77 km): *Aegli*, IV, 10 b. – LIMNI (53 miles/86 km): *Limni*, III, 91 b.; *Plaza*, III, 12 b.; *Avra*, III, 11 b. – ISTIAEA (80 miles/129 km): *Hermes*, III, 16 b. – NÉOS PÝRGOS (84 miles/135 km): *Akroyali*, IV, 46 b.; *Oasis*, IV, 36 b. – AIDIPSÓS (Loutra, 94 miles/ 151 km): *Aegli*, I, 154 b.; *Avra*, I, 133 b.; *Petit Palais*, I, 16 b.; *Hermes*, II, 78 b.; *Kerakleion*, II, 69 b.; *Khara*, II, 65 b.; *Galaxias*, II, 56 b.; *Kentrikon*, II, 56 b.; *Adonis*, II, 47 b.; *Anessis*, III, 97 b.; *Capri*, III, 87 b.; *Knossos*, III, 71 b.; *Nefeli*, III, 71 b.; *Mitho*, III, 69 b.; *Galini*, III, 68 b.; *Leto*, III, 65 b.; *Istiaea*, III, 63 b.; *Irene*, III, 55 b.; *Minos*, III, 41 b.; *Atlantis*, III, 38 b.; *Ilion*, III, 37 b.; *Mikra Epavlis*, III, 33 b.; *Artemision*, III, 27 b.

SOUTH OF CHALKÍS. – LEFKANTÍ: *Lefkanti*, III, 79 b. – MALAKÓNTA (2 miles/3 km): *Eretria Beach*, II, 453 b.; *Malakonta Beach*, II, 298 b. – ERÉTRIA (14 miles/ 22 km): *Chryssi Akti*, II, 193 b.; *Perighiali Eretrias*, II, 71 b.; *Delphis*, III, 168 b. – AMÁRYNTHOS (19 miles/ 31 km): *Blue Beach*, II, 399 b.; *Stefania*, II, 152 b.; *Flisvos*, III, 43 b.; *Artemis*, IV, 41 b. – ALMYROPÓTAMOS (48 miles/77 km): *Galazio Delphini*, III, 20 b. – NÉA STÝRA (60 miles/96 km): *Venus Beach* (bungalows), III, 154 b.; *Delphini*, III, 85 b.; *Aktaeon*, III, 79 b.; *Aegilion*, III, 51 b. – MARMÁRI (69 miles/111 km): *Marmari*, III, 188 b.; *Delphini*, III, 39 b. – KÁRYSTOS (77 miles/124 km): *Apollon Resort*, II, 150 b.; *Galaxi*, III, 136 b.; *Karystion*, III, 75 b.; *Plaza*, III, 68 b.; *Als*, III, 60 b.; *Louloudi*, III, 48 b.

INTERIOR AND NE COAST. – KÝMI (58 miles/93 km): *Beis*, III, 58 b.; *Khalkidis*, IV, 30 b. – STENI (20 miles/32 km): *Steni*, III, 70 b.; *Dirphys*, III, 35 b.

BATHING BEACHES. – At Paganítsa and Kourénti (to N) and Vasilikó (S of town).

TRANSPORTATION. – Rail and bus services from Athens ($1\frac{1}{2}$ hours either way); ferries from Rafína to Marmári and Kárystos, from Oropós to Erétria, from Glýfa to Ayiókambos, from Arkítsa to Aidipsós, from Kými to the Sporades.

**Euboea, whose coastal towns and villages have increasingly developed into tourist resorts, is the largest Greek island after Crete, larger than Lesbos and Corfu. It seems more like part of the mainland than an island, however, since it is separated only by a narrow strip of sea from the E coasts of Boeotia and Attica, with which it runs parallel for some 110 miles/175 km, varying in width between 4 miles/6 km and 30 miles/ 50 km.**

At its narrowest point the strait between Euboea and the mainland, *Evripos*, is only 200 ft/60 m wide, and the island's chief town, Chalkís, is connected to the mainland by a swing bridge. Compressed into this narrow channel, the tides – elsewhere in Greek waters barely perceptible – show a marked variation between ebb and flow, a phenomenon which created a hazard for ancient shipping and is still a danger to small modern boats. The landscape pattern of Euboea is set by its mountain ranges which reach a height of 4587 ft/1398 m in Mount *Ókhi*, to the S, and 5719 ft/1743 m in Mount *Dírfys*, in the center of the island, and by the alternation between its rich vegetation cover and areas of forest in the N, the sparser growth of the S and the barren upland regions.

Coastal scenery, Euboea

HISTORY. – In ancient times the rival cities of Chalkís and Erétria vied with one another for control of the island, until finally Athens established its authority. In 338 B.C. Euboea became Macedonian, in 194 B.C. Roman. – After the Fourth Crusade the island fell into the hands of Boniface of Montferrat, who divided it into three baronies. In 1306 Venice gained control of the island, now known as Negroponte. Occupied by the Turks in 1470, it finally became part of Greece in 1830. The present division into the eparchies of Istiáia, Chalkís and Kárystos corresponds to the medieval division into three territories.

THE ISLAND. – The chief town, **Chalkís** (alt. 33 ft/10 m; pop. 36,000), situated at the point where the Evripos is only 200 ft/60 m wide, was in ancient times a thriving city which established many colonies, and is still the administrative and economic center of Euboea. The Archeological Museum in Aristotle Street contains fine fragments of the frieze from the Temple of Apollo in Erétria, including a metope depicting Theseus and Antiope of about 510 B.C. The Historical Museum, containing medieval material, is housed in a former mosque in Platía Pesónton Oplitón. The Church of Aghia Paraskeví was the Catholic Cathedral during the period of Crusader occupation. A Turkish fortress occupies the site of the ancient acropolis.

On the mainland opposite Chalkís is the **Bay of Aulis**, where Iphigeneia was sacrificed at the beginning of the Trojan War. – On the way from Chalkís to *Steni* (21 miles/33 km NE; pop. 770; bus service) it is possible

Chalkís, Euboea

to climb Mount **Dírfys** (5719 ft/1743 m; about 6 hours), from the summit of which there are extensive views.

The attractive village of **Prokópion** (pop. 760; formerly known as *Akhmet Aga*), 36 miles/58 km from Chalkís in the N of the island, is noted for its handicrafts and for the Church of St John the Russian. – **Límni** (53 miles/86 km) lies on the W coast between two wooded hills. – **Artemísion** (73 miles/117 km; pop. 500) has the remains of a Sanctuary of Artemis (10 minutes N). Off Cape Artemísion there was a naval battle between Greeks and Persians in 480 B.C. The large bronze statue of Zeus now in the National Archeological Museum in Athens was found here in 1926–27. – **Loutrá Aidipsoú** (94 miles/151 km; pop. 1900) is a well-known spa recommended for the treatment of rheumatism, arthritis, sciatica and gynaecological conditions. A short distance N of the town is the little port of **Aghiokampos**, from which there is a ferry to **Glýfa** on the coast of Thessaly.

At **Lefkantí** (6 miles/10 km SE of Chalkís) a temple of the 10th–9th c. B.C. was excavated in 1981. – At **Erétria** (*Néa Psará*; pop. 1900), 14 miles/22 km from Chalkís in the S of the island, there are substantial ancient remains, including a theater (built about 430 B.C., altered after 330 and again about 200 B.C.), a gymnasion to the E of the theater and the walls of the acropolis. The site of a Temple of Apollo (about 510 B.C.) has also been located NE of the gymnasion. A museum on the site of the ancient agora contains local finds.

**Amárynthos** (19 miles/31 km; pop. 2400) is an attractive fishing port. – Green marble has been worked since ancient times at **Stýra** (26 miles/42 km; pop. 550) and **Kárystos** (77 miles/124 km; alt. 66 ft/20 m; pop. 3350). The present town of Kárystos was founded in 1833 in a bay near the site of the ancient city, now known as Palaiokhóra, where there is a Venetian castle. To the SE of the site are ancient marble quarries.

The little town of **Kými** (alt. 656 ft/200 m; pop. 3200) lies above the harbor of **Paralía Kýmis** (sandy beach).

# Famagusta
## See under Cyprus

# Formentera

Spain
Region and province: Balearics (Baleares).
Area: 39 sq. miles/100 sq. km. – Population: 3500.
ⓘ **Oficina de Información de Turismo,**
Vara de Rey 13,
**Ibiza;**
tel. (971) 30 19 00.

HOTELS. – ON CALA SAHONA: *Hostal Cala Sahona*, PII, 69 r. – IN ES PUJOLS: *Hostal Sa Volta* (no rest.), PI, 18 r.; *Hostal Cala Es Pujols*, PIII, 30 r. – ON PLAYA DE MITJORN: *La Mola*, I, 328 r.; *Formentera Playa*, II, 211 r.

EVENT. – *Fiesta Patronal* (July).

BOAT SERVICES. – Service from La Sabina to Ibiza (in summer several sailings daily; 1 hour).

**The unspoiled island of Formentera, the second largest of the Pityusas, lies between latitude 38° 40′ and 38° 49′ N and between longitude 1° 17′ and 1° 28′ E, to the S of Ibiza, from which it is separated by the Strait, usually stormy, of Els Freus, only 2½ miles/4 km wide and up to 30 ft/9 m deep. 14 miles/23 km long and 1–10 miles/1·7–17 km wide, with an area of 39 sq. miles/100 sq. km, it extends from E to W in the shape of an axe with a broad blade and a large knob at the end of the handle. The two main parts of the island are formed from massifs of unfolded Miocene limestones – to the E the Meseta de la Mola, with La Mola or Puig Pilar (630 ft/192 m) as its highest point, and to the W Puig Guillén (351 ft/107 m). The two ranges of hills are linked by a narrow spit of land 3 miles/5 km long with long stretches of dunes. Along the gently sloping S side of the island extends a magnificent sheltered sandy beach; along the N side the shore is mainly**

rocky, with many steep cliffs. – From the northern tip of Formentera a string of islets reaches out toward Ibiza. The largest are **Espalmador** (private property; good beach, naturists tolerated) and, to the E, **Espardell**. They can be reached, however, only by private boat.

Formentera has few sources of fresh water, and most of the island is covered with a sparse growth of macchia. The only patches of woodland (Aleppo pines, junipers) are on the hills of La Mola and Puig Guillén. The hot, dry climate and the incessant N winds promote the extension of steppe-like terrain, with trees distorted by the constant battering of the wind.

The 3500 inhabitants of the island (Formenterenses), who have the highest life expectancy of all Spaniards – perhaps in consequence of their bracing climate – live in four scattered settlements, gaining their subsistence from modest arable and horticultural cultivation, sheep- and pig-rearing and fishing.

Characteristic features of the Formentera landscape are the drystone walls built to shelter the crops from the wind, the wide-spreading fig trees with their branches supported by wooden props, and the windmills, now mostly either motor-driven or in a state of ruin. The large salt-pans on the N side of the island make a valuable contribution to its economy. In recent years there has been a considerable development of the tourist trade; and a pipeline bringing water from Ibiza and a substantial increase in hotel capacity are designed to cater for the increasing numbers of visitors.

> Formentera offers little in the way of entertainment for visitors; but it is an ideal place for those who seek unspoiled natural beauty, uncrowded beaches and clean water and are content with simple accommodation and amenities.

HISTORY. – Archeological evidence (finds dating from the Bronze Age) indicates that Formentera was already inhabited by man in the 2nd millennium B.C. Later it was successively occupied by Phoenicians, Carthaginians and Romans. The ancient Greek name of *Ophiusa* ("rich in snakes") and the Latin name of *Frumentaria* ("rich in corn") point to the island's former abundance of reptiles and the great fertility of its soil; for in ancient times it had abundant supplies of fresh water and a flourishing agriculture (mainly wheat). – After the Romans Formentera was held by a succession of different masters – Byzantines, Arabs, Normans, Catalans. At the same time, however, with little in the way of defenses apart from watch-towers at exposed spots, the island was constantly harassed by corsairs from North Africa, and by about 1400 was entirely depopulated. From this period date the legends of pirates' treasure hidden in the caves on the E and W coasts which are now the haunt of hippies. – When the waters of the Mediterranean became safer toward the end of the 17th c. Formentera was resettled from Ibiza. The first permanent settlement was San Francisco Javier, founded in 1726. Since then Formentera has shared the destinies of its sister island of Ibiza.

THE ISLAND. – The regular boat from Ibiza puts in – usually after a fairly rough crossing – in Formentera's only port, **Puerto de la Sabina**, from which the island's produce is shipped. To the W of the village of *La Sabina* is the *Estanque del Peix* (Fish Pond, from its abundance of fish), also known as the *Laguna*, which is linked with the sea by a narrow channel. To the E is the large *Estanque Pudent* (Stinking Pond), near which remains dating from the prehistoric period have been found.

From La Sabina a road 12 miles/19 km long, the **Vía Mayor**, runs along the whole length of the island to the light-house on the Cabo de la Mola. On this road, 2 miles/3 km S of La Sabina, lies the principal place on the island, **San Francisco Javier**, with a little fortified church. From here a surfaced road, gradually deteriorating as it goes, runs 6 miles/9 km S through hilly country with patches of woodland and later over the barren plateau of *Plá del Rey* to the new *lighthouse* (1971) above the precipitous **Cabo de Berbería**, the most southerly point on the island. About a third of the way there a side road runs W to a holiday village in the *Cala Sahona*, a sandy cliff-fringed bay on the steep W coast.

2 miles/3 km E of San Francisco Javier the main road comes to the farming village of *San Fernando*, from which a side road leads N to the seaside resort of **Es Pujols** (beach of fine sand $\frac{3}{4}$ mile/1 km long and 65 ft/20 m broad, with stretches of cliff) and then turns back toward La Sabina along the side of the Estanque Pudent with its salt-pans. – $\frac{3}{4}$ mile/1 km E of San Fernando a road branches off to the *Playa de Mitjorn, a sheltered beach of fine sand some 6 miles/10 km long and 100–130 ft/30–40 m broad on the S coast of the island, with several holiday com-

plexes. – 3 miles/5 km farther along the main road is the modest fishing village of *Es Caló*. The road then winds its way uphill for another 3 miles/5 km to a viewpoint from which there are extensive *views over the western part of the island; to the S is the *Puig de Nuestra Señora del Pilar* (or *La Mola*, 630 ft/192 m). – $1\frac{1}{4}$ miles/2 km farther on is the village of *Nuestra Señora del Pilar*, with a fine fortified church. – In another $1\frac{1}{4}$ miles/ 2 km the road ends at the *lighthouse* (1861) above the **Cabo de la Mola**, the steeply scarped eastern tip of the island.

See also **Majorca** (with *Cabrera*), *Minorca and *Ibiza.

# Gozo
## See under Malta

# Hvar

Yugoslavia
Republic: Croatia (Hrvatska).
Area: 116 sq. miles/300 sq. km. – Population: 20,000.
Telephone code: 058.
ⓘ **Turistički Savez Općine Hvar,**
Trg Maršala Tita 1,
YU-58450 **Hvar;**
tel. 7 40 58.
**Turistička Agencija Jelsa,**
na Obali,
YU-58465 **Jelsa;**
tel. 7 56 28.
**Dalmacijaturist Stari Grad,**
YU-58460 **Stari Grad;**
tel. 7 58 28.

HOTELS. – HVAR TOWN: *Amfora*, I, 745 b.; *Palace*, I, 145 b.; *Adriatic*, I, 116 b.; *Bodul*, II, 300 b.; *Sirena*, II, 300 b.; *Dalmacija*, II, 135 b.; *Delfin*, II, 112 b.; *Galeb*, II, 68 b. – JELSA: *Mina*, II, 387 b.; *Fontana* tourist complex, II, 376 b.; *Jadran*, II, 256 b. – JELSA VRBOSKA: *Adriatic*, II, 353 b.; *Madeira*, III, 44 b. – STARI GRAD: *Arkada*, I, 580 b.; *Helios*, II, 418 b., with annexe *Helios Bungalows*, II, 108 b.; *Adriatic*, II, 170 b.; *Jadran*, III, 33 b.

CAMP SITES. – STARI GRAD: *Jurjevac*. – JELSA: *Mina* (with facilities for naturists).

EVENTS. – International Fashion Festival in Stari Grad (June). – Open-air performances in summer in the ruins of St Catherine's Monastery above Hvar town, in the Arsenal and in the courtyard of Sv. Marko.

BATHING BEACHES. – On the beaches in front of the hotel complexes in Hvar town the rock has been covered with concrete and gangways into the water have been provided; there are only small stretches of shingle or sand. The Stari Grad hotels have a better beach (though swimming at the head of the inlet is not to be recommended.) The hotels at Jelsa also have a rocky beach.

CAR FERRIES. – Hydrofoils and fast motor-launches from Zadar to Vira, the harbor for Hvar town (Hvar itself is a pedestrian precinct); no cars on these services. Car ferries Split to Vira, Split to Stari Grad, Sućuraj (at the E end of the island) to Drvenik. Boat services between Jelsa and Bol and between Hvar and Korčula.

**\*Hvar, the longest Yugoslav island (42 miles/68 km), lies off the Dalmatian coast between Split and Dubrovnik. The S coast has bare hills falling steeply down to the sea; the flatter N coast is much indented. In the interior of the island are many vineyards, olive groves and plantations of rosemary and lavender.**

HISTORY. – Evidence of Neolithic occupation has been found in caves. In 385 B.C. Greeks from Paros founded the settlement of *Pharos*, and soon afterwards another settlement, *Dimos*, was established on the site of the present-day town of Hvar. In 235 B.C. an Illyrian King, Agron, gained control of the island. The Romans landed on Hvar in 219 B.C. and held the island until the 7th c. A.D. Thereafter it was occupied by Slavs from the Neretva Mountains. From 870 to 886 it belonged to the Byzantine Empire, and then fell back into the hands of the Neretvans. In the 11th c. it was controlled by the kings of Croatia, from 1145 to 1164 by Venice, from 1164 to 1180 by Byzantium, from 1180 to 1278 by the Hungaro-Croatian kings, then again by Venice. The Hungaro-Croatian kings regained control from 1358 to 1420, after which the island belonged to Bosnia and then to the Republic of Dubrovnik. From 1420 to 1797 it was again held by Venice, then from 1797 to 1806 by Austria, from 1806

to 1813 by France, and once again by Austria from 1813 to 1918. From 1918 to 1922 it was under Italian occupation, after which it was incorporated in the kingdom of Yugoslavia. In April 1941 the island was occupied by Italian troops, who were replaced by Germans after the Italian surrender in 1943. In September 1944 Hvar was recovered by Yugoslav Partisan units.

THE ISLAND. – Passenger ships and freighters, and the motor-launches and hydrofoils from Split, put in at the natural harbor of *Vira*, on the N coast of the island beyond Mount Trtdava, in order to keep cars, trucks and buses away from the town of Hvar, 2 miles/3 km S. Some vessels from Split also put in at Stari Grad, and there is a ferry service between the mainland town of Drvenik and Sućuraj, at the extreme easterly tip of Hvar.

The principal place on the island, **Hvar**, lies in a sheltered bay on the SW coast. The Sea Gate leads into the main square, to the left of which stands the 16th c. Cathedral, with a handsome 17th c. tower. It contains a number of valuable paintings, including a "Madonna with Saints" by Domenico Umberti (1692), a "Madonna and Child" (Pisan school, 13th c.), a "Pietà" (about 1520) and a "Madonna with Saints" by Palma Giovane (1626–27). The most valuable item in the

Hvar town

Treasury is the gilded staff of Bishop Pritić (1509).

In the square in front of the Cathedral stands the large Town Fountain of 1529. On the S side of the square is the Arsenal (13th–17th c.), with a wide arched entrance to admit a galley. On the first floor is a small theater (1612), now a museum.

Going toward the harbor, we see on the right the Palace Hotel, originally a Venetian palazzo, with a magnificent façade, loggia and clock-tower.

From the right-hand harbor basin paths lead through the beautiful municipal gardens to the modern hotel complexes on the N side of the town. On the hillside is a ruined monastery in which concerts and dramatic performances are given during the summer.

Returning to the harbor, we can make our way up to the Spanish fort above the town (cableway planned; bus service from harbor until 1 a.m.), from which there is a superb *view over the harbor to the Pakleni Oroci (Pitch Islands or Hell's Islands). Farther N, a little higher up, is a well-preserved old French fort, not open to the public (radar post, military installations).

From the main square it is 5 minutes' walk SE along the sea-wall to the Franciscan Friary, built in the 15th c. and restored after its destruction by the Turks in 1571; it has a fine church (pictures by Bassano, Palma Giovane and Santa Croce) and a museum housed in the refectory (*"Last Supper" by Matteo Rosselli, 1578–1650; pictures by Titian and Tiepolo; vestments, incunabula, etc.). Behind the refectory is a small garden with a 300-year-old cypress.

A winding hill road leads to **Stari Grad**, the ancient *Pharos*, at the head of a bay which reaches far inland. The hotels lie outside the old town, which possesses five churches, three of them half ruined. Many of the old houses have been renovated to provide accommodation for visitors. The town has many reminders of its long history – Cyclopean masonry of the Illyrian period, Roman mosaics, Early Christian fonts. Its most interesting building is a 16th c. house, erected within an old Turkish fort, which belonged to the

Croatian Renaissance poet Petar Hektorović. In the courtyard is a basin from which a pipe runs down to the harbor.

**Vrboska** is charmingly situated amid pine woods and vineyards at the innermost tip of a narrow inlet. It has two churches, one of which – a fortress as well as a church – contains a picture attributed to Titian.

**Jelsa**, half-way along the island, has remained a peaceful little village. The hotels are on the wooded slopes on either side of the harbor. An interesting trip is to the *Grapčeva Cave* (reached by boat from the harbor), in which evidence of prehistoric occupation was found.

# Hýdra
## (Idhra)

Greece
Nomos: Attica.
Area: 19 sq. miles/50 sq. km. – Population: 2550.
Telephone code: 0298.
ⓘ **Tourist Police** (summer only),
Navárkhou Vótsi;
tel. 5 22 05.

HOTELS. – ON HÝDRA: *Miramare*, I, 50 b.; *Miranda*, I, 26 b.; *Hydrousa*, II, 72 b.; *Delfini*, II, 20 b.; *Leto*, III, 74 b.; *Hydra*, III, 23 b.; *Argo*, IV, 16 b.

ON SPÉTSAI: *Spetses*, I, 143 b.; *Kasteli*, I, 139 b.; *Posidonion*, I, 83 b.; *Roumanis*, II, 65 b.; *Faros*, III, 84 b.; *Star*, III, 68 b.; *Ilios*, III, 51 b.

BATHING BEACHES. – Immediately W of the harbor (rock, with concreted surfaces) and in Mandráki Bay (pebbles and rock).

TRANSPORTATION. – Boats from Piraeus to Hýdra, and from Hýdra to the islands of Póros and Spétsai (Hovercraft).

**The long rocky island of Hýdra, lying off the NE tip of the Peloponnese, is now a popular summer holiday resort.**

The harbor, Hýdra

Boats in Spétsai Harbor

The chief place on the island, **Hýdra**, rises in a semicircle above its sheltered harbor. A number of handsome mansions belonging to shipowning families, among them the houses of the Tsamádos and Kountouriótis families, recall the powerful support given to the Greek struggle for independence by the wealthy shipowners of Hýdra. Other features of interest on the island are the Church of the Dormition (Kímisis Theotókou, 18th c.) in a former monastery by the harbor; the 15th c. Profítis Ilías Monastery (an hour's walk from the town); and the 16th c. Zourvás Monastery at the E end of the island (3 hours' walk; also accessible by boat).

To the W of Hýdra, opposite the southern tip of the Argolic Peninsula, lies the island of *Spétsai** (area 8 sq. miles/22 sq. km; pop. 3500), which attracts visitors with its gentle landscape and mild climate. The town of Spétsai has a number of handsome old mansions, three fine churches (in the Upper Town or Kastelli) and a local museum. – On the island are the remains of three Early Christian basilicas; and on the S coast a bay which offers good bathing and the *Bekiri* sea-cave.

# Hyères, Iles d'

France
Region: Provence – Alpes – Côte d'Azur.
Département: Var.
(i) **Office de Tourisme,**
Place Clemenceau,
F-83400 **Hyères;**
tel. (94) 65 18 55.

HOTELS. – ON PORQUEROLLES: *Mas du Langoustier*, II, 50 r.; *Relais de la Poste*, III, 30 r.; *Sainte Anne*, III, 15 r.; *Les Palmiers*, IV, 8 r. – ON PORT-CROS: *Le Manoir*, II, 30 r.– ON ILE DU LEVANT: *Brise Marine*, IV, 23 r.

**The *Iles d'Hyères, known as the Iles d'Or (Golden Islands), are a group lying SE of Toulon which, geologically, belong to the Massif des Maures and show a similar landscape pattern. The islands are largely forest-covered and have stretches of rugged cliff around their coasts; but they also possess beautiful natural harbors and inlets which provide refuge in a storm, and have excellent beaches.**

The three main islands can be reached by boat from Hyères (sailing from Hyères Plage); there is also a boat to Porquerolles from the Giens Peninsula.

THE ISLANDS. – The largest island in the group is **Porquerolles**, which is almost 5 miles/8 km long and some $1\frac{1}{4}$ miles/2 km wide. There are flat beaches on the N side of the island, but the S and E coasts fall steeply down to the sea. The chief place is **Porquerolles** (pop. 500), situated in the main bay on the N coast. From here it is a 45-minute walk S through beautiful Mediterranean vegetation to a lighthouse at the southern tip of the island, the *Phare de l'Oustaou* (315 ft/96 m). – A path runs NE through the forest and along the *Plage Notre-Dame* to the *Cap des Mèdes* (1 hour 15 minutes). Half-way there a track goes off on the right to the *Fort de la Repentance* and the *Sémaphore* (signal station; 466 ft/142 m; views).

To the E of Porquerolles is the island of **Port-Cros** (area 16,400 acres/6640 hectares), which has only a few inhabitants. Since 1963 it has been a National Park and nature reserve, with luxuriant Mediterranean vegetation and abundant animal life (natural forest, nesting-places of rare birds, fish). At the entrance to the harbor of *Port-Cros* (off which, to the W, is the little Ile de Bagaud, rising to 194 ft/ 59 m) is the 17th c. *Fort du Moulin*. There is a very attractive walk (1½ hours) south-eastward to the *Vallon de la Solitude* and the imposing *Falaises du Sud* (cliffs almost 650 ft/200 m high). Another good walk (3 hours) is eastward to the charming *Pointe de Port-Man*.

Still farther E is the lonely and geologically interesting **Ile du Levant**, a rocky island 5 miles/8 km long and up to 1 mile/1·5 km wide which formerly belonged to the Abbots of Lérins and is now well known for its naturist colony of **Héliopolis**, established in 1932. Much of the island is military territory and closed to the public.

# Ibiza

**Spain**
Region and province: Balearics (Baleares).
Area: 229 sq. miles/593 sq. km. – Population: 45,000.
(i) **Oficina de Información de Turismo,**
Vara de Rey 13,
**Ibiza Town;**
tel. (971) 30 19 00.

HOTELS. – IBIZA TOWN: *Torre del Mar*, I, 217 r.; *Los Molinos*, I, 147 r.; *Royal Plaza*, I, 117 r.; *Algarb*, II, 408 r.; *Goleta*, II, 252 r.; *Tres Carabelas*, II, 245 r.; *Ibiza Playa*, II, 155 r. – TALAMANCA: *Playa Real*, II, 237 r.

SAN ANTONIO ABAD: *Palmyra*, I, 160 r.; *Tanit*, II, 386 r.; *Pinet Playa*, II, 291 r.; *Hawai*, II, 210 r.; *San Remo*, II, 147 r.; *Tropical*, II, 142 r.; *San Diego*, II, 132 r.; *Helios*, II, 132 r.; *Arenal*, II, 131 r.; *Abrat*, II, 110 r.; *Acor Playa*, II, 110 r.; *Piscis Park*, III, 366 r.; *Pacific*, III, 156 r.; *Gran Sol*, III, 138 r.; *Ses Sevines*, III, 133 r.

SANTA EULALIA DEL RÍO: *Fenicia*, I, 191 r.; *Miami*, II, 370 r.; *Los Loros*, II, 262 r.; *S'Agamasa*, II, 217 r.; *Augusta*, II, 196 r.; *Don Carlos*, II, 168 r.; *Cala Llonga*, II, 163 r.; *Ses Estaques*, II, 159 r.; *Panorama*, II, 137 r.

CALA LLONGA: *Playa Imperial*, II, 268 r.; *Playa Dorada*, III, 266 r. – ES CANA: *Atlantic*, III, 195 r.; *Anfora Playa*, III, 81 r. – SAN JUAN BAUTISTA: *Hacienda Na Xamena*, I, 54 r.; *Imperio Playa*, II, 210 r.; *Cala San Vicente*, II, 120 b. – PORTINATX: *Presidente Playa*, II, 270 r.; *El Greco*, II, 242 r. – SAN JOSE: *Nautilus*, I, 168 r.; *Don Toni*, II, 328 r.; *Playa d'En Bossa*, II, 270 r.; *Milord II*, II, 218 r.; *Milord*, II, 153 r.; *S'Estanyol*, II, 135 r.; *Robinson Club Cala Vadella* (4 miles/6 km W), 320 b.

EVENTS. – *Fiesta Patronal* (January) in San Antonio Abad. – *Fiesta Patronal* (February) in Santa Eulalia. – *Fiestas de San Juan* (June), with folk events and fireworks. – *Sea Procession* (July) in Ibiza, with regatta and water sports. – *Fiestas Patronales* (August) in Ibiza. – *Fiesta Popular* (August) in San Antonio Abad. – *Semana Santa* (Holy Week), in almost every town and village on the island, with religious processions; in Ibiza procession on the night of Good Friday. – *Folk-dancing* in front of the parish church in San Miguel (every Thursday at 6 p.m.).

CASINO. – *Casino de Ibiza* at the new pleasure harbor (Ibiza Nueva).

BOAT SERVICES. – Car ferries to Palma de Mallorca and to the Spanish mainland (Barcelona, Valencia, Alicante).

**\*Ibiza (in the Ibizan dialect Eivissa), the largest of the Pityusas (221 sq. miles/572 sq. km), lies some 50 miles SW of Majorca between latitude 38° 50′ and 39° 6′ N and between longitude 1° 13′ and 1° 37′ E. Roughly oval in form, it extends from NE to SW for 30 miles/48 km, ranging up to 15 miles/24 km in width. It is traversed by two ranges of hills consisting of Mesozoic limestones and clays, with gently rounded summits – friendly hills, with little in the way of gullies or rugged rock faces.**

The southern range, with *Atalayasa de San José* (1562 ft/476 m) as its highest point, rises to greater heights than the more northerly one, which is broken up by a number of depressions. The two ranges are separated by a long low-lying area of terra rossa which cuts across the island from the Bay of San Antonio Abad in the W to the Cala San Vicente in the NE. The southern tip of Ibiza is occupied by a wide alluvial plain with salt-pans which have been worked since ancient times. The coast is much indented, with many *calas* (creeks, coves), which are sometimes sheltered, with sandy beaches, but are usually rocky and at some points in the NW have formidably steep cliffs. There are a number of secluded coves suitable for bathing (including naturist, which has been tolerated in recent years) which are accessible only by boat.

HISTORY. – Finds of Neolithic pottery and Bronze Age implements have shown that Ibiza had already been settled by man in the 2nd millennium B.C. The origin of these first inhabitants is uncertain: probably they were Iberian stock-herding peoples, who called their island *Aivis*. The sheltered harbor of what is now Ibiza town was already being used by seafarers and traders in ancient times as a port of call and base. In particular there are records of Phoenician and Greek traders, who gave the island the name of *Ebysos* or *Pityusa* (Island of Pines).

In 654 B.C. (or perhaps as early as about 720 B.C.) Carthaginians established the commercial and military post of *Ibosim* on the Isla Plana, on the E side of the harbor bay. This settlement minted its own coins and, as Diodorus tells us, was inhabited by foreigners of all kinds. It grew steadily in prosperity thanks to the manufacture of purple dye, the extraction of salt from the sea, agriculture and the mining of lead. The most impressive relic of this period is the Carthaginian necropolis of *Ereso*, on the Puig des Molins in Ibiza town. From this cemetery, and also from the Es Cuyeram Cave at San Vicente, which was a shrine of the goddess Tanit, came the abundance of Punic material, the finest items from which are now to be seen in the Archeological Museum in Barcelona.

After the defeat of Carthage by Rome and the conquest of Majorca and Minorca by Quintus Caecilius Metellus in 122 B.C. Ibiza seems to have been an ally of Rome; for the island preserved its Punic character into Roman times, and was not incorporated in the Roman Empire until A.D. 70, when it was given the honorific style of *Flavia Augusta*.

The pressures of the Iberian Peninsula during the period of the great migrations led to a considerable influx of population from the mainland into the Balearics and Pityusas, including Ibiza. In A.D. 426 the Vandals conquered and devastated the island, and it was not until 533–534, during the reign of Justinian, that Belisarius destroyed the Vandal kingdom and brought Ibiza back into Byzantine control.

After a bloody plundering expedition directed against Majorca in 707, the Arabs captured Ibiza, which they called *Yebisah*, in 711. In 798, however, they were driven out by Charlemagne; in 813 the island passed into the hands of the Franks, and in 817 it became part of the Frankish Empire. The Arabs recaptured it in 832, but were displaced by the Normans in 859; then in 901–902 they were finally able to establish themselves firmly on the island. Ruling Ibiza for some 500 years, with some interruptions, they left a lasting mark on its character and aspect. One legacy of the Arab period, for example, is represented by the *feixes* – an elaborate irrigation system which is still in operation.

The conquest of Ibiza by the Archbishop of Tarragona, Guillermo de Montgrí, and the expulsion of the Moors were followed by the re-Christianization of the island. The continuing Arab and Turkish raids, however, led in the 16th c. to the building of the fortified churches and watch-towers still to be seen in many places on the island and to the construction of the massive walls of Ibiza town. In 1652 Ibiza was ravaged by plague. The continuing threat from freebooters and pirates led to the arming of Ibizan ships, which then in the 18th c. themselves took to piracy. – In more recent times Ibiza has shared the destinies of Majorca. During the Spanish Civil War the island was held for a time by the Republicans.

# Ibiza town

**The town of Ibiza (officially Ciudad de Ibiza, Ibizan Eivissa; alt. 0–330 ft/ 0–100 m; pop. 22,000), in the S of the island, is its administrative and economic center and the see of a bishop. It is charmingly situated on the S side of the sheltered harbor bay which opens toward the SE, its characteristic cube-shaped white-washed houses climbing up the slopes of the hill crowned by a massive fortress.**

SIGHTS. – Although most visitors now arrive by air and reach the town on a road with little of interest to offer, the arrival in Ibiza by sea is still an impressive experience, for the **view of the town, visible from afar with its tiers of houses dominated by the mighty bastions of the fortress, is one of the most picturesque sights in the Western Mediterranean. The *Harbor* is protected by two breakwaters, and at the foot of the main one is an *obelisk* (erected 1915) commemorating the Ibizan corsairs and their Captain, Antonio Riquer, who in 1806 seized the brig "Felicity", sailing from Gibraltar under the British flag, and captured its commander, the notorious pirate Miguel Novelli. – Along the harbor runs Avenida Andenes (no cars), a lively and popular promenade. – In the northern harbor basin is the modern **yacht marina**, with the new Casino close by.

Ibiza town

To the S of the harbor is the LOWER TOWN, now the commercial and shopping quarter. In its western part, **La Marina**, are many shops, boutiques, eating-places and bars. In Plaza de la Constitución is the old *Fruit and Vegetable Market* (1872), and in Calle de Alfonso XII the octagonal *Meat and Fish Market*. In many narrow little streets are hippie markets. To the S of Plaza de José Pidal, in Calle del Obispo Cardona, is the Church of **El Salvador**, on the site of the fishermen's Church of San Telmo (originally 15th c.) which was destroyed during the Civil War. – *Sa Penya, the eastern part of the Lower Town and the fishermen's quarter, reaching up to the bastions of the fortress, is the oldest part of the town outside the fortress walls, an area of narrow little lanes and quiet nooks and crannies. It has preserved much of its original Oriental character. From the end of Calle de la Vista Alegra and from the E breakwater there are fine views of the town and the opposite side of the bay. – To the W of La Marina lies the modern part of the Lower Town, which is traversed by the wide **Paseo Vara de Rey (Rambla)**. In the center of the square can be seen a *monument* (1904) in honor of the Ibizan General, Joaquín Vara de Rey, who fell in battle during the Hispano-American War (1898). In the Rambla are the principal public buildings and banks, the *Museum* (No. 1) and the *Tourist Office* (No. 13). – In the northern part of the modern Lower Town is the **Bullring** (*Plaza de Toros*; 4000 seats), with a small *Bullfighting Museum*.

Above the Lower Town, to the S, rise the massive walls of the *Fortress (declared a national monument in 1942), which is unique for its form, its size and its excellent state of preservation. It was built between 1554 and 1585 at the behest of the Emperor Charles V. Designed by the Italian architect Calvi, it stands on the remains of earlier Arab walls of which only a few fragments have survived. The walls of the fortress, laid out in the form of an irregular heptagon with seven triangular **bastions** and three gates, enclose the UPPER TOWN or *D'Alt Vila, with its twisting stepped lanes (art galleries, restaurants), old public buildings and handsome mansions, the Castle, the Cathedral and the Bishop's Palace. – The Upper Town is reached from the Plaza de la Constitución by way of a broad ramp, *El Rastrillo*, and the **Puerta de las Tablas**,

the principal gateway of the fortress, once protected by a drawbridge. Flanking the gate are two badly damaged *Roman statues* discovered during the construction of the fortress. The gatehouse houses a *Museum of Contemporary Art*. – Above the *Santa Tecla Bastion* (*view of Sa Penya and the harbor) is the **Catedral** *de Neustra Señora de las Nieves* (Our Lady of the Snows). Of the original Gothic church, which was drastically altered in the 17th c., there remain only the *tower* (345 ft/105 m; *view) and the sacristy doorway. – The small *Cathedral Museum* contains a beautiful 14th c. monstrance of silver and enamel and Gothic paintings.

In the *Cathedral Square, to the NW, is the *Archeological Museum**, with a unique collection of Phoenician, Punic and Roman material from the surrounding area and the Es Cuyeram Cave. – On the W side of the square is the **Bishop's Palace**, with a Gothic doorway, a beautiful inner patio and a garden. Opposite it, to the N, is the old *Curia* (formerly the presbytery), also with a Gothic doorway (restored).

To the NE, near the outer fortress walls and on a considerably lower level than the Cathedral, stands the **Church of Santo Domingo** (popularly known as *El Convento*), begun at the end of the 16th c., which has Byzantine domes (frescoes) and beautiful tiled walls and floor; the Chapel of the Rosary has a notable Baroque altar-piece. – To the S, higher up, is the **Casa Consistorial** or *Ayuntamiento* (Town Hall), in a former conventual building. The Council Chamber is decorated with scenes from the history of the town. – From the *Santa Lucía Bastion*, to the N, there is a superb *view of the town and the harbor bay.

SW of the Cathedral, on the highest point in the town, once occupied by the Punic Acropolis and the Moorish Alcázar (Almudaina), is the **Castillo** (not open to the public), which reflects the architectural styles of several different periods; it has a medieval tower. From the *San Bernardo Bastion* behind it there are *views of the town and the southern part of the island, extending as far as Formentera. – In the western part of the Upper Town are a number of handsome mansions, including the *Casa de los Laudes* in Calle del Obispo Torres. In the same street, in the fortress's inner circuit of walls, are the *Portella*, an arched gateway which is believed to have been part of the Arab walls, and the little *Chapel of San Ciriaco*, at the spot where the Catalans broke through the walls in 1235. – The most westerly of the bastions, the **Portal Nou** (New Gate), affords fine views of the Puig des Molins and the western suburbs of the town.

From the Portal Nou the *Vía Romana*, on the line of an old Roman road, runs W to the **Puig des Molins** (Windmill Hill), with the dilapidated stumps of four 13th c. windmills and an astronomical *Observatory*. On the slopes of the hill excavation has revealed the largest known **\*\*Punic necropolis**, in use from the 7th c. B.C. down to Roman times, being reserved in the Christian era mainly for notable citizens of the town. Covering such a considerable area and such a long period of time, the necropolis has yielded a correspondingly rich harvest of grave-goods, including cult objects and military equipment, sarcophagi and death-masks, pottery, household articles, jewelry and coins. The finds are displayed in the **\*Museum** (*Museo Puig des Molins*) situated close to the necropolis in the Vía Romana.

Farther W, beyond the Puig des Molins, is the suburb of **Figueretas** (*Figueretes*), with many hotels lining the *Playa Figueretes*, a strip of beach of which some parts are rocky. $1\frac{1}{4}$ miles/2 km SW is the long sandy beach of the **Playa d'en Bossa**, which also has hotels. – $\frac{3}{4}$ mile/1 km W of the beach lies the village of *San Jorge*, which has a 14th c. fortified church. 2 miles/3 km farther SW is **Ibiza International Airport**; there are a number of windmills in the area.

THE ISLAND. – To the NE of the Ibiza town, separated from the harbor bay by a narrow isthmus leading to the *Isla Grossa* (\*view of town and harbor semicircular *Cala Talamanca*, with the hotel complexes of **Talamanca** and *Ses Figueres* and long stretches of beach (seaweed). – $1\frac{1}{4}$ miles/ 2 km inland is the little village of *Jesús*. The Church of Nuestra Señora de Jesús, built in the 14th c. as the chapel of a Dominican abbey and later fortified by Franciscans, has a Late Gothic \*retablo, perhaps by Juan Rodrigues de Osona (16th c.). – 4 miles/6 km N of Ibiza town is the little Church of *Monte Cristo*, with fine views toward the S.

**San Antonio Abad** (Ibizan *Sant Antoni de Portmany*) is the second largest town on the island and the administrative center of a district (pop. 9000) to which the villages of *San Rafael* (Sant Rafel, 5 miles/ 8 km E; 18th c. church, "Fantasylandia" leisure park), *Santa Inés* (Santa Agnès, 6 miles/9 km N) and the lonely hill village of *San Mateo* (11 miles/18 km NE) also belong. The town, with its ancient core, lies on the NE side of the wide *Bahía de San Antonio* (Bahía de Portmany), known to the Romans as Portus Magnus (Great Harbor), which reaches far inland from the NW, between the *Cabo Negret* to the N and the *Punta de Sa Torre d'en Rovira* (\*view from watch-tower) to the SW.

The once-modest little fishing village of San Antonio Abad has now developed into a lively (and noisy) tourist resort with much modern building and good beaches suitable for children in the immediate vicinity. The only features of interest are the fortified Parish Church of San Antonio, built in the 14th c. on the site of an earlier mosque situated on a low hill (92 ft/28 m), and an Ibizan local museum, the Museo Costumbrista. – A little way W of the town is a *Byzantine cemetery* excavated in 1906–07 (finds in Archeological Museum, Ibiza). $1\frac{1}{4}$ miles/2 km N is the Early Christian *rock-cut Church of Santa Inés* (national monument).

On either side of the town, flanking the bay, are many coves with sandy beaches, now developed to cater for vacationers. Immediately SE are several beaches; to the NW is the rocky **Cala Gració** (small sandy beach), fringed by woodland; and farther away on the S side, on the site of the Roman harbor (now almost entirely silted up), are **Port des Torrent** (shingle, with some rocks) and **Cala Bassa** (cliffs and sandy beach), both with sheltered anchorages. – Off the western end of the bay is the rocky 2 mile/3 km long **Isla Conejera** (*Conillera*; alt. 230 ft/70 m), with a lighthouse at its N end. Legend has it that Hannibal was born either on this island or on Es Vedrá (see below). To the S of Conejera are the islets of *Bosque* (goat-herding) and *Esparto*, to the W the uninhabited *Islas Bledas* (lighthouse on Bleda Plana).

6 miles/10 km N of San Antonio Abad (unsurfaced road, degenerating into a footpath) is the steeply scarped **Cabo**

**Nonó**, below the S side of which is the *Cueva de las Fontanellas*, a cave with Bronze Age rock-engravings.

**Santa Eulalia del Río** (Ibizan *Santa Eulària del Riu*; the Arabic name was *Xarc*), the third largest place on the island, administrative center of a district (pop. 11,000) and the principal tourist resort on the E coast of Ibiza with excellent facilities for visitors, lies 9 miles/15 km NE of Ibiza town on the *Río de Santa Eulalia*, the only river in the Balearics which flows throughout the year ("Río Balear"). The advantages of this site in the fertile Plain of *Plá de Vila*, sheltered on the N by the hills of the *Sierra de la Mala Costa* and *Furnás* (1345 ft/410 m) and provided by the river with a regular and abundant supply of water, led to the establishment of a flourishing settlement here in Roman times; and Santa Eulalia is still surrounded by the most extensive market-gardens on the island. – The simple cube-shaped houses of the little town are clustered loosely around the *Puig de Missa* (217 ft/66 m), on the summit of which is the conspicuous Church of Santa Eulalia, built in the 14th c. on the foundations of an Arab mosque and enlarged and fortified in 1568. Close by is a small museum devoted to the work of the Catalan painter Laureano Barau (1863–1957), who lived here for many years. – On the SW side of the town, below the modern road bridge, is a well-preserved Roman viaduct over the Río de Santa Eulalia and at the mouth of the river, at Ca'n Fita, a *Roman cemetery*.

Below the NE side of the Puig de Missa is the modern settlement of **Sa Vila**. In the Plaza de España in the center of the little town is the Town Hall (Ayuntamiento), and in front of this is a monolith set up in gratitude for the rescue of the passengers and crew of the steamer "Mallorca", which sank off Ibiza in 1913.

To the S of Santa Eulalia are the holiday villages of *La Siesta* (1 mile/1·5 km) and **Cala Llonga** (4½ miles/7 km), with a good beach extending along a deep sandy bay. Beyond these are the luxurious residential development of *Roca Llisa* (6 miles/10 km; golf-course), which extends along the rocky ridge of the *Puig d'en Vich* to the cliffs fringing the coast (rocky beach; no landing-place for boats), and the inland development, to the SW, of **Ca'n Furnet** (7 miles/11 km).

Beach in Cala Llonga, Ibiza

– Along the coast to the NE of Santa Eulalia del Río are the hotel colonies of **S'Argamassa** (2½ miles/4 km) and **Es Caná** (4½ miles/7 km), with a "hippie market", a good sandy beach, a small harbor (glass-bottomed boat) and the offshore *Isla de Caná*. On *Punta Arabí* is another hotel complex (rocky beach; diving), and off this, to the S, are the two little islets of *Isla de Santa Eulalia* and *Isla Redonda*.

4½ miles/7 km N of Santa Eulalia del Río lies the picturesque hamlet of **San Carlos** (*Sant Carles de Peralta*), with a small fortified church. 1¼ miles/2 km SW are *lead- and silver-mines* which were already being worked in Punic and Roman times and were closed down only in quite recent years. – E of San Carlos are many beautiful sandy coves and stretches of rocky coast; these, which provide a happy hunting ground for scuba-divers, include *Cala Nova* (2½ miles/4 km), *Cala Llenya* (3 miles/5 km), *Cala Mastella* (3 miles/5 km) with the residential development of *Ca'n Jordi* (2½ miles/4 km) and *Cala Boix* (4 miles/6 km), as well as the long *Playa Figueral* (2 miles/3 km), with holiday apartments. – From San Carlos an attractive *ridgeway (unsurfaced road) runs to Cala San Vicente and the Punta Grossa. – Off a long promontory ending in *Cabo Roig* (to S) and *Punta d'en Valls* (to N; old watch-tower) lies the rocky island of **Tagomago**, with a lighthouse and a restaurant (boat trips from Santa Eulalia del Río and Cala San Vicente).

**San Juan Bautista** (Ibizan *Sant Joan Baptista*) is a commune of 3500 people in the bleak and hilly northern part of Ibiza, which has offered little scope for the development of tourism. The inhabitants live in scattered cottages of the characteristic local type and in the four loosely clustered villages of San Juan Bautista, San Vicente Ferrer, San Miguel and San Lorenzo. Agriculture flourishes in the fertile valleys with their many springs. The administrative center of the commune is *San Juan Bautista*, some 14 miles/22 km NE of Ibiza town on the north-western slopes of the Sierra de la Mala Costa. On the highest point in the village, the Puig de Missa (643 ft/196 m), stands the simple Parish Church of San Juan Bautista (18th c., with later alterations), near which are the Town Hall and the cemetery. – **Mount Furnás** (1345 ft/410 m) offers a rewarding climb (2–2½ hours), with a *view which in good weather extends as far as Majorca and the Spanish mainland.

7 miles/11 km E of San Juan Bautista, beyond the village of *San Vicente Ferrer* (Parish Church; *view), is the charming holiday complex of **Cala San Vicente** (*Cala de Sant Vicent*), extending around the wide bay of the same name, which has one of the finest beaches on Ibiza, sheltered on the N by the rocky promontory of *Punta Grossa* (568 ft/173 m) and fringed by a pine wood which affords welcome shade. The road running up Punta Grossa is lined by trim villas and holiday houses. To the SE is a view of the island of Tagomago. – 1¼ miles/2 km N of Cala San Vicente is the **Es Cuyeram Cave**, in which a Carthaginian shrine dedicated to the goddess Tanit (Astarte) was discovered in 1907 and large numbers of Neolithic potsherds and a bronze tablet with inscriptions of the 4th and 2nd c. B.C. were found in 1913; material from the site can be seen in the Archeological Museum in Ibiza town. – There is a beautiful *ridgeway walk from Punta Grossa via Cala San Vicente to San Carlos.

In the extreme N of the island (3–6 miles/ 5–10 km from San Juan Bautista) two very picturesque fjord-like inlets cut deep inland: to the W *Cala Charraca* (Xarraca; small beach), to the E the narrow *Cala de Portinatx* (small sandy beach), fringed by beautiful pine woods, with the village of **Portinatx** (*Portinaitx*), also known as *Portinatx del Rey* since King Alfonso XIII landed here in 1929. On the W side of the inlet is the holiday complex *Ciudad Mar*.

6 miles/9 km SW of San Juan Bautista stands the simple *Church of San Lorenza* (18th c.). A short distance N is the ancient fortified village of **Balafi** (*Balafia*).

SW of San Juan Bautista (6 miles/9 km on an unsurfaced track or 15 miles/25 km by road via *Santa Gertrudis*; 18th c. church, barbecue site) and 10½ miles/17 km N of Ibiza town is the village of San Miguel (*Sant Miquel*). On the Puig de Missa (522 ft/159 m) is the fortified Church of San Miguel Arcángel (14th–15th c.; beautiful view from forecourt). A little way N (hard to find) is a small cave, *Sa Cova des Bon Nin*. – 2½ miles/4 km N of San Miguel we find the sheltered cove of **Puerto de San Miguel** (*Port de Balanzat*; no harbor), a landing-place which was already being used in ancient times. Above the W side of the cove is the stump of the *Torre del Mula*. Roman remains were found on the offshore islet of *Isla Murada*. – 2½ miles/ 4 km W of San Miguel, in a magnificent *situation 490 ft/150 m above the steep rocky coast, is the hacienda-style bungalow village of *Na Xamena*.

San Miguel beach, Ibiza

**San José**, a rural district in the SW of Ibiza with a population of some 7000 who make a good living from the extraction of salt from the sea, is a region of great scenic variety. In this area are both the highest and the lowest points on the island – rising to 1562 ft/476 m in Mount *Atalayasa de San José*, falling to 2·3 ft/0·70 m below sea-level at *Las Salinas*. To the W are picturesque cliff-fringed coasts, to the S broad beaches of fine sand. – Within this district are the villages of *San José* (pop. 850), the modest chief place of the district, which has an 18th c. church with a plain exterior and a Baroque interior; *San Jorge* (Sant Jordi); *San Francisco de Paula*; and *San Agustín* (Sant Agusti, 2 miles/3 km N), with a typical Ibizan church on a square ground-plan.

The principal tourist attractions in this area are the beautiful stalactitic Cave of **Cova Santa** (3 miles/5 km SE of San José, 330 yds/300 m S of the road to Ibiza town) and the very rewarding climb of **Atalayasa de San José** (1562 ft/476 m; *views of W and S coasts); on the way there is a cemetery in which the victims of an air crash in 1972 are buried. – On the rugged and much-indented W coast with its steep cliffs are a series of picturesque coves and holiday complexes – from N to S *Cala Conta* (rocks, sand), *Cala Codolá* (Codolar), *Cala Corral, Cala Tárida* (rocks, sand; woods), **Cala Molí** (cliffs; woods), **Cala Vadella** (a rocky cove with sand in its inner reaches), *Cala Carbó* and *Cala d'Hort* (sand, shingle).

From the *Mirador de Gaviña* above *Cabo Jue* (Jueu; watch-tower, the Torre del Pirata) there is a fine view of the steep and rocky island of *Es Vedrá (1253 ft/ 382 m; caves sacred to the goddess Tanit; lighthouse at W end) and the smaller and flatter islet, shaped like a horseshoe, of *Vedranell*. In the 13th and 14th c. falcons were reared on this barren rock; it is now inhabited only by goats which have reverted to the wild state.

On the flatter S coast of Ibiza are (from W to E) the coves and beaches of *Cala Llentrisca*, above which rears the hill of the same name (1355 ft/413 m; *view); *Es Cubells*, below the hermitage of that name (19th c.; now a religious seminary), with the Church of Nuestra Señora del Carmen; *Vista Alegre*; *Puerto Roig* (Purroig); and *Cala Jondal* (Yondal; rocks, sand).

The southern tip of the island is occupied by the area known as **Las Salinas (Ses Salines)**, with *salt-pans* which have been worked since Phoenician times. The salt is shipped from the little port of *La Canal*, in the extreme S of the area (Cala Jach). Amid the salt-pans lies the little village of *San Francisco de Paula*. Along the coasts are beautiful flat sandy beaches – *Playa Cavallet, Playa de Mitjorn* (Sa Trincha), *Playa Codolá*.

See also **Majorca** (with *Cabrera*), *Minorca and **Formentera**.

# Ikaria
## See under Samos

# Ionian Islands
## *(Iónii Nísi)*

Greece

**The Ionian Islands, also known as the Eptánisos (Seven Islands), are strung out along the W coast of Greece from the Albanian frontier to the Peloponnese. In this westerly situation, with more rain than most other parts of Greece, the islands have a mild climate and a lush growth of vegetation, with the exception of Kýthira, which lies apart from the others off the southern tip of the Peloponnese.**

The Ionian Sea, which was equated by ancient authors with the Adriatic and is now seen as its southern continuation, and the Ionian Islands owe their name, according to Aeschylus, to the wanderings of Io, and according to later sources to the Illyrian hero Ionics (spelled with omicron, the short *o*). They thus have no connection with the Ionian Greeks (derived from Ion with an omega, the long *o*), who left Greece in the 11th and 10th c. and settled on the Anatolian coast, giving this eastern Greek territory its name of Ionia.

HISTORY. – Evidence of settlement dating back to Mycenaean times has been found on the islands, but their first emergence into the light of history was in 734 B.C., when Corinth founded the city of Korkyra (later Kérkyra and now Corfu). In the 5th c. the islands came under Athenian influence, and in the 2nd c. B.C. all of them, including Kýthira, became Roman. Later they came under Byzantine rule, and in 1085 were conquered by the Normans; then in 1203–04 the fourth Crusade brought another change of masters.

Rocky coastal scenery at Palaiokastrítsa, Corfu

The islands now fell into the hands of Italian rulers, and then, one after the other, came under Venetian control – Kýthira in 1363, Kérkyra (thereafter known as Corfu) in 1386, Zákynthos in 1479, Kefallinía in 1500 (after a 21-year period of Turkish rule) and finally Lefkás (which had been Turkish since 1467) in 1684.

Venetian rule lasted until the fall of the Republic of St Mark in 1797. During this period the islands provided a refuge for many Greeks fleeing from the Turks, including artists from Crete who founded a school of their own here; and throughout these centuries they enjoyed a richer cultural life than the rest of Greece.

After an interlude of French rule the young "Republic of the Seven Islands" became a British Protectorate in 1815; and in 1864 Britain returned the islands to Greece.

*Corfu (Kérkyra): see page 53. – Paxí and Antípaxi: see p. 156. – Lefkás: see p. 117. – Kefallinía and Ithaca: see p. 108. – Zákynthos: see p. 201. – Kýthira and Antikythira: see p. 117.

# Ios
## See under Cyclades

# Iráklion
## See under Crete

# Ischia

Italy
Region: Campania. – Province: Napoli (Naples).
Area: 18 sq. miles/46 sq. km. – Population: 45,000.
Post code: I-80070. – Telephone code: 081.
ⓘ **AA,**
Via Iasolino,
I-80077 **Ischia**;
tel. 99 11 46.

HOTELS. – ISCHIA PONTE: *Hermitage Park*, II, 144 b., SP; *Miramare e Castello*, II, 82 b.; *Aragonese*, III, 41 b., SP.

ISCHIA PORTO: *Jolly – Grande Albergo delle Terme*, I, 368 b., SP; *Punta Molino*, I, 156 b., SP; *Majestic*, I, 135 b.; *Excelsior Belvedere*, I, 126 b., SP; *Parco Aurora*, I, 100 b.; *Moresco*, I, 100 b., SP; *Aragona Palace Terme*, I, 80 b., SP; *Bristol Palace*, I, 61 b.; *Continental Terme*, I, 357 b., SP; *Alexander*, II, 171 b., SP; *Flora*, II, 124 b.; *Royal Terme*, II, 116 b., SP; *Oriente*, II, 115 b.; *Solemar*, II, 104 b.; *Felix Terme*, II, 87 b., SP; *Ambasciatori*, II, 86 b., SP; *Floridiana*, II, 83 b., SP; *Regina Palace*, II, 81 b., SP; *Central Park*, II, 80 b., SP; *Parco Verde*, II, 77 b., SP; *Conte*, II, 72 b.; *Imperial*, II, 68 b.; *Nuovo Lido*, II, 68 b.

CASAMICCIOLA TERME: *Cristallo Palace*, I, 128 b., SP; *Manzi*, I, 119 b., SP; *La Madonnina*, I, 37 b.; *Elma*, II, 112 b., SP; *Gran Paradiso*, II, 85 b.; *L'Approdo*, II,

63 b., SP; *Stella Maris*, II, 58 b., SP; *Stefania*, II, 55 b.; *Candia*, III, 41 b.

LACCO AMENO: *Albergo della Regina Isabella e Royal Sporting*, L, 220 b., SP; *Augusto*, I, 185 b., SP; *San Montano*, I, 121 b., SP; *La Reginella*, I, 73 b., SP; *Grazia*, II, 90 b., SP; *Mediolanum*, II, 52 b.; *Antares*, II, 50 b.; *La Pace Terme*, III, 143 b., SP; two CAMP SITES.

FORIO: *Citara*, II, 97 b.; *Tritone*, II, 91 b., SP; *Green Flash*, II, 75 b.; *San Vito*, II, 68 b., SP; *Splendid*, II, 67 b., SP; *Punta del Sole*, II, 61 b., SP; *La Scogliera*, II, 60 b.; *Punta Imperatore*, II, 65 b., SP; *Santa Lucia*, II, 54 b.

SANT' ANGELO: *Cocumella*, I, 115 b.; *Parco del Sole*, II, 238 b., SP; *Majestic Palace*, II, 142 b.; *Caravel*, II, 141 b.; *Mediterraneo*, II, 108 b., SP; *Alpha*, II, 86 b.; *Milton*, II, 85 b.; *Cristina*, II, 73 b., SP; *Eliseo Parc's*, II, 59 b.

ON PROCIDA: *Arcate*, III, 72 b.; *Riviera*, III, 42 b.

BOAT SERVICES (including car ferries). – Several times daily to and from Naples, Capri, Procida and Pozzuoli. – Hydrofoil services. – HELICOPTER SERVICES.

**The volcanic island of *Ischia, lying at the entrance to the Bay of Naples, is the largest island in the vicinity of Naples. It was known to the Greeks as Pithekousa, to the Romans as Aenaria and from the 9th c. as Iscla.**

An island of luxuriant vegetation (vineyards, fruit orchards, pine woods), Ischia is of great scenic beauty, particularly on the N side. Its strongly radioactive hot springs attract many visitors seeking a cure for rheumatism or gout.

THE ISLAND. – The chief place on the island, in a picturesque situation on the NE coast, is the town of **Ischia** (pop. 17,000), which consists of two parts,

Ischia

Ischia Ponte and Ischia Porto. In *Ischia Ponte* is a formidable *Castle (about 1450) on a high craggy island (299 ft/91 m) approached by a stone causeway. 1¼ miles/2 km W is *Ischia Porto*, a spa and seaside resort with the oldest harbor on the island, a former crater lake. – 2½ miles/4 km W of Ischia Porto, half-way along the N coast of the island, is **Casamicciola Terme** (alt. 10 ft/3 m), situated on the lower slopes of Monte Epomeo and surrounded by gardens and vineyards, with hot springs (149 °F/65 °C) and a good beach. From here it is 4 miles/6 km SW, via the resort of **Lacco Ameno** (alt. 23 ft/7 m; pop. 3000; radioactive mineral springs, 122 °F/50 °C), to the little town of **Forio** (alt. 59 ft/18 m; pop. 8000; thermal springs), on the W coast.

From Forio a beautiful *road (12½ miles/20 km) runs through the southern part of the island. It passes above the *Gardens of Poseidon* (magnificent bathing facilities, with thermal springs) and continues via *Panza* (alt. 509 ft/155 m), where a road (2 miles/3 km) goes off to the village of *Sant' Angelo* (hot springs), picturesquely situated on the slopes of a promontory; then on to *Serrara* (1201 ft/366 m), *Fontana* (1483 ft/452 m) and *Barano d'Ischia* (696 ft/212 m; large beach of Maronti, with hot springs), past a 16th c. aqueduct and so back to Ischia Ponte. – From Fontana there is a rewarding climb (1 hour) up *Monte Epomeo (2589 ft/789 m), a massive volcano (extinct since 1302) with an almost vertical N face, in the center of the island (panoramic *views). – Another very attractive excursion is a boat trip around the island.

Procida

Half-way between Ischia and the mainland is the island of **Prócida**. Of volcanic origin, it is formed of the rims of two adjoining craters, the southern edges of which have been drowned by the sea; it is 2 miles/3·5 km long. – On the N side of the island, extending inland from the coast over a low hill, is the little town of **Procida** (alt. 105 ft/32 m), whose gleaming white houses have a rather Oriental aspect. Particularly picturesque are the *fishing harbor with its brightly colored boats and the *Corricella* quarter. On a precipitous crag above the town towers a massive Castle (now a prison), commanding extensive views of the neighboring islands and peninsulas. – From the town a narrow road runs 2 miles/3 km S to *Chiaiolella Bay*. To the E, higher up, is the old *Church of Santa Margherita*; offshore to the E is the little islet, planted with olives, of *Vivara* (alt. 358 ft/109 m; private property), which is connected with Procida by a bridge.

# Ithaca
## See under Kefallinia

# Jerba

Tunisia
Altitude: 0–184 ft/0–56 m.
Population: 100,000.
ⓘ **Office du Tourisme Régional,**
Place de la Poste,
**Houmt Souk;**
tel. (05) 5 00 16, 5 02 84, 5 05 81.

HOTELS. – *Dar Jerba*, I; *El Menzel*, I; *Ulysse Palace*, Plage Sidi Mehrez, I; *El Bousten*, Sidi Mehrez, I; *Les Sirènes*, Houmt Souk, II; *Palm Beach*, II; *Tanit*, Midoun, III; *Calypso Beach*, III; *El Jazira*, Sidi Mehrez, III; *Mennix*, III; *Sidi Slim*, III; *Yati*, Midoun, III; *Medina*, Plage Sidi Mehrez, IV; *Dar Faiza*, Rue de la République, Houmt Souk, IV; *Strand* (Chott), Plage Sidi Mehrez, IV. – HOLIDAY VILLAGES: *Club Méditerranée*, *Jerba la Fidèle*, *Jerba la Douce*, *Sidi Ali*. – YOUTH HOSTEL in Houmt Souk, tel. 5 02 04. – CAMP SITE: *Sidi Slim*.

RESTAURANTS: in hotels listed.

EVENT. – *Festival d'Ulysse* (August).

**The Tunisian island of Jerba or Djerba (area 198 sq. miles/514 sq. km) lies in the SE of the Gulf of Gabès, separated from the mainland by the little Bay of Bou Grara. A causeway 4 miles/6·4 km long carries a road from the mainland to El Kantara on the SE coast of Jerba, and there is also a ferry from the mainland town of Jorf to Adjim, on the SW coast of the island. The chief town of Jerba is Houmt Souk (pop. 12,000).**

Jerba is still an idyllic island which the 20th century seems to have passed by, an

**On the Tunisian island of Jerba**

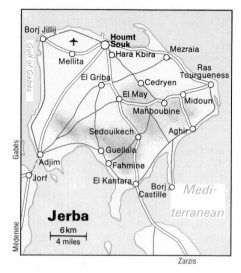

the water improves toward the interior of the island, and this is reflected in the pattern of agriculture, with relatively unproductive date-palms in the coastal regions, a more intensively cultivated zone of olive groves farther inland and large plantations of fruit trees in the center of the island.

About a quarter of the inhabitants, the Jerbi, still speak Berber dialects. In the past many of them left the island because its unproductive agriculture was insufficient to provide them with a subsistence, and Jerbi are now to be found in all the larger Tunisian towns, with a reputation as astute businessmen. The population also includes a sizeable minority of Jews, though their numbers have considerably declined as a result of emigration in recent years. After their expulsion from Palestine (presumably following the destruction of Jerusalem by Titus in A.D. 70) the Jews founded the two closed villages of Hara Kebira and Hara Seghira, with the famous Synagogue of La Ghriba, to which Jewish pilgrims from all parts of North Africa flock every year, 33 days after Easter.

island whose inhabitants still draw their main subsistence from extensive oases of date-palms, plantations of olives and irrigated garden crops, together with the traditional crafts of pottery and weaving, fishing and diving for sponges. The characteristic form of settlement is a widely scattered village, reflecting the low population density, which in turn is conditioned by the poor yields of the local agriculture.

Since the end of the Second World War, however, the centuries-old traditional economic structure has been supplemented by a new source of income in the northern coastal region. The dry, sunny and, thanks to the influence of the Mediterranean, very equable climate of this area, combined with its miles of sandy beaches, has led to the well-planned development of a tourist and holiday zone which, with the Oasis of Zarzis on the mainland, is the largest in southern Tunisia. A string of some 40 well-run hotels of European standard, with 10,000 beds, lines the coast at Sidi Mehrez and La Seguia; and the Mellita Airport, only 20 miles/30 km away, links the island with the European countries from which the visitors come.

One great problem on Jerba is the provision of water, for on this island of low rainfall (about 8 in./200 mm a year) and relatively flat terrain there are no surface watercourses. The resort area on the N coast is supplied with water by a pipeline from the mainland, but the rest of the island still depends mainly on some 3700 wells and 2000 cisterns, the water of which is slightly brackish. The quality of

HISTORY. – Legend makes Jerba the island of Calypso, who held Odysseus captive during his voyage home from Troy. The earliest firm historical evidence dates back to the 9th c. B.C., when Phoenicians established trading-posts on the island, known in ancient times as *Meninx*. In Roman times there were four cities on Jerba – Girba, Haribus, Tipasa and Meninx – and the island's present name is no doubt derived from the first of these. Even in these early days Jerba was connected with the mainland by a causeway, the remains of which form the foundations of the causeway carrying the modern road. The site of the Roman city is marked by a few columns still to be seen near El Kantara. The Romans were followed by a whole series of other foreign conquerors – Vandals, Byzantines, Arabs, Normans, Spaniards, Turks and French.

THE ISLAND. – The chief town, **Houmt Souk**, is full of interest for the visitor, with the picturesque little lanes of its *souk* (bazaar), in which a market is held on Mondays and Thursdays, when innumerable shopkeepers and stallholders offer a great variety of wares – clothes, shoes, silk, brassware, silver, leather goods, etc. In the old town there are three fine mosques, including the *Jama et-Turuk* (Turkish Mosque), with its seven domes and phallus-like minaret, and the *Jama Ghorba* (Strangers' Mosque), the minaret of which can be climbed. Close by is the *Regional Museum* (traditional costumes, jewelry, fine pottery). – On the harbor are a small *Spanish fort* (13th–14th c.) and the *Bordj el-Kebir* (Great Tower), originally erected in the 15th c., enlarged by the Spaniards in the 16th c. and renovated by the corsair Dragut soon afterwards. Beyond it is a pyramid marking the site of the *Tower of Skulls* which was demolished in 1848. This consisted of the skulls of 5000–6000 European Christians, members of a Papal army, which had been sent to destroy the pirates' lair on Jerba, who were murdered by Dragut in 1560.

Two interesting places to be seen on Jerba are the Jewish settlements of **Hara Kebira** and **Hara Seghira**, with the celebrated *Synagogue of La Ghriba*. Most of the 5000 Jews who lived here in 1956 have since emigrated, leaving only 700 in Hara Kebira and 280 in Hara Seghira. Farther S is the village of **El-May**, with a mosque which ranks as the finest on the island. On the S coast is **Guellala**, with several potters' workshops and shops selling their wares. On the way there can be seen many of the structures known as *fsaqia* – areas of sloping concrete, up to 360 sq. yds/300 sq. m in extent and usually whitewashed, which are designed, like the Roman impluvium, to collect rainwater for use in irrigation. They are often found near a mosque.

It is well worth taking a trip from Jerba to **Zarzis** (pop. about 20,000; Sangho Club, Zarzis, Sidi Saad and Zita Hotels), in an irrigated oasis on the mainland to the SE of Jerba, with 500,000 date-palms and 700,000 olive trees, in huge plantations which extend inland from the beautiful sandy *beaches edging the Jeffara coastal plain, surrounded by steppe-like desert terrain. The town was founded in the 19th c., under the French Protectorate, to provide settled homes for the Accara bedouin.

# Kalymnos
## See under Sporades

# Karpathos
## *(Kárpathos)*

Greece
Nomos: Dodecanese.
Area: 116 sq. miles/301 sq. km. – Population: 5400.

HOTEL. – *Porphyris*, III, 41 b.

BATHING BEACHES. – In Kárpathos Bay and on the SE and SW coasts.

Church on the island of Kárpathos

TRANSPORTATION. – Kárpathos is served by boats sailing between Rhodes and Aghios Nikólaos in Crete; also air services from Rhodes.

**Kárpathos, an island of great scenic attraction in the Dodecanese, SW of Rhodes, is 30 miles/48 km long by some 3 miles/5 km across, with heights up to 3986 ft/1215 m.**

The chief place, **Kárpathos** or *Pigádia* (alt. 82 ft/25 m; pop. 1200), lies in a wide curving bay on the E coast at the point of transition between the hills and the lower ground. It was built during the period of Italian occupation, from 1912 onwards, on the site of ancient *Poseidion*. – The insecurity of life in the Middle Ages is reflected in the hilltop sites of the island's villages which can be seen in a round trip from the port. In some of these villages the ancient Doric is still spoken and age-old traditions survive. Many houses are embellished, inside and outside, with elaborate designs.

The route runs via **Menetés** (4½ miles/ 7 km from Kárpathos; alt. 1150 ft/350 m; pop. 700) to **Arkássai** on the W side of the island (4 miles/6 km; alt. 154 ft/47 m; pop. 450; Early Christian basilica), then turns N to **Pylí** (4½ miles/7 km; alt. 1050 ft/320 m; pop. 300) and **Voláda** (3 miles/ 5 km; alt. 1445 ft/440 m; pop. 500), and finally returns via **Apérion** (1¼ miles/ 2 km; alt. 1050 ft/320 m; pop. 720) to the starting-point. Other villages in the N of the island (reached by a road from Pylí) are **Mesokhorió** (9 miles/14 km; alt. 425 ft/130 m), **Spóa** (4½ miles/7 km; alt. 1150 ft/350 m), **Ólympos** (17 miles/28 km; alt. 375 ft/114 m) and **Diafáni** (6 miles/ 10 km; alt. 100 ft/30 m).

To the SW of Kárpathos is **Kásos** or Kassos (area 25 sq. miles/65 sq. km; pop. 1400), a hilly island rising to 1970 ft/600 m, barren except for some fruit orchards. There are many caves and isolated beaches. The chief place, **Fry** (pop. 460), lies on the N coast, to the E of another coastal village, **Aghia Marína** (alt. 395 ft/ 120 m; pop. 550); at the local fair, textiles and embroideries for which the island is well known can be bought. From there it is possible to reach **Arvanitok-horió** (the "Albanian village") in the bare and hilly interior, in medieval times the chief place on the island.

# Kasos
See above under Kárpathos

# Kastellorizo (Meyisti)
See under Rhodes

# Kea
See under Cyclades

# Kefallinia
*(Kefallinía)*

Greece
Nomos: Kefallinía.
Area: 302 sq. miles/781 sq. km. – Population: 31,800.

HOTELS. – ARGOSTÓLI: *Xenia*, II, 44 b.; *Aenos*, III, 74 b.; *Tourist*, III, 38 b.; *Phokas*, III, 33 b.; *Ayios Gerasimos*, III, 28 b.; *Armonia*, III, 24 b.; *Aegli*, III, 17 b.; *Dido*, IV, 17 b.

SW OF ARGOSTÓLI. – LASSI (1¼ miles/2 km): *Méditerranée*, I, 430 b., SP. – PLATYS YIALÓS (2 miles/3 km): *White Rocks*, I, 190 b. – SVORONÁTA (6 miles/10 km): *Irinna*, II, 321 b.

EAST COAST (FROM N TO S). – FISKÁRDO (33 miles/53 km from Argostóli): *Panormos*, II, 10 b. – AGHIA EVFIMÍA (6 miles/9 km from Sámi): *Pylaros*, III, 17 b. – SAMI (13 miles/21 km from Argostóli): *Ionion*, III, 29 b. – PÓROS (16 miles/26 km from Sámi): *Iraklis*, II, 12 b.; *Atros Poros*, III, 18 b.

WEST. – LIXOURI: *Ionios Avra*, IV, 22 b.

NW COAST. – ASSOS (21 miles/34 km from Argostóli): *Myrto*, II, 10 b.

ON ITHACA: *Mendor*, II, 68 b.; *Odysseus*, II, 17 b.

BATHING BEACHES. – Platýs Yialós, Myrtós, Sámi.

TRANSPORTATION. – Air services from Athens; boat connections with Kérkyra and Pátras; ferry between Argostóli and Lixoúri; island buses.

**Kefallinía (commonly pronounced Kefalloniá) is the largest of the Ionian Islands, separated from Ithaca by a channel 1¼ miles/2 km**

An idyllic bay on Kefallinía

**wide. It is an island of mountains, rising to 5341 ft/1628 m in Mount Ainos, or Aenos, of fertile plains and of beautiful sandy beaches and long-stretches of rocky coast. On Mount Ainos are found the unique fir trees for which the island is renowned. The Gulf of Argostóli cuts deeply into the S side of the island, separating the western part from the main part to the E, which projects northwards to end in Cape Dafnoúdi.**

HISTORY. – In Mycenaean times Kefallinía was part of the kingdom of Odysseus – though Homer does not mention the island's name, referring only to Same and Doulikhion, which he believed to be two separate islands. In historical times Kefallinía shared the destinies of the neighboring islands. In the medieval period it was conquered by the Norman leader Robert Guiscard, who died here in 1185 and is commemorated by the place-name Fiskárdo in the N of the island. Later it was ruled by two Italian families, the Orsinis and the Tocchis. The island was occupied by the Turks for only 21 years, and was held by the Venetians from 1500 to 1797.

The chief place, **Argostóli** (pop. 8000) which is a popular yachting center, lies in a bay in the Gulf of Argostóli. Like other places on the island, it suffered earthquake damage in 1953 and was rebuilt in concrete but is still a place of charming squares and open-air cafés. The *sea mills* at the northern tip of the peninsula on which the town stands were driven until 1953 by sea water surging along a rocky passage; but the earthquake led to a rise in the level of the coast, and the mills no longer work. – The *Museum contains pottery of the Minoan, Mycenaean and later periods, Mycenaean gold and ivory objects, Greek, Roman and Byzantine coins, and a bronze statue of the Emperor Hadrian found at Sámi in 1959. – SW of the town are the sandy beaches of Makrís Yialós and Platýs Yialós.

6 miles/9 km S of Argostóli is the former capital of the island, **Aghios Gheorgios**, with a massive castle founded by the Byzantines and enlarged by the Venetians. In the plain below is the Convent of *Aghios Andréas* (St Andrew), which has a *reliquary containing the Apostle's foot. In the center of the fertile Livathó Plain are the picturesque villages of *Metaxáta* and *Lakíthra*. Between Argostóli and Lakíthra, to the left of the road (signpost), lies the *Cave of St Gerasimos*, the island's patron saint, whose feast is celebrated on August 16 and October 20.

The **Monastery of Aghios Yerásimos**, in a quiet valley to the E of Argostóli, is reached by taking the Sámi road, turning right in 4¼ miles/7 km and again into a road to the right beyond Frankáta. Continuing from Frankáta beyond the turning for Aghios Eleuthérios and taking a road to the right, we come to a mountain hut (4265 ft/1300 m) on **Mount Ainos** (5341 ft/1628 m): *views of Kefallinía and the neighboring islands of Ithaca and Zákynthos.

The principal harbor, **Sámi** (pop. 1000), where the island boats call, lies in the only bay of any size on the E coast. Near by are the remains of ancient *Same*. Immediately W of the village is an interesting *stalactitic cave*. To the N, on the way to the little coastal village of **Aghia Eyfimía** (6 miles/9 km from Sámi), is a cave, the roof of which has fallen in, containing an *underground lake* (Límni Melisáni) notable for its beautiful coloring.

In the N of the island is **Ássos** (21 miles/ 34 km from Argostóli), with a Venetian Castle built on a rocky peninsula and 11 miles/17 km beyond this, on the northernmost tip of the island, the fishing village of **Fiskárdo**.

# Ithaca/Ithaki *(Itháki)*

Off the NE coast of Kefallinía, separated from it by a channel 1¼ miles/2 km wide, lies the small and precipitous island of Ithaca (area 36 sq. miles/94 sq. km; pop. 4000), which has been renowned since ancient times as the home of Odysseus. It consists of a northern and a southern part linked by an isthmus only 660 yds/600 m wide. The chief place on the island and its principal port, Vathý officially Ithaki, lies in a sheltered situation in a long inlet which cuts inland from the NE.

HISTORY. – Excavators from the time of Schliemann (1868) onward have sought to identify places in the kingdom of Odysseus which are mentioned by Homer. The remains of buildings found by Schliemann on Mount Aetós (2195 ft/669 m), 3 miles/5 km from Vathý, which dominates the isthmus, belong to the post-Mycenaean settlement of Alalkomenai. Mycenaean walls and pottery of the right date for Odysseus were found by British archeologists from 1932 onward near the northern village of Stavrós, on Mount Pelikáta (¾ mile/1 km N, with views of several bays) and in Pólis Bay below the village. These were presumably the sites of the palace and the city. Finds from here are in the museums of Vathý and Stavrós. The Stavrós Museum contains a potsherd bearing the name Odysseus (8th c. B.C.) and an Attic lekythos depicting Athena, Odysseus and Telemakhos (5th c. B.C.).

The chief place on the island, **Vathý** (rebuilt after the 1953 earthquake), has a very beautiful situation. The museum contains a collection of Mycenaean vases. The village lies in an agricultural region (olives, wine); and Homer's "island of goats" still has very many goats. – An attractive run along the isthmus brings us to **Stavrós** (11 miles/18 km; bus), in the northern part of the island. Farther N is *Exoyí* (old church), and to the NE is the beautiful **Fríkes Bay**, beyond which is the village of Kióni. From Stavrós a road ascends through rugged scenery to the **Monastery of Katharón** (alt. 1970 ft/ 600 m), from which there are magnificent *views of Vathý Bay.

Other interesting trips from Vathý (on foot) are to the nearby **Cave of the Nymphs** and (guide advisable) to the *Fountain of Arethusa* at the S end of the island.

# Kerkennah Islands

Tunisia

HOTELS. – *Farhat*, II; *Grand*, II.

TRANSPORTATION. – Boats from Sfax (1½ hours).

The Kerkennah Islands lie due E of Sfax, 12 miles/19 km from the Tunisian mainland. Hannibal once lived here in voluntary exile. There are scanty Roman remains.

The two main islands in the group, **Gharbi** and **Chergui**, are linked by a 550 yd/500 m long causeway. From the landing-place at *Sidi Youssef*, at the SW end of Gharbi, a road runs for 20 miles/ 33 km to El Attaïa, at the NE end of Chergui. The inhabitants of the islands live mainly by fishing: agriculture is relatively unproductive on account of the lack of rain. The tourist and holiday trade has made little progress here, and visitors will find many miles of almost untouched beaches.

# Kérkyra
## See Corfu

Wind-surfer, Korčula

# Knossós
## See under Crete

# Koločep
## See Elaphite Islands

# Korčula

Yugoslavia
Republic: Croatia (Hrvatska).
Area: 108 sq. miles/279 sq. km. –
Population: 23,000.
Telephone code: 050.
ⓘ Turist-biro Putnik Marko Polo,
  YU-50260 Korčula;
  tel. 8 10 67.
  Turistički Biro,
  YU-50270 Vela Luka;
  tel. 8 20 42.
  Turističko Društvo,
  YU-50263 Lumbarda;
  tel. 8 36 05.

HOTELS. – KORČULA: *Bon Repos*, II, 720 b.; *Park*, II, 400 b.; *Marko Polo*, II, 430 b.; YOUTH HOSTEL. – RAČIŠĆE: *Mediteran* (pension), II, 20 b. – LUMBARDA: *Lumbarda*, II, 90 b., with annexes *Borik* and *Lovor*, II, 140 b. – PRIŽBA BLATO: *Alfier*, II, 120 b.; *Lipa*, II, 24 b. – SMOKVICA BRNA: *Feral*, II, 160 b. – VELA LUKA: *Poseidon*, II, 296 b., with annexe, 70 b.

CAMP SITES. – KORČULA: at Hotel Bon Repos. – SV. ANTUN: *Solitudo*.

EVENTS. – Every Thursday before and after the main season, twice daily in July and August, 16th c. sword dance, the Moreška. – Annually on April 23 (Liberation Day), performance of the Kumpanija, a battle dance, in Blato. – Summer concerts in Korčula town.

BATHING BEACHES. – Lumbarda has three large beaches of shingle and sand (particularly suitable for children); also facilities for diving; boat rental. – Vela Luka has a long beach and many coves; spa treatment establishment (curative mud).

CAR FERRIES. – Korčula town – Orebić, Prigradica–Drvenik, Korčula town–Split; also passenger boats to Split and Dubrovnik.

The island of *Korčula, lying halfway down the Dalmatian coast between Split and Dubrovnik, attracts many visitors with its beautiful scenery, picturesque little towns and excellent bathing. It has been popular with the Greeks for more than 2000 years. It is 29 miles/47 km long by 4–5 miles/6–8 km across, rising to a height of 1864 ft/568 m in Mount Klupča. Known in Antiquity as Corcyra, it was held by Venice from 1420 to 1797 and thereafter belonged to Austria until 1918.

HISTORY. – The first settlers were *Trojans*, led by the hero Antenor (1200 B.C.). In the 4th c. B.C. they were followed by *Dorians* from Knidos, and later by other Greeks from Syracuse. In 35 B.C. the *Romans* gained control of the island and of the mainland of Dalmatia. After the fall of the Western Roman Empire Korčula passed into the hands of the *Ostrogoths* under Theodoric in 493; then in 555 it fell to the Byzantines.

In the 9th c. a Slav people, the *Neretvans*, captured the island. About 1000 it came under *Venetian* control, and from 1180 it belonged to the *Hungarian-Croatian* Kingdom. In 1298 a Genoese fleet defeated a Venetian force near Korčula, and it is said to have been on this occasion that Marco Polo (1254–1324), who is claimed as a native of Korčula and not of Venice, fell into the hands of the Genoese. While in prison he dictated to a fellow prisoner his account of his journey to China, which lasted for 24 years (from 1271). In 1390 Korčula came under the control of the kings of *Bosnia*, and the battles of this period against the Turks are still commemorated in the Moreška, the dance-cum-drama which was formerly performed, against the backdrop of the old town, only on July 27 but is now put on twice daily during the main season.

An attempt by the Republic of Dubrovnik in 1413–17 to acquire Korčula as a further outpost in its defensive system was unsuccessful. Thereafter the island remained a dependency of Venice, with self-governing status, until 1797. It was then held in rapid succession by *Austria* (1797–1805), *France*

(1805–13) and *Britain* (1813–15). From 1815 to 1918 it belonged to *Austria*; from 1918 to 1921 it was claimed by Italy, but it was finally assigned to the kingdom of *Yugoslavia*. From 1941 to 1943 it was under Italian occupation; then in 1944 Yugoslav Partisans landed on the island.

The palaces and churches of the island's capital, **Korčula**, magnificently display the whole range of architectural styles from the 14th to the 16th c. The old town is still surrounded by high walls and towers.

The best starting-point for a sightseeing tour of the town is the waterfront at the harbor. The route passes two massive towers and a small and elegant 16th c. loggia (on the left); then through the Land Gate (just within the gate a handsome Triumphal Arch of 1650) into the main street. On the left is the Renaissance façade of the Prince's Palace, with a 16th c. loggia, and opposite it is the 17th c. St Michael's Church, also in Renaissance style.

Continuing in the direction of the Cathedral, we pass on the left a small Baroque church and on the right the former Bishop's Palace (14th c.), with a 17th c. Baroque façade; it now contains the Cathedral Treasury and paintings by Italian masters. To the left stands the Gabrieli Palace, a handsome Renaissance building which now houses the Municipal Museum. St Mark's Cathedral (to the right), begun in the 13th c. and completed some 300 years later, shows Romanesque, Gothic and Renaissance features, and contains behind the High Altar a painting ascribed to Tintoretto as well as some good pictures by artists of the

13th–15th c. – Beyond St Peter's Church, on the right, is a street leading to Marco Polo House, in which the great traveler is said to have been born.

Outside the town walls are a *Dominican Friary*, on the seafront to the W, and the two-aisled *St Nicholas's Church*, with a copy of Titian's "St Peter" above the High Altar.

At the SE end of the island, only 4 miles/6 km from Korčula town, is **Lumbarda**. On Koludrt Hill to the N of the village, by the medieval St John's Church, were found fragments of a stone tablet dating from the period of Greek settlement (copy in Korčula Municipal Museum, original in Archeological Museum, Zagreb) which contained information about landownership, mentioning Illyrian as well as Greek names. Lumbard is also noted for its golden "Greek" wine (Grk) and the skill of its stonemasons.

A drive along the 30 miles/48 km from Korčula to Vela Luka reveals the scenery of the island in all its variety – woodland, vineyards, olive plantations, with little in the way of inhospitable karstic terrain. Beyond the village of Pupnat the road passes the island's highest point, *Klupča* (1864 ft/568 m; good view, but strenuous climb). **Blato**, the largest town on the island (not on the sea), has its own pageant play, performed annually on April 23, the day on which the island was liberated in 1944. Here, too, is preserved the tradition of the "guslars", the folksingers who perform, to the accompaniment of a one-string fiddle, interminable melancholy sagas about battles, heroes and sorrows of long ago. The little town itself is of great interest, with many medieval buildings. In the Castle is a local museum, which also contains finds from the nearby Roman villa of Junium.

The road then continues to **Vela Luka**, which is sheltered by hills from both N and S winds. The area was already inhabited in the Stone Age. The little town is seeking to develop some industry (fish-canning, small boatyards).

There are attractive boat trips from Korčula town to the islands of **Badija** (Franciscan Friary of 1420, with arcaded cloister of 1477) and **Vrnik** (limestone quarries).

On the mainland NE of Korčula is the **Pelješac** Peninsula, with beautiful scenery and the interesting little town of *Orebić*.

Korčula town

# Kornati Islands/ Kornatski Otoci

Yugoslavia
Republic: Croatia (Hrvatska).
Altitude: 0–770 ft/0–235 m. – Uninhabited.
ⓘ Kornatturist,
YU-59243 Murter;
tel. (059) 7 52 15.

ACCOMMODATION. – Summer only, *tents* for visitors on a week's motor-boat trip among the islands; some supply-posts also operate then.

**Although the Kornati Islands are frequently described by foreign authors as comprising all the islands around Zadar, in Yugoslav usage the name is applied only to the islands of Kornat and Žut together with 145 small islets, all showing similar characteristics – formidable cliffs rising to 330 ft/100 m on the seaward side and a series of small coves on the inland side. Seen from the air, the islands appear almost exactly circular, and are covered with a sparse growth of vegetation. The whole archipelago, with an area of some 116 sq. miles/300 sq. km, is now a National Park.**

The islands have none of the obvious tourist attractions, and indeed at first sight appear bleak and inhospitable. According to the Yugoslav geographer Rubíc, however, the Kornati show rock forms not found on any other islands on the Yugoslav Adriatic coast. To the skipper of a boat approaching from the sea they present a harsh and forbidding appearance, but he has only to round an island to find on the other side a sheltered cove which provides anchorage for three or four boats and a safe haven in a storm. Almost every one of the islands has a refuge harbor of this kind. Here, too, land the shepherds who spend many months on the islands with their flocks, until the vegetation begins to dry up. There are also a few green valleys in which olives grow, but the peasants pay only rare visits to the islands to tend them.

For many centuries the islands have been inhospitable and barren, leading such inhabitants as there were to leave them. They are believed to have once been covered in forest; and at least in Roman times they must have been green and fertile, since wealthy Romans had villas here, as evidenced by the foundations which can still be seen under the surface of the sea. During the Second World War the islands could not be adequately policed by the occupation forces, and provided Tito's Partisans with an ideal operational base.

The barren Kornati Islands – a bird's-eye view

There are only a few houses on the islands, occupied only in summer. The favorite resort of fishermen and underwater divers is the S bay on the island of **Katina**, between *Dugi Otok* (see p. 85) and **Kornat**. The only source of fresh water is a meagre spring in the Bay of Luka Žut on the island of **Žut**. A number of inns on the islands bring in water by tanker, and in the coves used as anchorages there are cisterns which are filled in spring by the fishermen and shepherds; but these supplies are frequently insufficient to meet the increasing demand from visitors throughout the summer.

For many years now the Kornati have been popular with scuba-divers, and they are also well known – and indeed, on account of their dangerous shallows and reefs, notorious – to owners of motor-boats and yachts. Many wrecks, some of them dating from the Venetian period, lie off their coasts. Their waters are well stocked with fish, yielding larger catches than any other part of the Yugoslav Adriatic coast. Underwater fishing is, however, prohibited. For diving a permit is required, obtainable from the Harbor-master at Zadar or Biograd.

As a holiday area the Kornati will appeal to active and adventurous visitors who do not insist on having all their creature comforts.

# Kos
*(Kos)*

Greece
Nomos: Dodecanese.
Area: 112 sq. miles/290 sq. km. – Population: 16,650.
Telephone code: 0242.
(i) **EOT,**
on the Quay;
tel. 2 87 24.
**Olympic Airways,**
Odós Vasileos Pavlou 22;
tel. 2 83 31.

HOTELS. – KOS: *Atlantis*, I, 520 b., SP; *Ramira Beach*, I, 500 b., SP (2 miles/3 km); *Continental Palace*, I, 333 b., SP; *Kos*, II, 262 b.; *Alexandra*, II, 150 b.; *Theoxenia*, II, 78 b.; *Oscar*, III, 370 b.; *Elli*, III, 150 b.; *Milva*, III, 99 b.; *Zephyros*, III, 93 b.; *Kulias*, III, 51 b.; *Christina*, III, 41 b.; *Veroniki*, III, 36 b.; *Elisabeth*, III, 32 b.; *Ekaterini*, III, 24 b.; *Ibiscus*, III, 17 b. – Lambí (1½ miles/2·5 km N): *Irene*, II, 104 b. – AGHIOS FOKÁS (5 miles/8 km SE): *Dimitra Beach*, I, 261 b., SP. – MARMARI (N coast): *Caravia Beach*, I, 563 b., SP.

BATHING BEACHES. – Immediately E and N of Kos; to the SE at Aghios Fokás; on the S coast at Kardámena and Kéfalos; on the NW coast at Tingáki and Mastikhári.

TRANSPORTATION. – Air service from Athens; served by boats sailing between Piraeus and Rhodes and between Rhodes and Samos; island buses. A popular way of getting about is to hire a bicycle.

\***Kos, the largest island in the Dodecanese after Rhodes and the birthplace of Hippocrates, has become a popular holiday area, offering the attractions of its mild climate and beautiful scenery as well as an ancient Sanctuary of Asklepios of which there are extensive remains.**

HISTORY. – The Achaean Greek inhabitants of the island were followed by Dorian incomers, who combined with Knidos, Halikarnassos and the three cities on Rhodes to form the Hexapolis (League of Six Cities). In 477 B.C. Kos became a member of the First Attic Maritime League. In the 5th c. the island's medical school enjoyed great reputation through the work of Hippocrates. In 412–411 B.C. an earthquake destroyed the old city of Astypálaia (near Kéfalos on the S coast), and in 366 B.C., in a "synoecism" following the example of Rhodes, the population was concentrated in the city of Kos.

In the Hellenistic period Kos supported the Egyptian Ptolemies (Ptolemy II Philadelphos was born on the island in 308 B.C.), and benefited from their patronage, as it did in a later period from that of the Roman emperors. In 431 it became the seat of a bishop, and thereafter shared the destinies of the other islands in the Dodecanese.

# Kos town

The island's capital, **Kos**, has a population of 9000, including numbers of Muslims. The **Harbor**, guarded by the **Castle of the Knights of St John**, has modern port installations, various public offices dating from the Italian period and many tavernas. From here King Paul Street leads to the main square with its coffeehouses and Market Hall, the 18th c. *Defterdar Mosque* and the \***Archeological Museum**.

Going E from the Museum, we pass the site of the *Agora* (2nd c. B.C.) and come to a square with a mosque of 1786 and the famous \*\**plane tree* of Kos, many centuries old, its branches supported by props (including a small ancient circular altar). The tree is traditionally associated with the celebrated physician Hippocrates of Kos, but in fact the town of Kos was not founded until after Hippocrates's death.

From the square with the plane tree a bridge leads to the entrance of the mighty *Castle of the Knights*, above the gateway of which are the arms of knights and an ancient frieze of masks. The original 14th c. castle was enlarged in 1457 and equipped with crenelated walls and bastions for cannon. Immediately beyond the entrance an *open-air museum* displays ancient column capitals, carved medieval coats of arms, a Turkish prayer-niche, etc. A ramp leads down to the original castle, in the building of which many fragments of ancient masonry were used.

In Grigoriou Street is an excavation area of some size (Roman road and adjoining buildings; opposite this, a reconstructed Roman villa and a small Roman odeon). In the nearby Orthodox cemetery (beyond the Roman Catholic cemetery) is a *Chapel of St John* (5th–6th c.). At the corner of Grigoriou and Pavlou Streets are the excavated remains of a *Temple of Dionysos*.

Remains of the Asklepieion, Kos

The *Asklepieion (Sanctuary of Asklepios) lies 4 miles/6 km SW of the town. The sacred precinct, discovered and excavated in 1902 and further investigated in 1928, extends over three terraces. The oldest of these is the middle terrace, on which, about 350 B.C., an altar in honor of Asklepios, son of Apollo, was erected in a grove of cypresses sacred to Apollo. Opposite this there was built between 300 and 270 B.C. an Ionic temple in which the temple treasure was kept. The 2nd c. B.C. saw the addition of the lower terrace, with large stoas to accommodate the increasing numbers of visitors to the sanctuary, and the upper terrace, with a Doric temple dominating the whole complex.

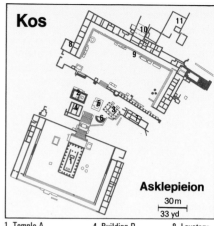

**Kos**

**Asklepieion**

30 m
33 yd

| | |
|---|---|
| 1 Temple A | 4 Building D |
| 2 Temple B | 5 Altar of Asklepios |
|    (Temple of Asklepios) | 6 Exedra |
| 3 Temple C | 7 Lesche |

| | |
|---|---|
| 8 Lavatory | |
| 9 Propylaion | |
| 10 Ramp | |
| 11 Baths | |

We enter the Asklepieion on the N side, passing on the left Roman **baths** with *hypocausts*. We then come to the *lower terrace*, which measures 305 ft/93 m by 154 ft/47 m. This was surrounded on three sides by stoas, with 67 columns each 12 ft/3·70 m high, containing treatment-rooms and living-quarters. On the S (uphill) side are a **fountain-house** (to the left of the steps leading up to the middle terrace) and (to the right of the steps) a *naiskos* (small shrine) donated by the Emperor Claudius's personal physician, C. Stertinius Xenophon of Kos. At the right-hand corner are another fountain and ablution facilities.

From this center of treatment and healing we go up the steps to the cult center on the *middle terrace*. Opposite the staircase is the *altar, originally erected in the 4th c. B.C. but sumptuously rebuilt in the 2nd c. on the model of the Great Altar of Pergamon. Oriented to face the altar is an Ionic **temple of antis**, two columns of which have been re-erected. To the left, beside the entrance to the cella, is a stone coffer in which the temple treasure was kept. Adjoining the temple on the S is a structure which has been identified as an *abaton*. At the E end of the terrace are the remains of a stoa open to the N. Between this, the altar and a semicircular exedra is a Corinthian *temple* of the 2nd c. A.D.

A broad **monumental staircase** leads to the *upper terrace*, 36 ft/11 m higher, from which there are extensive *views. Like the lower terrace, this was surrounded on three sides by stoas. It was dominated by a Doric peripteral temple (6×11 columns) erected in 170–160 B.C.

The road which runs W from Kos comes in 6 miles/9 km to a road on the left which ascends to the hill village of **Asfendíou** with its medieval castle. 8 miles/13 km from Kos another road on the left leads in 1¼ miles/2 km to **Pylí** (Byzantine church with remains of frescoes, 15th c.), continuing to **Kardámena** (16 miles/26 km), a little port on the S coast. The main road continues SW. At **Antimákhia** (15 miles/ 24 km; pop. 1500), with a castle of the Knights of St John, a road branches off on the right to **Mastikhári** (Early Christian church) on the N coast. The main road passes the airport (17 miles/27 km) and ends at **Kéfalos** (25 miles/40 km; pop. 1800), with another castle of the Knights. Near by are the remains of ancient Astypálaia.

# Krk

Yugoslavia
Republic: Croatia (Hrvatska).
Area: 158 sq. miles/409 sq. km. – Population: 20,000.
Telephone code: 051.

ⓘ **Turističko Društvo,**
YU-51513 **Omišalj;**
tel. 88 81 30.
**Turističko Društvo,**
Hotel Dražica,
Ružmarinoa 4,
YU-51500 **Krk;**
tel. 85 10 22.
**Turističko Društvo,**
YU-51523 **Baška;**
tel. 85 68 17.
**Turističko Društvo,**
YU-51511 **Malinska;**
tel. 88 55 07.
**Turističko Društvo,**
YU-51516 **Vrbnik;**
tel. 85 11 66.

HOTELS. – KRK: *Dražica*, II, 320 b., with annexes *Dubrava*, 67 b., *Koralj*, 398 b., *Lovorka*, 218 b.; and *Bor*, 50 b.; *Pećine* (pension), III, 28 b. – OMIŠALJ: *Adriatic I*, II, 653 b., with annexes *Adriatic II* and *III*, 364 b. – PUNAT: *Park I* and *II*, II, 528 b., with annexes *Kostarika*, 30 b., and *Kvarner*, 70 b. – BAŠKA: *Corinthia*, II, 244 b., with annexes *Adria*, 66 b., *Baška*, 55 b., *Zvonimir*, 152 b., *Velebit*, 56 b., and bungalows, 40 b. – MALINSKA: *Palace*, I, 464 b.; *Tamaris*, II, 654 b.; *Malin*, II, 166 b., with annexes *Adriatic*, 94 b., *Draga*, 59 b., and bungalows, 40 b.; *Slavija*, II, 144 b., with annexe *Kvarner*, 24 b.; *Triglav*, 70 b.

CAMP SITES. – KRK: *Ježevac.* – PUNAT: *Punat.* – BAŠKA: *Bunculuka*; *Zablaće.*

BATHING BEACHES. – At the holiday complex of *Haludovo* (1500 b.), near the quiet little village of Malinska.

TRANSPORTATION. – Rijeka's airport is on Krk. – Connected with mainland by bridge.

**The island of Krk in the northern Adriatic, lying opposite the town of Crikvenica, is the largest of the Yugoslav islands. Most of the population is concentrated in the lower and more fertile northern part of the islands; the limestone hills in the S have only a sparse growth of vegetation. The chief place on the island, Krk town, is on the W coast, sheltered from the bora (a cold, dry and gusty north-easterly wind which sweeps down from the mountains to**

**the Adriatic coast). The economy is based on agriculture and sheep-farming, with the tourist trade an important additional source of revenue.**

HISTORY. – Krk was occupied by an Illyrian tribe, the Liburni, and there was at least a temporary Greek settlement on the island. It was taken by the Romans in the 2nd c. B.C., and during the war between Caesar and Pompey there was a naval battle off the island in which Pompey's forces were victorious. In A.D. 395 when the Roman Empire split into two, Krk fell to Byzantium. In 480 Christians in what is now Krk town began to build a basilica on the site of a Roman bathhouse, and the external walls and columns of this church, which was repeatedly altered and enlarged, have survived the passage of 1500 years almost unscathed. – Between the 9th and 12th c. the island was ruled by the Croatian kings. Thereafter it came under the control of the Venetians, who appointed Count Frankopan, a Croatian, as ruler of the island; and the Frankopan family maintained their sway from 1118 to 1480. Then, in view of the increasing danger of Turkish occupation, Venice took over direct control, and continued to hold Krk until 1797. Napoleon incorporated the island in his Illyrian Provinces for a brief period, after which it passed to Austro-Hungary. The Treaty of Rapallo (1920) assigned Krk not to Italy, like the neighboring islands of Cres and Lošinj, but to the new kingdom of Yugoslavia. During the Second World War it was occupied by the Italians, later

GLAGOLITIC. – The Glagolitic script used in writing Old Slavonic, which resembles the Coptic and Armenian alphabets more than any other European script, was devised in the 9th c. by Cyril, the "Apostle of the Slavs": it is not certain whether this script or the other Early Slavonic script, Cyrillic, is the older. The Glagolitic script developed two distinct forms, the angular Croatian form and a more rounded form. It spread so rapidly that two Councils held at Split in 925 and 927 launched a vigorous attack on Churchmen who used the script and also preached in Croatian instead of Latin. Glagolitic soon became a symbol of the resistance by patriotic Slavs to the alien clergy under Roman control, and the pro-Slav priests, the *glagoljaši*, were persecuted. At a further Council in 1060 the adherents of Rome finally triumphed over their opponents, but the Glagolitic script and the Old Croatian language continued in use on the islands, particularly on Krk; and in the 13th c., by Papal Decree, the use of Glagolitic was permitted in the diocese of Senj and on Krk. By the end of the 15th c. books, charters, registers and statutes were being printed in Glagolitic; and the first printed book of the Southern Slavs, a Missal of 1483, is in Glagolitic script. At the beginning of the 16th c. there were Glagolitic printing-presses at Rijeka and on Krk; but from now on the script was used only for ecclesiastical purposes. A famous Codex of 1395 on which the French kings swore their coronation oath was written in Glagolitic. One of the oldest documents in the Croatian language is a charter, inscribed on a stone tablet, recording a donation by the Croatian King Zvonimir to the Benedictines. The original of the tablet is now in the Zagreb Archeological Museum; there is a copy in Baška. Another Glagolitic tablet can be seen in the village of Valun on the island of Cres (see p. 61).

(1943) replaced by Germans. After Krk became part of the new People's Republic of Yugoslavia in 1945 many of the Italian inhabitants left.

# Krk town

The chief place and principal port of the island is the town of **Krk**, in a bay on the W coast. It is still surrounded by remains of the old *town walls*, and the watch-tower at the main entrance to the town bears a carving of the Lion of St Mark. Continuing from the gate, past souvenir stalls, we come to Tito Square, beyond which, concealed from direct view by houses, is the **Frankopan Castle** (1197). To one side stands the Bishop's Palace, which contains a collection of 16th and 17th c. pictures. The **Cathedral**, originally built on the site of a Roman bath-house and subsequently enlarged, lies just off the square. Also worth seeing is a Gothic *Franciscan church* in the N of the town.

CIRCUIT OF THE ISLAND. – From Krk a hilly road follows the bay to the little town of **Punat**, with many weekend and holiday chalets on the slopes above it. Punat has a great tradition of seafaring and shipbuilding. Just before the town, on the right, are a small boatyard and a boating marina. Punat's principal feature of interest, a Franciscan Friary, lies away from the village in a wide bay on the islet of *Košljun*. Above the doorway is the Glagolitic inscription "Mir i dobra"

("Peace and goodness"). Visitors are shown the gravestone of one of the last of the Frankopan family, Princess Katherine, who died in 1529. In the library is a dugout boat, of a type still used at Punat at the end of the 19th c., together with costumes, kitchen equipment and Glagolitic vestments. The church contains a polyptych by Girolamo da Santa Croce and a "Last Judgment" by Ughetti.

From Punat a donkey-track leads to the next coastal village, **Stara Baška**, whose normal communications are by boat. The village, above the sea on the slopes of the island's highest hill, Obzova (1867 ft/ 569 m), is in a state of decline and many of the houses are mere ruins.

The next village, **Baška**, is connected with Krk town by bus. In the church was found the oldest Glagolitic inscription (see box above); the tablet now to be seen here is a copy. Baška has a long pebble beach, and there is good walking in the beautiful fertile plain inland from the village.

**Vrbnik**, opposite the town of Novi Vinodol on the mainland, lies at the top of steep cliffs, from which there is a breathtaking *view of the coastal mountain range. Much of the medieval town has been preserved, including old stone-built houses and churches. The altar-piece in the Church of the Assumption was painted in Venice by an artist from Kotor.

A rocky creek on the island of Krk

Here, too, there are Glagolitic inscriptions – one on the sacristy window, another in the Lady Chapel and a third on the rear wall of the cemetery chapel.

**Šilo**, where the ferries from Crikvenica put in, is no more than a huddle of houses on the coast and along the road running up into the hills.

**Omišalj**, the first village beyond the new bridge, situated on the cliffs, was in prehistoric times a fortified settlement controlling the seaway to Rijeka. It has a fine Romanesque Basilica (13th c.) with a notable Treasury.

**Njivice**, is a quiet little holiday village. Beyond it is **Malinska** surrounded by vineyards and olive groves, with the largest tourist complex on the island, Haludovo, notable for its ultra-modern architecture.

The island's other landing-place is at **Aghia Pelayía**, an open anchorage on the N coast 2½ miles/4 km below **Potamós** (pop. 780). Other places of interest are **Milopótamos** (Castle), on the W coast; the island's old medieval capital, **Palaiokhóra**, situated near the NE coast on a hill between two gorges, which was destroyed in 1536 by the Turkish Admiral, Khaireddin Barbarossa; and **Palaiókastro**, in Avlémona Bay on the E coast, with the remains of a Temple of Aphrodite and of the island's ancient capital, Skandeia, which is mentioned by Homer.

SE of Kýthira, about half-way toward Crete, is the little limestone island of **Antikythira** (area 8½ sq. miles/ 22 sq. km; alt. 1180 ft/360 m), the ancient *Aigila* or *Aigilia* (farming, fishing). In the channel between the two islands the wreck of a Roman ship was located and recovered in 1900. Its cargo, consisting of bronze and marble statues of the 5th–2nd c. B.C. (including the Ephebe of Antikythira), pottery, glass and an astronomical clock, is now in the National Archeological Museum in Athens.

# Kythira
## (Kíthira)

Greece
Nomos: Attica.
Area: 107 sq. miles/278 sq. km. – Population: 39,600.

HOTEL. – IN AGHIA PELAYÍA: *Cytheria*, II, 15 b.

TRANSPORTATION. – Boat services from Piraeus and Gýthion; island bus.

**Kýthira (the ancient Kythera, Cythera) was long regarded as one of the Ionian Islands, but it lies well away from the rest of the group, 9 miles/ 14 km S of the Peloponnese. It is now regarded as part of the SW Peloponnese and administratively, is no longer subordinate to Kérkyra (Corfu) but to Athens. On this rocky island the Minoans established a settlement at Kástri, and later it was settled by Phoenicians. Kýthira vies with Cyprus in claiming to be the birthplace of Aphrodite.**

**Kýthira** (pop. 850), chief place on the island and one of the most attractive of the little island towns, lies above Kapsáli Bay, 2 miles/3 km from its harbor. It has a small museum containing local finds. On a crag adjoining the town stands a Venetian Castle (view), with two churches, the Myrtidiótissa and the Pantokrátor.

# Kythnos
## See under Cyclades

# Lampedusa
## See under Pelagian Islands

# Lefkás
## (Lefkás)

Greece
Nomos: Lefkás.
Area: 115 sq. miles/299 sq. km. – Population: 23,000.
(i) **Tourist Police** (summer only),
Nidri (Lefkás);
tel. 9 52 07.

HOTEL. – *Nirikos*, II, 69 b.; *Santa Mavra*, III, 38 b.

TRANSPORTATION. – Bus service from Áktion Airport and from Athens.

**Lefkás, one of the Ionian Islands, is only just an island: it abuts the mainland, separated from it only by a canal which according to legend was cut in ancient times by the inhabitants and re-cut in 1905.**

HISTORY. – Human settlement on the island dates back to about 2000 B.C. In the 7th c. B.C. Corinth founded a colony here. In 197 B.C. the island passed into Roman hands. From 1204 it belonged to the

Despotate of Epirus, from 1331 to Venice, from 1362 to the Palatine County of Cefalonia (Kefallinía). Between 1467 and 1684 it was held by the Turks, after which it returned to Venetian rule. Thereafter it shared the destinies of the other Ionian Islands.

The chief town, **Lefkás** (pop. 7000), lies near the canal. Opposite it, amid the lagoons on the mainland, is the Castle of Santa Mavra, the name by which the island was known during the Middle Ages.

From Lefkás a road runs SW via Lazaráta and Aghios Pétros to Vasilikí Bay. To the W of this is the **Leucadian Rock**, a crag 230 ft/70 m high projecting far into the sea from which, according to an ancient tradition, the poetess Sappho sprang to her death in despair at her unrequited love. – On a hill 2 miles/3 km S of Lefkás is the site of ancient *Leukas* (remains of acropolis, etc.).

To the S of Lefkás is **Nídri**, in a beautiful setting at the mouth of Vlíkho Bay. Opposite it is a peninsula with the Chapel of *Aghia Kyriakí* and the grave of the German archeologist Wilhelm Dörpfeld (1853–1940), who died here. There is a monument to him on the quay at Nídri. Dörpfeld, who worked at Troy with Schliemann and later at Olympia and Pergamon, directed excavations at Nídri from 1901 to 1913 but failed to find any evidence supporting his theory that Lefkás and not Ithaca was the island of Odysseus. He brought to light circular structures, graves and walls dating from the Early Bronze Age (about 2000 B.C.), but nothing belonging to the time of Odysseus.

# Lemnos/Limnos
*(Límnos)*

Greece

Nomos: Lesbos.
Area: 183 sq. miles/475 sq. km. – Population: 23,000.
Altitude: 0–1542 ft/0–470 m.

HOTELS. – MÝRINA: *Akti Myrina* (Myrina Beach), L, 250 b., SP, bungalows; *Sevdalis*, III, 63 b.

AIR SERVICES. – Airfield at Varos, 13 miles/21 km E of Mýrina. – Athens–Lemnos, 1–2 flights daily (45 minutes); Salonikí–Lemnos, 5 flights a week (65 minutes).

BOAT SERVICES. – Weekly service from Kymi (6 hours; cars carried); seasonal service from Salonikí.

BATHING BEACHES. – *Akti Myrinas* and *Platis*, on W coast; in *Moúdros Bay*; *Kokkinas*, in Pourniá Bay.

ROADS. – Motor roads to all the larger places on the island. – Island bus. – Taxis.

EVENTS. – *St George's Day* (end of April); horse-races.

Lemnos is an island of relatively recent volcanic origin in the northern Aegean, with gentle hills in the W and S (rising to 1542 ft/470 m in Mount Skópia) and fertile low-lying land in the NE. It is a comparatively dry and waterless island.

The island is deeply indented by two inlets, *Pourniá Bay* in the N and *Moúdros Bay* in the S, forming a narrow isthmus only $2\frac{1}{2}$ miles/4 km between the eastern and western halves of the island. On this isthmus is the Hill of *Mosykhlos* (171 ft/ 52 m), believed to have been a volcano in prehistoric times, on which there was a temple dedicated to the blacksmith god Hephaistos, which is not surprising, as the earliest inhabitants were metal craftsmen. The "Lemnian earth" found here, credited with curative properties, was exported all over the Ancient World. – The considerable military presence on the island detracts from its attraction for visitors.

HISTORY. – During the Bronze Age Lemnos was settled by Tyrrhenians, who made the island a flourishing cultural and commercial center (reflected in the quantities of pottery and gold jewelry found here). In the 6th c. B.C. it was conquered by Miltiades, and until the end of the 2nd c. B.C. remained subject to Athens. Thereafter it was successively ruled by Rome, Byzantium and Venice, and in 1456 was taken by the Turks. The First Balkan War led to its incorporation in Greece in 1912.

The island's capital, **Mýrina** or *Kástro* (pop. 3500; museum), lies in the SW of the island, below a medieval castle (views). It occupies the site of ancient Myrina (scanty remains of town walls, Tyrrhenian necropolis). To the N of *Kokkinos* (ruined castle), in Pourniá Bay, is the site of ancient *Hephaistia* (necropolis, Roman theater). Near the village of *Kaminia*, on the E coast S of *Moúdros*, are the well-preserved remains of the Tyrrhenian city of **Polyokhni**, which flourished between 2800 and 2300 B.C. – There are warm radioactive sulfur springs in the W of the island and in the sea at *Pláka* off its north-eastern tip.

NE and E of Lemnos are the islands, now Turkish, of **Gökçeada** or *Imroz Adası* (area 231 sq. miles/597 sq. km) and **Bozcaada**, the ancient *Imbros* and *Tenedos*.

20 miles/30 km S of Lemnos lies the little island of **Aghios Efstrátios** (area 17 sq. miles/43 sq. km; pop. 1000). On the W coast, in the island's largest bay, is its chief place, *Aghios Efstrátios*, with a castle and a number of windmills on the hill above it. – Known in ancient times as Halonnesos, the island, held by the Athenians, secured the route to the islands of Lemnos and Imbros and the Hellespont.

# Leros
## See under Sporades

# Lesbos
## (Lésvos)

Greece
Nomos: Lesbos.
Area: 629 sq. miles/1630 sq. km. – Population: 97,000.
Telephone code: 0251.

(i) **Tourist Police,**
     Platía Teloníou,
     **Mytilíni;**
     tel. 2 27 76.
     **Olympic Airways,**
     Kavetsou 44,
     **Mytilíni;**
     tel. 2 86 60.

HOTELS. – MYTILÍNI: *Xenia* (1¼ miles/2 km from town), II, 148 b.; *Blue Sea*, II, 100 b.; *Lesvos Beach* (4 miles/6 km from town), II, 78 b.; *Lesvion*, II, 68 b.; *Sappho*, III, 56 b.; *Rex*, III, 34 b.

KRÁTIGOS: *Katia*, III, 76 b. – ERESSÓS: *Sappho Eressia*, III, 25 b. – MÍTHYMNA: *Delphinia*, II, 94 b. – PÉTRA: *Petra*, III, 34 b. – PLOMÁRION: *Oceanis*, III, 78 b. – SÍGRION: *Nisiopi*, II, 16 b. – THERMÍ: *Votsala*, II, 94 b.

BATHING. – In the S, Aghios Isídoros, Vaterá; in the W, Eressós, Sígri; in the N, Pétra, Míthymna, etc.

TRANSPORTATION. – Air service from Athens; boat service Piraeus–Chios–Lesbos (–Lemnos).

* **Lesbos, the third largest of the Greek islands in the eastern Aegean, is separated from the mainland of Anatolia by the 5–12 mile/8–20 km wide Sound of Mytilene and bounds on the SE the Gulf of Edremit, which cuts deep into the coast of Asia Minor.**

The inhabitants earn their living from agriculture, which produces rich crops in the island's fertile soil, and craft production (pottery, spinning, weaving).

HISTORY. – There is much archeological evidence to show that Lesbos was settled as early as the 3rd millennium B.C. From the 12th c. B.C. onward Aeolian Greeks established themselves on the island; by the 7th–6th c. their farming and trading activities brought great prosperity. In the 6th c. Lesbos was recognized as the principal center of the Aeolian Greeks of Asia Minor, and from its powerful capital of Mytilene settlers went out to establish colonies on the nearby mainland. – At the beginning of the 6th c. *Pittakos*, one of the Seven Sages, put an end to faction and arbitrary rule by good government and wise legislation. His contemporaries and opponents were the poet *Alkaios* and the great woman poet **Sappho**, who ran a school in Mytilene based on religious and esthetic principles. Her tender poems celebrating the charms of her pupils gave rise – probably without justification – to the idea of Lesbian love. – After a period of Persian rule Lesbos was liberated and became a member of the First Attic Maritime League, but lost its independence after the rising against Athens in 428–427 B.C. From 378 to about 350 it was a member of the Second Attic Maritime League. For a brief period (88–79 B.C.) it was held by Mithridates, King of Pontus, and then became part of the Roman province of Asia. Under the Byzantine emperors it was repeatedly harried and plundered by pirates, and thereafter alternated between Slav, Seljuk and Venetian rule. In 1354 it was granted to the Gattelusi family of Genoa, from whom it was captured by the Turks in 1461. After the Balkan War (1912–13) Lesbos was incorporated in Greece without any significant Turkish resistance.

The island's capital, **Mytilíni** or *Kástro* (pop. 25,000; museum), with many handsome houses, is picturesquely situated in a bay on the E coast, extending in a semicircle around the sheltered harbor. It occupies the site of ancient Mytilene. Above the town towers the massive Genoese and Turkish castle (ancient architectural fragments; * view), on a crag which was once separate from the main island and connected with it by bridges. To the W of the town, above a Turkish cemetery, is a Roman theater (3rd c. A.D.) built into the hillside, and below this is the House of Menander (3rd c. A.D.). N of the theater are fragments of the ancient town walls.

7½ miles/12 km NW of Mytilíni, in a small depression on the E coast, are the hot springs (high radium content) of *Thermi*, which in ancient times were sacred to Artemis Thermeia. – 6 miles/10 km NW the picturesque village of *Mantamádo* (pottery) has a church containing an icon of the Mother of God which is venerated as wonder-working.

There are rewarding excursions to be made in the area around the Gulf of Iera (ancient *Hiera*). To the W, above *Aghiasos* (pilgrimage church; pottery), is the island's highest summit, **Mount Ólympos** (3173 ft/967 m), from which a Roman aqueduct 16 miles/26 km long, still well preserved at some points, runs down to Mytilíni. – Around the Gulf of Kallóní, which cuts deep inland on the SW side of the island, extends the largest plain on Lesbos, extensively cultivated. Near the little town of **Kallonί** is the Monastery of *Límonos* (library).

In the W of the island are the remains of ancient *Eressos* (now called Palaió-kastro), home of Sappho. To the NW, at **Antissa**, are the remains of the ancient city of that name. In the N of the island, under a Genoese castle perched on a crag, is the picturesque little town **Míthymna** or *Mólyvos*, said to have been the home of the pastoral couple Daphnis and Chloe. – Near the village of *Sígrion* (ruined castle), in the extreme W of the island, is a petrified forest.

# Limassol
## See under Cyprus

# Lindos
## See under Rhodes

# Linosa
## See under Pelagian Islands

# Lipari Islands/Isole Lípari
## Aeolian Islands/Isole Eólie

Italy
Region: Sicily. – Province: Messina.
Principal island: Lipari. – Population: 13,000.
Post code: I-98055. – Telephone code: 090.
(i) **AA,**
Corso Vitorio Emanuele 239,
**Lipari;**
tel. 9 81 15 80.

HOTELS. – ON LIPARI: *Carasco*, II, 163 b., SP; *Gattopardo Park*, II, 99 b.; *Giardino sul Mare*, II, 60 b., SP; *Augustus*, III, 46 b. – ON VULCANO: *Eolian*, II, 162 b.; *Arcipelago*, II, 157 b., SP; *Garden Volcano*, II, 60 b.; *Les Sables Noirs*, II, 53 b.; *Mari del Sud*, III, 49 b. – ON FILICUDI: *Phenicusa*, II, 69 b. – ON PANAREA: *La Piazza*, III, 50 b. – ON STROMBOLI: *La Sciara Residence*, II, 122 b., SP; *La Sirenetta*, III, 52 b. – YOUTH HOSTEL in Lipari, Via Castello 17, 120 b.

BOAT SERVICES. – Regular services several times daily from Milazzo and Messina and several times weekly from Naples to Lipari, Vulcano, Salina and Panarea, with connections three times weekly to Filicudi and Alicudi; also weekly from Palermo to the Lipari Islands. – Hydrofoil services in summer (once or twice daily) from Milazzo and Messina.

**The Lipari Islands (Isole Lípari), also known as the Aeolian Islands (Isole Eólie) after the Greek wind god Aeolus, lying between 20 miles/ 32 km and 50 miles/80 km off the N coast of Italy, are an archipelago of seven larger islands and 10 uninhabited islets, the tips of mountains of volcanic origin rising from the sea-bed far below.**

The islands, with a total area of 45 sq. miles/117 sq. km and a present-day population of 12,000, were long used as penal colonies and places of banishment. In more recent times their mild climate and unusual scenery have attracted increasing numbers of visitors. They offer excellent scuba-diving.

THE ISLANDS. – The largest and most fertile of the islands is Lipari (area 15 sq. miles/38 sq. km; pop. 10,000). In the more southerly bay on the E coast lies the little town of **Lipari** (alt. 16 ft/5 m; pop. 4500), the chief place on the island. To the S of the harbor, on a rocky promontory, is the Castello, within which are the Cathedral (1654) and three other churches. Adjoining the Cathedral, in the former Bishop's Palace, is a *museum (Antiquarium) containing the rich finds of the Pre-Christian and Historical periods from recent excavations on the island (Greek painted vases, a statuette of Isis,

On the Lipari Islands

tombs, etc.). To the W of the Cathedral, on an excavation site in front of the Immacolata Church, can be seen a sequence of building-levels ranging in date from the Early Bronze Age (17th c. B.C.) through the Iron Age (11th–9th c. B.C.) and the Hellenistic period to Roman times (2nd c. A.D.). – N of the Castello is the fishermen's quarter; to the S the warehouses in which the island's exports (including pumicestone, currants, Malvasia wine, capers and figs) are stored while awaiting shipment.

2 miles/3 km N of Lipari, beyond *Monte Rosa* (784 ft/239 m), is the village of **Canneto** (alt. 33 ft/10 m), the center for the extraction, processing and export of pumice-stone. The pumice quarries in the Valley of the *Fossa Bianca*, NW of the village (45 minutes), are an interesting sight. – W of Canneto (1½–2 hours), beyond the massive lava flows at *Forgia Vecchia*, rises **Monte Sant' Angelo** (1949 ft/594 m), the island's highest peak. From its summit, roughly in the center of the archipelago, there are the best panoramic *views of the Lipari Islands. – At *Piano Conte*, in a valley near the W coast, are the *hot springs of San Calogero* (144 °F/62 °C; steam baths). – From Lipari there is an attractive walk (1½ hours) to *San Salvatore* (2 miles/3 km S), on the southern tip of the island, and from there back to Lipari along the W side of *Monte Guardia* (1211 ft/369 m).

To the S of the island of Lipari, separated from it by the Bocche, a strait ¾ mile/1 km wide, on the W side of which is the basalt cliff of *Pietralunga* (200 ft/60 m), is the smaller island of **Vulcano** (area 8 sq. miles/21 sq. km; pop. 400), which offers excellent opportunities for studying volcanic phenomena. On the N side of the island rises *Vulcanello* (404 ft/123 m), with three craters, which appeared out of the sea in 183 B.C. In the depression on the S side of the hill are the harbors of *Porto di Ponente* (to the W) and *Porto di Levante* (to the E). On the shore beside Porto di Levante is a curiously shaped rock, the remnant of an old volcano, riddled with caves for the extraction of alum. The sea water, here strongly radioactive, is warm and sometimes boiling as a result of underwater emissions of steam (recommended for the treatment of rheumatism and gout). – From the *Gran Cratere* (1266 ft/386 m; climbed from Porto di Levante in 1 hour), to the S of the depression, there

are superb *views; half-way up there are many fumaroles. The crater, which since the eruptions of 1880–90 has had the characteristics of a solfatara, measures 660 ft/200 m by 460 ft/140 m and is 260 ft/80 m deep. – Farther S is the cone of *Monte Aria* (1637 ft/499 m), the island's highest peak.

2½ miles/4 km N of Lipari is the island of **Salina** (area 10½ sq. miles/27 sq. km; pop. 2000), with two extinct volcanoes, *Monte de' Porri* (2822 ft/860 m) to the NW and *Monte Fossa delle Felci* (3156 ft/962 m) to the SE. – 12 miles/20 km W of Salina is the well-cultivated island of **Filicudi** (alt. 2545 ft/775 m; area 3½ sq. miles/9 sq. km; pop. 150). On its W coast a fine cave with basalt columns can be visited. – 8 miles/ 13 km farther W we come to the island of **Alicudi** (alt. 2175 ft/663 m; area 2 sq. miles/5 sq. km), with a population of some 130 shepherds and fishermen.

The small group of islands lying between 9 miles/14 km and 13 miles/21 km NE of Lipari may have been a single island before the volcanic eruptions of 126 B.C. The largest of the group, **Panarea** (alt. 1381 ft/421 m; area 1·4 sq. miles/3·5 sq. km; pop. 250) has hot springs At *Punta*

Panarea

*Milazzese*, the southernmost tip of the island, are the foundations (excavated 1948) of 23 huts belonging to a *Bronze Age village* (14th–13th c. B.C.), the best-preserved such site in Italy. – 2½ miles/ 4 km NE of Panarea is a small uninhabited rocky island, **Basiluzzo**, on which capers are grown.

9 miles/14 km NE of Basiluzzo is the island of **Stromboli** (area 4·8 sq. miles/

12·5 sq. km), reputed in ancient times to be the home of the wind god Aeolus. The population, which in 1935 was about 1800, has been reduced by emigration (particularly to Australia) to no more than 350. On the NE coast is the chief place on the island, **Stromboli** (alt. 65 ft/ 20 m), made up of the settlements of *San Bartolomeo, San Vincenzo* and *Ficogrande.*

Together with the Vulcano crater, *Strombóli (3038 ft/926 m), the red glow from which can be seen from a long way off, is one of the few European volcanoes that are still active. The Vulcano crater has given its name to all other volcanoes. The ascent (best undertaken from the N side; 3 hours) is a fascinating experience. The crater, on the N side of the highest peak, emits at frequent intervals huge bubbles of lava which explode with a thunderous noise, throwing up showers of stones which fall back into the crater or roll harmlessly down the *Sciara*, a slope descending on the NW side at an angle of 35° to the sea and continuing for some distance below the surface. Only every few years are there more violent eruptions which cause damage to the cultivated areas of the island. When the vapor is not too thick it is possible to go down to the brink of the crater and look in. – 1 mile/1·5 km NE of the village of Stromboli is the magnificent basalt cliff of *Strombolicchio*, rising 184 ft/56 m sheer from the sea (steps cut in rock).

# Lopud
## See under Elaphite Islands

# Lošinj

Yugoslavia
Republic: Croatia (Hrvatska).
Area: 29 sq. miles/75 sq. km. – Population: 8000.
Telephone code: 051.
(i) **Turist Biro,**
Obala Maršala Tita 7,
YU-51550 **Mali Lošinj;**
tel. 86 10 11.
**Turist Biro,**
YU-51551 **Veli Lošinj;**
tel. 86 12 83.
**Turističko Društvo,**
YU-51554 **Osor-Nerezine;**
tel. 86 50 07.
**Turističko Društvo,**
YU-51552 **Ilovik;**
tel. 86 12 31.

HOTELS. – MALI LOŠINJ: *Aurora & Vespera*, I, 1466 b., with apartments, I, 8 b.; *Bellevue*, II, 414 b.; *Helios*, II, 262 b., with annexes *Villa Karlovac*, II, 32 b., and *Villa Rijeka*, II, 48 b., and bungalows, II, 120 b.; *Alhambra*, II, 100 b., with annexes *Villa Dubrovnik*, II, 46 b., *Villa Sarajevo*, III, 11 b., *Villa Zadar*, III, 19 b., and apartments, III, 6 b.; *Čikat*, IV, 85 b., with annexe *Villa Flora*, III, 16 b.; *Istra*, IV, 43 b. – VELI LOŠINJ: *Punta*, II, 315 b. – NEREZINE: accommodation in private houses (apply to Tourist Office). – ON UNIJE AND SUSAK: accommodation in private houses (apply to Tourist Offices).

CAMP SITES. – MALI LOŠINJ: *Čikat; Poljana*, with yacht harbor. – VELI LOŠINJ: *Punta*. – NEREZINE: *Rapoca*, with a small harbor.

EVENTS. – *Winter Cup of the Nations* and *New Year's Cup of the Cities* (underwater fishing contests), end of December.

BATHING BEACHES. – The best-known bathing beach is in **Čikat Bay**, near the hotel complex in a wooded coastal area SW of Mali Lošinj; at the height of the season it is usually overcrowded. To the S, after a number of small coves belonging to hotels but also open to the public, is a naturist area (no shade). Beyond this, as far as the cape at the S end of the island, are other coves, some of them with small sandy beaches, which can be reached on bridle-paths but are more quickly and easily accessible by boat. On the E side of the island the bathing is not so good; the only good beaches are a few near Nerezine, to the N.

CAR FERRIES. – Connections with the mainland via the island of Cres (bridge); car ferries Porozina–Brestovo, Porozina–Rijeka, and also Pula–Lošinj–Zadar. Passenger services Pula–Ilovik–Unije–Mali Lošinj–Silba–Olib–Rab; also fast hydrofoil services.

**Subtropical vegetation and a climate in which the thermometer never falls below freezing-point have made the island of Lošinj (area 29 sq. miles/75 sq. km), lying 43 miles/70 km S of Rijeka, a popular resort frequented throughout the year. During the 19th c. asthma sufferers came to Lošinj to seek spa treatment for their complaint, but the spa aspect now plays a relatively minor role.**

HISTORY. – Like the neighboring island of Cres, Lošinj was already occupied by man in the Neolithic period, as has been shown by finds in caves on the steep W coasts of both islands. From the Bronze and Iron Ages date the remains of some 40 settlements with stone ramparts which have been found all over the area. About 1200 B.C. both islands were settled by Illyrians, who are described by contemporary writers as daring seamen and dreaded pirates. At the end of the 3rd c. B.C. the Romans established, on the channel between Lošinj and Cres, the fortified town of *Absorus* (present-day Osor), which soon had a population of 30,000. After the Slav occupation of the early 7th c. A.D. Osor continued under Byzantine sovereignty, which did not end until 842 when the Saracens captured and sacked the town. The early 10th c. saw the establishment of the first independent Croatian State under King Tomislav, of which Lošinj and Cres now became part. In 1018 Doge Orseolo II took Osor

The picturesque little town of Mali Lošinj

with a Venetian fleet, but 50 years later King Krešimir IV of Croatia recovered both islands.

In the following three centuries Lošinj and Cres alternated between Croatian and Venetian control. The victors always established themselves in Osor, but paid little attention to the now almost uninhabited island of Lošinj. During the 16th and 17th c. the Turks did not venture on to the islands, but there were frequent raids on the coastal settlements by pirates based at Senj. Better days for Lošinj began only after the Congress of Vienna (1815) gave Austria back its former possessions in Dalmatia and the northern Adriatic.

The Treaty of Rapallo in 1920 assigned Lošinj and Cres, together with the surrounding smaller islands, not to the new kingdom of Yugoslavia but to Italy, which pursued a radical policy of Italianization and suppressed the Croatian language and customs. In 1945 Yugoslav Partisans landed on Lošinj and Cres, and under the Treaty of Paris in 1947 both islands, together with Istria, were incorporated in the Republic of Yugoslavia.

THE ISLAND. – In **Mali Lošinj** a Venetian tower 112 ft/34 m high adjoining the church affords magnificent panoramic *views over the sea and the neighboring islands. St Mary's Church (1676), with a handsome Baroque façade, has a notable High Altar, with the reliquary of the martyred St Romulus, the Altar of the Cross (by the Venetian sculptor Ferrari),

A street in Mali Lošinj

and the Patronal Altar on the N wall, which has figures of the islands' patron saints – St Gaudentius (Crcs), St Quirinus (Krk) and St Christopher (Rab). From the church a path leads up to the 15th c. Castle. The churchyard of St Martin's Church contains the graves of shipowners and sea-captains. A Way of the Cross, with 14 Baroque stations, ascends the Calvary Hill (Kalvarija) to the SW of the town. In Čikat Bay is the little Pilgrimage Church of the Annunciation, the walls of which are covered with ex-votos depicting ships in peril on the sea.

Features of interest in **Veli Lošinj** a small maritime town with rich subtropical vegetation, are the Parish Church of St Anthony; the little Pilgrimage Church of St Mary on the promontory; a watch-tower of 1455 beyond the first row of houses on the harbor; the Church of Our Lady of the Angels (Gospa od Andjela), of 1510; and the former St Joseph's Monastery (Sveti Josip), now the presbytery. Above the town is a wooded park known as the Arboretum. Here, in 1885, Archduke Karl Stephan of Austria built his Palace of Wartsee, set in magnificent grounds (30 acres/12 hectares), which now belongs to a sanatorium.

The third largest place on Lošinj is **Nerezine**, now of growing importance as a summer resort. From here and from the nearby village of **Sveti Jakob** there are waymarked paths up the island's highest hill, *Televrina* (1929 ft/588 m), from the summit of which there are superb views over the sea to the neighboring islands and the mainland.

The three little islands to the S – Ilovik, Sveti Petar and Kozjak – are a kind of continuation of Lošinj.

**Ilovik**, with an area of barely 2·3 sq. miles/6 sq. km, is covered with an impermeable clay soil and accordingly, unlike Lošinj, has a number of springs with an abundant flow of water. The only settlement is the quiet and attractive little village of *Ilovik*. The Parish Church (1878) contains numbers of painted wooden figures made by a woodcarver in what is now the Val Gardena in Italy and presented to the church by local people who emigrated to America during the period of Austrian rule. – Ilovik produces rich crops of oranges, lemons and vegetables. There are regular boat services from Mali Lošinj and Zadar.

Opposite Ilovik lies the little island of **Sveti Petar**, covered with rich Mediterranean vegetation. In the channel between the two islands stands an old watch-tower built for protection against pirates. A large house on the coast is used by Franciscans from Zagreb as a convalescent home.

The third island, **Kozjak**, is uninhabited.

Off the W coast of Lošinj are two other islands of some tourist interest, Unije and Susak.

**Unije** (area 7 sq. miles/18 sq. km; pop. 280; accommodation only in private houses) is on the route of the regular boat services between Pula and Mali Lošinj. Consisting mainly of limestone, it has an area of fertile low-lying land on which olives and vines are grown. There are 300 beds available for visitors in private houses, and there is electricity but no piped water-supply: like Susak, Unije has to store its water in cisterns. As relics of the past there are the remains of Roman villas and the ramparts of prehistoric settlements.

**Susak** (area 2·4 sq. miles/6·3 sq. km; pop. 200; accommodation only in private houses) differs from the other Adriatic islands in having the form of a large hill of alluvial sand. On this remote and sequestered island noted for its wines and the national costumes which are still worn, there are no cars and no electricity, and the inhabitants draw their water from cisterns. In earlier days the main occupation was fishing, but now the few people left on the island earn their living by vine-growing. The beautiful old local costumes can still be seen. – From the harbor a footpath leads past beds of reeds to the upper part of the village, ending in a square in front of St Nicholas's Church (1770), which contains a Byzantine crucifix of painted wood (12th c.) salvaged from a wrecked ship. In front of the church is one of the cisterns which provide the island's water-supply, for there are no springs. The path continues to a *cemetery* with inscriptions in both Serbo-Croat and Italian which give a glimpse of the island's history. Finally from the lighthouse on Garba Hill there are fine views of the many neighboring islands and the open sea.

Traditional costumes on the island of Susak

The remoteness of the island no doubt explains the fact that here – and only here – the Old Croat dialect and the traditional laments for the dead have survived so long.

Every day throughout the summer Susak is a port of call for numbers of excursion vessels, and many sailing-boats seek the shelter of the harbor for an overnight stay. There are many lonely sandy beaches around the island.

# Majorca/Mallorca

Spain
Region and province: Baleares (Balearics).
Area: 1413 sq. miles/3660 sq. km. – Population: 420,000.

(i) **Oficina de Información de Turismo,**
Avenida de Jaime III 10,
**Palma de Mallorca;**
tel. (971) 21 22 16.
**Fomento del Turismo,**
Constitucio 1
(opposite Head Post Office)
**Palma de Mallorca;**
tel. (971) 22 45 37 and 21 53 10.

HOTELS. – PALMA DE MALLORCA: *Son Vida*, Castillo de Son Vida, L, 172 r., SP; *Victoria-Sol*, Avenida Joan Miró 21, L, 171 r., SP; *Valparaiso Palace*, Francisco Vidal, L, 138 r., SP; *Fenix-Sol*, Paseo Maritimo, L, 96 r., SP; *Bellver-Sol*, Paseo Maritimo 11, I, 393 r.; *Palas Atenea-Sol*, Paseo Maritimo 29, I, 370 r.; *Meliá Mallorca*, Monseñor Palmer 2, I, 239 r.; *Racquet Club*, Son Vida, I, 51 r.; *Cupido*, Marbella 32, II, 197 r.; *Majorica*, Garita 3, II, 137 r.; *Saratoga*, Paseo de Mallorca 6, II, 123 r.; *Reina Constanza*, Paseo Maritimo, II, 97 r.; *Alcina*, Paseo Maritimo 26, II, 89 r.; *Augusta*, Francisco Vidal, II, 88 r.; *Jaime III-Sol*, Paseo de Mallorca 14B, II, 88 r.; *Jumbo Park*, Can Tapara 3, III, 414 r.; *El Paso*, Álvaro de Bazán 3, III, 260 r.; *Horizonte*, Vista Alegre 1, III, 199 r.; *Isla de Mallorca*, Plaza Almirante Churruca 5, III, 110 r.; *César*, Cabo Martorell 19, III, 100 r.; *Hostal Santa Barbara*, Vicario Joaquín Fuster 285, P I, 46 r.

CALA MAYOR: *Nixe Palace*, L, 131 r., SP; *Santa Ana*, I, 190 r.; *Cala Mayor*, II, 93 r.; *Hostal Acor*, P I, 24 r.

CA'N PASTILLA: *Alexandra-Sol*, L, 164 r.; *Leo*, II, 285 r.; *Oleander*, II, 264 r.; *Gran Hotel El Cid*, II, 216 r.; *Caballero*, III, 308 r.; *Helios*, III, 305 r.; *Calma*, III, 190 r.; *Apolo*, III, 151 r.

ILLETAS: *De Mar-Sol*, L, 136 r., SP: *Bonanza Playa*, I, 294 r.; *Bonanza Park*, I, 138 r.; *Playa Marina*, LL, 172 r.; *Hostal Bella Playa*, P I, 35 r.

MAGALLUF: *Barbados-Sol*, I, 428 r.; *Antillas-Sol*, I, 332 r.; *Forte Cala Viñas*, I, 245 r.; *Meliá Magalluf*, I, 242 r.; *Coral Playa-Sol*, I, 184 r.; *Guadalupe-Sol*, II, 488 r.; *Samos*, II, 417 r.; *Magalluf Park-Sol*, II, 404 r.; *Trinidad-Sol*, II, 375 r.; *Jamaica-Sol*, II, 308 r.; *Barracuda*, II, 264 r.; *Dulcinea*, III, 198 r.

PALMA NOVA: *Son Caliu*, I, 239 r.; *Casa Blanca-Sol*, I, 171 r.; *Delfín Playa*, I, 144 r.; *Los Mirlos*, II, 336 r.; *Santa Lucía*, II, 332 r.; *Tordos*, II, 312 r.; *Treinta y Tres*, II, 275 r.; *Torrenova*, II, 254 r.; *Don Bigote*, III, 231 r.; *Olimpic*, III, 185 r.

EL ARENAL: *Río Bravo*, I, 200 r.; *Playa de Palma-Sol*, I, 113 r.; *Garonda Palace*, I, 112 r.; *Bahía de Palma*, II, 433 r.; *Arenal Park*, II, 343 r.; *Taurus Park*, II, 341 r.; *Bali*, II, 264 r.; *Gran Fiesta*, II, 241 r.; *Timor*, II, 241 r.; *Playa Golf*, II, 322 r.; *Tal*, II, 198 r.; *Obelisco Playa*, II, 192 r.; *Tropical-Sol*, II, 165 r.; *San Francisco*, II, 138 r.; *Lancaster*, III, 318 r.; *Luna Park*, III, 318 r.; *Orient*, III, 273 r.; *Bahamas*, III, 259 r.; *Concordia*, III, 200; *Hostal Golondrina*, P I, 59 r.

SANTA PONSA: *Rey Don Jaime*, II, 417 r.; *Pionero*, II, 312 r.; *Santa Ponsa Park*, II, 269 r.; *Bahía del Sol*, II, 162 r.; *Verdemar*, III, 254 r.; *Playa de Mallorca*, III, 218 r.; *Isabela*, III, 156 r.; *Hostal Oeste*, P I, 15 r.

PAGUERA: *Villamil*, I, 99 r.; *Sunna*, I, 75 r.; *Beverly Playa*, II, 413 r.; *Lido Park*, II, 236 r.; *Reina Paguera*, II, 183 r.;

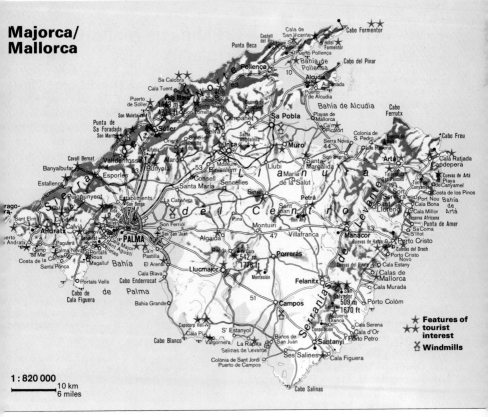

Majorca/
Mallorca

1 : 820 000
10 km
6 miles

★ **Features of tourist interest**
X **Windmills**

*Nilo*, II, 96 r.; *Paguera*, III, 247 r.; *San Valentín*, III, 158 r.; *Hostal Villa Font*, P I, 54 r.

BAÑALBUFAR: *Hostal Mary Vent*, P I, 15 r.

DEYÁ: *Es Moli*, I, 73 r.

SÓLLER: *Esplendido*, II, 104 r.; *Eden Park* (no rest.), II, 64 r.; *Porto Sóller*, III, 127 r.; *Hostal Es Port*, PI, 96 r.

PUERTO DE POLLENSA: *Pollensa Park*, II, 316 r.; *Illa d'Or*, II, 119 r.; *Uyal*, II, 105 r.; *Pollentia*, II, 70 r.; *Miramar*, II, 69 r.

CALA SAN VICENTE: *Molíns*, I, 90 r.; *Don Pedro*, II, 136 r.; *Simar*, II, 107 r.; *Cala San Vicente*, II, 44 r.

ON CABO FORMENTOR: * *Formentor*, L, 131 r., SP.

CA'N PICAFORT: *Exagon*, II, 285 r.; *Gran Vista*, II, 277 r.; *Clumba Mar*, II, 235 r.; *Tonga-Sol*, III, 322 r.; *Son Baulo*, IV, 251 r.; *Haiti*, IV, 234 r.

PORTO CRISTO: *Drach*, III, 70 r.; *Son Moro*, IV, 120 r.

CALA MILLOR: *Sumba*, II, 280 r.; *Playa Cala Millor*, II, 242 r.; *Flamenco*, II, 220 r.; *Borneo*, II, 200 r.

CALA RATJADA: *Lux*, II, 236 r.; *Aguait*, II, 188 r.; *Bella Playa*, II, 143 r.; *Son Moll*, II, 118 r.; *Carolina*, III, 198 r.; *Clumba*, III, 120 r.; *Regana*, III, 126 r.; *Na Taconera*, III, 120 r.

LLUCHMAYOR: *Maioris Palm*, I, 240 r.

CALA D'OR: *Tucan*, I, 155 r.; *Cala Esmeralda*, I, 151 r.; *Corfu*, II, 214 r.; *Rocamarina*, II, 207 r.; *Skorpios Playa*, II, 163 r.; *Centro*, II, 105 r.; *Costa del Sur*, II, 102 r.; *Robinson Club Cala Serena*, 202 r.

EVENTS. – *Los Reyes Magos* (January), in honor of the Three Kings, with presents for children. – *Semana Santa* (Holy Week), celebrated in many towns and villages, with impressive religious processions. – *Corpus Christi.* – *Fiesta San Pedro y San Pablo* (SS. Peter and Paul). – *Fiesta de Santiago*, in honor of St James, patron saint of Spain. – *Festival de Música* (August) in Pollensa. – *Moros y Cristianos* (August), the fighting between Moors and Christians, celebrated in many places. – *Día de la Hispanidad* (October). – *Dijous Bó* (November): "Good Thursday" in Inca, with agricultural show. – *Inmaculada Concepción* (December), with local celebrations.

**Casino:** *Casino Sporting Club Mallorca*, in Urbanización Sol de Mallorca, Magalluf.

BOAT SERVICES. – *Ferry services* from Barcelona, Valencia and Alicante (several times weekly) to Palma de Mallorca; also from Marseilles (France) and Algiers (Algeria) to Palma. – Within the Balearics there are ferry services between Puerto de Alcudia and Ciudadela or Mahón (Minorca) and Ibiza; also boat services (passengers only, no cars) between the islands.

**The largest of the Balearic Islands and the one which attracts the greatest numbers of visitors is ** Majorca (in Spanish Mallorca). The island is bounded on the NW by the Sierra del Norte, a long wooded range with peaks rising to 4741 ft/ 1445 m, and on the E by the much** lower Sierra de Levante, with hills of up to 1844 ft/562 m in height. Between the two ranges is an area of plain, deeply indented in the NE by the bays of Alcudia and Pollensa and in the SW by Palma Bay. The fields and fruit orchards on this plain are supplied with water by the characteristic local windmills.

Majorca (from Latin *Majorica:* i.e. the "larger" Balearic island) has, rather unfairly, tended to acquire a bad name as a land of mass tourism and overcrowded resorts. It is true that during the summer season some of the island's beaches and bays, flanked by huge hotels, are overrun with visitors; but Majorca still preserves, in the varied scenery of its inland regions and the remoter stretches of its coasts, the incomparable natural beauties which have attracted so many writers, artists and other creative minds. Visitors who break away from the most frequented tourist resorts and set out to explore the rest of the island – an exploration facilitated by Majorca's excellent roads, public transport and the ready availability of car rental – will find an abundance of artistic and historical interest as well as scenic beauty to reward the effort.

# Palma de Mallorca (Ciutat)

Palma, capital of Majorca and of the Spanish province of Baleares (Balearics), is picturesquely situated on the * Bahía de Palma (Palma Bay), which reaches some $12\frac{1}{2}$ miles/20 km into the SW coast of the island. This important Mediterranean port is a lively modern city of over 300,000

Palma de Mallorca

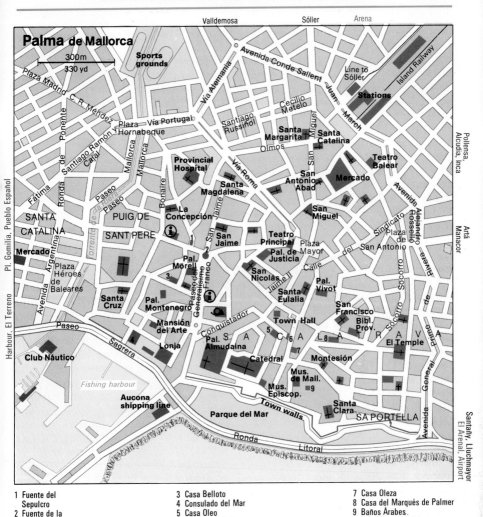

1 Fuente del Sepulcro
2 Fuente de la Princesa
3 Casa Belloto
4 Consulado del Mar
5 Casa Oleo
6 Almudaína Arch
7 Casa Oleza
8 Casa del Marqués de Palmer
9 Baños Árabes (Casa Font y Roig)

inhabitants (including many foreigners; about a third of the natives are Chuètas, i.e. originally of Jewish descent) which has grown far beyond its old boundaries. It is both the economic center (commerce, banking, industry and craft production) and the cultural focus (higher educational establishments and technical colleges, scientific institutes, artistic activities, literary circles; see of a bishop) of the Balearics and Pityusas (Ibiza and Formentera).

By the *Old Harbor* stands the palatial *Lonja, the old Stock Exchange (15th c.), with rich sculptural decoration. Adjoining it is the *Consulado del Mar*. A short distance away in Calle de Apuntadores, to the N, is the *Mansión del Arte* (House of Art), with a collection which includes all Goya's etchings in original prints and works by Picasso. – From the harbor the Avenida Antonio Maura leads to the *Cathedral or Seo, standing on higher

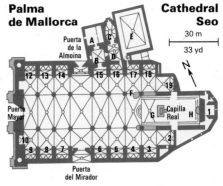

Palma de Mallorca
Cathedral Seo

30 m
33 yd

A Casa de la Almoina
B Tower
C New Chapter House
D Old Chapter House
E Cloister
F Pulpit
G Choir
H Bishop's throne

CHAPELS (Capillas)
1 Trinidad (sarcophagi)
2 San Pedro
3 San Antonio de Padua
4 Nuestra Señora de la Corona
5 San Martin
6 San Bernardo
7 Nuestra Señora de la Grada
8 Santa Corazón de Jesús
9 San Benito
10 Baptisterio
11 Almas (Animas)
12 Purísima
13 San Sebastián
14 San José
15 Todos los Santos
16 Piedad (above, organ)
17 Santo Cristo
18 San Jerónimo
19 Corpus Christi

ground. This magnificent building was begun in 1230 in Early Gothic style but not completed until the 17th c. Notable features are the W front with a fine rose-window (renewed in the 19th c.) and the richly decorated S doorway (14th c.), from which there is a magnificent *view. The interior (395 ft/120 m long, 185 ft/56 m wide, 145 ft/44 m high) has good stained glass and richly furnished chapels; the Old Sacristy contains a valuable collection of relics. Built on to the massive tower is the Gothic *Casa de la Almoina*. Immediately E of the Cathedral is the *Bishop's Palace* (1616), with the interesting *Diocesan Museum*.

Facing the Cathedral, to the W, we see the **Palacio de la Almudaina**, formerly the seat of the Moorish governors and the Christian kings. In the S wing is the *Museum of Art*, in the patio the Gothic *Capilla de Santa Ana*. – From the Plaza de la Reina the **Paseo del Borne**, the lively street which is Palma's main promenade, runs N, with many cafés and clubs and the *Palacio Morell* (1763). – From the N end of the Borne a street runs E to the *Theater* (1860; recently renovated). From here the tree-lined Vía Roma (Rambla) runs NW, with the *Plaza Mayor* (underground shopping center and car park) on higher ground at its SE end. From this square Calle San Miguel leads N to the Church of *San Miguel*, formerly a mosque. – SW of the Plaza Mayor is the Renaissance *Ayuntamiento* (Town Hall), and near this, to the E, are the Gothic churches of *Santa Eulalia* and *San Francisco* (1281–1317). San Francisco has a Plateresque-Baroque doorway, a charming Late Gothic cloister and the tomb of the medieval scholar Ramón Llull (1232–1315), who was born in Palma. Adjoining Santa Eulalia is the 18th c. *Palacio Vivot*.

EXCURSIONS FROM PALMA. – **To the Castillo de Bellver** (3 miles/5 km). – From the Lonja go W along the Paseo Maritimo and in ¾ mile/1 km turn right into Plaza Puente, continuing along Calle Andrea Doria to the *Pueblo Español* (Spanish Village, with reproductions of characteristic Spanish buildings; admission charge), in the villa suburb of *El Terreno*; then skirt the Parque de Bellver to reach the well-preserved *Castillo de Bellver** (alt. 427 ft/130 m), a royal castle dating from the 13th c., with a museum, an arcaded patio and a tower from which there are extensive views.

**To El Arenal** (7½ miles/12 km; bus service). – Two routes: either take the motorway to the airport and in 4½ miles/7 km turn right into the coast road, or leave on the coast road, passing the beaches of *Ciudad Jardín* and *Ca'n Pastilla*. The resort of **El Arenal** (pop. 400), with a beautiful beach on the sheltered E side of Palma Bay, is an extensive complex of hotels, with excellent entertainment, sport and shopping facilities – a good place for extended winter holidays.

**Circuit via Andraitx and Sóller** (76 miles/122 km; narrow-gauge railway to Sóller, 55 minutes, 4–5 trains daily). – Go W from Palma along the much-indented S coast with its many hotels and villas, passing below the Castillo de Bellver and through a series of suburbs with popular beaches – *Cala Mayor, Illetas, Bendinat* and *Palma Nova* (1¼ miles/2 km S of which is the *Playa de Magaluf*). The road then turns inland. – 12½ miles/20 km: road on the left to the picturesque bay of *Santa Ponsa*, with many beaches. – 2 miles/3 km: *Paguera*, with a beautiful beach. – 4½ miles/7 km: **Andraitx** (Majorcan *Andratx*), a finely situated little town (pop. 5000), 3 miles/4·5 km SW of which is the little harbor of *Puerto de Andratx*. – The road continues N at some distance from the coast, bypassing the western tip of the island, and traverses the coastal hills. Then follows a magnificent stretch of road above the steep NW coast, with a number of good viewpoints (*miradores*), to the village of *Estellencs* (Majorcan *Estallencs*). – 15 miles/25 km: *Bañalbufar* (Majorcan *Banyalbufar*), a village famous for its wine. – The road continues high above the sea. – 9 miles/15 km: **Valldemosa** (alt. 1395 ft/425 m), a beautifully situated hillside village dominated by the *Cartuja*

Cala Fornells, on Majorca's SW coast

(Charterhouse), founded in 1339 (now a museum), in which Chopin and the French novelist George Sand spent the winter of 1838–39 (see her account of their stay, "Un hiver à Majorque"). – The continuation of the coast road toward Sóller affords further superb views. – 3½ miles/5·5 km: on the left, the large apartment hotel of *El Encira*, with fine *views from a pavilion beyond it. Below the road on the left is the country house of *Miramar* (privately owned; brief conducted tour), built by the Austrian Archduke Ludwig Salvator (1847–1915), set in a large English-style park with cottages, marble temples and a chapel. – The road continues above the rocky coast, with extensive views. – 3 miles/5 km: **Deyá** (Majorcan *Deiá*; alt. 605 ft/185 m), a picturesque village, charmingly situated amid orange groves on the hillside, which attracts many artists. – 7 miles/11 km: **Sóller** (alt. 180 ft/55 m), a town of 12,000 inhabitants and a popular tourist center in a beautiful valley and surrounded by groves of oranges and lemons. 2½ miles/4 km N (tram from Sóller) are the harbor and beach of *Puerto de Sóller.* – The return to Palma is on a road which climbs S through a rocky valley, with many turns. – 5 miles/8 km: *Coll de Sóller* (1844 ft/562 m; views). Beyond the pass the road descends into the plain. – 5 miles/ 8 km: to the left, the *Alfabia Gardens* (admission charge). – 9 miles/14 km: **Palma**.

*From Sóller to Cabo Formentor** (51 miles/82 km). – Take the Puerto de Sóller road and in 1¼ miles/2 km turn right into a road which climbs through magnificent *scenery, passes a side road to the picturesque hill village of *Fornalutx* and continues uphill with many turns and extensive views (on the left, at the Bellavista Restaurant, the *Mirador de Ses Barques*). It then runs through a 660 yd/ 600 m long tunnel (alt. 2690 ft/820 m) and past a small reservoir, and descends slightly. – 10½ miles/17 km: *Son Torrella* (barracks), below the S side of **Puig Mayor** (pronounced *pooch*), the island's highest peak (4767 ft/1453 m; restricted military area). – The road continues past the *Gorch Blau* Reservoir and through another tunnel. – 4½ miles/7 km beyond Son Torrella a road known as *La Calobra* (The Snake) branches off on the left, crosses a hill and then winds its way down to the coastal hamlet of *La Calobra*, 9 miles/14 km N near a rocky gorge, the

Cala San Vicente, on the N coast of Majorca

*Torrente de Pareis* (rewarding walk, 2 hours). – In another 2 miles/3 km the main road reaches the *Mirador del Torrente de Pareis* (viewpoint, 2179 ft/ 664 m; refreshments). – 4½ miles/7 km farther on a road goes off on the left (¾ mile/1 km) to the hamlet of **Lluch** (pilgrimage church, museum, restaurant). – The road continues through karstic landscape and descends to the plain. – 12 miles/19 km: **Pollensa** (Majorcan *Pollença*; alt. 230 ft/70 m), a finely situated little town of 9000 inhabitants and a good center from which to explore the surrounding area (panoramic views from Calvary, reached by a flight of 365 steps). – 1¼ miles/2 km beyond Pollensa a road on the left (2½ miles/4 km) leads to the little resort of *Cala San Vicente* (Majorcan Sant Vicenç), magnificently situated in a rocky bay, with a good sandy beach. – 2½ miles/4 km: *Puerto de Pollensa*, a little port and seaside resort, beautifully set in the *Bahía de Pollensa.* – From here a boldly engineered *road (tunnels; fine viewpoints) runs along the Formentor Peninsula, much of which is wooded. – 6 miles/10 km: road on right (550 yds/500 m) to the *Hotel Formentor*, superbly situated above the sea. – From here it is another 7 miles/11 km to **Cabo Formentor** (alt. 620 ft/189 m), with a lighthouse 65 ft/20 m high (far-ranging views).

**From Palma to Alcudia** (34 miles/ 54 km). – The road runs NE through the huerta by way of *Santa María.* – 18 miles/ 29 km: *Inca* (alt. 125 ft/38 m), an old town of 18,000 inhabitants (bypass). – 8 miles/ 13 km: good road on left to Pollensa (10½ miles/17 km). – 7½ miles/12 km: **Alcudia** (alt. 30 ft/9 m), an old-world little port town (pop. 4000), prettily situated on the bay of the same name, with well-preserved 14th c. walls. To the W are the remains of a Roman amphitheater. 1¼ miles/2 km SE of the town center is *Puerto de Alcudia*, with a broad sandy beach extending around the bay for some 6 miles/10 km to the resort of *Ca'n Picafort*. – 5 miles/8 km NW of Alcudia (broad coast road) is *Puerto de Pollensa*.

**From Palma to the* stalactitic caves on the E coast** (about 60 miles/100 km). – Leave Palma by way of Plaza de San Antonio on a road which crosses the fertile plain. – 31 miles/50 km: **Manacor** (alt. 360 ft/110 m), an old town of 20,000 inhabitants (bypass) noted for the manufacture of artificial pearls. 9 miles/14 km S is the pottery-making town of *Felanitx* (pop. 12,000), from which a road leads (3 miles/5 km) to a pilgrimage chapel (1348) on the Hill of *San Salvador* (1670 ft/509 m; extensive* views in all directions from the tower of the chapel). A short distance S is the 13th c. *Castillo de Santueri*, on a rocky crag. – 7 miles/11 km E of Manacor lies the attractively situated little port and resort of **Porto Cristo**, ¾ mile/1 km S of which are the* **Cuevas del Drach** (Dragon's Caves; conducted tour 1½ hours), with crystal-clear lakes (concerts). 1 mile/1·5 km W of Porto Cristo are the *Cuevas dels Hams* (stalactites and stalagmites, colorfully floodlit; conducted tour 30 minutes). 3 miles/5 km N of Porto Cristo we come to the *Reserva Africana** (established 1969), an acclimatization and breeding reserve for large African animals (2½ mile/4 km long "photo safari" in visitors' own cars or in safari bus between 9 a.m. and 7 or 5 p.m.; admission charge). 7 miles/11 km NE of Porto Cristo in the Bahía de Artá is the hotel colony of **Cala Millor**. – The main road continues 13 miles/21 km NE from Manacor to the picturesque little town of **Artá** (alt. 560 ft/170 m; pop. 6000), from which a road runs NE via **Capdepera** (old fortifications; 4 miles/6 km N the beautiful sandy beach of *Cala Mezquida*) to the resort of **Cala Ratjada** (7 miles/11 km), charmingly situated amid pine woods (fine views from lighthouse), and another road runs SE (6 miles/10 km) to the *Cuevas de Artá** (conducted tour, 1 hour), situated on the sea, which are famous for long stalactites.

**From Palma to Santañy** (31 miles/ 50 km). – The road runs SE over the huerta and then enters a hilly region. – 15 miles/ 24 km: **Lluchmayor** (Majorcan *Lluc-mayor*), an old-world little country town of 11,000 inhabitants. 3 miles/5 km N is the *Puig de Randa* (1798 ft/548 m; extensive views), with the* *Ermita N.S. de la Cura*, which ranks with Lluch as one of Majorca's two principal pilgrimage centers. – From Lluchmayor a rewarding detour can be made to** **Capicorp Vey** (Majorcan *Capocorp Vell*), to the S. Here a short distance SE of the estate of *Capicorp* (admission charge; conducted tour), are remains of a settlement of the pre-talayot period (1000–800 B.C.), together with five talayots (stone-built towers). In the past the site was used as a convenient quarry of stone. – 8 miles/ 13 km: *Campos*. 8 miles/13 km: **Santañy** (Majorcan *Santanyi*; alt. 200 ft/60 m), a town of 5000 inhabitants near which are remains of prehistoric cult sites and fortifications. 7½ miles/12 km NE are the **Playa de Cala d'Or** and the *Playa Serena*, both with sandy bays. – 8 miles/ 13 km S of Santañy is the *Cabo de Salinas* (lighthouse).

10 miles/16 km SW of the southernmost point on Majorca, Cabo Salinas, and 35 miles/56 km SE of Palma, in latitude 39° 13' N and between longitude 6° 36' and 6° 40' E, is a small archipelago consisting of the main island of **Cabrera**, the uninhabited islands of **Conejera** (*Conillera*, Rabbit Island; also many lizards) and **Foradada** (lighthouse), to the N, and a number of small rocky islets. – The island of Cabrera is broken up by several irregularly shaped inlets. It has a total area of 6½ sq. miles/17 sq. km and maximum dimensions of 3–4½ miles/5–7 km. As a result of many years of over-grazing by goats which have reverted to the wild, this hilly island has been much eroded by karstic action, and large areas are covered with low cushions of rosemary.

There is nothing much to see on Cabrera, and in any case most of the island is a closed military area and it can offer no accommodation and little food. But visitors with their own boat will find in the harbour and in the inlets around the island sheltered anchorages and crystal-clear water for swimming, diving and fishing, as well as stretches of sandy beach at *Ganduf* (NW coast) and *Olla* (E coast) and at some points along the harbor pier.

The few non-military inhabitants of the island live in modest houses near the **Puerto de Cabrera**, a roughly circular natural harbor which is the most sheltered harbor in the Balearics after Mahón (Minorca), with an entrance only 360 yds/330 m wide.

During the several hours which the regular inter-island boat spends in harbor visitors can climb up on a steep and stony path to the ruined *Castillo* of the 14th–15th c. (caution required: crumbling walls, dangerous holes), near which are a small *seamen's cemetery* and a Guardia Civil post. From the castle and the rocky summit of the hill there are fine *views of the harbor, much of the island, several creeks and, to the N, Majorca. – On the small Peninsula of *Punta Anciola* to the SW, fringed by steep cliffs, is an important *lighthouse*.

In the center of the island (not at present accessible) is a stone *obelisk* erected in 1847–48 to commemorate the French prisoners of war who met a miserable end on Cabrera after the Battle of Bailén in 1808. It bears the inscription:

A la mémoire
des Français morts
à Cabrera
L'Escadre d'evolutions
de 1847
commandée par
S.A.R.
le Prince de Joinville

During the summer there are boat trips to the *Cueva Azul* (*Cova Blava*), 20 minutes' sail N of the harbor. This Blue Grotto, the most fascinating of the caves on Cabrera, can be reached only from the sea. The wide entrance leads into a high chamber measuring some 165 ft/50 m by 525 ft/160 m, shimmering with a bluish light.

See also *Minorca, p. 138; *Ibiza, p. 96; and **Formentera**, p. 91.

# Malta
*Republic of Malta*
*Repubblika ta' Malta*

Nationality letter: M.
Area: 122 sq. miles/315·6 sq. km.
Capital: Valletta.
Population: 340,000.
Religion: Roman Catholic (98%); Protestant and
     Jewish minorities.
Language: Maltese; English; some Italian.
Currency: Maltese pound (£M) of 100 cents.
Time: Central European (1 hour ahead of GMT).
Weekly day of rest: Sunday.
Travel documents: passport.
Traffic goes on left.

(i) **National Tourist Organization,**
     Harper Lane, Floriana;
     tel. 2 44 44.
**Malta Tourist Information,**
1 Citygate Arcade, Valletta;
tel. 2 77 47.
**Malta Government Tourist Office,**
Malta House,
24 Haymarket,
**London** SW1Y 4DJ;
tel. (01) 930 9851–5.
**Air Malta,**
285 Republic Street, Valletta;
tel. 2 12 07, 2 68 19.
**Air Malta,**
23–24 Pall Mall,
London SW1Y 5LP;
tel. (01) 839 5873–4, 930 2612–7.

DIPLOMATIC MISSIONS. – *United Kingdom*: High Commission, 7 St Anne Street, Floriana, tel. 2 12 85–87. – *United States*: Embassy, Development House (second floor), St Anne Street, Floriana, tel. 62 36 53, 62 04 24, 62 32 16.

**The independent State of Malta, a Republic within the British Commonwealth consisting of the main island of Malta (area 95 sq. miles/246 sq. km), the adjoining islands of Gozo (26 sq. miles/67 sq. km) and Comino (1 sq. mile/2·6 sq. km) and the uninhabited rocky islets of Cominotto, Filfla and Selmunett, lies in the Central Mediterranean at the E end of the Sicilian Channel, 60 miles/93 km from the southern tip of Sicily and 180 miles/288 km from the Tunisian coast to the W. The islands extend from NW to SE for a distance of some 27 miles/44 km, rising to a maximum height of 830 ft/253 m. The *Maltese Islands are the last remains of a land bridge which during the Late Tertiary era and the Glacial periods of the Pleistocene linked Sicily with North Africa and divided the Mediterranean into two.**

On the main island, **Malta**, the land rises in stages from NE to SW. In the E is a region of gently rolling hills never rising above 330 ft/100 m, which in the W, along a clearly marked fault line, gives place to a plateau of Tertiary limestones, much broken up by karstic action and reaching its highest points along the W coast. On the E side of the island there are a number of excellent natural harbors – drowned river valleys – while the W coast, edged by sheer cliffs, offers little shelter to shipping. The cultivable land is mostly in the larger basins in the eastern half of the island, and it is in these areas that the main concentrations of population and economic activity have developed.

The neighboring island of **Gozo** is separated from Malta by a channel some 3 miles/5 km wide, divided into two (the North Comino Channel and the South Comino Channel) by the little island of Comino. Like Malta, Gozo rises gradually toward the SW, though here the limestone hills are lower and the cliffs on the SW coast are correspondingly less formidable. The NE coast, with few indentations, has no natural harbors like those of the main island.

CLIMATE. – The Maltese Archipelago has a characteristically Mediterranean climate. During the summer it lies wholly within the subtropical belt of high pressure, but in winter this withdraws southward, so that during this period the whole of the Mediterranean may be reached by sub-polar troughs of low pressure. Accordingly the summers are hot and dry, while the winters are mild but rainy. In July the average temperature is 81 °F/27 °C; in January it is still as high

as 54.5 °F/12.5 °C. Frost is unknown on the islands. Most of the annual rainfall of barely 23.6 in./600 mm occurs in November and December; the month of lowest rainfall is July. From April to September the Maltese climate can be classed as arid: i.e. the total rainfall is less than the loss of moisture by evaporation.

**VEGETATION.** – The typically Mediterranean evergreen scrub known as macchia or garrigue is found all over Malta. Among its principal constituents are spurges, feathergrass, thyme, heaths, juniper and pistachio, which in the rainy spring period cover the ground with a carpet of flowers. The garrigue has replaced the original forest cover. About 900 B.C. the islands were still covered with trees, which provided the Phoenicians and Carthaginians with timber for shipbuilding. The destruction of the forests led to a sharp fall in the moisture content of the soil and to increased erosion – two factors which have greatly reduced the agricultural potential of the land. Characteristic elements in the vegetation of Malta apart from the macchia are other warmth-loving plants such as the carob tree, Aleppo pine, prickly pear, agave and oleander. These were introduced by man over the centuries, as was the olive, which was supplanted during the 19th c. by the more profitable cultivation of cotton.

**HISTORY.** – The Maltese Islands were inhabited by man during the Neolithic period, the oldest traces of settlement having been found in the small Cave of Ghar Dalam. The first radiocarbon determinations gave a date of about 3800 B.C., but more recent investigations indicate that the material found in the cave must be almost 7000 years old. A thousand years later, by about 4000 B.C., the original inhabitants, who are believed to have come from Sicily and the Aeolian Islands and who practiced agriculture and stock-farming, had developed an astonishingly advanced culture, building monumental megalithic temples and producing pottery notable for its beauty of form, unexampled anywhere else in western Europe. About

3000 B.C., however, this megalithic culture suddenly collapsed at the very peak of its achievement, presumably as a result of some unrecorded natural catastrophe. Some 600 years later, about 2400 B.C., Bronze Age peoples from Sicily and the Peloponnese came to Malta. War, which had been unknown to their predecessors, now played a part in their lives, and they built the islands' first fortifications to provide defense against attack from the sea.

In the 9th c. B.C. the **Phoenicians** established a colony and an important trading-post on Malta, giving it the name of *Melite*. Thereafter the islands, lying at the intersection of the shortest route between Sicily and Carthage in North Africa with the seaways between the countries of the Eastern Mediterranean and the Strait of Gibraltar, occupied a position of great political and strategic importance – as indeed they still do. The **Greeks** tried unsuccessfully to gain control of Malta in order to strengthen the position of the colonies they had founded in Sicily in the 8th and 7th c. What they failed to do was soon afterward achieved by the **Carthaginians**, who occupied the islands about 600 B.C. and held on to them until the outbreak of the Second Punic War (218 B.C.). They were then conquered by Titus Sempronius for **Rome**. Although Roman rule lasted for almost a thousand years and the people of Malta achieved a high degree of prosperity during this period, it has left surprisingly little in the way of architectural and artistic remains.

When the Roman Empire was split into two in A.D. 395 the Maltese Islands fell to the Byzantine (East Roman) Empire. In 429, however, they were apparently captured by the Vandals under Genseric. In 494 the Vandals were succeeded by the **Ostrogoths** under Theodoric; but 39 years later, in 533, the islands were recovered by the **Byzantines**. In 870 they were taken by the **Arabs** (Aghlabites). Although the Arabs held Malta for only 221 years they left an enduring mark on its language and culture. The present-day Maltese language consists of a mixture of various North

African dialects of Arabic with the addition, in terms of vocabulary, of bits and pieces taken over from Sicilian Italian and English. Many place-names and family names still recall the period of Arab rule, as do a variety of architectural details to be seen on Maltese buildings. The methods of irrigating the fields, which are strikingly similar to the methods used in Andalusia, also reflect Arab influence. Unfortunately, however, practically no examples of Arab architecture have survived, since the Order of St John systematically destroyed all traces of "Saracen" activity in the 16th c.

The Arabs were succeeded in 1091 by the **Normans**, coming from Sicily, under Count Roger I de Hauteville. In 1194 their kingdom fell by inheritance to the **Hohenstaufens**, who lost it in 1268 to Charles of Anjou. In 1284 Charles was displaced by Peter of Aragon, taking over the inheritance of the Hohenstaufens. In 1412 the Maltese Islands fell to the Habsburgs by marriage; and in 1530 the Emperor Charles V granted them to the **Order of St John**, which had been expelled from Rhodes by the Turks. This was an event of decisive importance in the history of Malta, which now, for the first time since the Norman period, emerged from limbo and began to feature on the world stage. Its heroic resistance to the Turkish siege of 1565, which held back the western advance of Islam, made it famed throughout Europe. The Order of St John, also known as the **Knights of Malta**, now received large grants of money and property, with the help of which the new capital of Valletta (named after the then Grand Master, J. P. de la Valette) was founded in 1566 to the design of Francesco Laparelli, the most celebrated military engineer of the day. In the course of the next two centuries the Order of St John brought Malta unprecedented prosperity, far exceeding the splendors of earlier periods. During these years were erected the magnificent buildings which are still the glory of Malta.

The rule of the Knights was brought to an end by Napoleon in 1798 at the beginning of his Egyptian Expedition; for the Order, whose members were recruited from great noble families, was a thorn in the flesh of Revolutionary France. The irresolute German Grand Master, von Hompesch surrendered the islands without a fight after two days. Two years later, in 1880, the Maltese drove out the French with the help of a British fleet, and in 1814 the Maltese Archipelago was assigned to **Britain** under the First Treaty of Paris and became a Crown Colony. The islands were now developed into an important naval base. In 1921 Malta was granted limited self-government, and in 1947, after its heroic resistance to mass German and Italian air attacks during the Second World War, full self-government. Full independence was achieved in 1964, and since December 13, 1974 Malta has been a **Republic** within the British Commonwealth. The last British troops were withdrawn on March 31, 1979, under a treaty signed in 1972. – On September 15 1980 Italy and Malta signed a treaty guaranteeing the neutrality of the island republic.

**POPULATION.** – The average density of population in Malta is about 2720 to the sq. mile (1050 to the sq. km), making it, after Monaco and Vatican City, one of the most densely populated countries in Europe and in the world. The main concentration of population is on the NE coast of the main island, around its two natural harbors, Marsamxett and Grand Harbour, which are surrounded by a ring of small towns with a total population of some 113,000. The overwhelming majority of the inhabitants are Roman Catholics.

The two large harbors are separated by a long tongue of land (alt. 200 ft/60 m) which is occupied by the capital, Valletta. With a population of 14,000, it ranks only fourth in order of size among Malta's towns, coming after Sliema (20,000), Birkirkara (16,800) and Qormi (14,600). In the central harbor area the population density reaches a peak of 20,000 to the sq. mile 7700 to the sq. km, but this figure falls rapidly farther inland, reaching 5950 to the sq. mile (2300 to the sq. km) on the outskirts of the harbor area. In the

Beach at Golden Sands Hotel, Malta

Mġarr, Gozo

N of Malta, the most thinly populated part of the island, the density is only 746 to the sq. mile (288 to the sq. km), a figure comparable with that for Gozo and Comino (808 to the sq. mile or 312 to the sq. km).

**ECONOMY.** – The high population density has long given rise to economic difficulties, since for many years there have been insufficient jobs to provide employment for all those of working age. Since the country achieved independence the problems have become increasingly acute, for the British withdrawal has meant the loss of the work in British military installations which in 1955 gave employment to 29% of the working population. Over the years, therefore, there have been a number of great waves of emigration to Australia, Canada, Britain and the United States, and for many decades the population of Malta tended to decline in spite of a relatively high excess of births over death. In more recent years there had been a slight improvement in the trend, and the rate of unemployment had been brought down to some 2%; but the return of Maltese "guest workers" from other European countries and the loss of the last few thousand military jobs after the final British withdrawal in 1979 have once again aggravated Malta's problems.

Many of the workers who lost their jobs as a result of the phased British withdrawal were able to find employment in the former naval dockyard, now converted to civilian use, and in a number of other newly established industries. The largest employer of labor is the dry dock at Fort Ricasoli, with installations for cleaning out tankers which are among the most modern and most efficient in the world. In addition, thanks to investments of foreign capital, several tens of thousands of new jobs have been created in the foodstuffs, textile and chemical industries and in engineering, supplementing the traditional small-scale and craft industries. In recent years, too, there has been a remarkable development of folk arts and crafts, and Maltese lace and silver, for example, are

much bought by visitors. Many of the unemployed are enrolled in State-financed labor corps and employed in emergency and infrastructure programs.

Malta has some 37,000 acres/15,000 hectares of cultivable land, representing about half its total area. The limestone soils in the karstic terrain of western Malta and Gozo have been brought into cultivation by the addition of good soil and artificial irrigation (about 1630 acres/660 hectares). The only fully irrigated areas (totalling about 250 acres/100 hectares), however, are in the Il Ghadira and Pwales valleys. In these areas the yields are more than double those achieved in the dry farming areas, since it is possible to take three crops a year with the help of irrigation. But the total area of cultivable land, irrigated and unirrigated, falls far short of what is required to feed the population of Malta; and antiquated farming methods, the fragmentation of holdings and lack of water for irrigation militate against any expansion of agricultural production. Some three-quarters of Malta's food-supply, therefore, has to be imported. The main Maltese products are wheat, barley, oil, carobs, vegetables, tomatoes and tobacco, together with figs and citrus fruits. The principal exports are early potatoes, wine grapes and garden produce.

Malta has an excellent network of roads, radiating from the Valletta area and from the town of Victoria on Gozo. There are no railways on the islands. There are, however, bus services from these two central points to almost every village in the country. Farther away from the centers, it is true, connections between the radial roads are sometimes lacking, so that to get from one peripheral village to another may involve a rather roundabout journey. The thinly populated areas in the W and SW are poorly served by roads. – Between Malta and Gozo there are two good and rapid ferry services, from Marfa to Mġarr and from Valletta to Mġarr (hydrofoil). International shipping traffic mostly uses the Grand Harbour of Valletta, which can take vessels of any size. There are also ferry services from Valletta to Catania, Syracuse, Reggio di Calabria and Naples, as well as to Libya, the main customer for Malta's exports.

The international airport at Luqa, 4½ miles/7 km SW of Valletta, is used by a number of airlines, and there are regular connections, mainly flown by Air Malta, with Britain, Austria, Switzerland, West Germany, Italy, Tunisia and Libya. Luqa Airport has gained increased importance with the rapid growth of the tourist trade, a welcome source of the foreign exchange which Malta so urgently requires. The Government has accordingly made great efforts to foster the development of tourism; and the successful marketing of Malta's mild and healthy climate and its monuments of the Neolithic period and the period of the Knights brought in 12% of the country's gross national product in 1975 and is likely to earn even more as a result of the increase in hotel capacity over the last few years.

THE MAIN ISLAND. – The part of Malta holding most interest for tourists is the **Valletta** area (see p. 195) with its historical associations and its many remains of the past. From here, however, it is easy to visit the rest of the archipelago, which also offers many sights of first-rate importance which no visitor to Malta should miss, especially the former Maltese capital of **Mdina** (pop. 930), picturesquely situated on a hill in the SW of the island – a place which the modern age seems to have passed by. There was a town here in ancient times, under the name of *Melite*. The Carthaginians and the

Romans were followed by the Arabs, who gave the town its present name. The construction of fortifications divided the town into two, and the part outside the walls developed into what is now the modern town of *Rabat*. The new masters who came to Malta from Sicily in 1427 renamed Mdina *Notabile*, a style which it bore only for a brief period. Under the Knights of St John Mdina rapidly lost its former importance, and its function as capital passed to Birgu (now Vittoriosa) and later to Valletta. The main features of interest in Mdina are the Baroque Cathedral designed by Lorenzo Gafà, with its treasures of art, the Baroque Seminary which now houses the Cathedral Museum, the Archbishop's Palace (1733), the Palazzo Santa Sophia and the Palazzo Falzon.

**Rabat** (pop. 12,000) has a Roman villa discovered in 1881, with a beautiful mosaic pavement; two Early Christian burial-places, St Paul's Catacombs and St Agatha's Catacombs; and St Paul's Church, built over the prison in which the Apostle was confined after his shipwreck off Malta in A.D. 60.

The town of **Mosta** (pop. 8500), NE of Mdina, is worth seeing for the sake of its

Characteristic houses and boats, Marsaxlokk

Neo-Classical Cathedral (by Grognet, 1833–63), with a dome which is one of the largest in the world. – In south-eastern Malta lies the picturesque fishing village of *Marsaxlokk* (pop. 1200), near which is the famous *Ghar Dalam Cave*, where the earliest evidence of Neolithic settlement on Malta was found. – Two other major sights are the prehistoric temples of *Hagar Qim and *Mnajdra, on the S coast. – Also of great interest are the enigmatic "cart-ruts" which criss-cross the higher parts of the western plateau like railway lines. Particularly striking examples are to be seen near the Dingli Cliffs. It is now known that these tracks were worn in the soft limestone by the runners of sleds used by the Bronze Age inhabitants of Malta and Gozo as a means of transport.

The best beaches for tourists on the main island of Malta are in the northern part of the **Valletta** area (see p. 195), in **St Paul's Bay**, scene of the Apostle's shipwreck, and in **Mellieha Bay** and the neighboring *Slug Bay*. Less well known are the beaches in *Anchor Bay* (NW coast), *Golden Bay* and around *Marfa* at the NW tip of the island.

GOZO. – It is well worth while making the trip to the smaller island of *Gozo (ferry from Marfa, 20 minutes), the history of which is bound up with that of the main island. At **Xaghra** is the most impressive Neolithic temple in the whole of the Maltese Archipelago, known as the **Ġgantija (Place of Giants) from the massiveness of the stones used in its construction. It dates from about 3600 B.C.

The chief place on Gozo is **Victoria** (pop. 6800), which has a handsome Cathedral (1697) built by Lorenzo Gafà. St George's Church has a number of pictures by Mattia Preti (1613–99). The Gozo Museum contains an interesting collection of antiquities found on the island.

# Marsala
## See under Sicily

# Melos (Mílos)
## See under Cyclades

# Messina

Italy
Region: Sicily. – Province: Messina.
Altitude: 0–16 ft/0–5 m. – Population: 250,000.
Post code: I-98100. – Telephone code: 090.
(i) **AAS,**
Via G. Bruno 121;
tel. 3 64 94.
**EPT,**
Via Calabria;
tel. 77 53 56.
*Information Office* at station;
tel. 77 53 35.
**ACI,**
Via L. Manara 125;
tel. 3 30 31.

HOTELS. – *Riviera Grand,* Via della Libertà, Isolato 516, I, 265 b.; *Jolly Hotel dello Stretto,* Via Garibaldi 126, I, 150 b.; *Royal,* Via Tommaso Cannizzaro, II, 166 b.; *Venezia,* Piazza Cairoli 4, II, 136 b.; *Excelsior,* Via Maddalena 32, II, 71 b.; *Monza,* Viale San Martino 63, III, 93 b.; *Commercio,* Via 1 Settembre 73, III, 90 b. – *Europa* (in Pistunina, 4 miles/6 km S), II, 186 b.

EVENTS. – *Fiera di Messina* (industrial, agricultural and craft fair), August.

**The active port of Messina, a university town and the see of an archbishop, lies near the NE tip of Sicily on the busy *Strait of Messina (the bridging of which is planned), with its western districts extending picturesquely along the foothills of the Monti Peloritani.**

After the great earthquake in 1908 which killed some 60,000 people – half the population – and destroyed 91% of its houses Messina was rebuilt with wide streets intersecting at right angles, and now presents the aspect of an entirely modern city.

HISTORY. – Messina was founded by Greek settlers about 730 B.C. on the site of an earlier Siculan settlement and named *Zankle* (Sickle) after the shape of the harbor. It was renamed *Messana* about 493 B.C., when it was occupied by Greek refugees from Samos and Miletus. It was destroyed by the Carthaginians in 396 B.C. and subsequently rebuilt, and became a Roman town in 264 B.C. – The town was captured by the Saracens in A.D. 843 and by the Normans in 1061. Under the Normans it enjoyed a long period of prosperity, which continued into the 17th c. under Spanish rule. Thereafter Messina suffered a rapid decline, due partly to internal conflicts but mainly to the town's bitter rivalry with Palermo, the process being hastened by a plague in 1740 and severe earthquakes, particularly in 1783. Its subsequent recovery was promoted by its favorable situation on one of the most important traffic routes in the Mediterranean.

SIGHTS. – From the Marine Station on the S side of the **Harbor** it is a short distance W to the northern end of the town's main

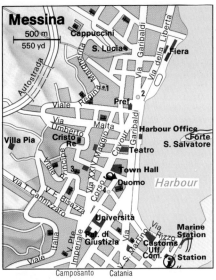

1 Osservatorio Meteorologico     3 Santuario di Montalto
2 Fontana di Nettuno              4 Fontana di Orione

A short distance SE of the Cathedral, in Corso Garibaldi, is the beautiful Norman Church of the **Santissima Annunziata dei Catalani** (12th c.; restored). Beside the church is a bronze *statue of Don John of Austria*, hero of the Battle of Lepanto (1571), by Andrea Calamech (1572).

NW of the Cathedral is the circular **Piazza Antonello**, with the *Palazzo della Provincia*, the *Town Hall* and the *Head Post Office*. From here Corso Cavour runs N, passing the *Teatro Vittorio Emanuele*, to the **Villa Mazzini** public gardens, on the N side of which stands the Prefecture. W of the gardens is the *Franciscan Church* (1254; rebuilt).

From the NE corner of the gardens the Viale della Libertà goes N past the halls of the Fiera di Messina and along the seafront (bathing establishments) to the **Museo Nazionale**, which contains material salvaged from the old Municipal Museum after the 1908 earthquake, together with sculpture and pictures from the hundred or so churches which were devastated at the same time. A particularly notable item (in Room II) is a *polyptych by Antonello da Messina (1479), the central panel of which depicts the Virgin Enthroned.

SURROUNDINGS of Messina. – There is a pleasant drive around Messina on the **Via della Circonvallazione**, which, under various names, describes a circuit above the W side of the city, passing the *Santuario di Montalto* (pilgrimage church) and the modern *Church of Cristo Rey*.

There is also a very attractive trip (35 miles/57 km) along the coast road, which runs NE, between villas and gardens (views), passes two salt-water lagoons, the *Pantano Grande* and *Pantano Piccolo* (also known as the *Laghi di Ganzirri*), and reaches the village of *Torre di Faro* on the *Punta del Faro*, Sicily's north-eastern tip (fine *view from the lighthouse). From Torre di Faro the coast road continues around the most northerly cape in Sicily; then the return to Messina is over the *Colle San Rizzo* (1526 ft/465 m).

street, Viale San Martino, which cuts through the southern part of the city. In 440 yds/400 m it crosses the tree-shaded **Piazza Cairoli**, Messina's busiest traffic intersection, and in another 1 mile/1·5 km leads into the spacious *Piazza Dante*, on the W side of which is the **Camposanto** (or *Cimitero*), one of Italy's most beautiful cemeteries, established in 1865–72. On top of the hill is an Ionic colonnade, the Pantheon of the town's leading citizens, from which there are fine *views of the city and the strait.

From Piazza Cairoli the broad Corso Garibaldi runs N. 1 mile/1·5 km along this street Via 1 Settembre leads left into the large Piazza del Duomo, the center of the old town, with the richly decorated *Orion Fountain* (1547–51) by Angelo Montorsoli, a pupil of Michelangelo. On the E side of the square, dominating the town, stands the **Cathedral**, originally built by Roger II in the 12th c., destroyed in 1908 and rebuilt in its original form in 1919–29, incorporating architectural fragments from the ruins, and again rebuilt after being damaged by fire in 1943. The interior is 305 ft/93 m long. In the apse is a beautiful mosaic, a reproduction of the 13th c. original which was destroyed in 1943. Adjoining the church is the 165 ft/50 m high *campanile* (1933), on the main front of which is an elaborate astronomical clock, with seven tiers and many moving figures. The lion, above, roars at 12 noon; the cock, below, crows. The clock was the work of the Strasburg clockmaker Ungerer.

# Meyisti (Kastellorizo)
See under Rhodes

# Mílos (Melos)
See under Cyclades

# Minorca/Menorca

**Spain**

Region and province: Baleares (Balearics).
Area: 265 sq. miles/686 sq. km. – Population:
50,000.

ⓘ **Oficina de Información y Turismo,**
Arco de San Roque,
**Mahón;**
tel. (971) 35 34 67.

HOTELS. – MAHÓN: *Port Mahón*, I, 74 r.; *Capri*, II,
75 r.

SON BOU: *Los Milanos*, II, 300 r.; *Los Pinguinos*, II,
300 r.

CIUDADELA: *Almirante Farragut*, II, 472 r.; *Cala'n
Bosch*, II, 169 r.; *Cala Blanca*, II, 147 r.; *Esmeralda*, II,
135 r.; *Cala Galdana*, III, 259 r.; *Cala'n Blanes*, III,
103 r.; *Los Delfines*, III, 96 r.

EVENTS. – *Semana Santa* (Holy Week), with an
impressive Good Friday procession in Mahón. –
*Fiestas de San Juan* (June) in Ciudadela, a striking
fiesta lasting several days, with a procession to the
Ermita de San Juan and riding contests in medieval
costume. – *Fiestas de San Martín* (July) in Mercadal,
with parades. – *Fiestas de San Jaime* (July) in
Villacarlos. – *Fiestas de San Lorenzo* (August) in
Alayor, with cavalcades of riders. – *Fiestas de Nuestra
Señora de Gracia* (September) in Mahón, with
traditional parades, festival of water sports, dance
festival, concerts and exhibitions.

BOAT SERVICES. – Car ferries to Mahón from
Barcelona and Palma de Mallorca and to Ciudadela
from Palma de Mallorca and Puerto de Alcudia
(Majorca).

**Some 25 miles NE of Majorca lies the
second largest of the Balearic Islands, \*Minorca, which attracts
visitors with its beautiful scenery,
many good beaches and a large
number of prehistoric remains. Its
highest point is Monte Toro (1181 ft/
360 m).**

Minorca (Spanish Menorca; Latin *Min-
orica*, the "smaller" of the Balearic
islands) is a quiet and unspoiled island
which has much of historical and artistic
interest to offer in addition to its beautiful
beaches. Particularly notable are its many
\*megalithic monuments – though the sites
of these are often difficult to find.

HISTORY. – Although Minorca has such an abundance of prehistoric remains (some 300 *talayots* or
stone-built round towers, 64 *navetas* or boat-shaped
chamber tombs and more than 30 *taulas* or T-shaped
stone structures) in an astonishingly good state of
preservation, nothing is known of events in this early
period. All that is known with certainty is that from
about 1000 B.C. Phoenicians and from about 800 B.C.
Phocaeans were visiting the island, which they knew
as *Nura* or *Melousa*, and trading with the farming
population. Much more intensive were the contacts
and the influence of the Carthaginians, who in the

3rd c. B.C. established on Minorca the military bases of
Jamma (Ciudadela) and Maghen (Mahón). With the
coming of the Romans in the 2nd c. B.C. we get the first
reliable accounts of the island, indicating that its
destinies were now closely bound up with those of the
larger sister island of Majorca. – From the 7th c. A.D.
Minorca was repeatedly harassed by Arab pirates, and
at the beginning of the 10th c. it fell wholly into the
hands of the Moors, who held on to it even after Jaime
I's conquest of Majorca in 1229. In 1287 Alfonso
recovered it for the Crown of Aragon, but the
inhabitants continued to suffer repeated raids by
bloodthirsty Moorish and Turkish corsairs. The period
of Arab rule, when the island was known as *Minûrga*,
has left its mark in many place-names incorporating
Arabic elements (Al, Bini, Rafal, etc.).

## Mahón

Mahón (or Port Mahón; Minorcan Maó or
Mahó; pop. 22,000), the attractive chief
town and port of Minorca, lies at the E end
of the island on a cliff-fringed table of rock
above the SW side of the **\*\*Puerto de
Mahón** (Minorcan Port de Maó), the
long inlet which reaches inland for some
3 miles/5 km, ranging in width between
330 and 1300 yds (300 and 1200 m), and
protected by various defense works. With
its strategically important situation, sheltered from wind and weather and easy to
defend, Mahón is perhaps the best natural
harbor in the whole of the Mediterranean,
and possession of it was hotly contested,
particularly during the 18th c. It is now a
Spanish naval base and quarantine station
and the most important commercial port
on the island. – Mahón can also claim to
have given *mayonnaise* (from *salsa
mahonesa*) to the world. It was discovered here by the French and thereafter
introduced to international cuisine.

SIGHTS. – From the harbor the winding
Rampa de la Abundancia and a stepped
lane flanked by gardens lead up to the
town. The ramp ends at the Plaza de
España and Plaza del Carmen (fish market), in which is the *Iglesia del Carmen*
(19th c.), originally the church of a
Carmelite convent now dissolved. The
cloisters now accommodate the *Market*.
To the NE, at the top of the stepped lane,
is the Plaza Miranda (\* viewpoint). – From
the Plaza de España the narrow Calle
Cristo leads into **Calle del General
Goded** (*Carrer Nou*), the town's principal
shopping street (pedestrian precinct),
which runs N into Plaza Franco. At the N
end of this square is the **Town Hall**
(*Ayuntamiento*; built 1613, rebuilt 1788),
on its E side the **Church of Santa
María**, founded by the Catalans in 1287

Although the quickest and easiest way to get to Mahón is by air, it is worth while arranging to arrive by sea for the sake of the magnificent sail up the fjord-like ** **Puerto de Mahón**. – The boat passes between the **Punta de San Carlos** (to the S; lighthouse), with the remains of the *Castillo de San Felipe*, and the **Cabo de la Mola** (to the N), with the *Fortaleza de Isabel II* (fortress and military prison), into the long inlet. Into this projects an elongated **Isla del Lazareto**, a peninsula which was transformed into an island in 1900 by the cutting of the Canal de Alfonso XIII (popularly known as the Canal de San Jordi). The buildings on the island are a convalescent home for staff of the Spanish Health Service. On the left are the coves of *Cala Pedrera*, *Cala Fons* (fishing harbor) and *Cala Corb*, and beyond these, above the shore, are the light-colored buildings of **Villa Carlos** (*Villacarlos*), founded in the 18th c. as a British military camp called Georgetown. – Opposite the N end of the Isla del Lazareto is the *Isla de la Cuarentena* or Isla Plana, the buildings on which were originally associated with the military hospital on the Isla del Lazareto. Beyond this point the inlet becomes wider, and on the right can be seen the *Cala Llonga*, fringed by holiday houses, and beyond this the *Cala de San Antonio*, with the landing-stage for the splendid Colonial-style mansion of *San Antonio* (Sant Antoni), known as the * **Golden Farm**, in which Nelson and Lady Hamilton stayed in 1799 and 1800. – The boat then sails past the **Isla del Rey** (formerly known as the *Isla de los Conejeros*), which was occupied by Alfonso III of Aragon in January 1287 and provided him with a base for the reconquest of Minorca. – Farther in, on the left, is the *Cala Figuera*, lined by quays and with a textile factory, and on the right the *Cala Rata*. – The boat then enters the inner harbor, the *Cala Serga*. On the right is the little *Isla Pinto* (submarine base), now linked with the mainland by a bridge; on the left the quays of the commercial harbor, with the picturesquely situated Upper Town of Mahón high above it.

and rebuilt in 1748–72 as an aisle-less hall-church in Neo-Classical style. It has a fine organ (3006 pipes), made in 1810 by the Swiss organ-builder Johannes Kiburz.

From Plaza Franco a narrow street runs E to Plaza Conquista, with a statue of Alfonso III of Aragon. On the N side of the square is the **Casa de la Cultura** (*museum*, library, archives). From the end of Calle del Punte del Castillo there is a good * view of the harbor.

From the Town Hall Calle de San Roque leads W to the **Puente de San Roque**, one of the old town gates (scanty remains of walls), and to Plaza Bastión. Then by way of Calle de San Bartolomé and Calle Cardona y Orfila to the **Ateneo** *Científico, Literario y Artístico* (founded 1905), with interesting natural history, prehistoric, historical and artistic collections. Beyond

this is the spacious Plaza del Ejército (Explanada). – From the Town Hall Calle Isabel II runs NW, past the Military Command Headquarters, to the **Church of San Francisco** (1719–92), which originally belonged to a Franciscan friary. From a viewpoint near the church there is a fine prospect of the harbor.

THE ISLAND. – 5 miles / 8 km NE of Mahón (private toll road from Sant Antoni) stands the **Cala Mezquida** (16th c. watch-tower), and 6 miles/10 km N the **Cala Grao** (near by, the new residential development of *Shangri-La*), two very beautiful coves on the E coast of the island.

From Mahón a road (6 miles/10 km) runs S by way of the village of **San Luis**, built by the French in 1756–63 (18th c. Parish Church, stumps of windmills; shoe manufacture), to the holiday area at the southern tip of Minorca. Here are the summer colonies of **S'Algar** (an attractive tourist village; no sandy beach), **Cala Alcaufar** (small and gently sloping beach, suitable for children), **Punta Prima** (flat sandy beach and rocky coast; good scuba-diving; offshore, the *Isla del Aire*, with a lighthouse), *Biniancolla* (rocky coast), * **Binibeca Vell** (an apartment village with traditional-style fishermen's houses; rocky beach), *Binisafúa* and *Cap d'en Font* (both with rocky coastline).

1 mile/1·5 km from Mahón on the road to the S a side road goes off on the left to the remains of the prehistoric settlement of **Trepucó** (excavated 1928–30), with a massive ** **taula** which is the largest and best preserved of its kind (base $13\frac{1}{2}$ ft/ 4·20 m high, 9 ft/2·75 m wide and 16 in./ 0·40 m thick; roof slab 11–12 ft/3·45– 3·65 m long, 59–63 in./1·50–1·60 m wide and 2 ft/0·60 m thick). Near by is a *talayot* (restored), surrounded by prehistoric dwellings.

From Mahón a good road runs SW to the international **airport** (on left, $2\frac{1}{2}$ miles/ 4 km) and continues past the *Talayot of Curnia* (on right) to a junction where a road goes off on the right to the excavated remains of an Early Christian Basilica at *Fornás de Torelló* (4th c.; fine mosaics); then on by way of the hamlet of *San Clemente* (3 miles/5 km) to the **Cala'n Porter** (6 miles/9 km; sandy beach). Above the cove is the *Cueva d'en Xoroi* (restaurant, bar), of which many legends are told; and to the E (unsurfaced side road from San Gabriel, 1¼ miles/2 km) is the *Cala Coves*, with many \***caves** hewn from the rock which are believed to have been inhabited in prehistoric times (*Cuevas Trogloditas*).

**From Mahón via Mercadal** (14 miles/23 km) **to Ciudadela** (29 miles/47 km) **or Fornells** (21 miles/33 km). – The main road along the center of the island runs W from Mahón. In 2 miles/3 km a dirt road goes off on the left to the prehistoric settlement of \**Talatí de D'Alt*, on the farm of that name (apply at the farm), with two fine *taulas* (the smaller one leaning against the larger one) within a well-preserved circuit of walls. – 3 miles/5 km farther on, off the road to the right, is the *Naveta of Rafal Rubí Nou*, one of the best preserved on the island. Soon afterward a road on the left (2 miles/3 km) leads to the *Taula of Torralba d'en Salort*. – 4 miles/6 km: **Alayor**, a little country town of whitewashed houses (vine-growing, charcoal-burning; shoe manufacture) under a ridge of hills, the administrative center of its district (pop. 5600). It has a massive parish church (Santa Eulalia, 1674–80) and another 17th c. church, San Diego, originally belonging to a Franciscan friary (cloister).

4 miles/6 km S of Alayor is the megalithic settlement of **Torre d'en Gaumés** (excavated 1942), with a *taula* and a unique hypostyle chamber. – 6 miles/10 km SW of Alayor, near the *San Jaume Mediterráneo* hotel colony to the E of the sandy beach of **Son Bou** (over 1¼ miles/2 km long; hotels), are the remains of an Early Christian aisled \**basilica* (4th–8th c.) with a cruciform font. Near here, to the SE, the remains of a settlement of the same period were found under the sea in 1954. This and other archeological finds made in the sea indicate that Minorca's coastline has changed considerably over the centuries as a result of erosion.

2 miles/3·5 km beyond Alayor on the main Mahón–Ciudadela road a side road on the left runs through the hamlet of *San Cristóbal* (4½ miles/7·5 km; parish church) and past the *Talayot of Sant Agusti Vell* to the new coastal settlements of *San Aldeodato* (8 miles/12·5 km) and *Santo Tomás* (9 miles/14 km; beautiful sandy beach). – 2½ miles/4 km farther on, on the left, is a bizarre rock formation known as

the *Cabeza de Indio* (Indian's Head). – 1¼ miles/2 km: **Mercadal** (*Es Mercadal*), a little country town at the foot of Monte Toro (pop. 2000; building, woodworking), an important road junction in the center of the island.

Mercadal is the starting-point of a rewarding drive 2 miles/3 km E on a winding road) up **Monte Toro** (1171 ft/357 m), Minorca's highest hill. On the summit are a statue of Christ on a large base and the *Santuario de Nuestra Señora de El Toro*, founded by Augustinians in the 17th c., with a pilgrimage church which contains a miraculous image of the Virgin, patroness of the island. From the terrace there are superb panoramic \*\*views of the whole island. There are pilgrimages to Monte Toro throughout the year, but the greatest occasion is the blessing of the country by the Bishop on the first Sunday in May.

From Mercadal a detour can be made, on a dirt road which at first is in reasonable condition but gradually degenerates and ends up as a rather arduous footpath, to the most northerly point on the island, the **Cabo de Caballería** (lighthouse; \*view). At the little harbor of *Sa Nitja* (which can also be reached by boat from Fornells) are the remains of a prehistoric settlement.

From Mercadal a road leads SW via San Cristóbal to Santo Tomás, and another, of excellent quality, runs 6 miles/10 km NE to the little fishing village of **Fornells** (pop. 250; crayfish), which grew up in the 17th c. around the Castle of San Antonio (now ruined). The village is situated on the W side of the entrance (protected by a watch-tower) into the *Bahía de Fornells* (salt-pans), a wide inlet which extends 2½ miles/4 km inland.

3 miles/5 km W of Fornells, in the **Cala Tirant**, lies a beautiful beach. – Near the *Punta na Giemassa*, the N end of the peninsula on the E side of the Bahía de Fornells, are the **Cova na Polida** (stalactites) and other small caves (accessible only by boat).

There is a direct road (about 13 miles/21 km) from Fornells to Mahón, running through an upland region of almost northern aspect. 7½ miles/12 km along this road a side road branches off on the left to the holiday settlements of **Arenal d'en Castell** (broad sandy beach below cliffs) and **Addaya**, on the NE coast of the island.

The main E–W road continues beyond Mercadal and comes in 5 miles/8 km to **Ferrerías** (*Ferreries*), an attractive village which is the chief place of a rural district (pop. 2700), in a sheltered situation under the S side of Mount *Inclusa* (S'Enclusa; 902 ft/275 m). The Parish Church is said to have been founded by Jaime III in 1331. 1¼ miles/2 km SE is the *Naveta of San Mercer de Baix.*

Ferrerías, Minorca

5 miles/8 km S of Ferrerías (by road, or on foot through the beautiful rocky Gorge of *Barranco de Algendar*) lies the *Cala Santa Galdana** (hotel colony), a semi-circular cove with a broad beach of fine sand below sheer cliffs which is one of the best on Minorca. Farther W is the quiet rocky Cove of *Cala Macarella*.

1½ miles/2·5 km beyond Ferrerías on the Ciudadela road is a *Roman bridge* (below road on right), and soon after this a road goes off on the right to the ruined *Castle of Santa Agueda*, on the hill of that name (853 ft/260 m), the last refuge of the Moors (who called it Sen Agayz) before the Christian Reconquest (1286–87). – 4 miles/6 km farther on a branch road on the left leads in ½ mile/1 km to the *Taulas de Torre Llafuda* and to the remains of the prehistoric settlement of *Torre Trencada* (Taula). In another 1½ miles/2½ km a left turn comes in ½ mile/1 km to the **Naveta of Es Tudóns,** the largest and best-preserved naveta on Minorca and the oldest building in Spain (*c.* 15th c. B.C.).

This boat-shaped chamber tomb of coursed Cyclopean masonry (46 ft/14 m by 21 ft/6·5 m; minor restoration work in 1960) stands in fairly open country

near the old Roman road which traversed the island and can easily be traced here. It is entered through a small opening in the flattened W end, originally closed by a slab of stone which fitted into cavities in the door-frame. This leads into a rectangular antechamber, from which another doorway (originally also closed by a stone slab) gives access to the main chamber (30 ft/ 9 m by 6½–10 ft/2–3 m). Above this, separated from it by stone arcades, is an upper chamber, which is also connected with the antechamber. – The bones and other objects found in the naveta point to its use during four different periods, illustrating the changing burial practices followed during the talayot period. The lowest level reflects the use of the naveta as the burial-place of clan chieftains and their immediate family. In the next phase practice was more liberal and the tomb was available for the burial of any member of the tribe. Then followed a period of declining interest in this form of burial; and in the final phase burial in the naveta was open only to those whose ancestors were already buried there. – These remotely situated burial-places have evidently inspired both fear and respect among local people over the centuries, thus preserving them from demolition for the sake of their stone.

3 miles/5 km beyond the turning for Es Tudóns the main road reaches Ciudadela, Minorca's second largest town, situated at the W end of the island.

In contrast to Mahón, **Ciudadela** *de Menorca* (Minorcan *Ciutadella*; pop. 17,000), which until 1722 was capital of the island and since 1795 has been the see of the Bishop of Minorca (a diocese instituted in the 5th c.), is a town of Moorish and Spanish creation which shows no traces of the periods of French and British rule. It is a thriving little town, noted for its shoe industry and for the manufacture of jewelry, but its port is of only local importance.

The town, which lies on the 40th parallel of latitude, is picturesquely situated above the long narrow inlet which forms its harbor, the Puerto. The many shallows, however, allow access only to small vessels. On the S side of the harbor entrance is a monument to Admiral Farragut, on a site once occupied by the Castillo de San Nicolás (late 17th c.).

From the harbor quay (Muelle) a broad and curving flight of steps and a steep street lead up to a large square, the Plaza del Borne, on the W side of which is the Town Hall (Casa Consistorial, Ayun-tamiento). In the center of the square stands an obelisk commemorating the destruction of the town by Turkish corsairs in 1558.

From the Plaza del Borne the Calle Mayor del Borne leads to Plaza Pío XII, with the Gothic Cathedral (since 1953 with the status of basilica), an aisle-less hall-church built between 1287 and 1362 with the Neo-Classical façade of 1813. On the N side is the Bishop's Palace (Palacio Episcopal).

From the Cathedral square a picturesque arcaded street, Calle José María Quadrado, runs NE to the Plaza Pablo Iglesias (Plaza de España), which is also surrounded by arcades.

Other features of interest are the former Augustinian Monastery of El Socós, in Calle Obispo Vila, with an archeological museum, a beautiful cloister and frescoes, which is now a theological seminary (concerts in summer); the churches of San Francisco (16th c.), Santo Cristo (Renaissance) and the Rosario (Churrigueresque façade, Baroque interior); and several palaces and mansions of different periods and styles of architecture and decoration, including the Palacio del Conde de Torre Saura (1697; Plaza del Borne), the Palacio de los Barones de Lluriach (Minorca's oldest noble family; Calle Santa Clara), the Palacio Martorell (Calle Santísimo), the Casa de Salort (Calle Mayor), the Casa de Sintas (Calle San Jerónimo), the Casa de Olives Beltrán (Calle San Rafael), etc.

5 miles/8 km NE of Ciudadela, in a charming setting, is the **Cala Morell** holiday complex, built around the sheltered cove of that name. – 2½ miles/4 km W of Ciudadela are the new resorts of **Cala'n Blanes** (rocky beach; scuba-diving), **Cala'n Forcat** (a rocky cove with a small sandy beach) and **Los Delfines** (rocky coast).

From Ciudadela a good road leads S to the beaches of *Son Oleo*, *Cala de Santandría* (2 miles/3 km; a rocky cove with sand) and **Cala Blanca** (2½ miles/4 km; gently sloping sandy beach; near which are the *Cuevas de Parella*, continuing to the **Cabo d'Artruch** (*d'Artrutx*, 6 miles/ 10 km; lighthouse), from which there are fine views, occasionally extending as far as Majorca, and to the nearby bungalow colony of *Playa Bosch* (7 miles/11 km), in the **Cala'n Bosch** (boating harbor). – Another road (unsurfaced) runs SE through beautiful scenery to *Torre Saura* (5 miles/8 km), where there have been a number of archeological excavations, and the excellent beach of *Son Saura* (6 miles/ 10 km). Another road leads to the new resort development at **Cala Turqueta** (7½ miles/12 km).

See also **\*\*Majorca** (with *Cabrera*) p. 125; **\*Ibiza**, p. 96; and **Formentera**, p. 91.

# Mljet

Yugoslavia
Republic: Croatia (Hrvatska).
Area: 38 sq. miles/98 sq. km. – Population: 2000.
Post code: YU-50226. – Telephone code: 059.

ⓘ **Mljet National Park,**
**Govedjari**,
tel. 8 90 10.
**Turističko Društvo**
**Saplunara–Okulje–Maranovići**,
YU-50224 **Maranovići**;
tel. 8 90 19
(rental of rooms in private houses).

HOTELS. *Odisej*, II, 317 b.; *Melita*, II, 86 b. (in the former monastery of Sv. Marija na Jezeru).

CAMP SITE. – Vrbovica.

BATHING BEACHES. – Coves (pebbles and rock) on either side of Pomina; large sandy bay at Saplurana. – The Vrbovica camp site is at Pristannište on the shores of the Veliko Jezero (also diving and fishing grounds).

FERRY SERVICES. – Polače–Sobra–Dubrovnik (cars carried); regular passenger service to Pelješac Peninsula.

**The island of Mljet, 24 miles/38 km long and 1½–2 miles/2–3 km wide, is the most southerly of the large Dalmatian islands, lying to the S of the Pelješac Peninsula, from which it is separated by the Mljetski Kanal. In Roman times Mljet (the ancient Melita) was a place of banishment.**

At the NW end of the island are two saltwater lakes created by karstic action. The smaller of the two, the *Malo Jezero* (area 60 acres/24 hectares), greatest depth 97 ft/29·5 m), is linked with the larger *Veliko Jezero* (area 360 acres/145 hectares), greatest depth 151 ft/46 m), which in turn is connected with the sea. A strong current flows through the channel between the lakes, altering direction every six hours in accordance with the ebb and flow of the tide. In the interior of the island are four other karstic depressions, with no connection to the sea, which fill up with fresh water after rain. The two sea-water lakes with their surrounding coniferous forests and some areas of agricultural land *form the Mljet National Park*, which has an area of 7400 acres/3010 hectares.

**The Church of Our Lady** belonging to the former Benedictine abbey on the island in the Veliko Jezero is in Apulian Romanesque style, an aisle-less building of regularly dressed stone with an apse, a dome and a frieze of round-headed arches on the outer walls. In front of the church is a Renaissance portico with the coat of arms of the Gundulić family (15th–16th c.). From the same period date the defensive tower, with loopholes, and the sacristy. There are two side chapels, with altars, added in the Baroque period. The monastic buildings (now a hotel) on the harbor side of the church date from the 16th c.

The largest village on the island, **Babino Polje**, lies 4 miles/6 km W of the port of Sobra, at the foot of Mljet's highest hill, *Veli Grad* (1686 ft/514 m). Near the village are a number of caves, the finest of which are the stalactitic *Movrica Cave* (110 yds/100 m long) and the *Ostaševica Cave* (440 yds/400 m long).

**Polače** takes its name from the remains of a Roman palace which can be seen, with other Roman remains, in the middle of the village. Adjoining are the ruins of an Early Christian basilica. On a hill to the E, *Nodilove Košare*, are the remains of another Early Christian church, buried in scrub.

# Murter

Yugoslavia
Republic: Croatia (Hrvatska).
Area: 7½ sq. miles/19 sq. km. – Population: 5540.
Telephone code: 059.
ⓘ **Turističko Društvo,**
YU-59240 **Tijesno;**
tel. 7 80 46.

**Turističko Društvo,**
YU-59242 **Jezera;**
tel. 7 80 20.
**Turističko Društvo,**
YU-59244 **Betina;**
tel. 7 52 31.
**Kornatturist,**
YU-59243 **Murter;**
tel. 7 52 15.

HOTELS. – MURTER: *Colentum*, II, 208 b. – TIJESNO: *Borovnik*, II, 160 b. – Also accommodation in private houses (apply to Tourist Offices).

CAMP SITES. – TIJESNO: *Jazine.* – BETINA: *Plitka Vala* – *Kosirina.* – JEZERA: *Lovišća.* – MURTER: *Slanica.*

BATHING BEACHES. – The hotel in Murter has a beach of clean fine sand in Slanica Bay (overcrowded at the height of the season). There is almost endless scope for bathing on the much-indented E coast of the island, facing the mainland.

TRANSPORTATION. – No car ferries; Murter is connected with the mainland by a swing bridge.

Murter, lying off the Yugoslav coast between Zadar and Šibenik, is one of the smaller Adriatic islands, with an area of barely 7½ sq. miles/19 sq. km The NW end of the island is an area of loess soil on which fruit, olives and vegetables flourish. The predominantly steep SW coast is broken up by a series of small coves. In those parts of the island which consist of limestone there is only a sparse covering of vegetation.

The road to the island branches off the Adriatic coastal highway between Pirovac and Vodice and crosses the Murterski Kanal (Murter Channel) on a swing bridge 40 yds/37 m long at the village of Tijesno, which is partly on the mainland and partly on the island. It then continues, with many turning and extensive views, to the little fishing port of Betina, skirts the

Murter, looking toward the neighboring islands of Prišnjak and Radelj

beautiful sandy beach of Hramina, comes to the village of Murter (which is not on the sea) and ends at the sandy beaches of Slanica.

HISTORY. – Murter was occupied by Illyrians and later by the Romans, who have left evidence of their presence at the village of Betina (ancient Colentum), where much archeological material has been recovered. In the 13th c. there were only two settlements on the island, Veliko Selo (now Murter) and Jezero. The villages of Betina and Tijesno were established during the period of Turkish attacks; Tijesno is first recorded in 1447.

**Tijesno** – a village of bright red-tiled roofs, like the other settlements on the island – has a Parish Church built in 1548, remodelled in Baroque style in 1640 and enlarged in 1840, with a handsome tower of 1680. The other little churches in the village date from the 17th c. – **Ivinj**, on the mainland SE of Tijesno, has a medieval church, St Martin's. At **Dazlina** are the ruins of a medieval watch-tower.

The village of **Betina**, on *Mount Gradina*, occupies the site of the Illyrian and later Roman settlement of *Colentum*. It has a medieval Church of the Mother of God (Gospa od Gradina).

The main place on the island, **Murter**, lies in a fertile plain some 770 yds/700 m from the sea. It has a fine beach and is noted for its wine. The medieval St Michael's Church (Sv. Mihovil) was restored in 1770 and enlarged in 1847. The Baroque High Altar has sculpture by Pio and Vico

dell'Acqua (1779). On a hill above the town stands the little St Roch's Church (1760).

# Mykonos
## (Míkonos)

Greece
Nomos: Cyclades.
Area: 33 sq. miles/85 sq. km. – Population: 3400.
Telephone code: 0289.

(i) **Tourist Police,**
Platía Apováthras;
tel. 2 24 82.

HOTELS. – MÝKONOS: *Leto*, I, 48 b.; *Rohari*, II, 99 b.; *Theoxenia*, II, 93 b.; *Despotika*, II, 40 b.; *Kouneni*, II, 36 b.; *Mykonos Beach*, III, 32 b.; *Mykonos*, III, 28 b.; *Manto*, III, 26 b.; *Marios*, III, 20 b.; *Bellou*, III, 16 b. AGHIOS STÉFANOS (2 miles/3 km): *Alkistis*, II, 182 b.; *Artemis*, III, 39 b. – PLATYS YIALÓS (2½ miles/4 km): *Petinos*, III, 55 b. – KALAFÁTI (6 miles/10 km): *Aphrodite Beach*, II, 180 b. – ÓRNOS: *Paralos Beach*, III, 76 b. – ANÓ MERÁ: I, 124 b. – YOUTH HOSTEL.

BATHING BEACHES. – *Ámmos*, immediately S of the town; on the *Diákofto* Isthmus, 2 miles/3 km SW; near *Aghios Stéfanos*, 2 miles/3 km N; in *Pánormos* Bay.

TRANSPORTATION. – Air service from Athens. – Mýkonos is served by boats sailing between Piraeus and Rhodes and between Piraeus and Samos. – Boat service to Delos.

**Easily accessible from Athens, the island of \* Mýkonos in the Cyclades has long been one of Greece's major holiday centers. The Gulf of Pánormos forms a deep indentation on the**

The town of Mýkonos

**Windmill, Mýkonos**

N coast, and at the W end of the island two smaller bays encroach on the land to form a peninsula. Mýkonos is built up of gneisses and granites and is poorly supplied with water, having no natural springs. The houses, freshly lime-washed every year, stand out in dazzling whiteness against the tawny brown of the earth.

THE ISLAND. – The chief town, Mýkonos (pop. 2800), on the W coast, is a picturesque little place, with cube-shaped whitewashed houses, churches and chapels with red and blue domes, windmills and pigeon-houses, shady lanes and a constant bustle of life around the harbor. The best known of the churches – many of them founded by private donors – is the picturesque *Paraportiani Church, with a domed upper church (the Chapel of the Panayía Paraportiani), and a lower storey (entered from the opposite side) which is known as the "tésseres ekklisíes" ("four churches") because of the four tiny chapels built side by side, dedicated respectively (from left to right) to Aghios Sóstis, Aghios Efstátios, the Aghii Anáryiri and Aghia Anastasía. The little *Museum in the N of the town contains archeological material from Mýkonos and the neighboring island of Rínia, including an Early Archaic pithos with relief decoration (scenes from the Conquest of Troy). Near the Paraportiani Church is a small Folk Museum.

In the interior of the island, 6 miles/10 km E of Mýkonos, is Anó Merá (pop. 700), with the Tourlianí Monastery. From here it is possible to continue to Anna Bay on Cape Kalafáta, to the SE, or to Cape Evros, to the E.

**Delos: see p. 81.

# Náxos
## (Náxos)

Greece
Nomos: Cyclades
Area: 165 sq. miles/428 sq. km. – Population: 14,200.

HOTELS. – Ariadne, II, 46 b.; Akroyiali, II, 27 b.; Coronis, III, 60 b.; Naxos Beach, III, 50 b.; Aegeon, III, 40 b.; Apollon, III, 34 b.; Panorama, III, 33 b.; Hermes, III, 32 b.; Nissaki, III, 30 b.; Zeus, III, 29 b.; Anessi, III, 27 b.; Renetta, III, 23 b.; Chelmos, III, 21 b.; Barbouni, III, 15 b.

BATHING BEACHES. – Small beach S of the town (15 minutes); at Aghia Ánna, on the S side of the Prokópios Peninsula, a long sandy beach; good swimming at the little port of Apóllona, on the N side of the island.

TRANSPORTATION. – Served by the Cyclades boats (Piraeus–Sýros–Páros–Náxos–Íos–Santorin). – Island bus Náxos–Apóllona.

Náxos, the largest, most fertile, and scenically the most attractive of the Greek Cyclades, is traversed from N to S by a range of mountains which fall steeply down on the E side but on the W side slope gradually down into fertile uplands and well-watered plains.

The range rises at the S end, in Mount Oxiá (the ancient Mount Drios), to 3291 ft/1003 m, and is crossed by two passes. Since ancient times the island has enjoyed a considerable degree of prosperity thanks to its agriculture, to the working of marble and emery and to the extraction of salt from the sea. In recent years the tourist trade has made an increasing contribution to the economy.

HISTORY. – Náxos is believed to have been the main center of the cult of Dionysos. The myth tells us that Theseus abandoned Ariadne here. – There is much archeological evidence of an early settlement of the island by Carians and Cretans and of the existence of a flourishing Cycladic culture in the 3rd–2nd millennium B.C. In the 1st millennium they were followed by Ionian Greeks, who in the 6th c. B.C. extended their authority to Poros, Andros and other neighboring islands. At this time, too, there grew up a famous school of sculptors (cf. the Apollo of Delos). A member of the First Attic Maritime League, Náxos took part in a rebellion against Athens, and when this failed it lost its independence, became subject to Athens and was compelled to accept Athenian settlers. Later it became a member of the Second Attic Maritime League. Conquered by Macedon, it was ruled from Egypt after Alexander's death; under Mark Anthony it came under the control of Rhodes, and thereafter passed to Byzantium. In 1207 the island was occupied by a Venetian nobleman named Marco Sanudo, who made it the center of his Duchy of the Archipelago. This Duchy of Naxos continued in existence until 1566 and rose to considerable prosperity and power; then in 1579 it was taken by the Turks. From 1770 to 1774 Naxos was under Russian administration but, like the other islands in the Cyclades, preserved a certain degree of autonomy. In 1830 it became part of the newly established kingdom of Greece.

THE ISLAND. – The island's capital, Náxos (pop. 2500), is situated in a fertile vine-growing and market-gardening region. Its houses climb picturesquely up the slopes of a rocky hill crowned by the ruins of the Venetian Kastro (1260), now occupied by a convent school (panoramic views). The town contains a number of

The town of Náxos

large emery-mines which were already being worked in ancient times.

Under the SE side of Mount Oxiá stands the Hellenistic *Kimaro Tower*, built of marble. On the W side of the hill is the *Cave of Zeus*, an ancient cult place.

Other features of interest on Náxos are the Venetian castles of *Apáno Kástro* (1¼ miles/2 km from Khalkí; 13th c.), *Áno Potamiá* (SE of Náxos town; guide required), *Apaliros* (in the SW of the island) and *Cape Panerímos* (in the SE). – At *Khalkí*, 9 miles/15 km E of Náxos town, and in the Drimália Valley can be seen the curious fortified tower houses known as *Pyrgi*. – Many of the island's churches have Byzantine wall-paintings. Particularly notable are those in the churches of *Aghia Kyriakí* at **Apíranthos** and Aghios Artémios at *Sángri* (frescoes of 9th c.).

dilapidated Venetian palazzos (Barozzi Palace, Sommaripa Palace, etc.), the Roman Catholic Church of Our Lady (13th c.) and St Anthony's Chapel (15th c.), on the harbor mole. The *Museum contains archeological material, including products of the Cycladic culture. – The modern town of Náxos occupies the site of the ancient city, among the remains of which are a 20 ft/6 m high marble doorway and the foundations of a Sanctuary (left unfinished) of Apollo or Dionysos (6th c.) on the rocky little islet of **Sto Paláti** (stone causeway). – NE of the town stands the *fortified Monastery of St John Chrysostom*. 6 miles/10 km NE of Náxos is the whitewashed *Faneroméni Monastery*, with a church of 1603.

26 miles/42 km N of Náxos town, above *Apóllona Bay*, which lies SE of *Cape Stávros*, the northernmost tip of the island, are a number of ancient quarries yielding the famous Naxian marble used for sculpture and architecture and also for roofing. In one of these, the ***Ston Apóllona**, is the unfinished figure, 34 ft/ 10·40 m long, of a kouros (youth), abandoned because of a defect in the stone. Above the quarry is a Venetian castle. The characteristic coarse-grained Naxian marble outcrops again farther S, between *Mélanes* and *Potamiá*, where there are other unfinished kouros figures and the upright of a doorway, probably intended for the temple on Sto Paláti. – In the hillsides flanking the Vothri Valley are

# Nicosia
## See under Cyprus

# Nisyros
## See under Sporades

# Olbia
## See under Sardinia

# Olib
## See Silba and Olib

# Pag

Yugoslavia
Republic: Croatia (Hrvatska).
Area: 110 sq. miles/285 sq. km. – Population: 10,000.
Telephone code: 051.
ⓘ **Kompas,**
Trg Loža 1,
YU-51291 **Novalja;**
tel. 89 35 15.
**Turist-biro,**
Obala Maršala Tita 1,
YU-51290 **Pag;**
tel. 89 11 31.

HOTELS. – NOVALJA: *Liburnija*, II, 248 b.; *Loža*, II, 74 b. – PAG: *Bellevue*, II, 302 b.

CAMP SITE. – *Straško*, Trg Loža 1, Novalja; part reserved for naturists.

EVENTS. – *Pag Summer Carnival* (July 26–29), with parades and folk performances.

BATHING BEACHES. – The 440 yd/400 m long pebble beach at Pag town is usually overcrowded, and the water lacks the clarity and purity usually found on the Yugoslav Adriatic coast, since there is little tidal movement in this narrow inlet with its restricted access to the open sea. It is better to look for a bathing-place on the open W coast of the island. There is also a public beach (pebbles) at Novalja; and the naturist beach of the camp site can also be used by non-campers.

CAR FERRIES. – Jablanac–Stara Novalja and Karlobag–Pag. Bridge connection with mainland.

**The northern Dalmatian island of Pag, which is separated from the mainland by the Velebit Channel, 1¼–3 miles/2–5 km wide, is Yugoslavia's third longest Adriatic island (37 miles/59 km). The coast has numerous bays and inlets, and the island itself is traversed by parallel ranges of bare karstic hills. Vines and olives are grown on the few areas of fertile land; and major contributions are made to the island's economy by sheep-farming and fishing.**

The E side of the island, facing the mainland, is without vegetation of any kind, as a result of the fierce onslaught of the bora (the cold, dry and gusty north-easterly wind which blows down from the mountains to the Adriatic coast). Even on the W side of the island the vegetation is sparse, but here at least there are a few olive groves, fields of vegetables and areas of green pastureland.

The tourist and holiday trade is concentrated in the little towns of Pag and Novalja and their immediate surroundings. The mud-baths at the Pag salt-pans have brought cure or relief to many patients; the waters around the island offer ideal sailing conditions; gourmets appreciate the local cheese (Paški sir); and the beautiful lace made on Pag is a favorite souvenir of a stay on the island.

HISTORY. – In prehistoric times Pag was occupied by an Illyrian people, the Liburni. In the 1st c. B.C. the Romans established a defensive system on the island, with fortified posts at Caska (*Cissa*) and the port of Novalja (*Novalia*) and a number of smaller forts. In the 6th c. A.D. the Slavs came to Pag. In 1071 King Krešimir IV of Croatia sowed the seeds of much further trouble when he presented the northern part of Pag to the church on Rab and the southern part to Zadar; for thereafter Rab and Zadar were constantly at odds,

each seeking to acquire the whole of the island. In 1311 the inhabitants of Pag rose against Zadar, but it was not until 1376 that the town of Pag was granted self-government. From 1409 to 1797 the Venetians held the island, which then passed to Austria together with the Dalmatian mainland. During the Second World War Pag was occupied by Italian and later by German troops.

The Parish Church (begun 1443) in the town of **Pag**, the chief place on the island, is an aisled basilica which shows a mingling of Romanesque, Gothic and Early Renaissance features. The same architect, Juraj Dalmatinac, designed the unfinished Bishop's Palace in the same square and laid out the town on an orthogonal plan centered on the square. The Late Gothic Rector's Palace is now occupied by a department store. St George's Church (Sv. Juraj) is also of interest. Outside the town are salt-pans in a lagoon which extends many miles inland from the S. In the lagoon, where the water is calm, can be seen the foundations of a Roman settlement swallowed up by the sea.

Parish Church, Pag

The former fishing village of **Novalja**, now a seaside resort, has a Roman aqueduct and remains of Early Christian churches. Apart from this its life revolves entirely round the tourist trade, its mild climate attracting visitors from May to the end of October. – Farther S is the interesting freshwater lake of *Velo Blato*, which is 3 miles/5 km long in winter but shrinks to no more than ¾ mile/1 km in summer. The reeds at the edge of the lake provide breeding-places for waterfowl, and its waters are well stocked with fish; turtles can also be seen on its shores.

From a hill NE of Novalja, *Komorovac* (653 ft/199 m) there are fine °views of the coast and the island of Rab.

# Palermo

Italy
Region: Sicily. – Province: Palermo.
Altitude: 0–65 ft/0–20 m. – Population: 650,000.
Post code: I-90100. – Telephone code: 091.

(i) **AA,**
Salita Belmonte 1;
tel. 54 01 41.
*Information Office* at harbour,
tel. 24 23 43.
**EPT,**
Piazza Castelnuovo 35;
tel. 58 38 47.
*Information Office* at Cinisi – Punta Raisi
Airport, 19 miles/31 km W;
tel. 23 59 13.
**CIT,**
Via Roma 320;
tel. 21 57 40.

HOTELS. – *Villa Igiea Grand Hôtel*, Salita Belmonte
I, L, 171 b., SP; *Jolly Hotel del Foro Italico*, Foro Italico
32, I, 468 b., SP; *Grande Albergo e delle Palme*, Via
Roma 398, I, 282 b.; *Politeama Palace*, Piazza
Ruggiero Settimo 15, I, 177 b.; *Ponte*, Via Francesco
Crispi 99, II, 270 b.; *Motel Agip*, Viale della Regione
Italiana 2620, II, 200 b.; *Centrale*, Corso Vittorio
Emanuele 327, II, 164 b.; *Europa*, Via Agrigento 3, II,
143 b.; *Mediterraneo*, Via Cerda 44, II, 99 b.; *Terminus*,
Piazza Giulio Cesare 37, III, 135 b.; *Elena*, Piazza
Giulio Cesare 14, III, 88 b.; *Sausele*, Via Vincenzo
Errante 12, III, 68 b.; *Regina*, Corso Vittorio Emanuele
316, III, 65 b.; CAMP SITE. – IN MONDELLO LIDO:
*Mondello Palace*, I, 124 b., SP; *Splendid Hotel La
Torre*, II, 266 b., SP; *Conchiglia d'Oro*, III, 69 b.

EVENT. – *Trade Fair* (May–June).

**Palermo, magnificently situated in a
beautiful bay on the N coast of
Sicily, is the capital of the island and
its principal port, a university town
and the see of an archbishop. It is
bounded on the S and W by the
artificially irrigated and fertile plain
known as the Conca d'Oro (Golden
Conch), with a wide arc of imposing
mountains as a backdrop.**

Palermo

Although Palermo now has the aspect of
an entirely modern city, it preserves a
distinctive character thanks to its Norman
buildings with their rather Oriental style,
the Baroque architecture it has inherited
from the period of Spanish rule, and the
urgent tempo of its traffic; and the old
town with its narrow and twisting side
streets is still the scene of a vigorous
popular life. Its many gardens and palm-
shaded promenades give the town a
particular charm.

HISTORY. – Palermo, founded by the Phoenicians
and known to the Greeks as *Panormos*, became the
principal Carthaginian base in Sicily until its capture
by the Romans in 254 B.C. In A.D. 353 the Byzantine
General, Belisarius recovered it from the Ostrogoths,
and thereafter it remained in Byzantine hands until its
capture by the Saracens in 830. The Saracens were
followed in 1072 by the Normans, who were in turn
succeeded in 1194 by the Hohenstaufens and in 1266
by the House of Anjou, whose brief period of rule was
ended by the popular rising known as the Sicilian
Vespers in 1282. Palermo then came under Aragonese
and Spanish rule, passed to the Bourbons in the
18th c. and was finally liberated by Garibaldi on May
27 1860.

SIGHTS. – The busiest traffic intersection
in the old town is the square, laid out in
1609, known as the *Quattro Canti*
(Four Corners) or *Piazza Vigliena*, at the
crossing of the Corso Vittorio Emanuele,
which runs across the city from NE to SW
for a distance of $1\frac{1}{4}$ miles/2 km, and the Via
Maqueda, which runs NW from the
railway station to the newer part of the
city, offering views of the Baroque townscape, with its long rows of uniform
buildings, and glimpses of attractive side
streets, all set against a background of
great scenic beauty. – At the S corner
of the Quattro Canti stands the **Church
of San Giuseppe dei Teatini** (1612–45),
a massive pillared basilica with a sumptuous Baroque interior. Adjoining it on the
S is the *University*, and beyond this the
imposing Baroque *Church of the Gesù*
(1564–1636).

From the Quattro Canti the Corso Vittorio
Emanuele goes SW past the handsome
Baroque *Church of San Salvatore* (on the
left) to the Piazza della Cattedrale. On the
NW side of this square, which is surrounded by a stone balustrade of 1761 with
16 large statues of saints, stands the
*Cathedral*, originally Romanesque but
frequently altered and enlarged, with a
beautiful S front (1300–59), but disfigured by a dome added between 1781
and 1801.

INTERIOR of the Cathedral. – In the S aisle are six *royal tombs – the majestic porphyry sarcophagi, surmounted by temple-like canopies, of the Emperor Frederick II (d. 1250; on the left), his father Henry VI (d. 1197; on the right), Roger II (d. 1154; behind, to the left), his daughter the Empress Constance (behind, to the right), William, son of Frederick II of Aragon (in a niche on the left), and Constance of Aragon, wife of the Emperor Frederick II (by the wall, to the right). – In the chapel to the right of the Choir is a silver shrine containing the *relics of St Rosalia*, the city's patron saint. – The Sacristy, at the end of the S aisle, houses the rich Cathedral *Treasury*. In the crypt are Antique and Early Christian sarcophagi containing the remains of early archbishops.

Immediately SW of the Cathedral is the **Archbishop's Palace** (*Palazzo Arcive-scovile*; 16th c.), with the *Diocesan Museum* (entrance in courtyard to the right). On the opposite side of the Corso Vittorio Emanuele is the Piazza della Vittoria, with the palm-shaded park of the *Villa Bonanno* (remains of Roman houses). At the SE corner of the square is the *Palazzo Scláfani* (1330), at the SW corner a *monument to Philip V* (1586). The W side of the square is occupied by the **Palazzo dei Normanni,** the former royal palace, a fortress-like building originally dating from the Saracen period which was remodelled by the Norman kings.

The last gateway on the left gives access to the palace courtyard (Renaissance arcades) and to the famous **Cappella Palatina** (on the first floor), dedicated to St Peter, which was built by Roger II in 1132–40. This is surely the most beautiful palace chapel in the world, with its splendid mosaic decoration and its mingling of Western and Oriental elements. The glass mosaics on a gold ground (some of them restored) which cover the walls depict scenes from the Old Testament, the life of Christ and the lives of the Apostles Peter and

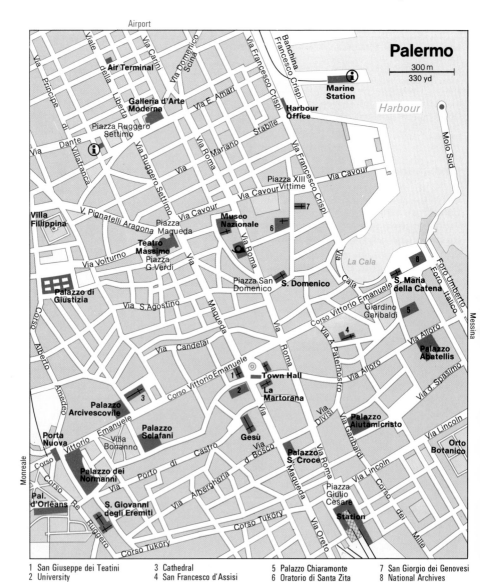

| | | | |
|---|---|---|---|
| 1 San Giuseppe dei Teatini | 3 Cathedral | 5 Palazzo Chiaramonte | 7 San Giorgio dei Genovesi |
| 2 University | 4 San Francesco d'Assisi | 6 Oratorio di Santa Zita | 8 National Archives |

Paul. – Adjoining the chapel is the **Torre di Santa Ninfa**, with a 50 ft/15 m high room on the ground floor which was probably the strong-room of the Norman kings. On the second floor is an *observatory*, from the roof of which there is a fine *view of Palermo. There are also good views from the balconies of various rooms in the palace (conducted tour).

Just beyond the Palazzo dei Normanni the Corso Vittorio Emanuele is spanned by the **Porto Nuova** (1535), the upper story of which (accessible from the palace) affords another magnificent view. – 1 mile/ 1·5 km W of the Porta Nuova, on the outskirts of the town, is the **Convento dei Cappuccini** (1621), with underground passages which, in spite of a fire in 1966, still contain the mummies or skeletons of ecclesiastics or well-to-do citizens in the clothes they wore during life (and which are still sometimes renewed by their descendants). No further burials of this kind have been permitted since 1881. – Some 550 yds/500 m N of the Capuchin Convent is a Norman palace known as **La Zisa**, a plain building based on Arab models which was erected by William I between 1154 and 1166. On the ground floor is a square garden room with a fountain, Byzantine mosaics and a high stalactitic ceiling.

Just S of the Palazzo dei Normanni is Palermo's most unusual ruined church, *San Giovanni degli Eremiti (1132), a building of decidedly Oriental aspect with its five tall red domes. Adjoining the church are the remains of a small mosque. On its N side is a picturesque cloister (tropical plants). – W of the church, in the Piazza dell'Indipendenza, is the *Villa d'Aumale* or *Villa d'Orléans*, now the offices of the Autonomous Region of Sicily, in a beautiful public park.

On the E side of San Giuseppe dei Teatini is the *Piazza Pretoria*, with a Florentine fountain (1550) in the center. On the S side of the square stands the **Palazzo del Municipio** (Town Hall). At the E corner is the side entrance to the *Church of Santa Caterina* (Baroque interior), with its main front on Piazza Bellini. Also in this square, approached by a flight of steps, is the little *Church of San Cataldo* (1161), in Byzantine style, with a dome. On its E side is the beautiful *Martorana Church* (1143), also known as *Santa Maria dell'Ammiraglio* after its founder Georgios Antiochenos, Grand Admiral of the Norman King Roger I (fine Byzantine mosaics and vault-paintings).

220 yds/200 m E of the Quattro Canti the eastern section of the Corso Vittorio Emanuele cuts across the busy Via Roma (a modern street driven through the old town from N to S), passes near the Gothic *Church of San Francesco d'Assisi*, off to the right, and the *Church of Santa Maria della Catena* (about 1500; beautiful portico) on the left, and leads into the Piazza Santo Spírito, which is closed on the seaward side by the ruins of the *Porta Felice*. – W of Santa Maria della Catena is the picturesque boating harbor of *La Cala*, and to the S is the Piazza Marina, almost entirely occupied by the tropical *Giardino Garibaldi*. On the E side of the square is the *Palazzo Chiaramonte*, usually known as *Lo Steri* (built 1307–80; later the residence of the Viceroy). – To the SE, in Via Alloro, which leads to the Foro Umberto I, is the *Palazzo Abatellis* (1495), with a crenelated tower and an unusual Gothic doorway. The palace now houses the *Galleria Nazionale Siciliana*, which gives a comprehensive view of Sicilian painting from the Middle Ages to modern times. Particularly notable is a magnificent *wall-painting, the "Triumph of Death", by an unknown 15th c. master (in Room II, the former chapel).

Along the seafront to the E and SE of the Porta Felice extends the *Foro Italico, a broad boulevard which affords magnificent views of Palermo Bay and is a favorite resort of the citizens on summer evenings. At the S end of the Foro Italico is the beautiful **Villa Giulia** Park, also known as *La Flora* (laid out in 1777). On the W side of this is the **Botanic Garden** (*Orto Botanico*), which has a magnificent variety of plants including date and coconut palms, banana trees and fine stands of bamboos and papyrus.

From the Quattro Canti Via Maqueda runs NW to the busy Piazza Giuseppe Verdi, lying between the old and the new town, with the *Teatro Massimo or *Teatro Vittorio Emanuele* (1875–97), one of the largest theaters in Italy, with seating for 3200. – From the Piazza Verdi Via Ruggiero Settimo continues the line of Via Maqueda through the newer part of the town to Piazza Ruggiero Settimo, with monuments to Sicilian patriots. On the NE side of the square, in the *Politeama Garibaldi*, is the **Galleria d'Arte Moderna** (works by Sicilian artists). From here the broad Via della Libertà continues NE for 1½ miles/2·5 km to the *Giardino Inglese*, a public garden. On the left is an *equestrian statue of Garibaldi* (1892).

From the theater Via della Bara runs E to the Piazza dell'Olivella, in which are the *Olivella Church* (1598) and the *Archeological Museum* (*Museo Archeologico*), one of Italy's finest museums, housed in a former monastery of the Campagnia di San Filippo Neri. In addition to prehistoric material and an Etruscan collection the museum contains many important Classical antiquities, among them the famous *metopes from Selinunte (about 550–450 B.C.), 56 lion's-head water-spouts from Himera (5th c. B.C.) and fine Greek bronzes (including Heracles and the Cerynaean Hind, a fountain group from Pompeii excavated in 1805 and a large ram from Syracuse).

From the E side of the museum Via Roma runs S past the *Head Post Office* (on the right) to the Piazza San Domenico, in which is a 100 ft/30 m high column bearing a *figure of the Virgin* (1726). On the E side of the square stands the **Church of San Domenico** (14th c., rebuilt 1636–40), which can accommodate a congregation of 8000. It contains a number of good pictures and many monuments to prominent Sicilians. In the chapel to the right of the choir is a charming relief of the Virgin with Angels by Antonello Gagini. Adjoining the church is a picturesque *cloister* (14th and 16th c.). – Beyond San Domenico, in Via Bambinai, is the *Oratorio della Compagnia del Rosario di San Domenico* (entrance at No. 16, to the right), with stucco decoration by Giacomo Serpotta (1656–1732). On the High Altar is Van Dyck's *"Madonna del Rosario"* (1624–25). – To the N of the Oratorio we come to the *Church of Santa Zita*, which has a triptych (1517) by Antonello Gagini. Behind the church, in Via Valverde, is the *Oratorio della Compagnia del Rosario di Santa Zita*, with stucco-work by Serpotta. – NE of Santa Zita is the *Church of San Giorgio dei Genovesi* (1591). From here Via Francesco Crispi runs N to the busy **Harbor** (*Porto*).

SURROUNDINGS of Palermo. – 8 miles/13 km SW of Palermo is the former Benedictine Monastery of **San Martino delle Scale** (alt. 1663 ft/507 m). The present buildings date from 1778 (church 1590). – From the former Minorite Monastery of **Santa Maria di Gesù** (alt. 165 ft/50 m), 2½ miles/4 km S of Palermo on the lower slopes of *Monte Grifone* (2730 ft/832 m), there is perhaps the finest °view of Palermo and the Conca d'Oro (seen at its best in morning light).

8 miles/13 km N of Palermo is the *Spianata della Sacra Grotta*, with the **Grotta di Santa Rosalia** (alt. 1408 ft/429 m; above the square, to the right), a cave which was converted into a church in 1625. According to the legend, St Rosalia (d. about 1170), daughter of Duke Sinibaldo and niece of King William II, withdrew to this hermitage at the age of only 14. In front of the church is a tablet commemorating Goethe's visit in 1787. From here a steep path runs SE (½ hour) to the summit of °**Monte Pellegrino** (1988 ft/606 m; two television towers), from which there are panoramic views. – From the Spianata della Sacra Grotta a good road descends, with many turns and fine views, to *Mondello* (5 miles/8 km).

There is also a very attractive trip **around Monte Pellegrino** (17 miles/27 km). The road runs N from Palermo past the former royal country house of **La Favorita** (park, orangery; camp site), near which is the little *Palazzino Cinese*, with the *Museo Etnografico Siciliano Pitrè* (folk traditions; puppet theater). From here it continues under the W side of Monte Pellegrino and through the northern suburbs of *Pallavicino* and *Partanna*, on the southern slopes of *Monte Gallo* (1729 ft/527 m), to **Mondello** (or *Mondello Lido*), Palermo's seaside resort (good sandy beach), lying on the Bay of Mondello between Monte Gallo and Monte Pellegrino. From here the return route runs along the coast, around the *Punta di Priola*, past the *Cimitero Monumentale* (or *Cimitero dei Rótoli*), Palermo's largest cemetery, and through the coastal suburbs of *Arenella* (with the magnificent *Villa Belmonte*) and *Acquasanta* to Palermo.

Another excursion, through country of great scenic beauty, is to **Piana degli Albanesi** (alt. 2380 ft/725 m; pop. 8000). 15 miles/24 km S via *Altofonte* (7½ miles/12 km; alt. 1161 ft/354 m; pop. 5500), which was known until 1930 as *Parco*, after a hunting-park of William II's. Piana degli Albanesi, formerly known as *Piana dei Greci*, was founded by Albanian settlers in 1488, and the people still preserve their distinctive dialect and the Eastern rite of the Roman Catholic Church. The town is the seat of a bishop whose diocese extends to all the Albanians in Italy. Picturesque Albanian costumes are worn on feast-days.

There is an attractive trip by boat (3 hours; 4–6 times weekly) or hydrofoil (1 hour 15 minutes; several times daily) to the volcanic island of **Ústica** (area 3½ sq. miles/9 sq. km; pop. 1100; wine, fruit, arable farming), 42 miles/67 km N. The highest point on the island is the *Punta Maggiore* (801 ft/244 m), a remnant of the old crater rim. Formerly a place of banishment and a penal colony, the island is now attracting increasing numbers of visitors with its beautiful scenery. On its eastern tip is the only settlement, **Ustica** (alt. 177 ft/54 m; Hotel Punta Spalmatore, II, 200 b.; Grotta Azzurra, II, 90 b., SP; Diana, II, 64 b.; Patrice, III, 74 b.), with the harbor. To the S, accessible only by boat, are a number of caves – the *Grotta Azzurra*, the particularly beautiful *Grotta dell'Acqua* and the *Grotta Pastizza*. There is also a very pleasant walk around the island, which is 3 miles/4·5 km long and almost 2 miles/3 km wide.

# Palma de Mallorca
## See under Majorca

# Pantellería

Italy
Region: Sicily. – Province: Trapani.
Area: 32 sq. miles/83 sq. km. – Population: 8500.

ⓘ **EPT,**
Piazzetta Saturno,
I-91100 **Trapani;**
tel. (0923) 2 90 00.

HOTELS. – *Francesco di Fresco,* II, 181 b.; *Punta Fram Mare,* II, 134 b.; *Punta Tre Pietre,* II, 122 b.; *Del Porto,* II, 86 b.; *Agadir,* III, 69 b.

BOAT SERVICES. – Ferry from Trapani (several times weekly); regular boats from Trapani and Marsala (several times weekly; cars not carried). – AIRFIELD.

The Italian island of Pantellería, known in Antiquity as Kossyra, lies S of the western tip of Sicily. Its highest point is in a volcanic massif, the Montagna Grande (2743 ft/ 836 m).

The coast is mostly rocky, offering excellent opportunities for scuba-divers. The island has radioactive mineral springs, and many people come here to take the cure.

The chief place on the island, **Pantellería** (alt. 65 ft/20 m; pop. 5500), has an old castle and a small harbor. – 2 miles/3 km SW are the remains of a Stone Age settlement at *Mursia,* near which are a number of megalithic chamber tombs, the *Sesi.* – An attractive excursion from Pantelleria is a boat trip along the coast (caves).

# Páros
*(Páros)*

Greece
Nomos: Cyclades.
Area: 75 sq. miles/194 sq. km. – Population: 7500.
Telephone code: 0284.

ⓘ **Tourist Police,**
Apovathra;
tel. 2 16 73 (summer only).

HOTELS. – IN PÁROS: *Xenia,* II, 44 b.; *Argo,* III, 83 b.; *Asterias,* III, 50 b.; *Alkyon,* III, 26 b.; *Georgy,* III, 43 b.; *Stella,* III, 38 b.; *Hermes,* III, 36 b.; *Argonaftis,* III, 27 b.; *Páros,* III, 22 b. – ALYKI: *Angeliki,* III, 26 b. – DRYÓS: *Annezina,* III, 26 b.; *Ivi (Hebe),* III, 23 b.; *Julia,* III, 23 b.; *Avra,* III, 18 b. – MÁRPISSA: *Logaras,* III, 16 b. – NÁOUSA: *Hippocambus* (bungalows), II, 94 b.; *Naousa,* II, 19 b.; *Mary,* III, 66 b.; *Minoa,* III, 51 b.; *Atlantis,* III, 40 b.; *Ambelas,* III, 32 b.; *Galini,* III, 22 b.; *Piperi,* III, 16 b. – PÍSO LAVÁDI: *Marpissa,* II, 21 b.; *Leto,* III, 28 b.; *Vicky,* III, 28 b.; *Piso Livadi,* III, 24 b.; *Lodos,* III, 20 b.

BATHING BEACHES at Páros, Dryós, Náousa and Píso Livádi.

TRANSPORTATION. – Páros is served by the Cyclades boats sailing between Piraeus, Sýros, Páros, Náxos and Santorin. – Boats to Antíparos and many other places. – Island buses.

**Páros, famed in Antiquity for its Parian marble, is one of the most beautiful of the Cyclades, the gentler sister of the larger neighboring island of Náxos.**

HISTORY. – On the hill now occupied by the town of Páros evidence of occupation since the Cycladic culture of the 3rd millennium B.C. has been found. In the 2nd millennium the island was settled by Mycenaean Greeks, in the early 1st millennium by Ionians. Its most flourishing period was in the 8th–6th c. In the 7th c. Páros established a colony on the island of Thásos, one of the founders being the poet Arkhilokhos (about 680–640 B.C.), later revered as a hero. The rich supply of gold on Thásos increased still further the prosperity of the mother island, based on the working of Parian marble. With the Persian Wars the political importance of Páros declined, but it was still able to found the colony of Pharos (Hvar) in the Adriatic in 385 B.C. In the Roman period the working of marble became an Imperial monopoly. During the Byzantine period Páros was sufficiently prosperous to build large churches, but in the 9th and 10th c. the island was plundered and the population decimated by Saracen pirates. In 1207 Páros became part of the Duchy of Náxos, and from 1389 to 1537 it was held as a fief of the Duchy by the Sommaripa family. Thereafter, until its liberation in the 19th c., it was under Turkish rule.

SIGHTS. – The chief town, **Páros** (pop. 2000), popularly known as *Paríkia,* lies in a flat bay on the W coast, on the site of the ancient capital. From the *Harbor* we go past a windmill into a large square, from which a street on the right runs past a fountain of 1777 and up to the medieval *Castle,* built in 1226 on the ancient acropolis, largely of fragments of ancient masonry. The apse of the castle chapel incorporates part of a handsome circular structure of the 4th c. B.C., and architectural elements from an Archaic *temple* can be seen in the neighboring lanes. They date from the time of the Naxian tyrant Lygdamis (about 540 B.C.) and have the

The fishing harbor, Páros

same dimensions as the contemporary temple on the Sto Paláti Peninsula on Náxos. – From here we continue through narrow lanes to the *Church of Aghios Konstantínos* (picturesque arcades) on the highest point of the hill. This was the center of the ancient settlement; the remains of the prehistoric period have been covered over, but part of the foundations of the Archaic temple can be seen immediately N of the church.

The main feature of interest in the town is the *Church of Panayía Ekatontapylianí*, the pride of Páros, which was restored to its original form in the 1960s. The white rendering and various additions which gave it the aspect of a typical Cycladic church were removed, and we can now see the masonry of the original structure (5th–6th c.) and a 10th c. renovation. The name Ekatontapylianí (Hundred-gated) comes from an icon of the Mother of God which is reputed to be wonder-working, and has been applied to the church itself only since the 18th c.; it is derived from the older name Katapoliani (Close to the town).

Outside the church, on the left, are ancient *sarcophagi* which have been reused and decorated with later reliefs. Passing through the *atrium* with its white-washed arcades, we enter the **principal church**, an aisled basilica with galleries and a central dome which dates from the time of Justinian (6th c.). Under the floor were found columns belonging to an earlier Christian building, and below this again remains of a large Roman house with a mosaic of Hercules (now in the museum). A striking feature of the spacious interior is the use of stones of different colors in the *choir vaulting*. This is part of the original structure, as are the *cherubim* in two of the pendentives supporting the dome. Behind the more recent *iconostatis* are an altar with a canopy borne on ancient columns, a side altar also incorporating ancient material and a *synthronon* (stone seats for clergy) in the apse such as is commonly found in churches of the Early Byzantine period.

From the N transept we enter the aisled **parekklisia** (subsidiary church), which appears to date from the 5th c. This church, too, has a synthronon behind the iconostatis, which dates from 1611. – From the S transept of the principal church a door leads into the **Baptistery** (6th c.), also an aisled basilica. In the chancel is the original cruciform *immersion font*.

A street immediately S of the church goes past a school to the *Museum* (signpost), housing material ranging from Early Cycladic idols to Late Antiquity. Notable exhibits are a *relief of Apollo and Artemis and a *mosaic of Hercules.

**North of the island** (7 miles/11 km; bus). – 1¼ miles/2 km E of the town of Páros are the **Tris Ekklisíes**, the ruins of a Christian basilica of the early 7th c., incorporating architectural elements from ancient buildings. An inscription found here indicated that the tomb of the poet Arkhilokhos was in this area. Finds from the site are in the museum. – Beyond this, on a hill to the right of the road, stands the **Langovárdas Monastery** (founded 1657, restored in the 19th c.), one of the few monasteries on the island which are still functioning; it has a school of painting. – **Naoúsa**, situated in a wide and much-indented bay, is a typical little Cycladic town of whitewashed houses.

**East and south of the island** (12½ miles/20 km). – 2 miles/3·5 km SE of Páros a footpath goes off on the right to the **ancient marble quarries** (signpost on the main road). After passing abandoned factory buildings the path comes to two entrances to the quarries. To the left of the second entrance is the figure of a *nymph* carved from the rock face. Parian marble was noted for its translucency. – The road continues via the very beautiful hill village of **Léfkes** (6 miles/10 km), with the modern Aghia Triáda Church, and **Márpissa** (9 miles/15 km) to the little port and seaside resort of **Píso Livádi** (10 miles/16 km), beyond which (12½ miles/20 km) is **Dryós**, with a beach of fine sand. The return route can be via Márpissa and Naoúsa.

**Walk to the Delion** (1 hour). – Going around the bay from Páros, we come to a small chapel, and from there follow a stony path which climbs N. the **excavations of the Delion** are on a hill, enclosed by a wall. The remains include an ancient *rock-cut altar* within the foundations of a *temenos* and a *temple* of the 6th c. B.C. dedicated to the divinities of Delos (Leto and her children Apollo and Artemis). From the site there is a far-ranging *view of the northern Cyclades. Near by are the remains of a *Sanctuary of Aphrodite*.

**To the island of Antíparos.** – It is a short trip by motor-boat across the narrow channel to the almost deserted village of **Antíparos** at the northern end of the island of Antíparos (area 13 sq. miles/ 34 sq. km). From there a road runs S down the E coast of the island to the Bay of *Ákra Akakós*, from which it is a 20-minute walk to an interesting stalactitic cave.

# Pašman

Yugoslavia
Republic: Croatia (Hrvatska).
Area: 22 sq. miles/56 sq. km. – Population: 1900.
Post code: YU-57262. – Telephone code: 057.

ⓘ **Turističko Društvo Jasenice,**
Pašman village;
tel. 8 31 25.

ACCOMMODATION. – At present only in private houses (apply to Tourist Office).

SPORT, BOATING and BATHING. – Boats can moor in Tkon Harbor, though at the height of the season it may be overcrowded. A sheltered anchorage (except when the bora is blowing) can be found in the Uvala Zaklopica, a cove just N of the southern tip of the island. Even boats with a shallow draft must keep a good lookout in the waters around Pašman, where there are many jagged rocks just below the surface. – The best bathing is at Tkon, which has a clean sandy beach. – The highest hill on the island, Bokolj (899 ft/ 274 m), can be climbed from Nevidjane. – Good facilities for water sports, fishing and walking.

TRANSPORTATION. – Car ferry from the mainland town of Biograd to Tkon. – Bridge from the neighboring island of Ugljan, which has a ferry service (several times daily) from Zadar.

**Pašman cannot yet compare with its neighbor, Ugljan, in the facilities it offers to visitors; but it has better beaches, still relatively untouched by tourism. It is an ideal place for a quiet holiday.**

HISTORY. – The island has been continuously occupied since prehistoric times. Tombs and hill-forts have yielded evidence of Illyrian occupation, and there were Roman settlements on the sites of the present-day villages of Pašman, Nevidjane and Banj. Like Ugljan, the island was never conquered by the Turks.

SIGHTS. – Roman remains have been found near **Pašman**, a little town on the NE coast. The *Parish Church*, originally built in the early medieval period, has an early 18th c. nave. The tower dates from 1750. The church contains two Late Gothic processional crosses and an altarpiece by C. Medović. – **Mali Pašman**, W of Pašman, has an aisle-less medieval church dedicated to St Roch.

On Čokovac, a hill NW of the village of **Tkon**, is a Romanesque *Benedictine Abbey*. After being rebuilt in the 14th c. this became a secret center of Glagolitic worship (see under Krk). There are a Glagolitic Crucifix in the church and a Glagolitic inscription in the refectory. – At **Kraj** is a 14th c. *Franciscan Friary*, partly remodelled in Baroque style. – At **Nevidjane** is the early medieval *Convent of St Neviana*.

# Pátmos
## (Pátmos)

Greece
Nomos: Dodecanese.
Area: 13 sq. miles/34 sq. km. – Population: 2430.

HOTELS. – IN PÁTMOS: *Patmion*, II, 42 b.; *Neon*, V, 14 b. – IN SKÁLA: *Chris*, III, 48 b.; *Astoria*, III, 26 b.

BATHING BEACHES. – In Kámbos Bay, at the N end of the island, and at other places on the coast.

TRANSPORTATION. – Pátmos is served by boats sailing between Piraeus and Rhodes and between Rhodes and Sámos. – Boats to the neighboring islands of Lípsi and Arkí.

**Pátmos lies in the eastern Aegean, S of Sámos and SE of Ikaría. The most northerly island in the Dodecanese, it is of volcanic origin – perhaps the rim of an extinct crater – and has a much-indented coastline.**

Pátmos has been associated since the Middle Ages with St John the Evangelist, who is believed to have lived in exile here in the year A.D. 95 and to have written the Book of Revelation while on the island.

HISTORY. – Ancient Pátmos was occupied by Dorian and later by Ionian Greeks, and had a Sanctuary of Artemis. Little is known of the early history of the island, which was of no economic or political importance. Like the barren neighboring islands, Pátmos was used by the Romans as a place of banishment. In the early medieval period it seems to have been abandoned and desolate. – A new phase in the island's history began in 1088, when Abbot Christodoulos fled from Asia Minor and moved his monastery from Mount Latmos near Miletus to Pátmos. This was a period of great religious and intellectual activity: enjoying almost complete independence, the island rose to wealth and influence thanks to the donations made to the monastery, which was granted extensive privileges and was governed by its own strict rule (*typikon*). It survived the period of Turkish rule unscathed, paying only an annual tribute. – Since 1946 Pátmos has been protected as a national monument.

SIGHTS. – The island is made up of three parts linked by narrow isthmuses. The busy port of *Skála* is situated in the deepest inlet on the E side; an hour away to the SW (bus service) is the chief place on the island, **Pátmos** or *Khóra*, its cube-shaped whitewashed houses huddled around the fortified *Monastery of St John the Theologian* (15th–17th c.; *view) on the top of the rocky hill which dominates the town. The monastery, originally founded in 1088, is surrounded by massive 15th c. walls. The refectory and the principal church date from the

Monastery of St John, Pátmos

## Pátmos
### St John's Monastery

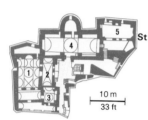

1. Katholikon
2. Chapel of Panayia
3. Chapel of Christodoulos
4. Refectory
5. Kitchen

10 m
33 ft

12th–13th c. In the church (18th–19th c. frescoes) is the tomb of the founder, Christodoulos. The library contains valuable early medieval manuscripts and icons; treasury.

N of Khóra, on the steep *Isthmos Kastelli*, are the remains of the ancient fortified city (4th c. B.C.). – Half-way between Skála and Khóra a road branches off on the left to the **Monastery of the Apocalypse** (now a theological college), built over the cave in which St John is said to have lived (conducted tour). The island is noted for embroideries and for its religious festivals, especially the re-enactment of the Last Supper by the monks at the monastery.

Some 7½ miles/12 km NE of Pátmos is the barren island of **Arkí** (ancient *Akrite*; area 2·7 sq. miles/7 sq. km; alt. 377 ft/115 m).

## Paxí
### *(Paxí)*

Greece
Nomos: Corfu (Kerkyra).
Area: 0·8 sq. mile/2 sq. km. – Population: 3000.
(i) **EOT,**
Governor's Building,
**Kérkyra** (Corfu);
tel. (0661) 3 03 60.

HOTEL. – *Paxos Beach*, II, 54 b.

TRANSPORTATION. – Boat connections with Kérkyra and Pátras.

The two quiet little islands of Paxí and Antípaxi lie immediately S of Corfu in the Ionian Sea. The villages of Paxí in the SE and Lákka in the N of the main island are linked by a road. In the SE are sulfur springs. Both islands have beautiful beaches and excellent *diving-grounds.

The islands' principal sources of income are farming (olive oil) and fishing. – On islets lying off the main port of **Paxí** or *Gaios* (pop. 500) are a Venetian fortress and the former Monastery of the Panayía (pilgrimage on August 15). – On the S coast is the Ipapanti *sea cave* (sea-lions).

SE of Paxí is its smaller sister island, **Antípaxi** (area 2·3 sq. miles/6 sq. km; alt. 351 ft/107 m; pop. 100; farming and fishing), a rocky island with beautiful beaches.

# Pelagian Islands/ Isole Pelagie

Italy
Region: Sicily. – Province: Agrigento.
(i) **EPT,**
Viale della Vittoria 255,
I-92100 **Agrigento;**
tel. (0922) 2 69 26.

HOTELS. – ON LAMPEDUSA: *Baia Turchese*, II, 94 b.; *Le Pelagie*, III, 24 b. Accommodation also available in private houses.

BOAT SERVICES. – Boats several times a week from Porto Empédocle (cars carried).

The islands of Lampedusa, Linosa and Lampione, together known as the Pelagian Islands (Italian Ísole Pelagie), lie SW of Sicily, only some 75 miles/121 km from the African coast. In recent years Lampedusa and Linosa have developed into popular holiday centers; Lampione is uninhabited.

**Lampedusa**, the main island of the group, has an area of 7·7 sq. miles/ 20 sq. km and a population of some 4000. The coast is mostly rocky, with good diving-grounds. Remains dating from the Bronze Age and the megalithic culture have been found in the interior of the island. The main sources of income are farming and fishing. The island has little water, and during the summer has to be supplied by tankers.

**Linosa**, 25 miles/53 km NE of Lampedusa, has an area of 2·1 sq. miles/5·5 sq. km. It is of volcanic origin, reaching a height of 640 ft/195 m in *Monte Vulcano*. It has no fresh water.

**Lampione**, the smallest island in the group with an area of only 7½ acres/3 hectares, lies 11 miles/16¼ km W of Lampedusa. It is uninhabited, but has a lighthouse.

# Pontine Islands/ Archipelago Pontino

Italy
Region: Lazio (Latium). – Province: Latina.
Population: 4000.
Post code: I-04027. – Telephone code: 0773.
ⓘ **EPT,**
Via Duca del Mare 19,
I-04100 Latina;
tel. 49 87 11.

HOTELS. – ON PONZA: *Chiaia di Luna*, I, 119 b.; *La Torre dei Borboni*, II, 64 b.; *Cernia*, II, 52 b.; *La Baia*, II, 54 b.; *Bellavista*, II, 30 b.

BOAT SERVICES. – From Formia to Ventotene according to requirements; from Anzio to Ponza several times a week; from Naples via Capri and Ischia to Ponza daily; also hydrofoils from Anzio.

**The Pontine Islands, lying off the coast of southern Latium, are of volcanic origin and are frequently subject to mild earth tremors. The inhabitants are mainly occupied in vine-growing and fishing, but there has also been a considerable development of the tourist trade in recent years, including the provision of camp sites.**

The north-western group of the Pontine Islands consists of the almost uninhabited islands of *Palmarola* (ancient *Palmaria*) and *Zanone* (ancient *Sinoinia*) and the well-cultivated main island of **Ponza**, 4¼ miles/7·5 km long, the rim of an old volcanic crater which rises to a height of 929 ft/283 m in *Monte della Guardia* at the S end and is fringed by picturesque bays and cliffs. Below the N side of the hill is the bay containing the island's harbor, with the villages of **Ponza** and *Santa Maria*. – The south-eastern group consists of the islands of *Ventotene* (2 miles/3 km long, ¾ mile/1 km wide), also part of an old

crater, with the village of Ventotene and a castle, and *Santo Stéfano*, a granitic island with a former penal establishment.

# Rab

Yugoslavia
Republic: Croatia (Hrvatska).
Area: 36 sq. miles/94 sq. km. – Population: 9000.
Telephone code: 051.
ⓘ **Turist-biro Rab,**
Maršala Tita 1,
YU-51280 **Rab**;
tel. 77 11 23.
**Generalturist Lopar,**
YU-51280 **Lopar**;
tel. 77 10 58.

HOTELS. – IN RAB: *Imperial*, II, 281 b.; *International*, II, 247 b.; *Istra*, II, 192 b.; *Beograd*, III, 94 b. – IN BANJOL: *Kontinental*, with annexes *Bellevue, Rio Magdalena, Margita* and *Marijan*, IV, together 132 b. – BARBAT: *Barbat*, III, 30 b. – LOPAR: *San Marino*, II, 1000 b. – SUHA PUNTA: *Eva*, II, 392 b.; *Carolina*, II, 292 b.; *tourist bungalow village*, II, 787 b.

CAMP SITES. – *Padova*, Banjol; *Rajska Plaža*, Lopar.

BATHING BEACHES. – Modest facilities for bathing on the coast road below the E side of Rab town walls. Naturist beach in *English Bay*, best reached by boat (admission charge; often overcrowded). The beaches at the *Suha Punta* hotel complex are better (facilities for naturists). – *Lopar* has a sandy beach 550 yds/500 m long. The *San Marino* hotel complex has attractive but rocky beaches (Rajska Plaža).

CAR FERRIES. – Senj–Baška/Krk–Lopar–Rab; Jablanac (mainland)–Rab. The fast passenger vessels from Rijeka to Dubrovnik (cars carried) also call in at Rab.

**The island of Rab, 14 miles/22 km long and up to 7 miles/11 km wide, lies near the northern Dalmatian coast between the islands of Krk and Pag. The most heavily wooded of the Yugoslav islands (holm oaks), traversed by three parallel ranges of hills, Rab attracts large numbers of visitors with its scenic beauty and attractive resorts; and one of these, the little town of Rab, offers the additional attraction of its fine old buildings.**

HISTORY. – Originally a Greek town, then a Roman settlement, after which it belonged successively to Byzantium, Hungary, Venice (1420–1797) and Austria, Rab became part of Yugoslavia in 1918.

The island's capital, **Rab**, lies on a narrow tongue of land, with the sea on either side. Its most conspicuous landmarks are four campaniles, the tallest and handsomest of which (85 ft/26 m) stands opposite St Mary's Cathedral.

SIGHTS. – From the landing-place it is a short distance, following the line of the town walls, to Tito Square, on the N side of which is the *Rector's Palace* (Knežev Dvor), with the Town Hall adjoining it. The old *Sea Gate* (Morska Vrata) leads into the main square (Plokata Gospi), which has been the hub of the town's life since the 14th c. The principal building in the square is the **Loggia** with its eight marble columns, once used as a law court. Adjoining the Loggia are a *clock-tower* and the little Gothic *Church of St Nicholas*. From here a flight of steps leads to the "Lower Street" (Donja Ulica, Ulica Marka Oreškovića), which runs past a number of fine old houses and the *Marčić Glazigna Palace* (Gothic windows and lions' heads) to the remains of the *Nemir Palace*, with a well-preserved doorway.

From the market square we continue to the "Upper Street" (Gorna Ulica, Ulica Rade Končara). To the right, adjoining the *Church of Sv. Križ* (Baroque stucco-work of 1798), can be seen *St John's Church* (Sv. Ivan Evangelist). The church itself, on the edge of steep cliffs, is in ruins, but the *campanile* survives. Farther along the street stands the 16th c. *St Justin's Church*, with a campanile topped by an

Rab, seen from the campanile

onion-shaped stone helm. The church has a Renaissance altar of carved wood and another altar (to the left) with a picture, the "Death of St Joseph", ascribed to Titian but probably by one of his pupils. Beyond this, on the right, is the 11th c. *St Andrew's Convent*, a house of Benedictine nuns which was converted into a private house in the 19th c.

The "Upper Street" leads into the Cathedral Square, with the fine *campanile* already mentioned, which can be climbed (fine view of the town). **St Mary's Cathedral** (*Crkva Sv. Marija*) is a predominantly Romanesque church dating from the 12th c. The W front has a fine *Renaissance doorway* with a Pietà of 1519.

Notable features of the INTERIOR are the 12th c. silver-gilt **Reliquary of St Christopher** above the High Altar, the carved *choir-stalls* (1445) by an unknown local master, part of a polyptych of the Venetian School (14th c.) on the altar in the S aisle, a Croatian *tabernacle* of about 1000 and a *font* of 1497.

At the N end of the town is the \***Komrčar Park**, planted with palms, pines, holm oaks and cypresses. Walking through the park or along the beautiful \*seafront promenade, we come to the **Franciscan Friary of St Euphemia**, with a fine *cloister* and *garden*. The church contains a number of notable *pictures*, including works by Antonio and Bartolommeo Vivarini (1458). NW of the friary is the forester's house of *Šuma Dundovo*.

7½ miles/12 km from the center of Rab (bus service) is **Lopar**, a small but beautiful village, which has only one historical association. It was the birthplace of a hermit named Marianus who retired to the mountains for the sake of his faith and in A.D. 301 founded San Marino, the smallest and oldest Republic in the world. Near the village lies the hotel complex of *San Marino*. There are several extensive sandy beaches.

# Rhodes/Rhodos
## (Ródhos)

Greece
Nomos: Dodecanese.
Area: 540 sq. miles/1398 sq. km. – Population: 60,000 (including some 2000 Turks).
Altitude: 0–3986 ft/0–1215 m.
Telephone code: 0241.
ⓘ EOT,
corner of Makarios and Papagos Streets; tel. 2 36 55 and 2 74 23.

HOTELS. – RHODES TOWN: \*Grand Hotel Astir Palace, L, 699 b., SB, SP, casino; Metropolitan Capsis, I, 1202 b., SP; Belvedere, I, 394 b., SP; Ibiscus, I, 383 b.; Blue Sky, I, 332 b., SP; Chavaliers' Palace, I, 319 b., SP; Mediterranean, I, 292 b.; Cairo Palace, I, 201 b., SP; Siravast, I, 170 b., SP; Park, I, 153 b., SP; Imperial, I, 151 b.; Regina, I, 144 b., SP; Riviera, I, 116 b.; Kamiros, I, 90 b.; Esperia, II, 362 b.; Cactus, II, 336 b.; Athina, II, 267 b., SP; Alexia, II, 257 b.; Constantinos, II, 246 b.; Plaza, II, 244 b.; Corali, II, 217 b.; Aglaia, II, 209 b.; Manousos, II, 204 b.; Acandia, II, 150 b.; Europa, II, 147 b.; Spartalis, II, 141 b.; Delphini, II, 135 b.; Despo, II, 122 b.; Angela, II, 118 b.; Marie, III, 245 b.; Semiramis, III, 230 b.; Flora, III, 188 b.; Soleil (hotel school), III, 160 b.; *Parthenon*, III, 150 b.; *Africa*, III, 144 b.; *El Greco*, III, 140 b.; *Carina*, III, 108 b.; *Colossos*, III, 99 b.

TRIÁNDA/IXÍA: *Rhodos Palace*, L, 1220 b., SB (sea water), children's zoo; *Olympic Palace* (adjoining), L, 552 b., SP; *Miramare Beach*, L, 330 b., SP, bungalows; *Rhodos Bay*, I, 611 b., SP, bungalows; *Oceanis*, I, 523 b., SP; *Golden Beach*, I, 431 b., SP, bungalows; *Electra Palace*, I, 400 b., SP; *Dionyssos*, I, 396 b., SP; *Avra Beach*, I, 353 b., SP, bungalows; *Bel Air*, I, 293 b., SP; *Solemar*, II, 194 b., SP; *Elisabeth*, I, 190 b., SP, apartments; *Leto*, II, 184 b., SP. – KALLITHÉA (5 miles/8 km SE): *Sunwing*, I, 738 b., SP. – KOSKINOÚ (6 miles/10 km SE): *Paradise*, I, 799 b., SP; *Eden Rock*, I, 720 b., SP, bungalows. – FALIRÁKI (11 miles/18 km SE): *Esperides*, I, 875 b., SP; *Colossos Beach*, I, 754 b., SP; *Faliraki Beach*, I, 550 b., SP; *Blue Sea*, I, 548 b., SP; *Apollo Beach*, I, 539 b., SP; *Rhodos Beach*, I, 517 b., SP, bungalows. – AFÁNDOU (15 miles/25 km SE): *Xenia*, II, 52 b., SP. – LÍNDOS: *Lindos Bay*, I, 364 b., SP. – THOLO (12½ miles/20 km SW): *Doretta Beach*, I, 546 b. – ON MOUNT PROFÍTIS ILÍAS: *Elafos-Elafina*, I, 127 b.

AIR SERVICES. – Airport at Kremasti, 10 miles/16 km SW of Rhodes town. – Regular flights from Athens to Rhodes (55 minutes); direct flights from London in summer; Rhodes–Iráklion (Crete) and Rhodes–Kárpathos in summer.

BOAT SERVICES. – Regular services from Athens (Piraeus), 1–3 sailings daily on weekdays (16–22 hours according to company and intermediate calls); also from Venice to Athens (Piraeus) and from Ancona via Katákolo, Iráklion and Santorin to Rhodes (seasonal). – *Local services* in Dodecanese: Rhodes–Sými–Tílos–Nísyros–Kos–Kálymnos–Léros Lípsi–Pátmos–Arkí–Agathonísi–Sámos; Rhodes–Kos–Kálymnos–Astypálaia; Rhodes–Kastellorízo (Meyísti); Rhodes–Khalkí–Diafáni–Kárpathos–Kásos.

ROADS. – The island is served by some 250 miles/400 km of roads, mostly of good quality, so that it is well worth while to bring your car or to rent one. – CAR RENTAL: *Avis*, 9 Gallias Street; *Hertz*, 10 Griva Street; *Hellascars*, Eth. Dodekanission Street; etc. – BUS SERVICES between the main places on the island.

BATHING BEACHES: around the peninsula on which Rhodes town is situated, along the E coast, particularly at *Faliráki*, *Afándou*, *Kharaki* and *Líndos*, and in the NW between *Trianda* and *Kremasti*. – BOAT RENTAL: several firms in Rhodes town. – WATER-SKIING SCHOOL: Rhodes Boat Club, 9 Koundouriotou Square. – DIVING SCHOOL. – GOLF-COURSE (18 holes) at Afándou.

EVENTS. – *Wine Festival* at Rodíni (July 15–September 30); *folk-dancing* (June–October) in Folk Theater, Rodíni Valley; many *church patronal festivals* (summer); *Mountain Road Race* and *Rhodes Rally* (both end of July).

**Rhodes, the largest of the Dodecanese, lies only 11 miles/18 km off the SW coast of Turkey. It is a wooded island with an abundance of water, rising to a height of 3986 ft/ 1215 m in Mount Atávyros. The agricultural land is mainly along the coasts. With its beautiful scenery, its excellent beaches and its fine old** buildings erected by the Knights of St John, Rhodes holds a wealth of attraction for visitors.

HISTORY. – The island of Rhodes was occupied in the Neolithic period, but its great cultural flowering came only with its settlement by Dorian Greeks. Their three cities of Líndos, Ialysos and Kámeiros were members of the *Hexapolis* (League of Six Cities) which became subject to the Persians in the 6th c. B.C. In the 5th c. Rhodes became a member of the Confederacy of Delos. About 408 B.C. the new capital city of Rhodes was laid out on a regular plan by the famous Greek town-planner Hippodamos of Miletus, and in the 4th c. it overshadowed Athens itself in commercial importance. Its great landmark, one of the Seven Wonders of the World, was the celebrated Colossus of Rhodes, a 100 ft/30 m high bronze statue of the sun god Helios standing on a stone base 35 ft/10 m high. Cast between 304 and 292 B.C. by Chares of Lindos, it stood at the entrance to the harbor and probably served as a lighthouse. It collapsed in an earthquake about 225 B.C. – With the extension of Roman control in the East the island's trade declined, but the city remained an important cultural center, with a well-known university (attended by Cicero and Caesar) and a major school of sculpture in which the famous Laocoön group now in the Vatican Museum was produced about 50 B.C. – During the Middle Ages the possession of Rhodes was contested by the Arabs, the Byzantines, the Venetians and the Genoese. In 1309 it was occupied by the *Knights of St John*, who developed the town into a powerful stronghold but were compelled to surrender it to the Turks under Suleyman the Magnificent in 1522. After almost 400 years of Turkish rule the island was occupied by Italy in 1912. In 1947, after the Second World War, it became part of Greece.

# Rhodes town

Picturesquely situated at the northern-most tip of the island, the town of **Rhodes** (pop. 32,000, including about 1000 Turks) has been capital of the island since ancient times. From 1309 to 1522 it was the residence of the Grand Master of the Order of St John. It consists of the Knights' town (Collachium) and the old medieval town in the center, the new town with its public buildings to the N and outlying districts to the S and W.

SIGHTS. – The old town, within which no Christian was allowed to live during the Turkish period, is surrounded by the magnificent 2½ mile/4 km long circuit of the 15th–16th c. **town walls**, one of the finest examples of the medieval art of fortification. Particularly impressive features are the *Amboise Gate* (with gardens and a deer-park adjoining), built by the Grand Master, Aimerie d'Amboise in 1512, in the NW, and the *Marine Gate* (1468; relief of the Virgin Mary) in the NE, by the Commercial Harbor.

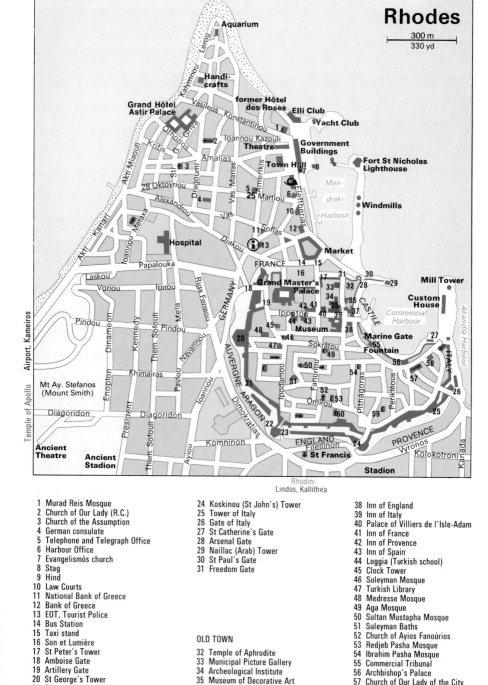

# Rhodes

300 m
330 yd

1 Murad Reis Mosque
2 Church of Our Lady (R.C.)
3 Church of the Assumption
4 German consulate
5 Telephone and Telegraph Office
6 Harbour Office
7 Evangelismós church
8 Stag
9 Hind
10 Law Courts
11 National Bank of Greece
12 Bank of Greece
13 EOT, Tourist Police
14 Bus Station
15 Taxi stand
16 Son et Lumière
17 St Peter's Tower
18 Amboise Gate
19 Artillery Gate
20 St George's Tower
21 Tower of Spain
22 St Mary's Tower
23 St Athanasius Gate

24 Koskinou (St John's) Tower
25 Tower of Italy
26 Gate of Italy
27 St Catherine's Gate
28 Arsenal Gate
29 Naillac (Arab) Tower
30 St Paul's Gate
31 Freedom Gate

OLD TOWN

32 Temple of Aphrodite
33 Municipal Picture Gallery
34 Archeological Institute
35 Museum of Decorative Art
36 Inn of Auvergne
37 Church of the Order of St John
   (museum)

38 Inn of England
39 Inn of Italy
40 Palace of Villiers de l'Isle-Adam
41 Inn of France
42 Inn of Provence
43 Inn of Spain
44 Loggia (Turkish school)
45 Clock Tower
46 Suleyman Mosque
47 Turkish Library
48 Medresse Mosque
49 Aga Mosque
50 Sultan Mustapha Mosque
51 Suleyman Baths
52 Church of Ayios Fanoúrios
53 Redjeb Pasha Mosque
54 Ibrahim Pasha Mosque
55 Commercial Tribunal
56 Archbishop's Palace
57 Church of Our Lady of the City
58 Hospice of St Catherine
59 Dolapli Mosque
60 Bourouzan Mosque

Visitors can take a fascinating walk around the old town on the walls, starting from the square in front of the Grand Master's Palace (entrance at Artillery Gate; guided walks) and continuing to the Koskinou Gate. A walk around the old town outside the walls is also full of interest.

The **Commercial Harbor** (*Emporiko Limani*), the town's principal harbor, used by the ships from Piraeus, and the old **Mandráki Harbor** to the N, the ancient harbor (from 408 B.C.), now mainly occupied by pleasure craft, are protected by long breakwaters. On the Mandráki Breakwater are three disused *windmills,*

Entrance to the Mandráki Harbor, Rhodes, with the stag and the hind

and at the northern tip are *Fort St Nicholas* (14th–15th c.), circular in plan, and a lighthouse. On either side of the harbor entrance stand stone columns topped by figures of a **stag** and a **hind**, the town's heraldic animals (and accordingly red deer are a protected species on Rhodes). On the E side of the old town is the **Akandia Harbor**, with a shipyard.

The *Freedom Gate*, at the S end of the Mandráki Breakwater, leads into the walled OLD TOWN with its labyrinth of narrow streets and lanes, its domes and its minarets set amid palms and planes. In Symi Square are the remains of a *Temple of Aphrodite* (3rd c. B.C.) and the *Municipal Picture Gallery* (modern art). Immediately S of this lies the picturesque Argyrokastro Square, in the center of which can be seen a small *fountain* constructed from fragments of a Byzantine baptistery. On the W side of the square is the former Arsenal (14th c.), now housing the *Archeological Institute* and the *Museum of Decorative Art*. A passage leads through to the former *Church of the Order of St John* (on the left), now a Museum of Early Christian and Byzantine Art. Diagonally across from this stands the massive *Hospital of the Order* (15th c., restored), now occupied by the **Archeological Museum**.

From the N side of the Hospital the *Street of the Knights* (*Odós Ippotón*) runs W. In this street, which still conveys an excellent impression of a Late Gothic

(15th–16th c.) street, were most of the "Inns" of the various nations ("Tongues") of the Order of St John. The finest of these is the *Inn of France* (on the right), built between 1492 and 1503. At the W end of the street, on the highest point in the town (to the right), stands the *Grand Master's Palace*, a massive stronghold which was defended by a triple circuit of walls. It suffered heavy destruction during the Turkish Siege, and was almost completely destroyed by an explosion in 1856, but during the period of Italian occupation (1912–43) was rebuilt on the basis of old plans (commemorative tablet at entrance). The interior arrangement does not, however, follow the original pattern. Notable features of the interior are the many *pebble mosaic pavements* from the island of Kos. On the NE side of the palace are beautiful gardens (entrance in Papagos Street). At its SW corner the **Artillery Gate** (*St Anthony's Gate*) gives access to the walls.

To the S of the Grand Master's Palace is a striking 19th c. **Clock-Tower**. Still farther S is the **Suleyman Mosque** (beautiful Renaissance doorway), the largest mosque on the island, and facing it, to the S, the *Turkish Library* (1794), with valuable manuscripts of the Koran. – From here the lively Socrates Street (Odós Sokrátous), flanked by bazaars, leads southward through the center of the old town toward the Commercial Harbor. SE of the Marine Gate are the *Commercial Tribunal* (1507) and the *Archbishop's*

*Palace* (15th c.). In the square in front of the palace can be seen the attractive *Seahorse Fountain*. – To the S of Socrates Street is a picturesque maze of streets and lanes, in particular Phanourios Street, Homer Street (Odós Omírou), both spanned by flying buttresses, and Pythagoras Street, with several mosques, including the **Ibrahim Pasha Mosque**, the oldest in the town (1531), and, opposite the magnificent **Suleyman Baths** with their many domes (open to visitors and bathers), the *Sultan Mustapha Mosque* (1765). In Phanourios Street is the little Orthodox *Church of St Phanourios*, partly built underground (founded 1335; converted into a mosque during the Turkish period). – On the W side of the old town, near St George's Tower, is the *Hurmale Medresse* (originally a Byzantine church), with a picturesque inner courtyard.

The town of Rhodes at night

The NEW TOWN, with Government offices and many hotels and restaurants, extends to the N of the old town, reaching almost to the northernmost tip of the island.

The massive **New Market** (*Nea Agora*) by the Mandráki Harbor has a large inner courtyard. From here Freedom Avenue (Eleftherías) runs N, past the Law Courts and the Post Office, to the **Evangelismós Church** (originally Roman Catholic, now Orthodox), a reproduction (1925) of the old monastic Church of St John, which originally stood beside the Grand Master's

Palace and was destroyed in the 1856 explosion. – Farther N are the Venetian-style **Government Buildings** (*Nomarchia*), the *Town Hall* and the *Theater*. Beyond these is the charming *Murad Reis Mosque*, surrounded by the old Turkish cemetery. – At the northern tip of the new town is an *Aquarium*, with a small museum of natural history. Some 550 yds/500 m SW the Grand Hotel Astor Palace has a casino.

Beach on the W side of the new town of Rhodes

SURROUNDINGS of Rhodes town. – Some 1¼ miles/ 2 km S of the old town, on the road to Kallithéa, are a number of **cemeteries** – two Orthodox (one large and one small) and a Roman Catholic, a Jewish and a new Turkish one. – Farther S is the beautiful *Rodini Valley*, with a park, a small zoo, a folk theater and a series of attractive footpaths.

2 miles/3 km SW of the new town, on **Mount Aghios Stéfanos** (also known as *Mount Smith*; 364 ft/ 111 m; views), are remains of the ancient *acropolis*, with fragments of temples. On the slopes of the hill are a *stadium* and a *theater* (restored).

9 miles/15 km SW of Rhodes (bus service) rises **Mount Filérimos** (876 ft/267 m; views), with the remains of the acropolis of ancient **Ialysos** (admission fee). On the site of a Temple of Athena (partly excavated) is a former *monastery* built by the Knights (reconstructed). Below this to the S, reached by a flight of steps in poor condition, is a charming Doric *fountain-house* (4th c. B.C.). To the NW is the partly subterranean *St George's Church* (15th c.; frescoes).

EXCURSIONS ON THE ISLAND. – **From Rhodes via Kámeiros to Líndos** (69 miles/111 km or 81 miles/131 km). – The road runs SW along the coast, and in 10 miles/16 km, beyond the airport, a road branches off on the left and runs via *Kalamónas* to (4½ miles/7 km) the *Valley of Butterflies (Petaloúdes)*, which in the height of summer is the haunt of thousands of reddish-brown butterflies. –

$7\frac{1}{2}$ miles/12 km: side road to Embónas, offering an attractive alternative route. – $2\frac{1}{2}$ miles/4 km: side road (1 mile/1·5 km) to the site, partly excavated, of ancient **Kámeiros** (6th c. B.C. to 6th c. A.D.). – Then on a beautiful *panoramic road above the coast to *Monólithos* (20 miles/ 32 km; alt. 920 ft/280 m). $\frac{3}{4}$ mile/1 km W there is a *view of a ruined castle of the Knights and the bay beyond. – From Monólithos it is another 29 miles/47 km eastward across the island to Líndos.

10 miles/16 km beyond the turning for Embónas a road goes off on the left to **Mount Profítis Ilías** (2618 ft/798 m; extensive *views; Foundoukli Church). – 5 miles/8 km: junction with the panoramic road, from which it is another 14 miles/ 22 km to Monólithos.

**From Rhodes via Arkhángelos to Líndos** (39 miles/62 km). – The road runs S, at some distance from the E coast for most of the way. $4\frac{1}{2}$ miles/7 km: road on the left (2 miles/3 km) to the beautifully situated resort (formerly a spa) of *Kallithéa*, with a rocky beach. – $1\frac{1}{4}$ miles/2 km: *Koskinoú*, a village of color-washed houses, picturesquely situated on a hill. – $4\frac{1}{2}$ miles/7 km: road on the left (2 miles/ 3 km) to *Faliráki* (good sandy beach; ceramic factory). – 6 miles/9 km: *Afándou* (sandy beach; large carpet factory). – 4 miles/6 km: *Kolýmbia*, with a beautiful bay (bathing). – 4 miles/6 km: **Arkhángelos**, a picturesque township with a ruined castle dominating it to the S. – $4\frac{1}{2}$ miles/7 km: *Malóna*, a modest little village surrounded by beautiful orange and lemon groves. – 11 miles/18 km: **Líndos**.

**Líndos** (alt. 130 ft/40 m; pop. 1500), situated on a promontory half-way down the E coast of the island, was a flourishing commercial port in ancient times. On a hill at the entrance to the large harbor is the domed tomb (open to the public) of the tyrant Kleoboulos. – Features of interest in the town are the Church of the Panayía (Byzantine wall-paintings) and a number of 17th c. houses, with small collections of Lindian faience (15th–17th c.), which is now rare. – On the NW side of the *Acropolis* (384 ft/117 m) can be seen the medieval Knights' Castle (later taken over by the Turks). On the rock face on the N side, at the foot of a steep flight of steps constructed by the Knights, is an ancient carving of a ship (about 200 B.C.), some 16 ft/5 m square. – On the highest terrace

Temple of Athena Lindia, Líndos

of the acropolis (*view), approached by a *monumental staircase*, with the Doric colonnade of a stoa, stands the *Temple of Athena Lindia* (partly rebuilt). – Immediately S of the town lies a small sheltered rocky harbor where the Apostle Paul is said to have landed (chapel).

W of Rhodes, at distances of up to 40 miles/64 km, lie the islands of **Alimniá** (pop. 25), with the ruins of a Genoese castle, and **Khalkí** (pop. 3000; chief place Nimbório), a rocky island with a medieval castle and the remains of a Temple of Apollo.

There is a weekly boat from Rhodes to **Meyísti** (*Kastellorízo*), Greece's most easterly island (pop. 500), lying off the S coast of Asia Minor. It has a medieval castle which was rebuilt by the Knights of St John.

### Lindos
#### Akropolis

1 Schiffsrelief
2 Johannitertreppe
3 Torbau
4 Ritterhaus
5 Burgkirche
6 spätantiker Tempel
7 Unterbau
8 dorische Säulenhalle
9 Freitreppe
10 Propylon
11 Vorhalle
12 Tempel der Athena Lindia

50 m

# Samos
## (Sámos)

Greece
Nomos: Sámos.
Area: 184 sq. miles/476 sq. km. – Population:
43,000.
Altitude: 0–4738 ft/0–1444 m.
Telephone code: 0273.

ⓘ **Tourist Police,**
Samos town (summer only);
tel. 2 79 80.

HOTELS. – SÁMOS: *Xenia*, II, 56 b.; *Samos*, III, 160 b.;
YOUTH HOSTEL. – PYTHAGÓRION: *Pythagoras*, III, 55
b. – KARLÓVASI: *Merope*, II, 152 b. – KOKKÁRI: *Kokkari
Beach*, III, 90 b.

AIR SERVICES. – Airport 2½ miles/4 km W of
Pythagórion. – Athens–Sámos twice daily.

BOAT SERVICES. – Athens (Piraeus)–Karlóvasi and
Athens (Piraeus)–Sámos, each six sailings a week
(14½–16 hours; cars carried). – *Local services*:
Rhodes–Sými–Tínos–Nísyros–Kos–Kálymnos–Léros–
Lípsos–Pátmos–Akrí–Agathonísi–Sámos     (Pytha-
górion); also to Turkish mainland (irregular).

ROADS: sometimes unsurfaced. – CAR RENTAL: in
Sámos. – BUS SERVICES. – TAXIS.

BATHING BEACHES. – Round Vathý Bay; *Psili
Amos, Phythagórion and Eraia on the S coast.

EVENTS. – Local *National Festival* (August 6); *church
festivals* in the Monastery of *Panayía Vrontianí*, the
oldest on the island (1566), 9 miles/15 km W of
Sámos (September 8), and *Timiou Stavroú*, 2 miles/
3 km W of Khóra (September 14).

**Sámos, a densely populated Greek
island in the southern Sporades,
separated from the coast of Asia
Minor by a channel 2100 yds/1900 m
wide, is well wooded, hilly and
abundantly supplied with watercourses.**

Farming (including vine-growing), timber for the construction of caiques (the
local fishing-boats) and fishing have been
from time immemorial the islanders' main
sources of income.

HISTORY. – The first inhabitants of Sámos, probably
Carians, were displaced at an early period by Ionians,
who used the island as a convenient base from which
to settle the neighboring coast of Asia Minor. Sámos
reached the peak of its political and economic power
in the 6th c. B.C. under the tyrant Polykrates, who, like
other tyrants of his time, was a great builder and
fostered the arts. The island took part in the Ionian
Rebellion, shook off Persian rule and became a
favored member of the First Attic Maritime League.
Having rebelled against Athenian rule (480 B.C.), it
was conquered by Perikles and until the end of the
Peloponnesian War became a base for the Athenian
fleet. Thereafter it came at different times under
Spartan, Attic and Persian influence. It took no part in
the Second Attic Maritime League. In 133 B.C. it

passed under Roman rule, but achieved freedom in the
time of Augustus and Tiberius (A.D. 17). – Later Sámos
was successively controlled by Byzantines, Arabs
(from A.D. 824), Venetians and Genoese. At the end of
the 15th c. it was plundered by the Turks, and in 1509
it was again devastated. In 1562, however, it was
resettled, and later was granted important privileges.
During the Greek War of Liberation (1821) the Turks
were unable to take the island. In 1832 the Conference
of London declared Sámos to be a principality
tributary to the Ottoman Empire, incorporating the
Greek cross in its flag. The Prince, though appointed
by the Sultan, was required to be a Christian. – During
the First Balkan War, in 1912, Italian troops drove out
the Turks, and later in the year Sámos became part of
Greece. – Sámos was the home of the Greek
philosopher Pythagoras.

The island's capital, *Vathý* also known by
its former name of **Sámos**, (Archeological Museum), lies in a semicircle
around the sheltered inner harbor, its
houses extending picturesquely up the
hillside with its vines and olive trees to the
Upper Town of *Apáno Vathý*. To the E of
the town are the beautifully situated
monasteries of *Aghia Zóni* and *Zoodókhos Piyí*.

On the island of Sámos

12½ miles/20 km SW of Vathý, near the
port of *Pythagórion* (until 1945 known as
*Tigáni*), is the **site of ancient Sámos**,
with remains of the harbor, the theater,
scattered remains of buildings and a
magnificent circuit of *town walls*,
4 miles/6·5 km long, with gates and 31
towers. A walk around the walls takes 2–3
hours, starting from the road to Khóra at
the W end of the site. The line of the walls,
built of polygonal blocks, runs up the hill
of *Kástro* (748 ft/228 m), with the early
19th c. Castle of Logothetis, which played
an important part in the defense of the
island during the War of Liberation. From
the top of the hill there are superb *views
– to the S of the site of ancient Sámos, to
the SW of the Heraion, to the N of the wide
fertile plain around the village of *Mytilíni*
(N of the village, slate-beds containing
fossils; Paleontological Museum) and the
Ayiades chapels, to the SE of the rich

Aghia Triás Monastery and to the W of Khóra, the old capital of the island. The wall, which is mostly of the Hellenistic period, then runs E along the northern edge of Mount Kástro, crosses a narrow valley with an ancient necropolis at Pythagórion and takes in the acropolis plateau (Astypálaia), which projects toward the NE. At both the E and the W end it extends down to the sea.

On the S side of Mount Kástro is the *Monastery of the Panayía Spilianí.* Farther W is the ancient *Theater,* and still nearer the western wall the S end of the *Eupalineion,* a tunnel $\frac{3}{4}$ mile/1 km long cut through the rock to carry a water channel. It is possible to walk through the tunnel, which is about 5 ft 9 in./1·75 m high and wide. 465 yds/425 m from the S entrance visitors can see the point where the two shafts, one driven from each end, met one another, making an almost perfect join.

The water was conveyed to the N end of the tunnel in a channel which was partly hewn from the rock and partly constructed of masonry, with a covering of horizontal stone slabs. The channel begins at a large reservoir fed by an abundant spring which is still used to supply water. The vaulted roof of this cistern is supported by 15 piers; on top of it is one of the three *Ayiades chapels.*

4 miles/6 km W of Pythagórion, at the W end of the rather marshy plain S of Khóra, is the **Heraion,** or Temple of Hera. Remains of an earlier Ionic temple (7th c. B.C.) are built into the foundations of the later temple. The older temple is believed to have been the first example of what later became the regular temple plan, with a cella enclosed within columns. The later temple (6th–5th c. B.C.), of which the foundations and part of the superstructure have survived, remained unfinished. The pronaos at the E end of the temple was square, divided into three aisles by two rows of five columns. The cella, though measuring 75 ft/23 m by 175 ft/54 m, had no columns in the interior. It was surrounded by a total of 123 columns – 2 × 24 along each side, 3 × 8 at the E end and 3 × 9 at the W end. Originally earth ramps led up to the temple, but during the Early Roman period a flight of marble steps was constructed at the E end, with the sacrificial altar standing at the foot. In the 1st c. B.C. the sanctuary was devastated by pirates and plundered by Roman officials (Verres, Antony), but it was apparently restored by Augustus during his stay on Sámos (21–10 B.C.).

$1\frac{1}{4}$ miles/2 km W of the Heraion, beyond the river, is the handsome "*Saracen Tower*", originally part of a medieval stronghold which, like the surrounding lands, belonged to the Monastery of St John on Patmos.

From Sámos it is possible to visit some of the ancient sites on the mainland of Asia Minor, such as *Priene, *Miletus or **Ephesus (which lies a short distance N of the Turkish port of Kuşadası).

SW of Sámos lies the island of **Ikaría** (area 98 sq. miles/255 sq. km; pop. 7700), named after Ikaros, who flew from Crete with his father Daidalos but plunged into the Icarian Sea which also bears his name.

The island is traversed by a ridge rising to 3280 ft/1000 m, with bare and treeless summits but slopes covered with macchia and forest. At the foot of the steep SE slope is the little port of **Aghios Kýrikos,** which in recent years has developed into something of a tourist center. From here a road runs $2\frac{1}{2}$ miles/4 km NE to **Thérmai,** on the site of the ancient city of the same name, with medicinal springs (recommended for rheumatism, arthritis and neuritis), continuing to the villages of Karavostámon, Évdilos and Armenísti on the N coast.

# Samothrace
## *(Samothráki)*

Greece
Nomos: Évros.
Area: 69 sq. miles./178 sq. km – Population: 3000.

HOTEL. – IN PALAIÓPOLIS: *Xenia,* II, 12 b.

TRANSPORTATION. – *Air service:* Athens–Alexandroúpolis. *Ferry* Alexandroúpolis–Samothrace.

*Samothrace is a rocky island of great scenic beauty lying S of the Hellespont some 20 miles off the Thracian coast in the north-eastern Aegean (Sea of Thrace). Its highest point is Mount Fengári (6037 ft/ 1840 m). The regular coastline with few inlets offers little in the way of sheltered harbors for shipping. The population's main source of income is the growing of fruit and vegetables (onions).

HISTORY. – Samothrace has been inhabited since Neolithic times. About 1000 B.C. incomers from mainland Thrace settled on the island, bringing with them the cult of the deities known as **Kabeiroi** (or

Cabira) to which Samothrace owed the high status and extensive autonomy it enjoyed from ancient times until the coming of Christianity. – About 700 B.C. a further wave of settlers from Aeolia and Ionia came to Samothrace. Later, after periods of Macedonian and then Egyptian rule, it was occupied by Rome in 163 B.C. The Romans were succeeded by the Byzantines, who in turn gave place to Venetians and Genoese; and finally the Turks gained control of the island in 1457. – The First Balkan War led to the incorporation of Samothrace in Greece. During the Second World War it was occupied by Bulgarian troops.

The island's capital, **Samothráki** or *Khóra* (pop. 1500; museum), lies in the hills 2 miles/3 km E of the port of *Kalamiotissa* (ruined castle). 2½ miles/4 km NE, near the coast, is the site of the island's ancient capital, now known as Palaiópolis. Above this is the *Sanctuary of the Great Gods (or *Sanctuary of the Kabeiroi*), which has only recently been completely excavated. In spite of repeated destruction by pirates, wars and earthquakes the sanctuary continued in existence until the 4th c. A.D.; then during the Middle Ages the ruins were used as a source of building stone for medieval strongholds. The divinities worshiped here were Axieros, the Great Goddess of nature, with her youthful attendant god Kadmilos, two male deities, the Kabeiroi, and the god and goddess of the Underworld, Axiokersos and Axiokersa.

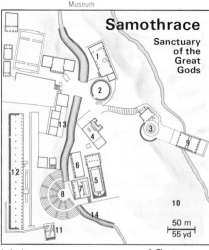

Museum

## Samothrace

Sanctuary of the Great Gods

| | |
|---|---|
| 1 Anaktoron | 8 Theater |
| 2 Arsinoeion | 9 Ptolemaion |
| 3 Circular building | 10 Necropolis |
| 4 Temenos | 11 Find-spot of Nike |
| 5 Hieron | 12 Stoa |
| 6 Hall of Votive Gifts | 13 Ceremonial hall |
| 7 Altar Court | 14 Cyclopean wall |

On a promontory between two streams are the remains of the *Old Temple* (7th–4th c. B.C.) and, S of this, the *New Temple* (3rd c. B.C.). Both temples have libation-pits. – Other buildings, dating from the Late Hellenistic period, are a **Stoa**, a niche (above the temple to the W) which once contained the *Victory of Samothrace*

now in the Louvre, the **Arsinoeion** (a rotunda built about 285 B.C. by Arsinoe, wife of King Lysimachos of Thrace, to house assemblies of the initiate) and, to the E of this, the **Ptolemaion**, built by Ptolemy II. – N of the Victory niche is a *theater* of the 2nd c. B.C. – In 168 B.C. Perseus, the last King of Macedon, sought refuge in the Sanctuary of the Kabeiroi when being pursued by the Romans.

To the SE of the sanctuary lies the *ancient cemetery* (7th c. B.C. to 2nd c. A.D.); *Archeological Museum*.

Above the sanctuary to the NE is the site of the city established by the Aeolian settlers (7th c. B.C. onwards). The colossal *town walls* (6th c. B.C.) reach high up on to the mountain ridge. Little is left within the walls, but on the acropolis hill are the ruins of a castle which belonged to the Genoese family of Gattelusi. – On a 33 ft/10 m high sinter cone at *Therma*, E of Palaiókastro, is a hot spring (131 °F/55 °C). – **Mount Fengári** offers a rewarding climb (6037 ft/1840 m; 6 hours, guide advisable; panoramic *views).

# Santorin (Thíra)
## *(Santoríni/Thíra)*

Greece
Nomos: Cyclades.
Area: 29 sq. miles/76 sq. km. – Population: 6200.
Telephone: 0286.

ⓘ **Tourist Police,**
  in **Firá**

HOTELS. – FIRÁ: *Atlantis*, I, 47 b.; *Kavalari*, III, 39 b.; *Panorama*, III, 34 b. – KAMÁRI: *Kamari*, III, 104 b. – MESARIÁ: *Artemidoros*, III, 30 b. – FIROSTÉFANO: *Kafieris*, III, 20 b. – YOUTH HOSTEL.

Accommodation can also be had in *Atlantis Villas* (old island houses, restored) at Ia (Oia).

BATHING BEACHES. – Kamári and Monólithos on the E coast, Périssa on the S coast (buses from Firá).

TRANSPORTATION. – *Air service:* Athens–Santorin; *boats*: Piraeus to Santorin (cars carried), and to Iráklion (Crete).

BOAT TRIPS. – From Skála to Mikrá Kaiméni in the caldera, with the 1925 crater; to the neighboring island of Thirasía; in good weather to **Anáfi**, 12 miles E of Santorin (area 14 sq. miles/35 sq. km; pop. 450), with the hilltop village of Khóra and the Panayía Monastery.

**Santorin (also known as Thíra), the most southerly of the larger Cyclades, and the neighboring islands of Thirasía (area 3½ sq. miles/9 sq km; alt. 968 ft/295 m) and Aspronísi (area 0·8 sq. mile/2 sq. km; alt. 233 ft/71 m) are relics of a volcanic crater engulfed by the sea.**

Wall of the crater, Santorin

the explosion of the volcano the island remained uninhabited for some 500 years.

At the beginning of the 1st millennium B.C. Thíra was occupied by Dorians, who settled mainly on a limestone ridge SE of Mount Profítis Ilías. In 630 B.C. their king, Grinos, founded Kyrene, the largest Greek colony in North Africa. From 275 to 146 B.C. Santorin was occupied by an Egyptian garrison, which held it on behalf of the Ptolemies; thereafter it came under Roman rule. In 1207, after the Fourth Crusade, it was conquered by Marco Sanudo, ruler of Náxos, and remained in Italian hands for three centuries. From this period date the name Santorin (=Santa Irene) and the ruined Castle of Skáros. In 1539 the island was taken by the Turks. It was finally reunited with Greece in 1830.

The eruption which led to the collapse of the crater can be dated to about the middle of the 2nd millennium B.C. The inhabitants, warned by the preceding volcanic activity, were evidently able to get away in time. The severe earthquakes and seaquakes accompanying the eruption may have been the cause of the sudden collapse of the Minoan civilization on Crete. The rim of the caldera now emerges from the sea to form a ring, open on the NW and SW sides, around a basin up to 1280 ft/390 m deep, out of which there rose in Historical times the peaks of a new volcano, now represented by the **Kaiméni Islands**. Hot springs and emissions of gas still bear witness to continuing volcanic activity (last eruption in 1956). – In the SW of Santorin is its highest hill, *Mount Profítis Ilías* (1916 ft/584 m). The crater rim itself falls steeply down to the central basin in sheer rock faces 650–1300 ft/200–400 m high, formed of greyish-black lava with layers of white pumice and reddish tuffs. On the outer slopes the land falls gradually away toward the sea, with a deep layer of fertile pumice soil on which vines flourish. There is insufficient water, however, to support trees. The inhabitants have attained a modest degree of prosperity by the export of wine, pulses and tomato purée and of "Santorin earth" (pozzolana), a pumice ash used in the manufacture of hydraulic cement. In recent years the tourist trade has also made great strides, thanks to the island's unusual scenic attractions and the archeological excavations, which are among the most important in Greece. Visitors whose only interest is bathing and sunbathing, however, will not come to Thíra

HISTORY. – In ancient times Thíra was known as *Kalliste* (the Fairest island) or as *Strongyle* (Circular). In the 3rd millennium B.C. (the period of the Cycladic culture) it was probably inhabited by Carians, but about 1900 B.C. it was settled by Achaeans, who in turn were displaced by Phoenicians about 1500. After

The volcanic force which originally built up the island around the older limestone cone of Mount Profítis Ilías (1916 ft/584 m) and then destroyed it shortly after 1500 B.C. continued to manifest itself in later centuries. In 197 B.C. the islet of Palaiá Kaiméni (the old burnt-up island) rose out of the drowned crater, followed in A.D. 1570 by Mikrá Kaiméni and in 1707–11 by Néa Kaiméni, which in 1925–26 joined up with Mikrá Kaiméni and is still active. The last violent volcanic phenomena, combined with earth tremors which caused considerable damage, took place in 1956.

SIGHTS. – The *entrance into the caldera by boat is highly impressive. After the gentle green slopes on the outside of the crater rim visitors find themselves suddenly enclosed within a ring of steep cliffs encircling the huge basin of the crater. At the northern tip of the main island the village of *Ia* (Oia) can be seen clinging to the edge of the cliffs, with a steep path zigzagging up from the little Bay of *Aghios Nikólaos*. As the boat sails on, the island of Thirasía (on the right) and the southern tip of Thera, visible in the distance beyond the Kaiméni Islands, close the ring around the basin.

The chief place on the island, **Thíra** (alt. 675 ft/205 m; pop. 1000), now comes into sight on the top of the cliffs beyond a promontory. From the little port of *Skála* a steep road winds its way up to the town

Firá (Santorin).

(20 minutes; donkeys). There is an interesting *museum* (material found on the island).

The road from Thíra to the ancient city of **Thera**, capital of the island, runs S to *Pýrgos* (bus service), from there SE up *Mount Aghios Ilías* (1857/566 m; monastery of 1711; panoramic *views, extending S as far as Crete) and then E down to the saddle of *Selláda*, on both sides of which are the cemeteries of ancient Thera. From here roads branch off on the left to *Kamári*, with the site of ancient *Oia* lying by the sea, and on the right (S) to Périssa. Straight ahead the road winds its way up the Hill of *Mesa Vouno*, passes the Church of *Aghios Stéfanos*, built over an Early Christian Basilica (5th c.) and incorporating some elements from ancient buildings, and comes to the *Evangelismós Chapel* (alt. 974 ft/297 m), adjoining which is an ancient heroon (2nd c. B.C.).

The **site of ancient Thera** extends from the Selláda saddle along the rocky ridge of Mésa Vounó, which falls steeply down on three sides. The layout of the city, which was occupied until Byzantine times, follows the pattern normal at the time of its foundation in the Hellenistic period.

From the Evangelismós Chapel a path winds up to the retaining wall of a terrace on which are the remains of a *Temple of Apollo Kameios* (6th c. B.C.). NW of this is a temple consisting of a pronaos, naos (outer and main halls) and two chambers built on to the SW wall of the naos. The terrace to the S (6th c. B.C.), built up for the purpose, afforded space for the performance of ceremonial dances. Between the temple and the corner of the wall are the foundations of a rectangular building, within which the names of deities (NW side; some dating from the 8th c. B.C.) and citizens of Thera (SE side) are inscribed on the rock. – At the SE end of the ridge is the *Gymnasion of the Ephebes* (2nd c. B.C.), with the Grotto of Hermes and Herakles on the NE side of a large courtyard and a hall and rotunda at the E end. Above the remains are rock-cut inscriptions, some of them erotic in content.

Alongside the main road are the foundations of a number of Hellenistic private houses with plans similar to those found on Delos. Here, too, is the **Theater**, with a stage of the Roman period; below the stage are remains of the Ptolemaic proscenium, adjoining which was the circular orchestra (the "dancing-place" for the chorus). At the entrance to the theater a track branches off the main road and runs up to the **rock sanctuary** of the Egyptian divinities *Isis*, *Serapis* and *Anubis*. – On the main road beyond the theater is an open *market hall*, and beyond this again Roman *baths*. Then comes the *Agora* (market-place), a long irregular open space with a number of streets running into it. On the SE side is the **Stoa Basilike** (1st c. B.C.), with two inscriptions in the name of Kleitosthenes opposite the entrance. The interior is divided into two aisles by a row of Doric columns along its longitudinal axis; the pilasters along the walls and a structure to the N (a law court?) are later additions. – Farther along, on the left, is a terrace with a **temple** originally dedicated to *Dionysos*, later to the *Ptolemies* (2nd c. B.C.) and finally to the cult of the Roman Emperors. Opposite it is the **Temple of the goddess Tyche** (Fortune).

Beyond the Agora the main road continues N. A side road on the left runs up to the *Barracks* and the *Gymnasion* (to the S) of the Ptolemaic garrison, on the Hill of Mésa Vounó. – At the lower end of the main road, near the Selláda, is the **Temple of Arte-midoros** (3rd c. B.C.), with rock-cut reliefs.

From the Selláda it is a 30-minute walk S to the picturesque Church of **Périssa** (19th c.). Beyond the church, to the right of the churchyard, are the foundations of a circular structure of the Early Imperial period with cadastral (land-registry) inscriptions (3rd–4th c. A.D.). – From Périssa the return to Thíra is by way of **Empório**, passing close to the *Temple of Thea Basileia* (1st c. B.C.), excellently preserved by its conversion into the Chapel of *Aghios Nikólaos Marmarenios*, with the ancient roof, a handsome door-frame and a niche in the interior.

At **\*\*Akrotíri**, 12½ miles/20 km S of Firá on the S bay of Santorin, recent excavations have revealed a Mycenaean settlement with astonishingly well-preserved remains of buildings and wall-paintings, together with the ruins of a Minoan palace of the 2nd millennium B.C. Evidence of a similar settlement has also been found on the S coast of Thirasía.

The **Kaiméni Islands** (boats from Firá) are worth visiting for the sake of their still-active volcano. There are ancient accounts of the emergence and disappearance of small islets on this spot in 197 B.C. and A.D. 19 and 46. In the year 726 volcanic changes took place here, probably on **Palaiá Kaiméni** (to the SW), and in 1457 there was a rock collapse of non-volcanic origin. In 1570–73 **Mikrá Kaiméni** (to the NE) emerged from the sea; and in 1650 there was an eruption to the NE of Thera (Columbus Bank); in 1707–11 **Néa Kaiméni** was formed; and in 1866–70 there were further violent eruptions on this island, when lava surged up on its SW shore to form the island of *Afroessa*, which later joined up with Néa Kaiméni. On the SE coast is the George Crater (named after King George of Greece; 420 ft/128 m), which still emits sulfurous fumes at some points (last eruption 1956); it can be climbed on the N side (20 minutes), from the bay between Néa and Mikrá Kaiméni. – Boat-owners like to put in at Néa Kaiméni for a day or two in order to expose their boat's hull to the warm sulfurous water and thus get rid of seaweed, barnacles, etc.

11 miles/18 km SW of Santorin are the islets of *Khristianá* (alt. 915 ft/279 m) and *Askania* (alt. 469 ft/143 m), the most southerly of the Cyclades.

# Sardinia/Sardegna

Italy
Region: Sardinia.
Provinces: Cágliari, Nuoro, Oristano and Sassari.
Area: 9265 sq. miles/24,000 sq. km. – Population: 1,628,000.

**ⓘ Ente Sardo Industrie Turistiche,**
Via Mameli 97,
I-09100 **Cágliari**;
tel. (070) 66 85 22.
**EPT,**
Piazza Matteotti 1,
I-09100 **Cágliari**;
tel. (070) 65 16 04.
**EPT,**
Piazza d'Italia 9,
I-08100 **Nuoro**;
tel. (0784) 3 00 83.

**Pro Loco Oristano,**
Vico Umberto I 15,
I-09025 **Oristano;**
tel. (0783) 7 06 21.
**EPT,**
Piazza d'Italia 19,
I-07100 **Sassari;**
tel. (079) 23 01 29.

HOTELS. – CAGLIARI: *Mediterraneo*, II, 280 b.; *Jolly Regina Margherita*, II, 191 b., SP; *Italia*, II, 184 b.; *Sardegna*, II, 152 b.; *Moderno*, II, 138 b.

NUORO: *Grazia Deledda*, I, 108 b.; *Paradiso*, II, 148 b.; *Moderno*, II, 102 b.; *Motel Agip*, II, 102 b.

MACOMER: *Motel Agip*, II, 192 b.; *Marghine*, III, 31 b.; *Nuraghe*, III, 31 b.

SASSARI: *Jolly Grazia Deledda*, I, 228 b., SP; *Frank*, II, 85 b.; *Turritania*, III, 133 b.

CASTELSARDO: *Peddra Ladda*, II, 244 b., SP; *Riviera*, III, 55 b.; *Castello*, III, 40 b.

TEMPIO PAUSANIA: *Petit Hôtel*, II, 82 b.; *San Carlo*, III, 89 b.

OLBIA: *President*, I, 60 b.; *Mediterraneo*, II, 133 b.; *Royal*, II, 129 b.; *Motel Olbia*, II, 40 b.; *Minerva*, III, 59 b.

ON COSTA SMERALDA: *Abi d'Oru*, in Golfo di Marinella, I, 102 b.; *Cala di Volpe*, I, 235 b., SP, and *Nibaru*, II, 60 b., SP, both in Cala di Volpe; *Cervo*, I, 176 b., SP, *Luci di la Muntagna*, II, 136 b., SP, and *Le Ginestre*, II, 102 b., SP, all in Porto Cervo; *Pitrizza*, in Liscia di Vacca Bay, I, 52 b., SP; *Ringo*, II, 272 b., SP, *Smeraldo Beach*, II, 248 b., SP, *Delle Vigne*, II, 158 b., *Cormorano*, II, 112 b., SP, and *La Biscaccia*, II, 110 b., SP, all in Baia Sardinia.

CALA GONONE: *Villaggio Palasera*, II, 650 b.; *Mastino delle Grazie*, III, 88 b.

ARBATAX: *Telis*, III, 416 b.

BOAT SERVICES. – Regular services (cars carried) several times daily from Civitavecchia to Porto Aranci (8–9 hours) and daily from Genoa to Porto Torres (13 hours), Genoa to Olbia (14 hours), Civitavecchia to Olbia (7 hours) and Civitavecchia to Cágliari (12 hours); also five times weekly from Genoa to Porto Torres (13 hours) and Cagliari (20 hours).

AIR SERVICES. – Cágliari International Airport, $2\frac{1}{2}$ miles/4 km W of town; airfields for domestic services at Olbia and Alghero.

*Sardinia is the second largest island in the Mediterranean (area 9265 sq. miles/24,000 sq. km), separated from the neighboring French island of Corsica only by the narrow Strait of Bonifacio. The population, which from the late medieval period until the beginning of this century was decimated by malaria, is concentrated in the fertile and well-cultivated coastal areas.**

Geologically the island is a remnant of a rump mountain range composed of gneisses, granites and schists, overlaid by a band of limestones running from N to S and partly covered with recent volcanic deposits. The only plain of any size, the Campidano, lies between the Iglesiente uplands to the SW, with their rich mineral resources, and the rest of the island, a hilly region with gentler slopes in the W and more rugged country in the E, rising in Mount Gennargentu to a height of 6017 ft/1834 m and falling steeply down to the sea in the sheer cliffs on the E coast. The summers are hot and dry; the winters bring heavy rain.

In recent years tourism has become an important element in the island's economy. In addition to the established tourist areas around Alghero and Santa Teresa a new holiday region has been developed on the Costa Smeralda.

On the Costa Smeralda, Sardinia

HISTORY. – Evidence on the earliest inhabitants of Sardinia is provided by the remains of many prehistoric settlements, in particular the **nuraghi** (singular *nuraghe*), massive towers characteristic of the island culture of the Bronze and Iron Ages which show a striking similarity to the talayots of the Balearics (see p. 44). Like the talayots, they no doubt served as fortresses, watch-towers and burial-places, and can be dated to the period between 1500 and 500 B.C..

From the 9th c. B.C. onward Phoenicians and later Carthaginians established settlements on the coasts. In 238 B.C. the island was occupied by the Romans, attracted by its rich deposits of minerals. About A.D. 455 it fell into the hands of the Vandals, and later became subject to Byzantine control. Between the 8th and 11th c. it was frequently ravaged by Saracen raids; but these piratical activities were repressed by Pisa and Genoa following an appeal by the Pope, who rewarded them with the grant of the territory; the traditional system of rule by four *giudici* (judges) in the districts of Torres, Gallura, Cagliari and Arborea was, however, maintained. In 1297 Sardinia was granted by the Pope to the Crown of Aragon. Under the Treaty of Utrecht in 1713 it was assigned to Austria, and in 1720 was exchanged with Sicily and passed to the Dukes of Savoy as the kingdom of Sardinia. In 1948 it was given the status of an autonomous region within the Republic of Italy.

Thanks to the ruggedness and remoteness of much of the island its old customs and traditions are still vigorously alive. The Sardinian language is a Romance tongue which has developed independently of mainland Italian and preserves certain Archaic features.

## Cágliari

Cágliari (in Sardinian Casteddu; pop. 240,000), capital of the autonomous region of Sardinia, the island's principal port and commercial center, a university town and the see of an archbishop, lies on the S coast of the island in the wide Gulf of Cágliari.

The oldest part of the town, which was founded by the Phoenicians and became the Roman *Carales*, is known as the *Castello* (Sardinian *Castedd' e susu*). It clings picturesquely to the slopes of a steep-sided hill, at the foot of which are the newer districts and suburbs of the town. To W and E are two large lagoons, the *Stagno di Cagliari* and the *Stagno di Molentargius*, with extensive salt-pans.

Cágliari

SIGHTS. – The tree-shaded Via Roma runs along the busy harbor quay, with the *railway station* and the twin-towered modern **Town Hall** (murals by F. Filgari in the interior) at its NW end. From the Town Hall the wide Largo Carlo Felice goes NE, gently uphill, to Piazza Yenne, from which the lively Corso Vittorio Emanuele runs NW. – Via G. Manno, a shopping and commercial street popularly known as the *Costa*, descends SE from Piazza Yenne to the Piazza della Costituzione. Off Via Garibaldi, which begins

here, is the *Church of San Domenico*, with a beautiful cloister. – Farther E, in the wide Via Dante, is the *Church of Santi Cosma e Damiano* (founded in the 5th c., enlarged in the 11th–12th c.), the oldest Christian building on the island.

From the Piazza della Costituzione the beautiful *Viale Regina Elena*, affording fine views, runs N below the sheer E side of an old bastion to the *Giardino Pubblico*.

A flight of marble steps, the Passeggiata Coperta, climbs to the *Bastione San Remy (officially Terrazza Umberto I), a magnificent terrace (views) laid out on the medieval bastion (partly preserved). Higher up, to the N, is the *Bastione Santa Caterina*, which also commands extensive views. From here Via dell'Università leads NW to the *University* (founded 1956; good library) and the massive *Torre dell'Elefante* (1307). – From the Bastione San Remy the gate of the old *Torre dell'Aquila* gives access to the narrow Via Lamarmora, the main street of the old town, which runs N along the steep hillside, linked with parallel streets to right and left by steep lanes or dark archways and flights of steps. Half-way along is the terraced Piazza del Palazzo, above the E side of which is the **Cathedral** of Santa Cecilia, built by the Pisans in 1312, with beautiful old doorways in the transepts. Inside, on either side of the entrance, are the two halves of a *pulpit from Pisa Cathedral which was presented to Cágliari in 1312. This masterpiece of 12th c. Pisan sculpture (by Master Guillelmus) is decorated with New Testament scenes. There are a number of tombs in the crypt of the Cathedral.

At the N end of Via Lamarmora we come to the Piazza dell'Indipendenza, in which are the *Torre San Pancrazio* (1305; view) and the *Museo Nazionale Archeologico**, with Punic, Greek and Roman material as well as the largest collection of Sardinian antiquities. Of particular interest are the *bronzes found in the *nuraghi*, of crude and primitive workmanship but with a distinctive character of their own (Room 1). On the upper floor are pictures of the 14th–18th c.

From the Museum Viale Buon Cammino runs N through the outer courtyard of the Citadel and along the ridge of the hill. In 550 yds/500 m a road leads down on the left to the Roman **Amphitheater** (290 ft/

88·5 m by 240 ft/73 m; arena 165 ft/50 m by 112 ft/34 m), constructed in a natural depression in the rock, and which is now used as an open-air theater. SW of the amphitheater is the *Botanic Garden*, with luxuriant Southern vegetation.

SURROUNDINGS of Cágliari. – There is an attractive trip (4½ miles/7 km SE), passing close to *Monte Sant'Elia* (456 ft/139 m; fine views) and the extensive *Molentargius* salt-pans, to the **Spiaggia di Poetto**, Cágliari's popular beach, which extends for 6 miles/10 km along the *Golfo di Quartu*. – From here it is possible to continue for another 30 miles/50 km to the SE tip of the island. The road traverses an extensive agricultural development area; then beyond the hamlet of *Flúmini* a beautiful stretch of road keeps close to the coast, running through beech woods and passing many old watch-towers and *nuraghi*, to *Capo Carbonara*, the extreme south-easterly point of Sardinia (views), with the 17th c. *Torre Santa Caterina* (alt. 377 ft/115 m) and the *Fortezza Vecchia*, which also dates from the 17th c.

Another rewarding excursion is a tour of the *Iglesiente*, the hilly region in the SW of the island. – Leave Cágliari on SS 195, which runs SW along the spit of land between the *Stagno di Cágliari* and the sea and past the S. Gilla salt-pans. – At the village of *Sarroch* (12½ miles/20 km) is a very characteristic *nuraghe*. – 4½ miles/7 km farther on is *Pula*, from which a road leads 2½ miles/4 km S to the remains of the Phoenician and later Roman town of **Nora**, situated on a narrow peninsula (forum, amphitheater, temples, foundations of villas, well-preserved mosaic pavements). – After some time the road leaves the coast. 24 miles/38 km from Pula it crosses a pass (988 ft/301 m) with the *Nuraghe of Mesu*, and comes in another 9 miles/14 km to the attractively situated little town of **Teulada** (alt. 207 ft/63 m), chief place in the southern part of the Iglesiente, known as *Sulcis*. – 22 miles/36 km beyond Teulada SS 195 joins SS 126 at *San Giovanni Suergiu*.

From San Giovanni Suergiu there is an interesting excursion (7 miles/11 km SW) to the large volcanic island of **Sant'Antioco** (area 42 sq. miles/109 sq. km), with the little town of **Sant'Antioco** (alt. 50 ft/15 m; pop. 13,000), a popular seaside resort. On either side of the castle is a well-preserved Phoenician cemetery (about 550 B.C.), with a small museum. Many of the tombs – sometimes enlarged by knocking down party walls – are occupied as dwellings. 6 miles/9 km NW of Sant'Antioco is *Calasetta* (alt. 95 ft/29 m), a little place of rather Oriental aspect which was originally established by settlers from Carloforte, on the neighboring island of San Pietro, who, like the inhabitants of that island, have preserved the language and customs of Genoa. There are boats to Carloforte (30 minutes) several times a day.

Beyond San Giovanni Suergiu the tour of the Iglesiente continues N on SS 126, which in 4 miles/6 km reaches **Carbonia** (pop. 35,000), a new town founded in 1938 in the middle of the Sardinian coalfield. In another 7 miles/11 km a road branches off on the left to the little ports of *Portoscuso* (tuna-fishing) and *Portovesme*, from which there are boats (including car ferries) several times daily (45 minutes) to **Carloforte** (alt. 33 ft/10 m; pop. 8000), the chief place on the island of **San Pietro** (area 20 sq. miles/52 sq. km), built up of trachytes (light-colored volcanic rock). Carloforte was founded in 1736 by Genoese settlers from an island off Tunisia which had

been held by Genoa since the 13th c., and their descendants still preserve their distinctive language and costume. – An interesting trip (though not for the squeamish) is a visit to the tuna-fishing grounds (*tonnare*), off the northern tip of the island near the little *Isola Piana* and Portoscuso, during the fishing season (May and early June). The tuna grows to a length of 6½–13 ft/2–4 m and a weight of 330–660 lb/150–300 kg; canned in oil, the fish are much prized in Italy. The tuna live primarily in the Mediterranean, move E in spring to spawn, traveling in dense shoals which are often accompanied by sharks, and are caught in large nets and killed – rather messily – off the coasts of Sardinia and Sicily. Thousands of people are employed during the season on the catching, cutting up, cooking and canning of the fish.

7½ miles/12 km beyond the turning for Portoscuso and Portovesme is *Iglesias* (alt. 623 ft/190 m; pop. 23,000), an old episcopal town in the heart of the Iglesiente which still preserves remains of its medieval walls and has a Mining College (museum). In the Piazza del Municipio stands the Cathedral, built by the Pisans in 1285, and to the S of the square is the medieval Church of San Francesco. Above the town to the E can be seen the Castello Salvaterra.

From Iglesias it is 35 miles/56 km E on SS 130 to Cágliari. Shortly before reaching the town the necropolis of ancient *Carales* can be seen in the limestone cliffs on the left of the road, with Punic and Roman tomb chambers hewn from the rock in vertical shafts.

TOUR OF THE ISLAND (about 450 miles/720 km). – Leave Cágliari on SS 131 (the Sássari road), which runs NW and comes in 12½ miles/20 km to *Monastir* (alt. 272 ft/83 m), a village of Oriental aspect on the slopes of a volcanic hill (rock-cut tombs). 3½ miles/5·5 km SW, at *San Sperate*, is an open-air museum of modern sculpture. Beyond Monastir the road follows the eastern edge of the Campidano Plain. – 14 miles/23 km: **Sanluri** (alt. 443 ft/135 m; pop. 8000), with a 14th c. Castle containing a small military museum.

15 miles/24 km NE of Sanluri is the village of **Barúmini**, near which ¾ mile/1 km W, to the left of the road to Tuili) is the largest nuraghic settlement in Sardinia, **Su Nuraxi**, with 396 houses and a massive central structure flanked by many towers.

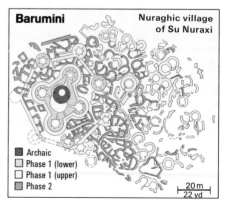

**Barumini**          Nuraghic village of Su Nuraxi

■ Archaic
□ Phase 1 (lower)
□ Phase 1 (upper)
■ Phase 2

20 m
22 yd

Su Nuraxi, near Barúmini, Sardinia

From Sanluri SS 197 runs W to the wooded *Costa Verde*, a coastal region now being developed as a popular holiday area, with new roads, villas, hotels and sports facilities.

6 miles/9 km beyond Sanluri on the main road is *Sárdara* (alt. 535 ft/163 m). By the little Church of Santa Anastasia is an underground spring sanctuary of nuraghic type. 2 miles/3 km W is the little spa of *Terme di Sardara* (hot springs, 122 °F/50 °C and 154 °F/68 °C). – 22 miles/36 km: *Santa Giusta* (alt. 33 ft/10 m), on the N side of a marshy lake, the Stagno di Santa Giusta, with a beautiful Pisan-style 12th c. church (ancient columns). – 2 miles/3 km: **Oristano** (alt. 30 ft/9 m; pop. 30,000), which is noted for its pottery. It still preserves a number of towers belonging to its medieval defenses. The Cathedral (18th c.) occupies the site of an earlier church of the 13th–14th c. The Archeological Museum contains finds from the site of ancient Tharros, which lay to the NW of the Gulf of Oristano. Beautiful traditional costumes can often be seen here on market days. – 10 miles/16 km: *Bauladu* (alt. 95 ft/29 m), on the northern edge of the Campidano Plain. The road now continues up the Bobólica Valley.

4 miles/6 km farther on SS 131d branches off on the right. Running diagonally across the island, this is the quickest and shortest route from Cágliari or Oristamo to Olbia (192 miles/309 km and 113 miles/182 km respectively). In 36 miles/58 km it bypasses the provincial capital of **Nuoro** (alt. 1814 ft/553 m; pop. 37,000), charmingly situated on a hillside between limestone hills of Alpine type to the S and the peak of *Ortobene* (3265 ft/995 m; *views) to the E. Beautiful local costumes

are worn on the Feast of the Savior (August 29–31). Nuoro was the birthplace of the writer Grazia Deledda (1893–1936; Nobel Prize 1926). – On the SE side of the town is the Neo-Classical *Cathedral* (19th c.). The most conspicuous building is the prison, a reminder of the days when brigands were active in the area. – 1 mile/1·5 km NE are the Pilgrimage Church of *Nostra Signora della Solitudine* (*view) and, beyond the *Colle di Sant'Onofrio* (1949 ft/594 m), the *Sardinian Museum of Costume*, housed in over 20 buildings in the style of Sardinian peasants' houses. Near the town are several *nuraghi*.

From Nuoro there is a beautiful drive S to **Mamoiada** (alt. 2113 ft/644 m; costumes) and **Fonni** (alt. 3280 ft/1000 m; pop. 5000), the highest village on the island. In the surrounding area are many *nuraghi* and "fairies' houses" (*domus de janas*, rock-cut tombs). Fonni is the starting-point for the ascent (4 hours, with guide) of **Bruncu Spina** (6001 ft/1829 m; panoramic views), the northern peak of the *Gennargentu Massif*, from which the southern peak, **Punta la Mármora** (6017 ft/1834 m) can be climbed (45 minutes).

Sardinian costumes, Fonni

Continuing on SS 131, we see on the left, shortly after the turning for Nuoro, the well-preserved *Nuraghe of Losa*, with a number of subsidiary structures. – 1¼ miles/2 km: **Abbasanta** (alt. 1027 ft/313 m), the largest livestock market in Sardinia, on the southern edge of the Abbasanta Plain, an area of black basaltic rock. 6 miles/10 km SE is the *Tirso Dam*, once Europe's largest dam, which has impounded the water of the island's principal river to form *Lago Omodeo*, 14 miles/22 km long and up to 3 miles/ 5 km wide. – 10 miles/16 km: **Macomer** (alt. 1847 ft/563 m; pop. 10,000), situated on a bleak plateau of basalts and trachytes on the slopes of the Catena del Marghine, with beautiful far-ranging views.

In front of the church are three Roman milestones found in the area. Some of the best-preserved *nuraghi* in Sardinia can be seen in the immediate surroundings of the town. Particularly fine is the *Nuraghe of Santa Barbara* (alt. 2126 ft/648 m), a conical structure on a high square base (a torch should be taken).

2 miles/3 km beyond Macomer SS 129 bis goes off on the left to the village of *Suni* (14 miles/23 km; extensive views) and, 4 miles/6 km beyond this, the little port of **Bosa** (alt. 33 ft/10 m; pop. 8000), with the ruined Castle of *Serravalle* (about 1100). 10 miles/16 km S of Suni is **Cuglieri** (alt. 1572 ft/479 m; pop. 5000), on the lower slopes of *Monte Ferru* (3445 ft/1050 m), an extinct volcano. – 1¼ miles/2 km: on the left of the road, the almost completely preserved *Nuraghe of Succoronis (Muradu)*. – 17 miles/27 km: road on the right (¾ mile/1 km) to the three-story *Nuraghe of Sant'Antine*, 52 ft/ 16 m high. – 3 miles/5 km: *Bonnánaro* (alt. 1329 ft/405 m), where a road goes off on the left (2½ miles/4 km SW) to the richly ornamented *Church of San Pietro di Sorres* (Pisan period, 12th c.). Beyond Bonnánaro the road traverses the beautiful wooded uplands of **Logudoro**. – 13 miles/21 km: SS 597, the direct road from Sassari to Olbia, goes off on the right. 1¼ miles/2 km along this road is the former Abbey Church of **\*\*Santissima Trinità di Saccargia**, the finest example of Pisan architecture in Sardinia (13th c. frescoes). – 9 miles/15 km: **Sássari** (alt. 738 ft/ 225 m; pop. 120,000), Sardinia's second largest town, lies on a limestone plateau which falls steeply down on the E side. A town of predominantly modern aspect, it is the chief town of its province and the see of an archbishop, with a university founded in 1617. Two interesting annual events are the Processione dei Candelieri (August 14) and the Cavalcata Sarda (Assumption; picturesque traditional costumes). – The hub of the town's traffic is the palm-shaded Piazza Cavallino de Honestis, immediately SE of which is the large Piazza d'Italia, with a monument to Victor Emmanuel II and a modern Prefecture. – From the Piazza d'Italia the tree-lined Via Roma runs SE to the Museo

Nazionale G. A. Sanna, with the collections assembled by Giovanni Antonio Sanna, a Member of the Italian Parliament (prehistoric, Punic and Roman antiquities; over 350 pictures of the 16th–19th c.). – NW of the Piazza Cavallino de Honestis, reached by way of Piazza Azuni, is the Corso Vittorio Emanuele, Sássari's principal street. From this we turn left along Via del Duomo to reach the Cathedral of San Nicola, with a Baroque façade (interior restored). E of this in Via Santa Catarina is the handsome Palazzo del Duca, now the Town Hall. – To the W of the Cathedral, in the spacious Piazza Santa Maria, is the Church of Santa Maria di Betlém, rebuilt in modern style but still preserving its severe Gothic façade of the Pisan period. – The pretty Fonte del Rosello on the N side of the town has a Baroque fountain-house of 1605.

From Sássari a pleasant road through the coastal district of *Nura* leads (12 miles/19 km NW) to the little industrial town of **Porto Torres** (alt. 33 ft/10 m; pop. 21,000), the port of Sássari, situated in the *Golfo dell'Asinara*. On the E side of the town stands the Church of San Gavino, in Pisan Romanesque style (11th–13th c.; fortified in the 18th c.); in the interior are 22 antique columns and six pillars, and in the crypt the tomb of San Gavino. To the W of the harbor a seven-arched Roman bridge spans the little Rio Turritano, and near this are the remains of a large Temple of Fortuna, popularly known as the Palazza del Re Bárbaro (Palace of the Barbarian King). – 18 miles/ 29 km NW of Porto Torres lies the charmingly situated fishing village of **Stintino** (alt. 30 ft/9 m). 3 miles/ 5 km beyond this on a road offering extensive views is the *Punta del Falcone*, the north-western tip of Sadinia. Lying off the promontory to the N is the little **Isola Piana** (79 ft/24 m), and beyond this is the long *Isola Asinara* (11 miles/17·5 km long, area 20 sq. miles/52 sq. km; alt. 1339 ft/408 m), with many bays and inlets.

Another very attractive trip from Sássari is to the charmingly situated town and seaside resort of **Alghero** (alt. 23 ft/7 m; pop. 38,000), 23 miles/37 km SW, the inhabitants of which still speak a Catalan dialect. Features of interest are the Cathedral (1510; Spanish Gothic doorway), the Church of San Francesco (cloister), the picturesque Spanish bastions and towers, and many old houses. – 9 miles/ 14 km W of Alghero (also by motor-boat, 3 hours), on the W side of the precipitous *Capo Caccia*, is a beautiful stalactitic cave, the *Grotta di Nettuno*.

For the next section of the tour, from Sássari to Olbia and La Maddalena, there are alternative routes – either the direct road on SS 597 (63 miles/101 km) or the more interesting SS 127. – 9 miles/14 km: **Ósilo** (alt. 1970 ft/600 m; pop. 6000), which is renowned for the beautiful costumes of its women. From the ruined Malaspina Castle and the nearby Cappella di Bonaria there are fine views. The road continues through the wooded *Angola* district. – 24 miles/39 km: road on left, through delightful scenery, to the village of *Sédini* (16th c. church), picturesquely situated above a gorge, and the little walled port town of **Castelsardo** (alt. 374 ft/114 m; pop. 5000), in a magnificent *situation on a promontory which falls sheer down to the Golfo dell'Asinara. This is the main center of basketwork in Sardinia. In the Parish Church is a beautiful 15th c. Madonna, a masterpiece of the Sardinian-Spanish School. From the ruined castle there are fine *views.

Some 2½ miles/4 km beyond the turning for Castelsardo, at *Pérfugas* (just off SS 127), a fortified village of the nuraghic period and a spring sanctuary have been excavated. – 16 miles/26 km: **Tempio Pausania** (alt. 1857 ft/566 m; pop. 9000), formerly chief town of the Gallura district, situated below the N face of the jagged *Monti di Limbara* (cork industry). – 6 miles/10 km: *Calangiánus* (alt. 1700 ft/518 m; pop. 6000), an old town surrounded by forest, with a pretty Parish Church.

22 miles/35 km: **Olbia** (alt. 50 ft/15 m; pop. 31,000), formerly known as *Terranova Pausania*, lying at the W end of the deeply indented *Gulf of Olbia*. A causeway 1 mile/1·5 km long carrying the road and the railway links the town with the little *Isola Bianca*, where the ships from Civitavecchia come in. Beside the town railway station is the 11th c. Church of San Simplicio, in Pisan style, with a collection of Roman inscriptions (particularly milestones) and a sarcophagus with a decoration of garlands. From the church and from the harbor there are fine views of the bay and the large rocky island of *Tavolara* (alt. 1821 ft/555 m; area 2·3 sq. miles/6 sq. km).

To the N of Olbia, extending along the shores of a large peninsula, is the beautiful *Costa Smeralda (Emerald Coast), with beaches of fine sand which are being developed as a holiday area by the construction of new roads and the provision of facilities for vacationers. The roads to the various resorts branch off SS 125, which runs N from Olbia to Palau. – 4 miles/6 km: road (5 miles/8 km) to the *Golfo di Marinella*. – ¾ mile/1 km: road along the coast to *Cala di Volpe* (9 miles/ 15 km) and **Porto Cervo** (29 miles/ 47 km), the chief place on the Costa Smeralda. 2 miles/3 km N, beyond *Capo Ferro*, is the Bay of *Liscia di Vacca*, and 3 miles/5 km farther on *Baia Sardinia*. – At the S end of the Costa Smeralda is the holiday center of *Portisco*. SS 125 continues to *Arzachena* (10½ miles/17 km). – 7½ miles/12 km: *Palau* (alt. 16 ft/5 m).

From Palau there is a boat service (several times daily; 15 minutes) to **La Maddalena** (alt. 95 ft/29 m; pop. 11,000), on the island of the same name (alt. 515 ft/ 157 m; area 7·7 sq. miles/20 sq. km), a port which until the Second World War was strongly fortified, commanding the Strait of Bonifacio between Corsica

Porto Cervo, Sardinia

and Sardinia. – The island is traversed by a *panoramic road* 4½ miles/7 km long which is carried by a swing bridge over the *Passo della Moneta*, a strait fully 550 yds/500 m wide, on to the neighboring island of **Caprera** (Goat Island; alt. 696 ft/212 m; area 6·1 sq. miles/15·8 sq. km). 1 mile/1·5 km E of the bridge is a house once occupied by Garibaldi, who died here on June 2, 1882 (collection of mementoes). In front of the house is a monument to Garibaldi, and behind it is an olive grove containing his tomb, which attracts visitors from all over Italy, particularly on the anniversary of his death.

The return from Olbia to Cágliari is on SS 125, which runs SE past a number of salt-water lagoons, with the rocky island of *Tavolara* lying offshore on the left. Thereafter the road continues at varying distances from the coast. – 35 miles/ 57 km: **Siniscola** (alt. 138 ft/42 m; pop. 9000), at the W end of a large coastal plain, from which a *panoramic road (unsurfaced) runs along the rocky ridge of *Monte Albo* (3698 ft/1127 m), through a region well stocked with wildlife, to *Bitti* (alt. 1801 ft/549 m; pop. 6000). 4 miles/ 6 km NE of Siniscola is the developing resort of *La Caletta*.

From Siniscola it is possible to return to Cágliari either by taking the shorter but less interesting road via Nuoro and Oristano or by continuing on the coast road. – 22 miles/36 km: **Orosei** (alt. 62 ft/ 19 m; pop. 4000), on the right bank of the River *Cedrino*, with a ruined castle. – 13 miles/21 km: **Dorgali** (alt. 1270 ft/ 387 m; pop. 8000), a little town famous for its wine, situated on the slopes of *Monte Bardia* (2894 ft/882 m); local costumes. In the surrounding area are a number of beautiful stalactitic caves (*Grotta Toddeittu, Grotta del Bue Marino*, etc.) and some of the rock-cut tombs known as "fairies' houses" (*domus de janas*). 7 miles/11 km NW of Dorgali is the nuraghic village of *Serra Orrios*. – 1¼ miles/ 2 km: we reach a side road (4½ miles/7 km) which winds its way down to the little port of *Cala Gonone* (alt. 80 ft/25 m).

Beyond Dorgali the road traverses beautiful mountainous country. – 38 miles/ 61 km: **Tortolì** (alt. 50 ft/15 m; pop. 8000), at the beginning of an extensive plain. 3 miles/5 km E is the attractively situated little port of **Arbatax** (pop. 1000), formerly also known as *Tortolì Marina*, which ships the agricultural produce and minerals of the Ogliastra region. Near by are picturesque red porphyry cliffs. – From Tortolì there is a very attractive alternative route to Cágliari,

first on SS 198 through the **Ogliastra** uplands, with hills of crystalline limestone, sometimes in bizarrely contorted shapes, to **Lanusei** (alt. 1952 ft/595 m; pop. 6000), prettily situated amid vineyards, **Seui** (alt. 2625 ft/800 m) and the *Cantoniera di Santa Lucia* (roadmen's depot); then on SS 128 and SS 131 to Cágliari.

Beyond Tortolì SS 125 follows a winding course through the south-eastern part of the Ogliastra region. – 6 miles/10 km: *Barì Sardo* (alt. 165 ft/50 m), from which there is a view of the Gennargentu Massif. The road continues, with many turns, through lonely hill country. – 75 miles/121 km: **Quartu Sant'Elena** (alt. 20 ft/6 m; pop. 42,000), a thriving town in an area which produces the famous white wine, Malvasia. On the Feast of St Helena (May 21) there is a picturesque procession of richly decked pairs of oxen. – 5 miles/8 km: **Cágliari**.

# Sássari
## See under Sardinia, above

# Selinunte

Italy
Region: Sicily. – Province: Trapani.
Altitude: 243 ft/74 m.
ⓘ EPT,
   Corso d'Italia 10,
   I-91100 **Trapani**;
   tel. (0923) 2 72 73.

**The ruins of *Selinunte, lying on both banks of the little rivers Modione (ancient Greek Selinon) and Gorgo di Cotone, near the SW coast of Sicily, are one of the most striking and interesting sites on the island.**

HISTORY. – *Selinous*, the most westerly Greek colony in Sicily, was founded about 628 B.C. on a hill near the sea, and later extended on to the plateau to the N. A sacred precinct was established on the hill to the E during the 6th c. In 409 B.C. the flourishing city was destroyed by the Carthaginians; and a new fortified town built on the western hill from 407 onward was in turn destroyed, again by the Carthaginians, in 250 B.C., during the First Punic War.

The size and importance of the ancient city is attested by the extent and scale of the ruins, in particular the massive remains of eight Doric temples (6th–5th c. B.C.), which probably collapsed as a result of earthquakes between the 5th and 8th c. A.D. and were then gradually covered with blown sand. Since 1925 restoration work and further excavation has been steadily carried on; two temples have been re-erected, and others are to follow.

THE SITE. – On the western hill are the remains of the *Acropolis (490 yds/450 m long and up to 380 yds/350 m across), formerly surrounded by walls and traversed by two principal streets, one running N–S, the other E–W. In the SE sector are the remains of the small *Temple A* and the foundations of the very similar *Temple O*. Immediately N of the E–W street is the tiny *Temple B*, of which no columns remain erect, and to the N of this, on top of the hill, is *Temple C* (columns re-erected in 1925 and 1929), the oldest on the Acropolis and one of the two most striking features of the site (the other being Temple E, referred to below). Farther N again is the rather later *Temple D*. – On the northern edge of the Acropolis are the excavated remains of the Greek **defensive walls** (restored in 407 B.C.), an excellent example of the highly developed Greek art of fortification. Beyond this, on the *Manuzza* Plateau to the N of the Acropolis, extends the town proper, of which only a few remains have been preserved.

Following the E–W street westward from the Acropolis, we cross the River Modione (at the mouth of which was the W harbor) and come to the Hill of *Manicalunga*, on the slopes of which is the sacred precinct, with the remains of the **Temple of Demeter**, dedicated to Demeter Malophoros (the Fruit-Bringer). At the N corner of the precinct is the little *Shrine of Zeus Meilikhios* (the Forgiving). – To the W of the Temple of Demeter is a necropolis extending for some 1¼ miles/2 km.

From the Acropolis a road runs 1 mile/1·5 km E over the River Gorgo di Cotone

(at the mouth of which was the E harbor) to the eastern hill, with the remains of three large temples which even in their present state of ruin are overwhelmingly impressive. To the S is *Temple E (the Heraion or Temple of Hera), which was re-erected in 1959 with its 38 columns. To the N are *Temple F* and the adjoining *Temple G*, probably dedicated to Apollo, which is the second largest of all Greek temples (364 ft/111 m long), exceeded in size only by the Temple of Zeus at Agrigento.

# Serifos
## See under Cyclades

# Sicily

Italy
Region: Sicily.
Provinces: Agrigento, Caltanissetta, Catania, Enna, Messina, Palermo, Ragusa, Siracusa (Syracuse) and Trapani.
Area: 9926 sq. miles/25,708 sq. km. – Population: 5,000,000.

ⓘ EPT,
Piazza Castelnuovo 34,
I-90100 **Palermo**;
tel. (091) 58 38 47.
EPT,
Viale della Vittoria 255,
I-92100 **Agrigento**;
tel. (0922) 2 69 26.
EPT,
Corso Vittorio Emanuele 109,
I-93100 **Caltanissetta**;
tel. (0934) 2 17 31.
EPT,
Largo Paisiello 5,
I-95100 **Catania**;
tel. (095) 31 77 20.
EPT,
Piazza Garibaldi,
I-94100 **Enna**;
tel. (0935) 2 11 84.
EPT,
Via Calabria,
I-98100 **Messina**;
tel. (090) 77 53 56.
EPT,
Via Natalelli,
I-97100 **Ragusa**;
tel. (0932) 2 14 21.
EPT,
Corso Gelone 92,
I-96100 **Siracusa**;
tel. (0931) 6 76 07.
EPT,
Piazzetta Saturno,
I-91100 **Trapani**;
tel. (0923) 2 90 00.

HOTELS. – MILAZZO: *Silvanetta Palace*, II, 245 b.; *Residenzial*, II, 124 b.; *Riviera Lido*, II, 67 b.; *Saverly*,

Temple E, Selinunte

II, 64 b. – CASTROREALE TERME: *Grand Hotel Terme*, I, 122 b.; *La Giara*, III, 151 b. – PATTI: *Santa Febronia*, II, 88 b.; *La Plaja*, II, 82 b. – CAPO D'ORLANDO: *La Tartaruga*, II, 70 b., SP; *Villaggio Testa di Monaco*, II, 82 b.; *Bristol*, III, 100 b.; *Villaggio Nettuno*, III, 99 b. – RANDAZZO: *Motel Agip*, III, 30 b. – CEFALÙ: *Le Sabbie d'Oro*, II, 420 b., SP; *Kalura*, III, 117 b., SP; *La Caletta*, II, 100 b., SP; *Santa Dominga*, II, 92 b.; *Tourist*, II, 92 b.; *Santa Lucia*, III, 85 b. – TERMINI IMERESE: *Grande Albergo delle Terme*, II, 180 b. – BAGHERIA: *Motel A'Zabara*, II, 128 b., SP.

PALERMO: see p. 149.

MONREALE: *Carrubella Park*, II, 44 b.; *Il Ragno*, III, 28 b. – ALCAMO: *Centrale*, IV, 37 b.; *Miramare*, IV, 33 b. – SAN VITO LO CAPO: *Robinson Club Cala'mpiso*, 600 b. – TRAPANI: *Nuovo Rosso*, Via Tintori 6, II, 48 b.; *Vittoria*, Via F. Crispi 4, III, 77 b. – ON FAVIGNANA: *Punta Fanfalo Village*, II, 729 b., SP; *L'Approdo di Ulisse*, II, 156 b. – MARSALA: *Stella d'Italia*, II, 83 b.; *Motel Agip*, II, 62 b. – MAZARA DEL VALLO: *Hopps*, II, 489 b., SP. – CASTELVETRANO: *Zeus*, II, 77 b.; *Selinus*, II, 68 b. – SCIACCA: *Delle Terme*, I, 126 b., SP; *Garden*, II, 120 b.; *Motel Agip*, II, 76 b.; *Sciaccamare* holiday center.

AGRIGENTO: see p. 39.

LICATA: *Baia d'Oro*, II, 144 b.; *Al Faro*, II, 60 b. – GELA: *Motel Gela*, II, 180 b.; *Mediterraneo*, II, 110 b. – VITTORIA: *Europa*, III, 27 b.; *Sicilia*, III, 27 b. – RAGUSA: *Mediterraneo*, II, 174 b.; *Ionio*, II, 69 b.; *San Giovanni*, II, 42 b.; *Tivoli*, III, 54 b.; *Village* holiday center, II, 1684 b., SP, and *Palace*, II, 516 b., SP, both 20 miles/ 30 km SW at Kamarina. – MODICA: *Motel di Modica*, II, 63 b. – NOTO: *Eloro*, II, 398 b., at Pizzuta, to SE.

SYRACUSE: see p. 188.

LENTINI: *Carmes*, III, 34 b. – AUGUSTA: *Kursaal Augusteo*, III, 71 b.; *Centrale*, IV, 20 b.; *Villaggio Valtur*, II, 894 b., SP, at Brucoli, to N.

CATANIA: see p. 49.

ACI CASTELLO: *Baia Verde*, I, 254 b., SP, at Cannizzaro; *I Faraglioni*, I, 123 b., and *Eden Riviera*, II, 66 b., both in Aci Trezza. – ACIREALE: *La Perla Ionica*, II, 1659 b., SP; *Santa Tecla*, II, 494 b., SP; *Aloha d'Oro*, II, 162 b., SP; *Maugeri*, II, 68 b.

TAORMINA AND MESSINA: see pp. 191 and 136.

**\*\* Sicily, the largest and most populous island in the Mediterranean (area 9926 sq. miles/25,708 sq. km; pop. 5,000,000), is a largely autonomous Italian region with its capital at Palermo and nine provinces. It is an almost entirely mountainous island, bearing the marks of vigorous volcanic activity. Its most notable landmark is the massive snow-covered cone of Mount Etna (10,913 ft/3326 m), Europe's largest active volcano, which rises above the E coast, visible from afar. The main concentrations of population are on the well-watered and fertile coastal plains.**

Sicily's productive and rapidly developing agriculture gives it a leading place among the farming regions of Italy. Intensive vegetable-growing (tomatoes, cucumbers, early potatoes, etc.), fruit orchards (citrus fruits, almonds, olives) and (particularly at the western tip of the island around Marsala) wine production

Etna in eruption

predominate in the fertile coastal areas; the dry and hilly interior is suitable only for extensive arable cultivation (wheat alternating with beans) and some pastoral farming (sheep, goats). The feudal system inherited from the past and the (often inefficient) working of the land by small tenant farmers which is its legacy stand in the way of the more rapid development which the potential of the land would permit. – Contributions to the economy are also made by the coastal fisheries (tuna, anchovies, cuttlefish, swordfish) and the extraction of salt in the Trapani area.

Sicily has little industry. The only industrial activities of any consequence are petrochemicals (around Syracuse and Gela), the mining of potash (which has superseded the once-considerable sulfur workings) and the working of asphalt (around Ragusa) and marble. In recent years, however, there has been a significant development of industry which has helped to stem the drift of population to the highly industrialized states of northern Europe.

Sicily's magnificent scenery and its beautiful beaches, particularly on the N and E coasts, its great range of ancient remains, including the best-preserved Greek temples to be found anywhere, and the very remarkable art and architecture of its Norman rulers have long made the island one of the great Meccas of travelers and tourists; and the development of a modern tourist industry is now making rapid progress.

CIRCUIT OF SICILY (580 miles/930 km). – The first part of the circuit, from Messina to Palermo, is partly on the A 20 motorway and partly on SS 113 (the Settentrionale Sicula road), following the coast of the Tyrrhenian Sea through scenery of great beauty and variety. – The road runs NW from Messina through garden suburbs, crosses the *Colle San Rizzo* Pass (1526 ft/ 465 m; motorway tunnel) in the wooded *Monti Peloritani* (4508 ft/1374 m) and descends to the sea. – 23 miles/37 km: *Milazzo/Isole Eolie* motorway exit. 4 miles/6 km N is the little town of **Milazzo** (alt. 100 ft/30 m; pop. 31,000; good beaches; boat services to Lipari Islands), founded by Greek settlers in 716 B.C., which has a Norman Castle. 4½ miles/7 km farther N is the *Capo di Milazzo*. – 7½ miles/12 km along SS 113 is the spa (sulfur springs) of *Castroreale Terme*. 2 miles/3 km beyond this SS 185 goes off on the left and follows a winding course to the little town of *Novara di Sicilia* (alt. 2215 ft/675 m), 12¼ miles/20 km inland; then over the *Portella Mandrazzi* (3691 ft/1125 m) to the ridge of the Monti Peloritani; on, with a magnificent *view of Etna,* to *Francavilla di Sicilia* (1083 ft/330 m); and from there another 14 miles/22 km, passing close to the *Gola dell'Alcantara (Alcantara Gorge), to *Giardini*, below Taormina.

Some 7½ miles/12 km beyond the Milazzo motorway access a road branches off SS 113 on the right, passes the *Monastery of the Madonna del Tíndari*, traverses the village of Tíndari and comes in 1¼ miles/2 km to the remains of **Tyndaris**, the last Greek colony in Sicily, founded by Dionysius I in 396 B.C. and probably destroyed by the Saracens (remains of town walls, a theater and a Roman basilica; mosaic pavements; museum).

18 miles/29 km beyond Milazzo/Isole Eolie on the motorway is the exit for **Patti** (alt. 502 ft/153 m; pop. 12,000), with large monasteries and a Cathedral which occupies the site of an earlier castle and contains the Tomb of Adelasia of Montferrat (d. 1118), mother of King Roger of Sicily. – 6 miles/9 km: tunnel through the precipitous **Capo Calavà**; beyond this a fine view of the fertile coastal area, with *Capo Orlando* (305 ft/93 m) reaching far out to sea. – 15 miles/24 km: exit for **Capo d'Orlando** (alt. 40 ft/12 m; pop. 11,000), a little town which is also a seaside resort. From here SS 116 runs S via *Naso* (alt. 1631 ft/497 m) and over the *Portella del Zoppo* (4147 ft/1264 m), a pass on the ridge of the *Monti Nébrodi* (6060 ft/ 1847 m), to **Randazzo** (alt. 2474 ft/ 754 m; pop. 15,000), which, with its old houses built of dark-colored lava, still preserves much of its medieval character. At the E end of the main street, Via Umberto I, is the Church of Santa Maria (1217–39); Baroque interior, with columns which are each hewn from a single block of black lava. From here the picturesque Via degli Archi runs W to the Church of San Nicolà (originally Norman; remodelled in the 16th c.; badly damaged during the Second World War), which contains a statue of St Nicholas by Antonello Gagini (1523). Beyond the church, to the NW, is the Palazzo Finocchiaro (1509). At the W end of Via Umberto I is the Church of San Martino, with a 14th c. campanile; diagonally opposite the church is a tower of the old Ducal Palace.

From Capo d'Orlando SS 113 continues over the fertile coastal plain, the Piana del Capo, and then through the *Bosco di Caronia*, the largest area of woodland in Sicily (mainly scrub). – 30 miles/49 km: SS 117 branches off and runs S via *Mistretta* (alt. 3117 ft/950 m; pop. 11,000) and over the *Portella del Contrasto* (3675 ft/1120 m), a pass on the ridge of the Monti Nébrodi, to **Nicosia** (29 miles/46 km; alt. 2362 ft/720 m; pop. 20,000), with the 14th c. Cathedral of San Nicolà, the 18th c. Church of Santa Maria Maggiore (marble reredos 26 ft/8 m high by Antonello Gagini, 1512) and a Castle. – Beyond the junction with SS 117 the coast road skirts the foot of the *Madonie* Mountains (*Pizzo Carbonaro*, 6493 ft/ 1979 m) and in 23 miles/37 km reaches Cefalù.

The little port of **Cefalù** (alt. 100 ft/30 m; pop. 14,000) is picturesquely situated below a massive bare limestone crag which falls sheer down to the sea. On the E side of the main street, the Corso Ruggero, which runs N toward the sea, is the spacious Piazza del Duomo, with the Town Hall and the *Cathedral, one of the finest buildings of the Norman period in Sicily, which was begun by King Roger in 1131–32. The interior (245 ft/74 m long, 95 ft/29 m wide) has 15 granite columns and one of cipollino, with beautiful capitals. In the apse are magnificent mosaics, including one of the *Savior (1148), the Virgin with the Four Archangels, and the Twelve Apostles. In the S aisle is a fine 12th c. font. The cloister (fine

Cefalù

capitals) is entered from the N aisle. – W of the Piazza del Duomo is the little Museo Mandralisca (antiquities from the Lipari Islands, pictures). – Cefalù has an excellent beach.

At the N end of the Corso Ruggero is the starting-point of the climb (45 minutes–1 hour) up the **Rocca**, a crag of fossiliferous limestone 971 ft/269 m high, with the ruins of a medieval castle and an ancient polygonal structure known as the Tempio di Diana. From the highest point, on which there are remains of a Norman castle, there are magnificent views. – 9 miles/15 km S of Cefalù, in a situation affording panoramic views, is the *Santuario di Gibilmanna* (17th–18th c.), above which is an observatory (3297 ft/1005 m; *views). – Another attractive excursion from Cefalù is a hydrofoil trip to the **Lipari Islands** (see p. 120).

Beyond Cefalù the route continues on the motorway. – 9 miles/15 km: junction with the A 19 motorway to Enna and Catania. $1\frac{1}{4}$ miles/2 km S on A 19 is the *Buonfornello* exit, where we continue on SS 113. A short distance along this, on the right, are the remains of the Greek city of *Himera*, founded in 648 B.C. and destroyed by the Carthaginians in 409 B.C. (Doric temple of about 480 B.C.; temple of 6th c. B.C.). The Targa Florio car-race (45 miles/ 72 km) is held at Buonfornello annually in May. – 8 miles/13 km: exit for **Términi Imerese** (alt. 371 ft/113 m; pop. 26,000), finely situated on a promontory. In the Lower Town is the spa establishment (radioactive saline springs, 108 °F/42 °C) in the Upper Town the Cathedral and the Belvedere Park, on the site of the ancient Forum; Museo Civico. 6 miles/10 km S, on a rocky crag above the Fiume San Leonardo, perches the township of *Cáccamo* (alt. 1709 ft/521 m; pop. 11,000), with a well-preserved 12th c. castle. – $2\frac{1}{2}$ miles/4 km: exit for **Trabia** (pop. 6000), a little town on the coast, with a battlemented castle. – 10 miles/16 km: exit for *Casteldaccia*, from which we continue on the coast road to *Santa Flavia*, where a road goes off on the right via *Porticello* and *Sant'Elia* to *Capo Zafferano* 9 miles/14 km; 738 ft/225 m; lighthouse). From this road a side road 1 mile/1·5 km) winds steeply up to the remains of **Soluntum** (Greek *Solous*; Italian *Sólunto*), a Phoenician settlement and later a Roman town, situated on the SE slopes of *Monte Catalfano* (1234 ft/ 376 m). Particularly notable is the re-erected part of a peristyle belonging to a building known as the Gymnasium. From the top of the hill there are superb views westward of Palermo Bay and eastward, on fine days, as far as Etna.

2 miles/3 km beyond Trabia on the motorway is the exit for **Bagheria** (alt. 279 ft/85 m; pop. 42,000), notable for its Baroque villas (18th c.). At the end of the Corso Butera, the town's main street, is the Villa Butera (1658; Certosa, with wax figures in Carthusian habits). A little way E is the Villa Palagonía (1715), with an extraordinary series of grotesque sculptured figures. Still farther E is the Villa Valguarnera (*views from terrace and from the nearby hill of Montagnola). – 7½ miles/12 km: exit for **Palermo** (see p. 149).

The next part of the circuit, from Palermo to Trapani, can be done either direct on the A 29 and A 29d motorways or on the coast road (SS 187) via the little port town of Castellammare del Golfo and Erice. Longer, but well worth the extra distance, is the route following SS 186 and SS 113, leaving Palermo by the Porta Nuova and Corso Calatafimi.

5 miles/8 km: **Monreale** (alt. 985 ft/300 m; pop. 25,000), the see of an archbishop, beautifully situated above the Conca d'Oro. On the left-hand side of the main street stands the **Cathedral with its two massive towers, the finest example of Norman architecture in Sicily. Basilican in form, 335 ft/102 m long by 130 ft/40 m wide, it has a beautiful choir with intersecting pointed arches of dark grey lava which preserves the structure of the Byzantine church. The main doorway has a fine bronze door by a Pisan artist named Bonannus, with reliefs from Scriptural history and inscriptions in Early Italian (1186). The left-hand doorway, under a porch of 1569, has a bronze door by Barisanus of Trani (12th c.). The interior has 18 antique columns with fine capitals, and the walls are covered with magnificent mosaics (1182) which have a total area of 68,250 sq. ft/6340 sq. m (the largest area of mosaics in Sicily), with scenes from the Old Testament and the life of Christ and the Apostles. In the S transept are the sarcophagi of William I and II, son and grandson of Roger II. In the S aisle is the 18th c. Cappella di San Benedetto (marble reliefs), in the N aisle the Cappella del Crocifisso (1690), with fine carved scenes from the Passion on the side doors. It is well worth climbing to the roof of the Cathedral (172 steps) for the sake of the view. – To the right of the Cathedral is the former Benedictine Monastery. Of the original buildings

nothing is left but the *cloister (Chiostro di Santa Maria Nuova), the largest and finest in the Italian Romanesque style, with 216 columns. The cloister is overshadowed on the S side by a ruined wall of the original monastery.

13 miles/21 km beyond Monreale on SS 186 is **Partinico** (alt. 620 ft/189 m; pop. 25,000), dominated by an ancient tower. Continue on SS 113. – 12½ miles/20 km: **Álcamo** (alt. 840 ft/256 m; pop. 44,000), a town founded by the Arabs. In the main street is the 17th c. Cathedral, with paintings by Borreman (1736–37) and sculpture by Antonello Gagini and his School (also to be seen in the Church of San Francesco d'Assisi). In the Church of Santa Chiara and the Badia Nuova are stucco figures by Giacomo Serpotta. There is also a 14th c. Castle. Above the town rises *Monte Bonifato* (2707 ft/825 m; *view), which can be climbed in 2 hours. – 9 miles/15 km: the road on the right leads to the remains (2 miles/3 km W) of ancient **Segesta** or *Egesta* (alt. 1000 ft/305 m), one of the oldest towns in Sicily, founded by the Elymians in pre-Greek times. It was almost incessantly at war with its Greek neighbors, particularly Selinous (Selinunte); later it became Carthaginian and then Roman, and was finally destroyed by the Saracens. From the end of the access road a stepped path leads up to the *temple, standing in majestic solitude on a levelled hill ridge below the W side of the ancient city. Begun in 430 B.C. but left unfinished, it is one of the best-preserved temples in Sicily (200 ft/61 m long by 85 ft/26 m wide), with 36 Doric columns still supporting the entablature and pediments. – From the end of the access road a track winds its way up to the site of the ancient city, 1 mile/1·5 km SE on *Monte Bárbaro* (1414 ft/431 m), with remains of fortifications, houses (mosaic pavements) and a *theater hewn from the rock.

2 miles/3 km beyond the turning for Segesta is *Calatafimi* (alt. 1017 ft/310 m; pop. 13,000), with a castle on a hill to the W of the town. – ¾ mile/1 km: minor road (2 miles/3 km SW) to the Ossario, a conspicuous monument erected in 1892 to commemorate Garibaldi's first victory over numerically superior Bourbon forces on May 15, 1860. – ¾ mile/1 km farther on the road forks. SS 188A, to the left, runs via *Salemi* (6 miles/10 km; alt. 1450 ft/442 m; pop. 17,000), with a castle built in

the time of Frederick II in which Garibaldi proclaimed his dictatorship of Sicily in 1860 (commemorative column), to Castelvetrano (another 16 miles/26 km). The road to the right leads to Trápani (22 miles/35 km).

The coast of Sicily near Trápani

**Trápani** (pop. 72,000), situated on a sickle-shaped peninsula on the NW coast of Sicily, and accordingly named Drepanon (Sickle) by the Greeks, was the port of ancient Eryx, the modern *Érice*, lying 9 miles/15 km inland to the NE (magnificent ** views over land and sea), and is still a port of some consequence, shipping salt, wine and tuna meat. The town's main street is the Corso Vittorio Emanuele, in the eastern half of which are the 17th c. Cathedral of San Lorenzo and the Chiesa del Collegio or Chiesa Nazionale (1638), which was elaborately adorned with marble and stucco in the 18th c. At the E end of the Corso is the Old Town Hall (17th c.; now the Registry Office), with a fine Baroque façade. The former Church of Sant'Agostino to the SE has a beautiful rose-window, and once belonged to the Templars; it is now a concert and lecture hall. Farther E is the Church of Santa Maria di Gesù (15th c.). – From the Old Town Hall Via Torre Arsa leads S to the harbor (attractive seafront promenade) and N to Via Garibaldi, which in turn leads NE to the Villa Margherita (public gardens) and the busy Piazza Vittorio Emanuele. From here the wide Via Fardella runs E to the Borgo Annunziata quarter. In this part of the town is the Santuario dell'Annunziata (founded 1332), with a 13th c. Virgin (in the Cappella della Madonna di Trapani), richly decorated with jewelry and other

votive offerings, which is venerated as miraculous (candle procession on August 16). The old conventual buildings (beautiful cloister) house the Museo Nazionale Pepoli (paintings, sculpture, decorative art, prehistoric and Classical antiquities).

A pleasant trip from Trápani is by boat (daily; 45 minutes – 2 hours 45 minutes) or hydrofoil (several times daily; 15 minutes – 1 hour) to the **Ísole Égadi**, the main tuna-fishing area. The boats call in at the islands of *Favignana* (alt. 991 ft/302 m; area 7·6 sq. miles/19·8 sq. km). *Lévanzo* 978 ft/298 m; 2·3 sq. miles/6 sq. km) and *Maréttimo* (2244 ft/684 m; 4·7 sq. miles/12·3 sq. km) only twice weekly.

The third part of the circuit of Sicily, from Trápani to Syracuse, is on SS 115. – 20 miles/32 km: **Marsala** (alt. 40 ft/12 m; pop. 80,000), a port and commercial town situated at the western tip of Sicily, best known for its rich golden-yellow dessert wine (13–16° alcohol); visitors can see around some of the wine-making establishments. – The hub of the town's traffic is the Piazza della Repubblica, with the beautiful 18th c. Old Town Hall, built in the form of a loggia, and the Cathedral, dedicated to St Thomas of Canterbury, which contains fine sculpture by Antonello Gagini and eight magnificent 16th c. Flemish tapestries, displayed only on certain feast-days. – From the Piazza della Repubblica the town's main street, Via XI Maggio, runs NW past the Monastery and Church of San Pietro (16th c.) to the Porta Nuova. On a house on the left is a plaque commemorating a visit in 1862 by Garibaldi, whose victorious campaign against the Bourbons had begun two years earlier with his landing in Marsala harbor on May 11, 1860. Beyond the Porta Nuova, to the right, are public gardens, at the N end of which is a belvedere affording fine views. Below the belvedere and along the Viale Vittorio Veneto, which continues the line of Via XI Maggio, are the remains of ancient *Lilybaeum*, including fragments of the town walls. Off the road to the right are the ruins of the Insula Romana, a Roman apartment block of the 3rd c. A.D., with a fine animal mosaic in the associated * baths. From the end of the avenue there is a beautiful view of the sea and the coast; and from **Capo Boeo** or *Capo Lilibeo*, a short distance SW, there are even more extensive views NE over the old harbor to Monte Érice and NW to the Isole Egadi. – Half-way between the cape and the Porta Nuova, off the road to the right, is the Church of San Giovanni Battista, from which steps lead down to the Grotta della Sibilla (Roman Mosaic).

12 miles/19 km: **Mazara del Vallo** (alt. 25 ft/8 m; pop. 44,000), with an 11th c. Cathedral (remodelled in 17th and 20th c.) founded by Count Roger and a number of other fine churches and palaces. – 9 miles/15 km: *Campobello di Mazara* (alt. 330 ft/100 m; pop. 12,000). 2 miles/ 3 km SW are the ancient quarries known as the *Rocche di Cusa or Cave di Campobello which supplied the building material for Selinous (Selinunte). – 5 miles/8 km: **Castelvetrano** (alt. 625 ft/ 190 m; pop. 32,000), with the churches of San Giovanni (Statue of John the Baptist by Antonello Gagini, 1512, in choir), San Domenico (stucco figures by Antonio Ferraro, 1577, and marble Madonna by Domenico Gagini) and the Chiesa Madre (16th c., with Renaissance doorway). 2 miles/3·5 km W of the town is the restored Norman *Church of Santa Trinità della Delia* (12th c.), in Byzantine style on a centralized plan. – 6 miles/9 km: road on right (SS 115D) to *Selinunte* (see p. 175). – 23 miles/37 km: **Sciacca**, or *Sciacca Terme* (alt. 200 ft/60 m). At the W entrance to the town is the Porta San Salvatore. Just beyond it, to the right, stands the 16th c. Church of Santa Margherita (marble N doorway, 1468), and to the left the Chiesa del Carmine. NE of the Porta San Salvatore, at the W end of the Corso Vittorio Emanuele, we come to the Gothic Casa Steripinto, with a façade of faceted stones. Beyond this is the Cathedral (Madonna by Francesco Laurana, 1467, in the fourth chapel on the right). Farther E are the public gardens (view) and the Terme Selinuntine, the spa establishment (sulfur baths), on the site of the ancient baths. Higher up, on the line of the town walls, are the remains of the Castle of Count Luna. – From the Porta San Salvatore a road runs 4½ miles/7·5 km NE to the limestone hill of **Monte San Calógero** (1273 ft/388 m), with the *Santuario San Calogero* on its summit *view). Below the monastery are caves with vapor baths, known as the *Stufe* (93–104 °F/34–40 °C). – 12½ miles/20 km NE of Sciacca lies the little town of *Caltabellotta* (alt. 2460 ft/750 m; pop. 7500), dominated by its castle, with a Cathedral of the Norman period.

14 miles/23 km beyond Sciacca on SS 115 a road goes off on the right to the remains (4 miles/6 km SW on Capo Bianco) of ancient *Eraclea Minoa*, destroyed in the 1st c. B.C. – 25 miles/41 km: *Porto Empédocle*, the port of Agrigento. – 4 miles/6 km: road on the left to **Agrigento** (see p. 39), running between the temples of Zeus and Hera and then winding its way up to the town. – 20 miles/32 km: **Palma di Montechiaro** (alt. 525 ft/160 m; pop. 20,000), with a handsome Baroque church. On the hill beyond it, to the right, can be seen the 14th c. *Castello* (938 ft/286 m). – 12½ miles/20 km: **Licata** (alt. 40 ft/12 m; pop. 42,000), beautifully situated on the hillside at the mouth of the River Salso, an expanding port which is the principal commercial town on the S coast of Sicily (export of sulfur). Above the town to the W stands the 16th c. *Castel Sant'Angelo* (restored). 7 miles/11 km: on the coast, to the right, the 15th c. *Castello di Falconara* (restored). – 14 miles/22 km: **Gela** (alt.

Licata, on the S coast of Sicily

150 ft/45 m; pop. 76,000), a port formerly known as *Terranova di Sicilia* (oil-refineries) which is also frequented as a seaside resort. To the W of the town are the extensive cemeteries of the ancient city (founded by Dorian settlers in 688 B.C.) and the Zona Archeologica di Capo Soprano, with the imposing remains of Greek *defensive walls of the 5th–4th c. B.C. (220 yds/200 m long, built of regular stone blocks in the lower part and sun-dried bricks in the upper part – the earliest known use of such bricks) and Greek baths of the 4th c. B.C. At the E end of the town is the *Museo Archeologico, and near this are the most recent excavations (houses and shops of the 4th c. B.C.). To the S of the Museum, on the Molino a Vento (Windmill) Hill, is the ancient acropolis (now a public park), with the remains of two Doric temples (6th and 5th c. B.C.).

21 miles/33 km beyond Gela on SS 115 is **Vittoria** (alt. 550 ft/168 m; pop. 45,000), the principal center of the Sicilian wine trade. In the main square are the Neo-Classical Teatro Vittorio Emanuele and the Church of the Madonna delle Grazie (18th c.). – 5 miles/8 km: **Cómiso** (alt. 805 ft/245 m; pop. 27,000), with two 18th c. domed churches, the Chiesa Madre and the Chiesa dell'Annunziata, and a beautiful Fountain of Diana in the Piazza del Municipio. – 10 miles/17 km: **Ragusa** (alt. 1680 ft/512 m; pop. 67,000), a provincial capital, pictur-esquely situated above the gorge of the River *Irminio*, with a Baroque Cathedral (18th c.) and the splendid Baroque Church of San Giorgio (18th c.) in the old part of the town, the Ibla quarter to the E (steep winding streets). From the bypass to the S of the town there are fine *views. – Near the town are deposits of bitumi-nous limestone, and 1¼ miles/2 km S, on the road to the rising seaside resort of *Marina di Ragusa* (17 miles/28 km), are large asphalt-mines. In recent years, too, oil has been worked here.

9 miles/15 km beyond Ragusa is **Módica** (alt. 1445 ft/440 m; pop. 48,000), built on the slopes on both sides of the Módica Valley. In the lower town, approached by a flight of steps, are the churches of San Pietro (18th c.) and Santa Maria di Gesù (about 1478), and adjoining them a former monastery with a fine cloister. In the upper town is the imposing 18th c. Church of San Giorgio. – 4½ miles/7 km:

road on the left into the picturesque Valley of *Cava d'Íspica*, in the rock walls of which are many caves which were used as dwellings and tombs in Byzantine times. – 20 miles/32 km: **Noto** (alt. 518 ft/158 m; pop. 24,000), attractively laid out on terraces, with Baroque churches and handsome palaces. The present town was built from 1703 onward to replace the older town of Noto, 7 miles/11 km SE, which was destroyed by an earthquake in 1693. Along the town's main street, the Corso Vittorio Emanuele, which traverses it from W to E, are three monumental squares. In the first of these, the Piazza Ércole (officially Piazza XVI Maggio), are the Baroque Church of San Domenico (18th c.) and an ancient statue of Hercules. In the second, the Piazza del Municipio, are the Cathedral (imposing Baroque façade), the Palazzo Ducezio (Town Hall) and the Church of San Salvatore. In the third, the Piazza XXX Ottobre, are the Church of the Immacolata (or San Francesco) and the Monastery of San Salvatore. To the N, 1000 ft/300 m above Via Cavour, is the Chiesa del Crocifisso, with a Madonna by Francesco Laurana (1471).

6 miles/9 km beyond Noto is **Ávola** (alt. 130 ft/40 m; pop. 28,000). The road then crosses the River *Cassibile*, the ancient *Kakyparis*, where Demosthenes and his 6000 Athenians were compelled to sur-render to the Syracusans in 413 B.C. Upstream, in the rock faces of the Cava Grande, can be seen a *Siculan necropolis*. – 14 miles/23 km: **Syracuse** (see p. 188).

The last part of the circuit of Sicily, from Syracuse to Messina, is on SS 114 (the Orientale Sicula road; from Catania also the A 18 motorway), running close to the sea for most of the way. – 9 miles/14 km from Syracuse the road forks. Straight ahead (the old and more interesting) road via **Lentini** (alt. 233 ft/71 m; pop. 35,000) to Catania; to the right the new road, SS 114, which is 18 km/11 miles shorter and much faster. This road runs past large oil-refineries and in 4½ miles/7 km reaches the turning for **Augusta** (alt. 45 ft/14 m; pop. 38,000), the principal Italian naval base in Sicily. – 39 miles/63 km: **Catania** (see p. 49; starting-point for the ascent of **Etna).

6 miles/9 km beyond Catania on SS 114 is the little town of **Aci Castello** (alt. 50 ft/15 m; pop. 13,000), dominated by a picturesque ruined castle on a high crag.

Just beyond the town, out to sea, can be seen the seven **Isole dei Ciclopi** (Cyclops' Islands) or *Faraglioni*, traditionally the rocks which the blinded Cyclops hurled after Odysseus's ship ("Odyssey", IX, 537). On the largest of the islands, the *Isola d'Aci*, is a marine biological station. – $4\frac{1}{2}$ miles/7 km: **Acireale** (Sicilian *Iaci*; alt. 528 ft/161 m; pop. 50,000). At the near end of the town, on the right of the road, are the *Terme di Santa Vénera* (warm radioactive water containing iodine, sulfur and salt). From here the town's main street , the Corso Vittorio Emanuele, runs N, with the Church of San Sebastiano (Baroque façade) on the right. Beyond this, in the Piazza del Duomo, are the Cathedral, the Town Hall (small museum) and the Church of Santi Pietro e Paolo. From the municipal park at the N end of the town there are fine views. – 11 miles/ 18 km: *Mascali*, a little town which formerly lay farther W but was destroyed by lava in 1928 and rebuilt on its present site. – 9 miles/15 km: \***Taormina** (see p. 191). – 30 miles/48 km: **Messina** (see p. 136).

# Sifnos
## See under Cyclades

# Silba and Olib

Yugoslavia
Republic: Croatia (Hrvatska).
Altitude: 0–260 ft/0–80 m. – Population: 700.
Telephone code: 057.
(i) **Turističko Društvo Silba,**
YU-57295 **Silba.**

ACCOMMODATION. – In private houses.

CAMP SITE. – Naturist site on Silba (no caravans).

FERRIES. – Passenger services from Zadar (no cars; there are no motor roads on either of the islands).

**The islands of Silba and Olib lie in the Adriatic some 30 miles NW of Zadar, beyond the island of Pag. They are renowned for excellent wines, cheese and fish.**

HISTORY. – The history of the two islands is almost identical. Both were occupied in Roman times, and both are referred to by the Emperor Constantine VII Porphyrogenitus in his historical writings, under the names of *Selbo* and *Alope*. In the 15th c. the islands were leased by Venice to families from Zadar, who used them mainly for grazing sheep. During the 17th and 18th c. Silba enjoyed a considerable measure of prosperity through the activities of its seamen and shipowners, while Olib and the small neighboring islands remained mere sheep-grazings. No settlements of any size could develop on either island, since they had no natural springs or watercourses and depended for their water-supply (as they still do) on storing water in cisterns. The decline of the Adriatic fisheries in the 20th c. led to a further exodus of population from the islands. Their prospects for the future depend on the tourist trade and the discovery of the islands as nature reserves free of motor traffic.

The 17th c. Parish Church in the village of **Silba** has paintings by the Venetian artist Carlo Ridolfi. The Church of Our Lady (Gospa od Karmena), built in 1752, belonged to a Franciscan Friary founded in 1660, now abandoned. Of the old fortifications there remains a ruined 16th c. tower. Beside the Post Office is a 19th c. outlook tower.

The only settlement on the island of **Olib** is in the Bay of Luka Olib. The Parish Church was built in 1632 and renovated in 1858. The presbytery preserves 20

The little port of Olib on the island of the same name

Glagolitic codices (see under Krk) of the 16th–19th c. The other church in the village is older than the parish church. Outside the village is a watch-tower of the 17th–18th c., and in Banve Bay to the S are the remains of a Roman settlement (foundations of buildings), a ruined church and a monastery destroyed about 1200.

# Šipan
## See under Elaphite Islands

# Skiathos
## See under Sporades

# Skopelos
## See under Sporades

# Skyros
## See under Sporades

# Šolta
## See under Brač

# Spetsai
## See under Hydra

# Sporades
*(Sporádhes)*

Greece

HOTELS. – ON SKIÁTHOS: *Skiathos Palace*, L, 382 b.; *Esperides*, I, 300 b.; *Nostos*, I, 208 b.; *Alkyon*, II, 152 b.; *Xenia*, II, 64 b.; *Belvedere*, III, 95 b.

ON SKÓPELOS: *Rigas*, II, 71 b.; *Xenia*, II, 8 b.; *Aeolos*, III, 79 b.; *Avra*, III, 51 b.

ON ALÓNNISOS: *Galaxy*, III, 73 b.; *Marpunta Bungalows*, III, 200 b.

ON SKÝROS: *Xenia*, II, 38 b.

ON LÉROS: *Xenon Angelou*, II, 16 b.; *Panteli*, III, 48 b.; *Alinda*, III, 41 b.; *Leros*, III, 35 b.

ON KÁLYMNOS: *Armeos Beach*, II, 61 b.; *Drosos*, III, 97 b.; *Olympic*, III, 81 b.; *Thermai*, III, 23 b.

ON SÝMI: *Aliki*, I, 28 b.; *Nireus*, II, 12 b.

**The Sporades are, etymologically, the "scattered" islands. The northern Sporades, lying off the Peninsula of Magnesia, N of Evia extend SE from Skiáthos by way of Skópelos and Alónissos to Skýros, with the smaller islands of Pélagos, Ghioúra and Pipéri to the N. The southern Sporades include the islands around Sámos and the Dodecanese.**

HISTORY. – The Sporades played no great part in history or in art, either in Antiquity or in later centuries. In the 5th c. Athens gained control of the whole group; in 338 B.C. the islands became Macedonian, and in 168 B.C. Roman; thereafter they were under Byzantine rule. From 1207 to 1263 they were ruled by a Venetian family, the Ghisi, whose seat was on Skýros; later they returned to Byzantine control and then again to Venice before falling under Turkish rule. They were united with Greece in 1828–29.

The main islands in the northern Sporades have recently become popular as holiday resorts offering peace and quiet, beautiful scenery and excellent beaches. The two islands nearest the mainland, Skiáthos and Skópelos, are particularly well equipped with holiday facilities; the others are attractive to those who prefer the simple life.

## Northern Sporades

The NORTHERN SPORADES lie between Euboea (Evia) (see p. 89) and the Chalcidice Peninsula in the northern Aegean.

**Skiáthos** (area 19 sq. miles/48 sq. km; pop. 3900) is the closest to the mainland of the northern Sporades, lying only $2\frac{1}{2}$ miles/4 km off the Peninsula of Magnesia. This green, wooded island is an attractive and popular holiday resort. – The pretty little town of **Skiáthos** (pop. 3000), the chief place on the island, lies in a bay on the SE coast which is picturesquely dotted with a number of small islets. At the E end of the town the rocky *Boúrdzi* Peninsula projects into the sea. At the base of the peninsula is a monument to the short-story writer Alexandros Papadiamantis (1851–1912), whose house can be seen in the street just off the harbor. From the little hill on which stand a clock-tower and the Chapel of St Nicholas there are extensive views. Another good view-point is the Church of Aghios Fanoúrios, reached on a road which goes off on the W side of the town (30 minutes).

A road runs W from Skiáthos to the beaches of **Akhládes** (2½ miles/4 km), **Tzaneriá** (3 miles/ 4·5 km) and **Koukounariés** (8 miles/13 km). The beach of Koukounariés, backed by a pine wood, is one of the most beautiful in the Aegean.

The medieval capital of **Kástro**, abandoned only in 1825, lies on an impregnable crag on the N coast (accessible by boat or by a steep climb of some 3 hours).

**Skópelos** (area 37 sq. miles/96 sq. km; pop. 4500), like Skiáthos, is a green and pleasant island. It was known in Antiquity as *Peparethos*. – The chief town, **Skópelos** (pop. 3000) is beautifully situated on the slopes above a north-facing bay, along the E side of which are gardens and a sandy beach. Its courtyards abound with a multitude of flowers mirrored in the beautiful, embroidered traditional dresses worn by many of the women. The islanders have a pleasant custom of greeting a visitor with a sweet cake or prune and a glass of "raki" and when one leaves they usually present one with a gardenia or sprig of basil to say "please come again". Among the many churches St Michael's is of particular interest. The medieval castle is built on part of the site of ancient Peparethos. The other ancient settlements on the island were *Selinous* (present-day Glóssa) and *Panormos* (present-day Klíma).

Skópelos

Near the town are the **monasteries** of *Episkopí, Aghia Evangelistría* and *Aghia Varvára*. There is a road from the town to the bays of **Stáfilos** (3 miles/5 km; sandy beach) and **Agnóndas** (6 miles/9 km) and to **Glóssa** (alt. 785 ft/240 m), situated in the W of the island above the landing-place of **Skála Glóssas**.

NE of Skópelos is **Alónnisos** (area 25 sq. miles/72 sq. km; pop. 1500). The villages

on this long narrow island are in the SW, opposite Skópelos. Among them are the chief place, **Alónissos** (pop. 500), situated on a hill, and the little harbor town of **Patitíri** (pop. 400), on the S coast, which offers the best prospect of finding accommodation. From here there are boat trips E to the neighboring island of *Peristéra* 5·4 sq. miles/14 sq. km; pop. 65) and NE to the islands of *Kyrá Panayía* (or Pélagos; 9·7 sq. miles/25 sq. km; pop. 70; monastery), *Ghioúra* (4·2 sq. miles/11 sq. km; ruined monastery, goatherds looking after wild goats) and *Pipéri* (2·7 sq. miles/ 7 sq. km).

Fishermen, Skýros

**Skýros** (area 81 sq. miles/209 sq. km; pop. 3000), the most easterly of the northern Sporades, is barer and less fertile than the other islands in the group. There are beautiful beaches in the many inlets around the coast. Attractive handicrafts (hand-weaving, furniture). – From the port of *Linariá* (pop. 250), on the W coast, a road runs across the island to its picturesque chief town, **Skýros** also called *Orio* (pop. 2500), on the E coast (bus service). This little town of white cube-shaped houses lies on the slopes of the formidable crag once occupied by the ancient acropolis and now crowned by a Venetian castle, with remains of ancient masonry incorporated into its walls. Below the summit plateau is a monastery dedicated to St George. In Platía Kýprou can be seen a monument to Rupert Brooke, who died on his way to the Dardanelles in 1915 and is buried in the Bay of Tris Boukes. There is a small local museum, and many of the little houses are virtually living museums, filled with hand-made artefacts, embroidery and sculpture.

From both Linariá and Skýros boat trips can be arranged to the island's many bays and inlets. There are also pleasant walks from Skýros – for example to *Mount Ólympos* (1207 ft/368 m), at the foot of which is the *Olympianí Monastery* (5 miles/8 km W).

# Southern Sporades

The SOUTHERN SPORADES, off the W coast of Asia Minor, consist mainly of the islands around Sámos and the Dodecanese.

**Sámos:** see p. 164.

**Pátmos:** see p. 155.

**Léros** (area 20 sq. miles/53 sq. km; pop. 8500) is a hilly island with deeply indented bays lying between Pátmos and Kálymnos. From the port of **Lakkí** (pop. 1700; medieval church) in the SW there is a road to the chief place on the island, **Aghia Marína** (2 miles/3 km; pop. 2600), with a Byzantine castle which was restored by the Knights of St John. From here it is 7½ miles/12 km to **Parthénion**, in a beautiful situation in the NW of the island. In the plain S of Lakkí is the village of *Xerokambos*, above which lies the ancient site of *Palaiókastro*, with the remains of a fortress of the 4th c. B.C..

**Kálymnos** (area 43 sq. miles/111 sq. km; pop. 13,000) is best known as the island of the sponge-fishers. Visitors can see the establishments in which the sponges are processed in the port town of **Kálymnos**. – There is a road from Kálymnos to **Vathý**, in a deep inlet on the E coast (4 miles/6 km; bus). Another road runs W, passing a *Castle* of the Knights of St John perched on a sheer crag on the left, to **Khorió** (2 miles/3 km) and then down to **Pánormos** or **Linariá** (6 miles/9 km; sandy beach, restaurants). From Khorió it is possible to continue to **Myrtiés** and **Emborió**, at the northern tip of the island, where a Mycenaean tholos tomb was found. From Linariá a boat trip can be made to the little island of **Télendos** (ancient remains, medieval castle, ruined monastery).

**Kos:** see p. 113.

**Nísyros** (area 16 sq. miles/41 sq. km; pop. 1250) lies S of Kos, with which it is linked by myth. It is said to be a part of Kos which Poseidon hurled at the Titan, Polybotes. – Thanks to its good natural water resources the island is fertile. On the N coast is the port of **Mandráki**, with a cave monastery in the crag which rears above the village. A little way inland (30 minutes; some signposts) is the *Kastro* – the ancient acropolis, with long stretches of wall 12 ft/3·60 m thick and still standing fully 20 ft/6 m high, built of dressed stone. To the right of the gate, still completely preserved, is an ancient flight of steps leading up to the wall-walk (fine views). – 1¼ miles/2 km E of Mandráki is the little seaside resort of **Loutrá**. – The center of the island is occupied by a volcanic crater 2½ miles/4 km in diameter, which is reached from Mandráki by way of **Emborió** (pop. 260). A narrow track leads to the fumaroles and sulfur deposits inside the crater. The outer slopes of the volcano are covered with carefully terraced fields.

**Sými** (area 22 sq. miles/58 sq. km; pop. 2500) lies N of Rhodes between two long promontories projecting from the Anatolian coast. The chief town and port, **Sými**, in a beautiful bay on the N coast, has houses rising in a semicircle on the slopes of the hill. In a house by the harbor (commemorative tablet) the surrender of the Dodecanese to the Allies was signed on May 8, 1945. There are many tavernas around the little harbor. – On a hill above the town is a *Castle of the Knights of St John*, built over remains of the walls of dressed stone of the ancient acropolis. From the castle there are views of the *Windmill Hill*, on which, above the windmills, is an ancient circular tomb, and (to the E) of the next bay, with the village of **Pédion** and the only stretch of flat fertile land on the island. – In a bay at the S end of the island, 2½ miles/4 km from Sými, is the Monastery and Pilgrimage Center of *Aghios Panormítis*.

**Tílos** (**Télos**; area 23 sq. miles/60 sq. km; pop. 600) lies between Rhodes and Kos. Two large inlets cut into the island from N and S. The landing-place at *Livádia* is in the north-eastern bay, the principal settlement, **Megalokhorió** (pop. 300), 7½ miles/12 km away in the north-western bay, below a *Castle of the Knights of St John*. In the interior of the island is the little village of *Mikrokhorió*.

**\*\*Rhodes:** see p. 158.

**Kárpathos** and **Kásos:** see pp. 107/108.

# Stromboli
## See under Lipari Islands

# Susak
## See under Lošinj

# Symi
## See under Sporades

# Syracuse/Siracusa

Italy
Region: Sicily. – Province: Syracuse.
Altitude: 0–16 ft/0–5 m. – Population: 118,000.
Post code: I-96100. – Telephone code: 0931.

ⓘ **AA,**
Via Maestranza 33;
tel. 6 52 01.
**EPT,**
Corso Gelone 92C;
tel. 6 76 07.
**ACI,**
Foro Siracusano 27;
tel. 2 46 55.

HOTELS. – *Jolly*, Corso Gelone 45, I, 146 b.; *Fontane Bianche*, Via Mazzario 1, II, 196 b., SP; *Grand Hotel – Villa Politi*, Via M. Politi Laudien 2, II, 164 b., SP; *Motel Agip*, Viale Teracati 30, II, 152 b.; *Park*, Via Filisto 80, II, 144 b.; *Panorama*, Via Necropoli Grotticelle 33, II, 90 b.; *Aretusa*, Via F. Crispi 75, III, 67 b.

EVENTS. – Performances of Classical plays in the Greek Theater (alternate years in spring).

\***Syracuse, capital of its province and the see of an archbishop, is largely situated on an island off the E coast of Sicily, separated by a narrow channel from the Sicilian mainland, on which are the modern town and the principal remains of the ancient city. The Bay of Porto Grande, which cuts deep inland to the S of the town, is perhaps Italy's largest and best natural harbor. The town's situation, its beautiful surroundings and the monuments and relics of its splendid past make Syracuse one of the most fascinating places in Italy.**

HISTORY. – Syracuse (Greek *Syrakousa*, Latin *Syracusae*) was founded on the island of *Ortygia* in the second half of the 8th c. B.C. by settlers from Corinth, and rapidly rose to prosperity. From the 5th c. onward it was ruled mostly by tyrants, the first of whom were Gelo (485–478) and Hiero I (478–467). Some of Greece's greatest poets, including Aeschylus and Pindar, lived at Hiero's Court. Syracuse was drawn into the conflict between Athens and Sparta, but an Athenian expedition against the city (415) ended in the total annihilation of the Athenian army and fleet in 413. During the struggle with Carthage,

Syracuse rose under Dionysius I (406–367) and his successors to become the most powerful Greek city, with a perimeter, according to Strabo, of 180 stadia (20 miles) and a population of half a million. Among the eminent men who lived in Syracuse during this period was the mathematician and physicist *Archimedes.* – After the First Punic War, in which Syracuse was allied with Rome, the city went over to the Carthaginian side: whereupon it was besieged and captured by the Romans (212 B.C.), and Archimedes was killed by a soldier. Thereafter Syracuse shared the destinies of the rest of Sicily, but never recovered its former importance.

THE TOWN. – The OLD TOWN, with its narrow winding streets and its old houses and palaces – many of them with handsome balconies – lies, as it did in Greek times, on the island of Ortygia. Its busiest traffic intersection is the *Piazza Archimede*, on the W side of which is the *Banca d'Italia*, with a 15th c. courtyard; a little way NE is the *Palazzo Montalto* (1397), with magnificent Gothic windows. – From here Via Dione runs N to the **Temple of Apollo** (early 6th c. B.C.), which was also dedicated to Artemis (the Roman Diana). The oldest Doric temple in Sicily, it was excavated in 1933 and has recently been partly re-erected.

SW of Piazza Archimede lies the elongated *Piazza del Duomo*, with the *Palazzo del Municipio* (Town Hall, 13th c.) and next to it the \***Cathedral**, built in the 7th c. on the site of a Temple of Athena of the 5th c. B.C., enlarged in the 17th c. and provided with a handsome Baroque façade between 1728 and 1757. The pillars of the temple were incorporated into the Cathedral wall. – Opposite the Cathedral is the \***Museo Archeologico Nazionale**, with a large collection of antiquities, mostly of Sicilian origin, ranging in date from prehistoric to Early Christian times. Particularly notable items are (ground floor, Room XIV) the \*Sarcophagus of Valerius and Adelfia (4th c. A.D.) from the Catacombs of San Giovanni, with carvings of scenes from the Old and New Testaments, and (Room IX) the Landolina Venus (Venus Anadyomene), with a dolphin by her side, a copy (2nd c. A.D.) of a fine Hellenistic work.

From the S end of the Piazza del Duomo Via Picherale continues S to the semicircular basin of the **Fountain of Arethusa** (*Fonte Aretusa*) with its papyrus plants. The legend of the nymph Arethusa, pursued by the river god Alpheus from Olympia to here, reflects the idea that the Peloponnesian River

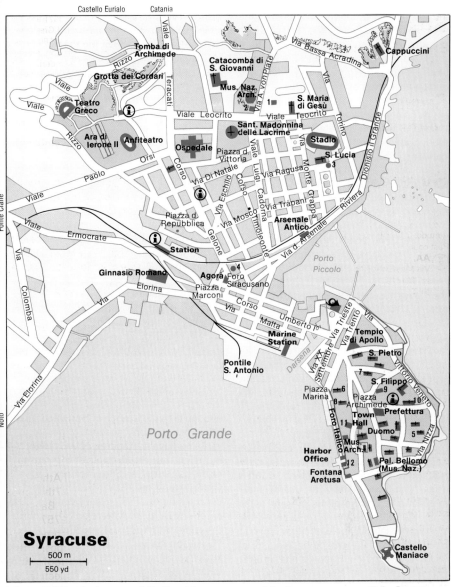

1  Catacombe di Vigna Cassia     4  War Memorial            7  San Tommaso           10  San Francesco
2  Villa Landolina               5  San Giovanni Battista   8  Chiesa del Collegio   11  Palazzo Beneventano
3  Cappella del Sepolcro         6  Santa Maria dei Miracoli 9  Palazzo Montalto     12  Acquario Tropicale

Alpheus continued flowing under the
sea and emerged at this point. – To the N of
the fountain extends the *Foro Italico, a
fine seafront promenade with views of
the harbor and of Etna. At the S end of the
Foro, in a small park, is the entrance to the
*Acquario Tropicale, with rare fishes
from tropical seas. At the N end of the Foro
are the Porta Marina, with Hispano-
Mauresque ornament (16th c.), and the
Church of Santa Maria dei Mirácoli
(1501). – A little way E of the Fountain of
Arethusa, at the S end of Via Roma (which
runs down from Piazza Archimede), we
come to the Palazzo Bellomo (15th c.),
which houses the Museo Nazionale

(medieval collections and a small picture
gallery).

At the southern tip of the island is the
Castello Maniace, a Hohenstaufen
stronghold built about 1239, with a
handsome gateway. From the S bastion
there is a fine view.

At the N end of the island, W of the Temple
of Apollo, is Piazza Pancali, from which
there is a bridge over the Dársena (the
channel between the island and the
mainland) to the NEW TOWN, with the
railway station and the impressive remains
of the ancient city. The Corso Umberto I,

the main street of the modern town, runs W from the bridge to the **Foro Siracusano**, on which remains of the ancient *Agora* can be seen. To the W are remains of the *Ginnasio Romano* (Gymnasium), once surrounded by colonnades.

¾ mile/1 km NW of the Foro Siracusano, to the left of the Corso Gelone (the Gatania road, SS 114), is the Augustan **Amphitheater** (153 yds/140 m long, 130 yds/119 m across), in the part of the Roman town known as Neapolis. 110 yds/100 m W of the Amphitheater is the *Altar of Hiero II* (Ara di Ierone II), a gigantic structure 220 yds/200 m long by 25 yds/22·5 m wide which originally rose in two tiers to a height of 35 ft/10·5 m. Here probably was performed the annual sacrifice of 450 oxen. Opposite the altar is the entrance to the **Latomía del Paradiso**, an ancient quarry 100–130 ft/30–40 m deep, now covered with a luxuriant growth of vegetation, which was used, like the other *latomíe* in Syracuse, as a prison for offenders condemned to stone-breaking and also for the confinement of prisoners of war. Keeping left immediately inside the entrance archway along the garden wall, we come to the so-called *Ear of Dionysius*, an S-shaped cave hewn from the rock, 213 ft/65 m deep, 75 ft/23 m in height and 16–36 ft/5–11 m wide, contracting toward the top, in which sound is considerably amplified without any recurring echo. It has borne its present name since the 16th c., reflecting the belief that the tyrant Dionysius was thus able to overhear even the whispered remarks of State prisoners confined in the quarry. Farther to the right, below the W wall of the quarry, is the *Grotta dei Cordari*, named after the rope-makers who carry on their trade there. – Immediately E is the *Latomía di Santa Vénera*, with a particularly lush growth of vegetation.

Immediately W of the Latomía del Paradiso is the *Greek Theater (5th c. B.C.),* with a semicircular auditorium hewn from the rock, the largest and most impressive in the Greek World (diameter 454 ft/138·5 m; cf. Athens, 330 ft/100 m). Two tunnels under the auditorium give access to the orchestra (diameter 78 ft/24 m, the same as Athens). In this theater Aeschylus (d. 456 B.C.) directed the performance of his ''Persians'' (about 472 B.C.); and it is still used for the performance of Classical plays (in spring, in alternate – even-numbered – years). From the top of the

theater there is a magnificent *view at sunset of the town, the harbor and the sea. – In the rock face above the theater is the so-called *Nymphaeum*, a cave which was the terminal point of an ancient aqueduct. From the left-hand side of the Nymphaeum the **Street of Tombs** (*Via dei Sepolcri*) runs up in a curve for some 165 yds/150 m, with cavities and tomb chambers of the Late Roman period in its walls.

Greek Theater, Syracuse

550 yds/500 m NE of the Amphitheater, to the right of the Catania road (SS 114), can be seen the little Church of **San Giovanni alle Catacombe**, the western part of the early medieval Cathedral, of which nothing is left but the W front of the present church, with a conspicuous rose-window, and the 15th c. porch. From the church a flight of steps leads down to the cruciform *Crypt of St Marcian* (4th c., with the remains of frescoes) and the adjoining *Catacombs, which are among the finest known, far more extensive than the catacombs of Rome. – SE of San Giovanni, in a small *latomía*, is the *Villa Landolina*, with the tomb of the 19th c. German poet August von Platen in the garden. From here, going N along Via Augusto von Platen, with the entrance to the *Catacombs of Vigna Cassia*, and then 550 yds/500 m E aong Via Bassa Acradina, we come to a Capuchin Monastery and beside it the *Latomía dei Cappuccinni, one of the wildest and grandest of the ancient quarries, in which the 7000 Athenian prisoners taken in 414 B.C. were probably confined.

SURROUNDINGS of Syracuse. – 5 miles/8 km NW of the Foro Siracusano, at the western end of the outlying district of ancient Syracuse, *Epipolae*, on higher ground, is the *Fort of Euryalus (*Castello Eurialo*). Built between 402 and 397 B.C. at the meeting of the N and S edges of the plateau; this is one of the best-preserved works of fortification to have come down to us from ancient times.

A pleasant outing from Syracuse is a boat trip (3–4 hours there and back) from the harbor up the little River *Ciane* (on a hill to the left two columns of the Olympieion, a Temple of Zeus of the 6th c. B.C.), between tall stands of papyrus, to the **Fountain of Cyane** (*Fonte Ciane* or *Testa della Pisma*), the "azure spring" into which the nymph of that name was metamorphosed for opposing Pluto in his rape of Proserpina.

21 miles/33 km W of Syracuse lies the interesting town of **Palazzolo Acréide** (alt. 2287 ft/697 m; pop. 11,000), the ancient *Akrai* (Roman *Placeolum*, Arabic *el-Akrat*), which was founded by settlers from Syracuse in 664 B.C. On the nearby Hill of *Acremonte*, the site of the ancient city, is a *Cinta Archeologica* containing the remains of a Late Greek theater (seating for 600), to the W of this the Bouleuterion (Council Chamber), to the SE *latomie* containing Greek and Early Christian tombs, and two tomb chambers known as the Templi Ferali (funerary temples). – From here it is a 15-minute walk to the Valley of *Contrada dei Santicelli*, near the large cemetery of *Acrocoro della Torre*, to see the *'''San-toni''*, cult images carved in niches in the rock (mutilated in the 19th c.). Most of them represent a seated goddess, presumably Cybele, with Hermes beside her. On the far side of the valley is *Monte Pineta*, with many small tomb chambers. – 21 miles/34 km NE of Palazzolo Acreide is the *Necrópoli di Pantálica*, the cemetery of the Siculan town (12th–8th c. B.C.) which lay on the hill to the N, with thousands of small tomb chambers hewn from the rock faces in the Ánapo Valley. During the Middle Ages many of the tombs were used as dwellings. Jewelry and ornaments found in the tombs are displayed in the Museo Nazionale in Syracuse.

# Syros
## See under Cyclades

# Taormina

Italy
Region: Sicily. – Province: Messina.
Altitude: 820 ft/250 m. – Population: 10,000.
Post code: I-98039. – Telephone code: 0942.

(i) **AA,**
   Piazza Santa Caterina;
   tel. 2 32 43.
   **TCI,**
   Corso Umberto I 207;
   tel. 2 49 57.
   **CIT,**
   Corso Umberto I 101;
   tel. 2 33 01.

HOTELS. – *San Domenico Palace*, L, 177 b., SP; *Jolly Hotel Diodoro*, I, 202, SP; *Excelsior Palace*, I, 166 b.; *Vello d'Oro*, I, 105 b.; *Bristol Park*, I, 99 b., SP; *Méditerranée*, I, 93 b., SP; *Timeo*, I, 93 b.; *Imperial Palace*, II, 136 b.; *Grande Albergo Monte Tauro*, II, 134 b., SP; *Sole Castello*, II, 94 b.; *President Hotel Splendid*, II, 87 b.; *Continental*, II, 80 b.; *Sirius*, II, 77 b.; *Ariston*, III, 207 b.; *Residence*, III, 50 b. – MAZ-ZARÒ: *Grande Albergo Capo Taormina*, I, 415 b., SP; *Mazzarò Sea Palace*, L, 146 b., SP; *Atlantis

Bay*, I, 174 b., SP; *Lido Méditerranée*, II, 110 b. – CAMP SITE.

EVENTS. – *Costume Festival*, with gaily painted Sicilian carts (*carretti*; end of May); *International Film Festival* (July); *Summer Festival* in Greek Theater.

**The picturesque little town of Taormina, the ancient Tauromenium, enjoys a magnificent** \*\***situation on a terrace high above the Ionian Sea on the E coast of Sicily. Still higher up are a ruined castle on a rocky crag and the little hill town of Castelmola, and in the background is the majestic cone of Etna. There are many who would claim Taormina to be the most beautiful place in the whole of Sicily.**

From the coast a steep and twisting road leads up to the town (4½ miles/7 km). The nearest beaches, at *Mazzarò* (cableway) and *Isola Bella*, are of only moderate quality; the sandy beaches at *Sant'Alessio Siculo* (9 miles/14 km N) and *Santa Teresa* (12½ miles/20 km N) are to be preferred.

THE TOWN. – The road which winds its way up from the coast, Via L. Pirandello (views), terminates at the *Porta Messina*, at the NE end of the town. A little way NE of the gate is the *Church of San Pancrazio*, occupying the cella of a Greek temple. To the S of the Porta Messina lies the Piazza Vittorio Emanuele, with the Gothic *Palazzo Corvaia* (1372) and the little *Church of Santa Caterina*. Behind the church are the remains of a Roman *Odeum*. – From the square Via del Teatro Greco runs SE to the *Greek Theater*, which was reconstructed in Roman style in the 2nd c. A.D. With a diameter at the top of 358 ft/109 m, it is the largest theater in Sicily after the one at Syracuse. It is renowned for its excellent acoustics (performances of Classical plays). The \*\*view from the top of the theater of the precipitous E coast of Sicily, with the gigantic cone of Etna, snow-covered for most of the year but always "steaming" and frequently fiery, and of the Calabrian coast is one of the most breath-taking in Italy.

From the Piazza Vittorio Emanuele the town's principal street, Corso Umberto I, flanked by handsome old houses, runs SW to the Largo IX Aprile (view), with the *Church of San Giuseppe* and the deconsecrated Church of *Sant'Agostino*. It

Taormina

then curves W, past the Palazzo Ciampoli (on the right), and joins the Piazza del Duomo, where a beautiful 12th c. fountain can be seen. The small **Cathedral** (13th–16th c.) has a number of fine altarpieces and, to the right of the High Altar, a 15th c. Madonna.

On the hillside to the N of the Piazza del Duomo are the ruins of the Gothic *Badia Vecchia* (14th c.). To the S, on the edge of the terrace, is a fine old *Dominican Monastery*, now the Hotel San Domenico Palace (cloister). From the tower of the church (destroyed 1943) there is a beautiful °view. – To the W of the Piazza del Duomo, beyond the *Porta Catania* or *Porta del Tocco*, is the *Palazzo Santo Stéfano* (1330), its vaulting supported on a massive granite column. Below the former monastery Via Roma (fine views) runs E to the *Villa Comunale* (public gardens), in a commanding situation, from which Via Bagnoli Croci continues to the °*Belvedere* (superb views). From here we can return on Via Luigi Pirandello, passing below the Greek Theater, to the Porta Messina.

SURROUNDINGS of Taormina. – From the W end of the town, near the Badia Vecchia, a road winds steeply uphill, with sharp turns, to the Chapel of the Madonna dell Rocca (1¼ miles/2 km), from which it is a few minutes' climb to the **Castello di Taormina**, on *Monte Tauro* (1306 ft/398 m). – Even more attractive is the further stretch of road (2 miles/3 km) to the village of **Castelmola** (1475 ft/450 m), perched on a precipitous crag, which commands panoramic °views from its various terraces, but particularly from its highest point near the ruined castle.

A very rewarding excursion from Taormina is the ascent of °°**Etna** (see p. 89).

# Thasos
## *(Thásos)*

Greece

Nomos: Kavála.
Area: 146 sq. miles/379 sq. km. – Population: 13,500.
Telephone code: 0593.

ⓘ **Tourist Police,**
tel. 2 25 00
(only in summer).

HOTELS. – THÁSOS: *Roula*, I, 12 b., apartments; *Timoleon*, II, 54 b.; *Xenia*, II, 50 b.; *Villa Meressi*, II, 46 b.; *Angelika*, III, 50 b.; *Laios*, III, 32 b.; *Lido*, III, 30 b.; *Panorama*, III, 16 b.

EAST COAST. – MAKRYÁMMOS (2 miles/3 km): *Makryammos Bungalows*, I, 402 b. – POTAMIÁ (7½ miles/12 km): *Blue Sea*, III, 23 b.; *Atlantis*, III, 12 b. – KÍNYRA: *Gerda*, III, 24 b.

WEST COAST. – PRÍNOS (9 miles/14 km): *Crystal*, III, 20 b. – LIMENARIÁ (26 miles/42 km): *Menel*, III, 34 b.; *Sguridis*, III, 27 b.

CAMP SITE. – Rakhóni.

BATHING BEACHES. – At Makryámmos, SE of the town of Thasos; in the bays of Potamiá Skála and Kínyra on the E coast; between Limenariá and Potós, and elsewhere on the W coast.

**Thásos is an attractive and fertile island off the coast of eastern Macedonia in the northern Aegean (here known as the Sea of Thrace N of Samothrace; oil deposits). The northern and eastern parts of the island have an abundance of water.**

The island is occupied by a range of wooded hills slashed by deep valleys, reaching their highest point in Mount Ypsári (3947 ft/1203 m). The northern and eastern slopes fall steeply down to the sea; on the S and W coasts the hills have a gentler slope and form deep sandy bays. The inhabitants earn their living from agriculture, mining (copper, zinc) and increasingly from the tourist trade.

HISTORY. – About the middle of the 2nd millennium B.C. the island was settled by Phoenicians, who were later displaced by Thracians. – In the 7th c. B.C. Ionian Greeks from Paros captured Thásos from the Thracians and rose to great prosperity by the mining of gold and silver and by trade. Between 464 and 404 B.C., after putting up fierce resistance, the island became subject to Athens and later to Philip II of Macedon. – After being successively held by the Romans, the Byzantines, the Venetians and the Bulgarians Thásos was taken by the Turks in 1455. In 1841 it was presented to the Khedive of Egypt by Sultan Mahmud, and remained in Egyptian hands until 1902. In 1912, during the First Balkan War, it was occupied by the Greeks.

The modern town of **Thásos** (*Limín*, pop. 2000), the island's capital and port, occupies the western part of the site of ancient Thasos.

SIGHTS. – The extent of the ancient city is indicated by the surviving walls of the old naval harbor (now the fishing harbor), stretches of the town walls of the 7th–5th c. (originally 3850 yds/3515 m long) and the foundations of houses and temples which extend SE from the beach to the hill which was the ancient *Acropolis* and is now occupied by the ruins of a medieval castle, the *Kastro* (1431). Near the N gate, to the SE of the ancient naval harbor, is the *Agora* (4th c. B.C.), with a stoa (colonnaded hall). Just off the E corner is the *Thereon*, residence of the Commandant of the city, and farther SE is the *Sanctuary of Artemis Polo* (6th c. B.C.). – At the S corner of the Agora is the *Odeion* (2nd c. A.D), and beyond the Roman road is a paved courtyard. Farther SW are the remains of a *triumphal arch* erected in honor of the Emperors Caracalla and Septimius Severus in A.D. 213–217 and of a Temple of Heracles (6th c. B.C.).

In the northern part of the ancient city are the *sanctuaries of Poseidon and Dionysos* (both 4th c. B.C.), the *Theater* (3rd–2nd c. B.C.), a *sanctuary of foreign deities* and, at the most northerly point, a *Sanctuary of the Patrooi Theoi* (6th c. B.C.). In the sea to the N of this last sanctuary are remains of the breakwater of the ancient commercial harbor. – To the SW, above the Kastro, lie the foundations of a *Temple of Athena* (5th c. B.C.; panoramic views).

In the SE of the island, at **Alyki**, are ancient marble quarries, near which are the remains of Archaic cult sites and tombs.

# Thera
### See Santorin

# Tílos (Télos)
### See under Sporades

# Tínos (Tenos)
### See under Andros

# Trapani
### See under Sicily

# Tremiti Islands/ Ísole Trémiti

Italy
Region: Puglia. – Province: Foggia.
Area: 1·2 sq. miles/3·06 sq. km. – Population: 350.
Post code: I-71040. – Telephone code: 0382.
(i) **Ufficio Turistico,**
    Town Hall,
    San Nicola;
    tel. 6 30 02.

BOAT SERVICES. – 3–6 times weekly from Rodi Garganico on the Italian mainland (1½ hours); also from Termoli and Ortona Vieste and Pesichi. The boats put in at San Nicola; services from there to San Domino according to requirements. Hydrofoil from Ortona, Termoli and Vasto to Tremiti.

**The Tremiti Islands (Ísole Trémiti) are a rocky archipelago (limestones) of great scenic beauty, still largely unspoiled, lying in the Adriatic some 13 miles off the N coast of the Monte Gargano Promontory. The rocky coasts, mostly falling steeply down to the sea, with innumerable caves and cavities in the rock, offer ideal conditions for underwater sports.**

The most westerly and scenically most attractive of the three larger islands in the group is the pine-covered **Isola San Domino** (alt. 381 ft/116 m; area 0·8 sq.

Tremiti Islands, San Nicola

mile/2 sq. km; many camp sites), which served until 1943 as a place of banishment and is now increasingly being developed for tourism. The principal place on the island, *San Domino*, lies above the E coast. There are a number of interesting sea-caves, in particular the *Grotta delle Viole* and the *Grotta Bue Marino* (both with a beautiful interplay of light and shade). – NE of San Domino is the smaller **Isola San Nicola** (alt. 246 ft/75 m; area 0·2 sq. mile/0·5 sq. km), with the little walled town of *San Nicola*, the "capital" of the Ísole Trémiti. Its main features of interest are the Castle (rebuilt in the 15th c.) and the Church of Santa Maria (1045), all that remains of an abbey founded in the 9th c., with a beautiful Renaissance doorway and remains of a Romanesque mosaic pavement (11th–12th c.).

To the N, between San Domino and San Nicola, are the islet of **Il Cretaccio** and a number of isolated rocks and crags. – The most north-easterly of the three main islands is the almost uninhabited **Isola Caprara** or **Capraia** (alt. 174 ft/53 m; area 0·2 sq. mile/0·5 sq. km).

# Ugljan

Yugoslavia
Republic: Croatia (Hrvatska).
Area: 18 sq. miles/46 sq. km. – Population 11,000.
Post code: YU-57275. – Telephone code: 057.
ⓘ **Turističko Društvo Ugljan,**
   tel. 8 80 12.
   **Turist Biro Preko,**
   tel. 8 60 12.

HOTELS. – UGLJAN TOWN: *Zadranka*, III, 176 b.; also accommodation in private houses. – PREKO: *Zelena Punta* hotel complex, II, 460 b.; also accommodation in private houses. – Accommodation in private houses also available at Kukljica, Kali, Poljana, Sutimišća and Lukoran.

BATHING BEACHES. – The best beaches are at **Preko**, which also has a small harbor and an attractive promenade. The beaches consist partly of specially laid concrete or of stones, partly of areas of grey sand. The islet of Galovac (Franciscan Friary), 90 yds/80 m offshore, has a pine wood which affords shade. – The *Zelena Punta* holiday complex, near Kukljica, has a pebble beach, some stretches of sand and a naturist area (reached by boat). – Near the little town of **Ugljan** are lonely coves with crystal-clear water, suitable also for naturists.

CAR FERRY. – Zadar–Preko.

**Ugljan, an island of typical Mediterranean character and vegetation, has a steep and inaccessible SW coast and a N coast which slopes gently down to the sea. Its limestone hills are bare or covered only with a sparse growth of vegetation; elsewhere the island is green and fertile, with plantations of olives, figs, vines and fruit and areas of woodland. It is a densely populated island of great variety which attracts many weekend visitors from Zadar but has so far developed little in the way of a tourist trade, except at Preko and the fishing village of Kukljica.**

HISTORY. – The island was occupied in the Neolithic period; and Illyrian occupation is attested by the remains of a number of fortified settlements. During the Roman period there was a considerable population, and the remains of many ancient buidings have been found in the NW of the island. The name Ugljan first appears in the records in 1325. After the Turks occupied the whole hinterland of Zadar and advanced to the very walls of the town Ugljan supplied vegetables to feed the beleaguered inhabitants. – The two neighboring islands of Ugljan and Pašman were originally so close together that there was no room for ships to pass between them, and a channel 13 ft/4 m deep, now spanned by a bridge, was cut to provide a passage.

SIGHTS. – On the promontory on the N side of Ugljan Harbor is a *Franciscan Friary* founded in 1430, with an aisle-less Gothic Church of 1447. The cloister has interesting Romanesque capitals, probably brought here from Zadar. In the courtyard of the friary is the Tomb of Bishop Šime Kožičić Benja (d. 1536), who established a Glagolithic printing-press (see under Krk) at Rijeka. Near the Cove of *Batalaža* the remains of a Roman villa have been found. SE of Ugljan, on Mount *Kuran*, are the remains of a prehistoric fort. At *Mulin* are the ruins of Early Christian buildings (4th–6th c.), including a memoria, a cemetery basilica and a mausoleum.

Otherwise there are only a few features of relatively minor importance on the island

– the remains of Roman buildings and tombs in the farming and fishing village of *Lukoran*, a 17th c. Baroque church at *Kali* (2 miles/3 km SE of Preko). The island's principal holiday resort, *Kukljica*, has no buildings of historical interest.

# Unije
## See under Lošinj

# Ustica
## See under Palermo

# Valletta/Il-Belt Valetta

Malta
Altitude: 0–200 ft/0–60 m.
Population: 14,000 (urban region 113,000).
(i) **National Tourist Organization,**
Harper Lane, Floriana;
tel. 2 44 44.
**Malta Tourist Information,**
1 Citygate Arcade;
tel. 2 77 47.

DIPLOMATIC MISSIONS. – *United Kingdom:* High Commission, 7 St Anne Street, Floriana, tel. 2 12 85–87. – *United States:* Embassy, Development House (second floor), St Anne Street, Floriana, tel. 62 36 53, 62 04 24 and 62 32 16.

HOTELS. – *Hilton International Malta*, St Julian's, L, 400 b., SP; *Grand Hotel Excelsior*, Great Siege Road, Floriana, L, 376 b., SP; *Dragonara Palace*, St Julian's, L, 357 b., SP; *Phoenicia*, The Mall, Floriana, L, 179 b., SP; *Preluna*, 124 Tower Road, Sliema, I, 406 b., SP; *Fortina*, Tigné Sea Front, Sliema, I, 198 b., SP; *Cavalieri*, Spinola Road, St Julian's, I, 164 b., SP; *Eden Beach*, St George's Bay, St Julian's, I, 115 b., SP; *Tower Palace*, Tower Road, Sliema, I, 94 b.; *Metropole*, Dingli Street, Sliema, II, 234 b.; *Kennedy Court*, The Strand, Sliema, II, 172 b.; *Tigné Court*, Quisi-Sana, Sliema, II, 166 b., SP; *Imperial*, 1 Rudolph Street, Sliema, II, 153 b., SP; *Plevna*, 2 Thornton Street, Sliema, II, 143 b., SP; *Marina*, Tigné Sea Front, Sliema, II, 120 b.; *Osborne*, 50 South Street, Valletta, II, 119 b.; *Capua Court*, 60 Victoria Avenue, Sliema, II, 117 b., SP; *Plaza*, 251 Tower Road, Sliema, II, 114 b.; *Europa*, 138 Tower Road, Sliema, II, 108 b.; *Sliema*, 59 The Strand, Sliema, II, 107 b.; *St Julian*, Dragonara Road, Paceville, St Julian's, II, 99 b.; *Adelphi*, Victory Street, Gzira, II, 96 b.; *Promenade*, 121 Tower Road, Sliema, II, 92 b.; *Green Dolphin*, St George's Bay, St Julian's, II, 88 b.; *Sa Maison*, 22 Marina Street, Pietà, II, 80 b.; *Balluta*, Main Street, St Julian's, II, 76 b.; *Eden Rock*, 117 Tower Road, Sliema, II, 76 b.; *Meadowbank*, 164 Tower Road, Sliema, II, 76 b.; *Astra*, 127 Tower Road, Sliema, II, 72 b.; *Crown*, 166–167 Tower Road, Sliema, II, 72 b.; *Patricia*, New Howard Street, Sliema, II, 65 b.; *Delphina*, 72 Dragonara Road, St Julian's, II, 56 b.; *Eagle Court*,

New Street of St George's Road, St Julian's, II, 54 b.; *Caprice*, 2 Victoria Gardens, Sliema, II, 53 b.; *Midas*, 45 Tigné Street, Sliema, II, 52 b.; *Castille*, St Paul's Street, Valletta, II, 44 b.; *Grand Harbour*, 47 Battery Street, Valletta, II, 44 b.; *Carina*, 83 Windsor Terrace, Sliema, II, 34 b.; *Debonair*, 102 Howard Street, Sliema, II, 31 b.; *Olympic*, Paceville Avenue, Paceville, St Julian's, II, 30 b.; *Elba*, 52 New Street, Sliema, II, 24 b.; *British*, 267 St Ursula Street, Valletta, III, 87 b.; *Continental*, St Louis Street, Msida, III, 60 b.; *Adelaide*, 229–231 Tower Road, Sliema, III, 50 b.; *Spinola*, Upper Ross Street, Paceville, St Julian's, III, 47 b.; *Belmont*, Mrabat Street, St Julian's, III, 45 b.; *Angela*, Antonio Sciortino Street, Msida, III, 44 b.; *Isola Bella*, Clarence Street, Msida, III, 42 b.; *Cumberland*, 111 St John Street, Valletta, III, 23 b.; *Kent*, 24 St Margaret Street, Sliema, III, 19 b.; *Astoria*, 46 Point Street, Sliema, IV, 17 b.; *Regina*, 107 Tower Road, Sliema, IV, 49 b.; *Happy*, 6–7 Ponsonby Street, Gzira, IV, 40 b.; *Seacliff*, 225 Tower Road, Sliema, IV, 31 b.

RESTAURANTS. – *Chains*, Grenfell Street, St Julian's; *Eating House*, Ross Street, St Julian's; *Fortizza*, Tower Road, Sliema; *Il Bancinu*, Piazzetta, Tower Road, St Julian's; *Tigullio*, Spinola, St Julian's; *Wyndham's*, Tigné Street, Sliema.

EVENTS. – *Good Friday procession*; *Carnival parade* (second week-end in May); *rowing regatta* in Grand Harbour and great *firework display* (first week-end in September); *theatrical performances* (October–June); *Republic Day (December 13)*; *church patronal festivals* in surrounding area (May–October).

Casino (roulette, baccarat, blackjack): Dragonara Palace, St Julian's.

SPORT. – In the immediate surroundings of Valletta there are numerous sports clubs which offer temporary membership to visitors: *bowling* (Enrico Mizzi Street, Gzira); *tennis and squash* (Malta Sports Club, Marsa, and Union Club, Sliema); *riding and polo* (Darmanin Stables, Marsa); *horse-racing* (Malta Racing Club, Marsa; October–May); *archery* (Malta Archery Club, Marsa); *cricket and golf* (Malta Sports Club and Royal Malta Sports Club); *sailing* (Royal Malta Yacht Club and Vella Charles Boatyard, Marsamxett Harbour; also Yacht Marina, Ta' Xbiex); *water-skiing* (Dragonara Water Sports Centre, St Julian's).

*Valletta (officially il-Belt Valetta, formerly known as La Valeta), capital of the island Republic of Malta, occupies a fine strategic situation on the Sciberras Peninsula (200 ft/ 60 m) on Malta's NE coast, surrounded by what are surely the mightiest fortifications in the world. The peninsula, 2 miles/3 km long and up to 770 yds/700 m wide, extends between the country's two largest and economically most important harbors, Marsamxett Harbour and Grand Harbour – long inlets which reach far into the interior of the island and enclose the town on the N, E and S. These are the best and most beautiful natural harbors in Europe.*

The whole harbor area around the center of Valletta is enclosed by a semicircle of densely populated little towns which combine with the capital to form the conurbation of Valletta. Running into one another along the S side of the Grand Harbour are Kalkara, Vittoriosa, Cospicua, Senglea, Paola and Marsa, and to the N, around Marsamxett Harbour, are Floriana, Pietà, Msida, Ta' Xbiex, Gzira and Sliema.

As capital of the Maltese Archipelago, Valletta is the country's administrative center, the seat of its parliament (House of Representatives) and Supreme Court. It is also the cultural center of the Republic, with the see of a bishop, a University (founded 1769), the Malta College of Arts, Science and Technology, the Malta Cultural Institute, the Agrarian Society, the Observatory and a number of higher educational establishments. The National Museum of Malta is an institution of recognized status.

The urban region of Valletta, with its two harbors, is the economic center of the Maltese islands. The main source of employment is the former British naval dockyard, which was converted to civilian use in 1958 and nationalized in 1968. There are five dry docks in which passenger vessels are built and overhauled and tankers of up to 300,000 tons are repaired and cleaned. The shipyards provide employment for more than 5000 people. The Grand Harbour, modernized in 1961, handles almost the whole of the country's commercial and passenger traffic. It has a deep-water quay which can take vessels of up to 92,000 GRT, with a large grain elevator (capacity 12,500 tons) and many transit warehouses. The harbor has an annual turnover of more than 400,000 tons of freight.

In recent years efforts have been made to restructure the country's economic life, which in the past was exclusively centered on the British naval base, and the phased British withdrawal gave rise to an acute shortage of jobs. Even after their conversion to civilian use the two harbors have retained their dominant place in the economy; but in addition it has been possible to develop other industries, in particular foodstuffs, chemicals, textiles and engineering. Most of the new industrial undertakings have been established in Marsa, at the innermost tip of the Grand Harbour. The former overconcentration of employment in the services sector has been much reduced in the course of time by the promotion of the tourist trade.

HISTORY. – As the regular grid plan of Valletta still indicates, the town was a planned foundation, laid out after the Great Siege of Malta by the Turks in May–September 1565. Although the Knights of St John, who had been granted possession of the Maltese Islands in 1530, successfully beat off the attack by greatly superior Turkish forces, it was recognized that the rebuilding of the existing fortifications which had been destroyed or severely damaged during the siege – Fort St Elmo, at the tip of the then unbuilt-on Sciberras Peninsula; Fort St Angelo, fronting the Knights' Headquarters in Birgu (now Vittoriosa); and Fort St Michael, on the peninsula now occupied by Senglea – would be inadequate to provide protection against a further Turkish attack. Accordingly the then Grand Master of the Order of St John, *Jean Parisot de la Valette*, founded the town of Valletta which bears his name on March 28, 1566 in order to secure the defense of Grand Harbour. The site on Mount Sciberras, above Fort St Elmo, was selected as the one offering the best strategic qualities. The plans were drawn up by Francesco Laparelli da Cortona, one of the finest military engineers of the time, who had been sent to Malta by Pope Pius IV in recognition of the Knights' achievement in defending the Christian cause. Thanks to the contributions which poured in from all over Europe, Laparelli was able to revert to an earlier plan which had previously been turned down on financial grounds, and within three years the work of building the town was so far advanced that Laparelli left its completion to his assistant Gerolamo Cassar. Cassar was responsible for the construction of *auberges* ("inns") in Renaissance style occupied by Knights of different nations (of which only four still survive), the Grand Master's Palace, St John's Co-Cathedral and the Verdala Palace at Rabat. Most of the older buildings of Valletta, however, were erected in the Early Baroque style, which reached Malta from Italy about 1650 and left its mark on the architecture of the whole of Malta. The best-known architects of this period were Lorenzo Gafà (1630–1704), Giovanni Barbara (1660–1730) and Giuseppe Bonnici (1707–about 1780). After 1722 the Iberian style came increasingly to the fore, for from then until 1775 the Order of St John was headed by Grand Masters from Spain and Portugal. Under their rule Domenico Cachia (1710–90) rebuilt Cassar's Auberge de Castille, with a sumptuous façade which reflects the prosperity of Valletta and the whole of the Maltese Archipelago in the closing years of the Knights' rule. This era, however, came to an end under a Grand Master of German origin. Ferdinand von Hompesch (from 1797), who surrendered Valletta without offering any resistance when Napoleon Bonaparte sailed into Grand Harbour with a French fleet in 1798 on his way to Egypt. On June 18 of that year all members of the Order of St John were compelled to leave Malta; but French rule lasted only two years, for in 1800 Valletta was occupied by British forces. Under the Treaty of Paris (1814) Britain was given possession of the whole group of islands, which became a Crown Colony; and until the middle of the 20th c. Valletta was one of the major British naval bases. During the Second World War the town suffered heavy damage from air attacks by the Axis Powers. In 1964 it became capital of the independent State of Malta.

SIGHTS. – In the center of Valletta is **Palace Square**, with the *Grand

A  Freedom Square          B  Great Siege Square     C  Palace Square          D  Independence Square
1  Auberge d'Aragon        2  Auberge de Bavière      3  Auberge d'Italie       4  Auberge de Castille et Léon

**Master's Palace**, built by Gerolamo Cassar between 1568 and 1574. This Renaissance palace with its two entrances on the main front now houses the Maltese Parliament, the residence of the President of Malta and various Government offices. In Neptune Court, the larger of the two inner courtyards, is a fine bronze figure of the sea god; in the tree-planted Prince Alfred's Court is a clock, installed by the Grand Master, Manuel Pinto de Fonseca (1741–73), on which two figures clad in Moorish costume strike the hours with large hammers.

In the INTERIOR of the palace is the famous Council Chamber, hung with valuable Gobelins tapestries woven in France for the Grand Master, Ramón Perellos y Roccaful (1697–1720). They depict exotic scenes from the then little-known Caribbean area and from South America. The other rooms and passages of the palace are also splendidly furnished with *objets d'art* and old arms and armor. Particularly notable are the former Hall of the Supreme Council of the Knights (fine frescoes), the Hall of the Ambassadors (portraits of Grand Masters and European rulers) and the Yellow

State Room, its walls hung with yellow brocade. On the basement floor is the very interesting Armory, one of the largest collections of its kind in the world, though reduced to a fraction of its former size by the depredations of the French. Among its principal treasures are a suit of armor made in Milan for the Grand Master, Adrien de Wignacourt (1690–97) and a full-length panoply made for the Grand Master, Martin Garzes by Sigismund Wolf of Landshut.

Opposite the Grand Master's Palace is a Classical-style building with Doric columns, the **Main Guard**, which formerly housed the Grand Master's bodyguard and is now occupied by the Libyan and Italian Cultural Centers. On the NE side of Palace Square is the 17th c. *Hostel de Verdelin*. From here the 1000 yd/900 m long **Republic Street**, the town's principal commercial and shopping street (pedestrian precinct), runs in a dead straight line to **Fort St Elmo**, (380 yds/ 350 m away at the tip of the peninsula. The fort, designed to protect the entrance to Grand Harbour, was built in 1553 under the Spanish Grand Master, Juan de Homedes (1536–53), incorporating parts of a medieval Spanish fortress, which itself had succeeded an earlier Norman fortification on the same site. About the same time were built *Forts St Angelo and St Michael*, on the other side of Grand Harbour. (The Headquarters of the Knights were then in Birgu, present-day Vittoriosa.) Fort St Elmo was destroyed during the 1565 Siege and rebuilt at the time of the foundation of Valletta. During the Second World War it successfully repelled a German naval attack. The Lower Fort now houses a *War Museum*, with relics of the two world wars, including one of the gallant Gladiator fighters which defended Malta during the last war.

Parallel with Republic Street to the SE is Merchants Street, which also begins at the bastions of Fort St Elmo. Some 130 yds/120 m along it is crossed by Old Hospital Street, in which, to the left, is the **Hospital of the Order**. Its situation on the south-facing slope of Mount Sciberras was perhaps climatically unsatisfactory, but enabled sick and wounded to be brought easily and quickly into hospital from ships anchored in the adjoining Grand Harbour. The building was erected in the time of the Grand Master, Jean l'Evêque de la Cassière (1572–81) by an unknown architect. It now houses the **Mediterranean Conference Center** ("multi-vision" display on the history of Malta). – From the Hospital St Paul Street runs parallel to Merchants Street. Some distance along, on the right-hand side, is the **University of Malta**, which developed out of the old Collegium Melitense, a higher educational establishment of the Knights of St John which was founded by Grand Master, Hugues Loubenx de Verdalle (1581–95). On the same side of the street, beyond the *Market*, is the **Church of St Paul Shipwrecked**, with a sumptuous *interior containing a fine altar-piece depicting the shipwreck by Paladini (1544–1614).

Beyond the church a stepped lane, St Lucia Street, runs up on the right to **Great Siege Square**, on the line of Republic Street. In the center of the square is the bronze *Monument of the Great Siege* (by Antonio Sciortino), and on the NW side are the new Law Courts, built on the ruins of Gerolamo Cassar's *Auberge d'Auvergne*, which was destroyed during the Second World War. – Immediately NE is Queen's Square, bounded on the S side by the **National Library of Malta**, in the last building erected by the Knights (1796). The Library was founded by the Knights in 1650, and soon developed into one of the largest public libraries in the world. In addition to 30,000 modern books and portraits of benefactors of the library it contains valuable collections of old manuscripts and documents relating to the Order of St John, including a Bull by Pope Paschal II establishing the Order and the Act of Donation by which the Emperor Charles V granted possession of Malta to the Order.

Diagonally opposite the Library is the end of Old Theatre Street, which runs between Queen's Square and Palace Square. On the right-hand side, between Old Bakery Street and Old Mint Street, is the **Manoel Theatre**, named after Grand Master Antonio Manoel de Vilhena, who built it in 1731. It has a sumptuous interior, with gilded boxes and seats upholstered in green velvet. – Passing the *Church of Our Lady of Carmel*, beyond Old Mint Street, and turning right into West Street, we come to the Anglican **St Paul's Cathedral**, in Independence Square, with a tower which is one of Valletta's landmarks. It was built in 1844 on the site of the old *Auberge d'Allemagne*, which had been pulled down in 1839 to make way for it. Facing the Cathedral is the **Auberge d'Aragon**, now occupied by the Ministry of Education and Culture. This is the oldest (1571) of the seven auberges built by Gerolamo Cassar, and one of only two (the other being the Auberge de Provence) which have survived in their original condition. Externally plain, it contains fine Renaissance rooms. Immediately adjoining, in Archbishop Street, is the **Archbishop's Palace**, an imposing edifice of 1624.

Going along Mint Street, a picturesque little lane with a magnificent *view of Manoel Island and Fort Manoel in Marsamxett Harbour, and its continuation St Charles Street, we come to the section of wall known as the *English Curtain*, above the SW side of St Elmo Bay. Opposite the *Jews' Sally Port* is the **Auberge de Bavière** (1696), originally built as a private palace, which from 1784 was used for the accommodation of Bavarian and English Knights. From here the English Curtain can be followed E to St Nicholas

Street, which runs into Republic Street. Turning right along this, we return by way of Palace Square and Queen's Square to Great Siege Square.

On the S side of Great Siege Square is the famous **St John's Co-Cathedral** (1573–77), one of Europe's finest churches, designed by Gerolamo Cassar, the first architect of the Order of St John. Dedicated to St John the Baptist, it was built at his own expense by the French Grand Master, Jean l'Evêque de la Cassière as the conventual church of the Order. In 1816 Pope Pius VII granted it the status of Co-Cathedral, ranking equal with Mdina Cathedral. The façade, flanked by two square Renaissance towers, is relatively austere, and the doorway, surmounted by a balcony on which the Grand Masters presented themselves to the Knights after their election, is also very modest.

After this simple exterior the richness and the breathtaking magnificence of the *INTERIOR are of overwhelming effect. Particularly impressive are the *side chapels of the various *langues* ("tongues" or nations) of the Order; for the nations were in competition with one another, each seeking to decorate their part of the church with finer pictures and sculpture than the others. The floor is paved with 400 inlaid marble tombstones, under which several generations of the great nobility of Europe, members of the Order of St John, lie buried. The six sections of the vaulted ceiling contain 18 Baroque frescoes by the Italian painter Mattia Preti commissioned by the Grand Masters, Raffael and Nicola Cotonor, depicting scenes from the life of St John the Baptist. The finest work in the Cathedral, however, is one of Caravaggio's masterworks, the "Beheading of St John" (1608), one of the greatest Baroque paintings. Also very fine is the *High Altar* (1686), with a "Last Supper" by Lorenzo Gafà and a marble group, the "Baptism of Christ" by Giuseppe Mazzuoli. On either side of the altar are the thrones of the Grand Master and the Archbishop of Malta. In the *Crypt* are the sarcophagi of 12 Grand Masters, including the Monument of Philippe Villiers de l'Isle Adam, who brought the Order of St John from Rhodes to Malta. Adjoining is the Tomb of Jean Parisot de la Valette, founder of Valletta. In the *Sacristy*, to the left of the main entrance, can be seen old vestments and some fine paintings by Preti. In the *Oratory* beside the Cathedral are three other pictures by Preti, the "Bearing of the Cross", "Ecce Homo" and the "Crowning with Thorns". The *Cathedral Museum* also contains a number of notable items, including 14 Flemish tapestries after cartoons by Rubens and Poussin.

From the main entrance of the Cathedral St John Street goes down toward the Grand Harbour. Going down a flight of steps at the end of the street and passing the Renaissance *Church of St Mary of Jesus* (16th c.), designed by Gerolamo Cassar, we come to the *St Barbara Bastion*, from which it is only a few paces,

by way of the *Victoria Gate*, to the **Harbor**. From the end of the street called Liesse Hill we continue through a tunnel under the fortifications to the old *Customs House*, with the landing-stage used by the gondola-like dghajjes (singular dghajsa) which ply in Grand Harbour. From the foot of the bastion it used to be possible to take a lift up to the beautiful *Upper Barracca Gardens**, 200 ft/60 m above, laid out on part of the old fortifications. From the gardens, in which there are several statues (including one of Churchill), there are magnificent views of Grand Harbour. Since the lift is not at present operating, the best plan is to return to the Victoria Gate and turn left past the Church of St Mary of Jesus into St Ursula Street. The entrance to the Upper Barracca Gardens is at the end of the street, which leads into the spacious Castile Place.

Castile Place is named after the famous *Auberge de Castille (et de Léon)**, one of Valletta's most magnificent buildings, the splendid façade of which dominates the square. Originally designed by Gerolamo Cassar, it was rebuilt in masterly Baroque style by Domenico Cachia for the Grand Master, Manoel Pinto de Fonseca (1741–73). Finely proportioned and strictly symmetrical, the building was badly damaged during the Second World War but was later carefully restored. The dominant feature of the two-story façade is the doorway, surmounted by a bust of the Grand Master, flanked by paired columns and old cannon, and approached by a grand staircase. Formerly occupied by the British military headquarters, the auberge is now the official residence of the Prime Minister.

Near by, in Merchants Street, is the 18th c. *Palazzo Parisio*, now occupied by the Ministry of Foreign Affairs. Napoleon Bonaparte stayed here briefly after taking Valletta on June 11, 1798. Opposite is the **Auberge d'Italie**, built by Gerolamo Cassar in 1574 and altered at the end of the 17th c. in the time of Grand Master, Gregorio Carafa (1680–90), whose coat of arms appears above the doorway. Adjoining is the *Church of St Catherine*, originally the church of the Italian Knights and now a parish church, with its S side flanking Victory Square. On the other side of the square is the *Church of Our Lady of Victories*. Here the foundation-stone of Valletta was laid in 1566.

From Victory Square the narrow South Street runs NW to Marsamxett Harbour. Turning right off this street into Republic Street, we come, at the intersection with Britannia Street, to the ** **National Museum of Archaeology**, with a collection which is unique in the world. It is housed in the former Auberge de Provence, an imposing building erected by Gerolamo Cassar in 1571.

The most notable exhibits are in the PREHISTORIC SECTION, which contains all the material recovered from the Neolithic temples of the Maltese Islands – 6000–7000-year-old pottery, ornaments, altars, limestone statuettes, terracottas, cult utensils, etc., from the Ġgantija site on Gozo, the cult sites of Haġar Qim, Mnajdra and Hal Tarxien and the Hypogaeum. One room contains interesting models of the five best-preserved temples. Other sections are devoted to Phoenician, Punic, Roman and Arab material and to the Order of St John.

At the intersection of South Street and Scots Street, at the NE corner of the town, is the **National Museum of Fine Arts**, with pictures by Maltese artists, including a "Self-Portrait" by Giuseppe Grech (19th c.), Giorgio Bonavia's "Portrait of a Woman" and a plaster group by Antonio Sciortino, "Arab Horses". The collection also includes pictures of the Spanish, French and British schools, among them works by Mattia Preti (1613–99), Tiepolo (1727–1804), Palma Giovane, Mathias Stomer (1600–50) and Andrea Vaccaro (1598–1670).

From the Museum it is well worth taking a stroll through the nearby *Hastings Gardens*, named after a former Governor-General, the Marquess of Hastings (1824–26). To the SE is the *City Gate*, in front of which is Freedom Square, at the end of Republic Street. Outside the gate is a large square, in the center of which is the *Triton Fountain*. Here, too, is the *City Gate Bus Terminus*, starting-point of all Malta's bus routes. The carefully tended gardens on the far side of the square are within the area of FLORIANA, a suburb established in the early 18th c. (architect Pietro Floriani) to protect the landward side of Valletta. Features of interest are the fortifications (*Porte des Bombes*), the *Church of St Publius* (dedicated to the first Bishop of Malta), *Sarria Church* and the Chapel of *Our Lady of Lourdes*. It is also worth paying a visit to the beautiful Argotti Botanic Gardens, which contain an interesting collection of cacti and a number of monuments.

SURROUNDINGS. – From Valletta and its suburb of Floriana two short but rewarding excursions can be made to the little neighboring towns around Grand Harbour and Marsamxett Harbour which form part of the Valletta conurbation.

**Grand Harbour, between Floriana and Ricasoli Point.** – **Marsa**, the next little township to Floriana, lies at the end of Grand Harbour. Here are concentrated most of the industrial establishments founded after the British withdrawal in order to reduce the unemployment resulting from the loss of the naval base. The town has no features of particular tourist interest.

There is more interest to be found in **Paola** (pop. 12,000), lying S of Marsa ¾ mile/1 km from Grand Harbour, a modern town with streets laid out on a regular grid plan. Its principal attraction is the ** *Hypogaeum of Hal Saflieni*, a Neolithic cult site of a type unique in the world which was discovered during the construction of a cistern in 1902. The sanctuary, entered through a modern doorway of dressed limestone, consists of a complex of catacombs hewn from the native rock with stone tools over a period of many centuries to a depth of 30 ft/9 m below the ground – a system of chambers, passages and stairways on three levels dated by the experts to at least 5000 years ago, and on the basis of the latest studies to as much as 7000 years ago. In this underground labyrinth the early inhabitants of Malta performed religious rituals and consulted oracles. The catacombs were also used for burial, as the remains of some 6000–7000 people found here have shown. In the National Museum of Archaeology can be seen unique clay figures from the Hypogaeum, together with stone figures of birds and – most notable of all – a female figure (probably a priestess) lying on a couch.

The largest, most recent and best-preserved prehistoric cult site in Malta is at * **Tarxien**, just over ¾ mile/1 km SW of Paola. The site, originally covering an area of 6500 sq. yds/5400 sq. m, was excavated and restored in 1914. The stone reliefs and sculpture found here are now in the National Museum of Archaeology in Valletta, and are represented on the site by excellent reproductions. The stone walls of the four adjoining temples are decorated with spiral patterns and animal figures, of types found on other Maltese cult sites. In the southernmost temple are the remains of a statue, originally 9 ft/2·75 m high, of a fertility goddess with grotesquely swollen legs, disproportionately small feet and a pleated skirt.

2 miles/3 km N of Tarxien are two promontories reaching out into Grand Harbour, with the port towns of Senglea and Vittoriosa and their extensive docks and shipyards. On the mainland between them is the town of **Conspicua** (pop. 9000), with the Church of the Immaculate Conception, one of the most richly furnished churches on the island.

**Senglea** (pop. 5000) also has a notable church, Our Lady of Victories. On the tip of the promontory is an old watch-tower, a relic of Fort St Michael. From here there are fine * views of the Grand Harbour and the town of Valletta beyond it.

**Vittoriosa** (pop. 4000) is the second oldest town in Malta. Under the name of *Birgu*, which it bore before the Great Siege of 1565, it was already known in ancient times. The Phoenicians built a temple here, the remains of which are overlaid by the ruins of a Roman temple. Originally the port of Malta's former inland capital, Mdina, Birgu was already protected by modest fortifications before the coming of the Knights. Dating from the Aragonese period, these were strengthened

View of Vittoriosa

in the time of the Grand Master, Juan de Homedes (1536–53); the bastions of Fort St Angelo were built, separated from the town by a moat with a drawbridge. Thanks to this fort, together with Fort St Elmo on the opposite side of the harbor and the neighboring Fort St Michael, the Knights were able to beat off the Turkish attack. Birgu then became the Headquarters of the Order, previously in Mdina. From the period of the Knights there remain a number of auberges (inns), the Inquisitor's Palace and St Lawrençe's Church, the first conventual church of the Order. The church contains the sword and hat of the Grand Master, La Valette, founder of Valletta.

To the N of these "three cities" is the picturesque little township of **Kalkara** (pop. 2200). Here are built the dghajjes, the gondola-like boats which ply across the harbor to Valletta. – At the tip of the promontory which reaches out into the sea N of Kalkara is the 17th c. **Fort Ricasoli.**

**Marsamxett Harbour, between Floriana and Sliema.** – Valletta's second natural harbor, Marsamxett Harbour, to the N, is also lined by a string of little towns, and Malta's busiest road is the one running around the harbor to Sliema. Beyond Floriana the road first comes to **Pietà** (pop. 4500), with St Luke's Hospital and the beautifully situated Villa Portelli, in which Queen Elizabeth II once stayed.

Farther N is **Msida** (pop. 6000), with the University of Malta. Beside the fishing harbor is a fine church, St Joseph's. On both sides of Msida Creek, an inlet opening off Marsamxett Harbour, are moored many of the many yachts which give the harbor its characteristic atmosphere.

On a promontory at the W end of the harbor is the select residential area of **Ta' Xbiex**, with Lazzaretto Creek, in which some of Marsamxett's most expensive yachts lie at anchor. – Immediately N of this is the industrial town of **Gżira** (pop. 9000), from which there is a causeway leading to **Manoel Island** and Fort Manoel, built by the Knights in 1730.

To the N Gżira merges imperceptibly into **Sliema** (pop. 20,000), the largest, most modern and busiest Maltese town. It is Malta's principal shopping and tourist center, with many hotels, restaurants and cafés flanking its long seafront promenade and beach (mostly stony). It has a fine Romanesque-style

church, St Gregory's. SE of the town is Fort Tigné, built by the Knights in 1730.

The old fishing village of **St Julian's** immediately N of Sliema, made up of the districts of *Paceville* and *St George's Bay*, has made great efforts in recent years to develop its tourist facilities, and now competes with Sliema as a holiday center. It has long sandy beaches, first-class hotels, a casino and several night-clubs. The modern parts of the town form an attractive contrast to the picturesque old fishermen's quarter.

See also \* **Malta** (including \* *Gozo*), p. 131.

The fishing harbor of St Julian's

# Zákynthos
## *(Zákinthos)*

Greece
Nomos: Zákynthos.
Area: 155 sq. miles/402 sq. km. – Population: 30,200.

ⓘ **Tourist Police,**
   Eleftheriou Venizélou;
   tel. 2 25 50.

HOTELS. – ZÁKYNTHOS: *Strada Marina*, II, 91 b.; *Xenia*, II, 78 b.; *Phoenix*, III, 70 b.; *Diana*, III, 69 b.; *Angelika*, III, 32 b.; *Adriana*, III, 18 b.; *Apollon*, III, 17 b.; *Aegli*, III, 16 b.; *Astoria*, III, 15 b.; *Zenith*, III, 14 b. – ALYKÁ (10 miles/16 km NW): *Montreal*, III, 56 b.; *Asteria*, III, 16 b. – ARGÁSI (2½ miles/4 km SE): *Chryssi Akti*, II, 106 b.; *Mimosa Beach*, II, 60 b.; *Argassi Beach*, III, 26 b. – LAGANÁS (5 miles/8 km SW): *Zante Beach* (hotel and bungalows), II, 494 b.; *Galaxy*, II, 152 b.; *Ionis*, III, 91 b.; *Alkyonis*, III, 37 b.; *Eugenia*, III, 27 b.; *Panorama*, III, 26 b.; *Selini*, III, 24 b.; *Asteria*, III, 23 b.; *Zephyros*, III, 22 b.; *Atlantis*, III, 20 b.; *Blue Coast*, III, 20 b.; *Medikas*, III, 20 b.; *Hellenis*, III, 17 b.; *Ilios*, III, 16 b. – PLANOS (2½ miles/4 km NW): *Tsilivi*, III, 105 b.; *Cosmopolit*, III, 27 b.; *Anetis*, III, 23 b.

TRANSPORTATION. – Air connections with Athens; ferry from Kyllíni; bus from Athens.

**Zákynthos, also known as Zanthe (Xanthe) is the most southerly of the main group of Ionian Islands, lying off the Peloponnese opposite Kyllíni and Olympia. During the period of Venetian rule (1479–1797) it was known as Zante, and its mild climate**

earned it the name of "Zante – fior di Levante". **The W coast is steep and rugged, the E coast hilly; the lower ground between the two is like one large garden.**

The chief town, **Zákynthos** or *Zante* (pop. 10,000), lies on the E coast below a Venetian castle which occupies the site of the ancient acropolis (panoramic views). Many of the town's old churches were destroyed in the 1953 earthquake: notable among those that survived or have been restored are Kýra ton Ángelon and Aghios Dionýsios (which is dedicated to the island's patron saint and preserves his relics). By the harbor is the Church of Aghios Nikólaos, on the N side of Solomós Square. In the center of this spacious square stands a monument to Dionýsios Solomós. On the W side of the square is the *Museum, with a very fine collection of icons, wall-paintings and iconostases which illustrates the development of icon-painting of Zákynthos in the 16th and 18th c. under Italian influence. Of particular interest are the frescoes in popular style from the Church of Aghios Andréas at Vólimes and works by Michael Damaskinos and two other refugees from Crete, Angelos and Emmanuel Lombardos. NW of the Museum is the Mausoleum of Dionýsios Solomós (1798–1857), who together with Ugo Fóscolo and Andréas Kálvos represents the island's contribution to modern Greek literature and is honored as the author of the national anthem.

Near the town is the beach of **Tsiliví**. There is also a long beach at **Laganás**, 6 miles/9 km from Zákynthos in the wide bay at the S end of the island. The road to Laganás continues to the pitch springs of Kerí (12$\frac{1}{2}$ miles/20 km), which have been known since ancient times.

# Practical
# Information

When to Go
Inoculations, etc.
Travel Documents
Summer Weather
Currency
Time
Car Ferries
Mediterranean Harbors
Yacht Harbors and Marinas
Shipping Lines
Language
Accommodation
Bathing Beaches
Airports
Information

Island of Kos

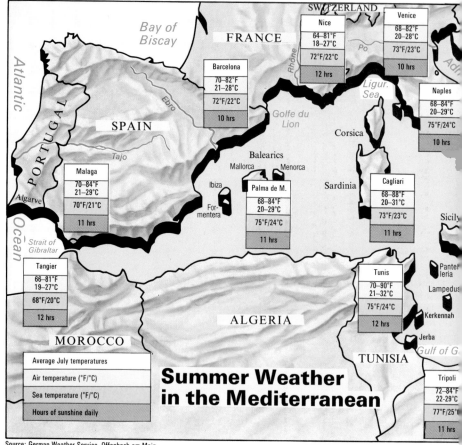

The map contains the following weather data boxes:

**Nice** 64–81°F 18–27°C | 72°F/22°C | 12 hrs

**Venice** 68–82°F 20–28°C | 73°F/23°C | 10 hrs

**Barcelona** 70–82°F 21–28°C | 72°F/22°C | 10 hrs

**Naples** 68–84°F 20–29°C | 75°F/24°C | 10 hrs

**Malaga** 70–84°F 21–29°C | 70°F/21°C | 11 hrs

**Palma de M.** 68–84°F 20–29°C | 75°F/24°C | 11 hrs

**Cagliari** 68–88°F 20–31°C | 73°F/23°C | 11 hrs

**Tangier** 66–81°F 19–27°C | 68°F/20°C | 12 hrs

**Tunis** 70–90°F 21–32°C | 75°F/24°C | 12 hrs

**Tripoli** 72–84°F 22-29°C | 77°F/25°C | 11 hrs

| Average July temperatures |
| Air temperature (°F/°C) |
| Sea temperature (°F/°C) |
| Hours of sunshine daily |

**Summer Weather in the Mediterranean**

Source: German Weather Service, Offenbach am Main

# When to Go

The best time to visit the more northerly islands in the European part of the Mediterranean (Iles d'Hyères, Corsica, Elba, Pontine Islands, the Yugoslav islands) is from early summer to the early fall (autumn) (June to September). For the Balearics, Sardinia, Sicily and the other southern Italian islands, Malta, the Greek islands and Cyprus the best times of year are spring and the fall; the Balearics are also popular for long winter vacations. Jerba is pleasant in the late fall and early spring; the winter is mild, with a fair amount of rain.

# Inoculations, etc.

For all the islands described in this Guide vaccination against typhoid and polio-myelitis is recommended, but not compulsory; in addition visitors to the Tunisian island of Jerba are recommended to have a cholera vaccination and to take precautions against malaria (tablets). Since the vaccinations take time to become effective you should consult your doctor 6–8 weeks before departure.

# Travel Documents

Visitors to the islands described in this Guide from the United Kingdom, British Commonwealth countries and the United States must have a valid *passport* but do not require a visa in most cases, the U.S. visitors will need a visa for Yugoslavia, Algeria and Libya. Travel to the last two countries is restricted.

National *driving licenses* are accepted in Cyprus, France, Greece, Malta and Yugo-slavia; they are accepted in Italy, if accompanied by an Italian translation (obtainable in Britain from the Auto-mobile Association); and they are

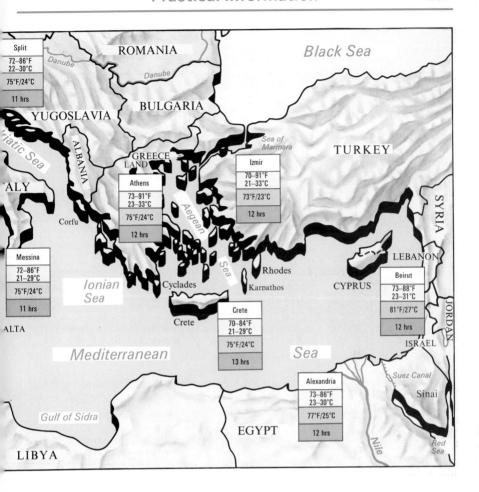

Split
72–86°F
22–30°C
75°F/24°C
11 hrs

Messina
72–86°F
21–29°C
75°F/24°C
11 hrs

Athens
73–91°F
23–33°C
75°F/24°C
12 hrs

Izmir
70–91°F
21–33°C
73°F/23°C
12 hrs

Crete
70–84°F
21–29°C
75°F/24°C
13 hrs

Beirut
73–88°F
23–31°C
81°F/27°C
12 hrs

Alexandria
73–86°F
23–30°C
77°F/25°C
12 hrs

accepted in Spain if accompanied by an official translation stamped by a Spanish consulate (but it is easier and cheaper to obtain an international driving permit). In Malta the license must be endorsed (free of charge) at the police headquarters in Floriana, but endorsement is not necessary if you are driving your own car. An international driving permit is recommended in Tunisia (Jerba).

If you are driving you own car you should carry the *car registration document*. British visitors to other EEC countries do not require to produce an *international insurance certificate* ("green card") but are recommended to have one; other visitors to EEC countries and all visitors to countries not in the EEC must have a green card. It is advisable in any event to take out a short-term insurance providing fuller cover.

*Health cover*. – British visitors to other EEC countries are entitled to medical treatment free or at reduced cost on presentation of form E111 (obtainable from the Department of Health and Social Security before departure). They may also be able to obtain such treatment under reciprocal arrangements with other countries (see the leaflet "Medical Costs Abroad", also obtainable from the DHSS). Here, too, it is advisable to take out additional short-term insurance cover.

Sunset over the Aegean

# Currency

| Country | Currency | Rate of exchange of £ sterling and US dollar (subject to fluctuation) | Max. permitted import of foreign/local currency | Max. permitted export of foreign/local currency |
|---|---|---|---|---|
| **Cyprus** | Cyprus pound (C£) | C£1=£1·22<br>£1=C£0·820<br>C£1=$1·84<br>$1=C£0·540 | unlimited/<br>C£10 | $500 US/<br>C£10 |
| **France** | Franc (F) | 1 F=£0·08<br>£1=12 F<br>1 F=$0·13<br>$1=7·80 F | unlimited/<br>unlimited | as declared/<br>5000 F |
| **Greece** | Drachma (dr) | 100 dr=£0·71<br>£1=140 dr<br>100 dr=$1·18<br>$1=85 dr | unlimited/<br>1500 dr. | as declared/<br>1500 dr |
| **Italy** | Lira (l) | 1000 l=£0·42<br>£1=2400 l<br>1000 l=$0·65<br>$1=1530 l | unlimited/<br>200,000 l | as declared/<br>200,000 l |
| **Malta** | Malta pound (£M) | £M1=£1·50<br>£1=£M0·67<br>£M1=$2·28<br>$1=£M0·44 | unlimited/<br>£M50 | as declared/<br>£M25 |
| **Spain** | Peseta (pta) | 100 ptas=£0·44<br>£1=225 ptas<br>100 ptas=$0·68<br>$1=148 ptas | unlimited/<br>50,000 ptas | unlimited/<br>20,000 ptas |
| **Tunisia** | Tunisian dinar (DT) | 1 DT=£1<br>£1=1 DT<br>1 DT=$1·41<br>$1=0·71 DT | unlimited/<br>prohibited | unlimited/<br>prohibited |
| **Yugoslavia** | Yugoslav dinar (din) | 100 din=£0·65<br>£1=155 din<br>100 din=$1<br>$1=100 din | unlimited/<br>1500 din | unlimited/<br>1500 din |

The major *credit cards* are widely accepted. *Traveler's checks* can often be cashed only in banks.

# Time

| | New York time | Normal time | Summer time |
|---|---|---|---|
| **Cyprus** | GMT−5 | GMT+2 | GMT+3 |
| **France** | GMT−5 | GMT+1 | GMT+2 |
| **Greece** | GMT−5 | GMT+2 | GMT+3 |
| **Italy** | GMT−5 | GMT+1 | GMT+2 |
| **Malta** | GMT−5 | GMT+1 | GMT+2 |
| **Spain** | GMT−5 | GMT+1 | GMT+2 |
| **Tunisia** | GMT−5 | GMT+1 | − |
| **Yugoslavia** | GMT−5 | GMT+1 | GMT+2 |

# Car Ferries

| SERVICE | FREQUENCY | COMPANY |
|---|---|---|
| **Balearics from Spain** | | |
| Alicante–Ibiza | 3 times weekly | Trasmediterránea |
| Alicante–Palma de Mallorca | 3 times weekly | Trasmediterránea |
| Valencia–Ibiza | 3 times weekly | Trasmediterránea |
| Valencia–Palma de Mallorca | 6 times weekly | Trasmediterránea |
| Barcelona–Ibiza | 3 times weekly | Trasmediterránea |
| Barcelona–Palma de Mallorca | 6 times weekly | Trasmediterránea |
| Barcelona–Mahón | 3 times weekly | Trasmediterránea |
| | | |
| **Balearics from France** | | |
| Marseilles–Palma de Mallorca | weekly | Cie Nat. Algérienne |
| | | |
| **Balearics from Algeria** | | |
| Algiers–Palma de Mallorca | weekly | Cie Nat. Algérienne |
| | | |
| **Balearics (Inter-Island)** | | |
| Ciudadela–Alcudia | twice weekly | Trasmediterránea |
| Palma de Mallorca–Cabrera | weekly | Trasmediterránea |
| Palma de Mallorca–Ibiza | 3 times weekly | Trasmediterránea |
| Palma de Mallorca–Ciudadela | weekly | Trasmediterránea |
| | | |
| **Corfu from Greece** | | |
| Patras–Corfu | sev. times weekly | Karageorgis |
| Patras–Igoumenitsa–Corfu | daily | Epirus Line |
| Patras–Igoumenitsa–Corfu | daily | Adriatica |
| Patras–Igoumenitsa–Corfu | daily | Hellenic Med Lines |
| Patras–Igoumenitsa–Corfu | 5 times weekly | Fragoudakis |
| Igoumenitsa–Corfu | daily | Libra Maritime |
| Patras–Kefallinia–Ithaca–Corfu | 3 times weekly (June 2–Sept. 26) | Ionian Lines |
| Patmos–Iraklion–Korfu | weekly | Med Sun Lines |
| | | |
| **Corfu from Italy** | | |
| Ancona–Corfu | sev. times weekly | Karageorgis |
| Bari–Corfu | daily | Epirus Line |
| Brindisi–Corfu | daily | Hellenic Med Lines |
| Brindisi–Corfu | 5 times weekly | Fragoudakis |
| Brindisi–Corfu | daily | Libra Maritime |
| Brindisi–Corfu | 3 times weekly (June 2–Sept. 26) | Ionian Lines |
| Otranto–Corfu | 5 times weekly | R Line |
| | | |
| **Corsica from France** | | |
| Marseilles–Bastia | daily | SNCM |
| Toulon–Bastia | sev. times weekly | SNCM |
| Nice–Ajaccio | daily | SNCM |
| Nice–Bastia | daily | SNCM |
| Nice–Calvi | daily | SNCM |
| Nice–Ile-Rousse | daily | SNCM |
| Nice–Propriano | sev. times weekly | SNCM |
| | | |
| **Corsica from Italy** | | |
| San Remo–Calvi | sev. times weekly | Corsica Line |
| San Remo–Bastia | sev. times weekly | Corsica Line |
| Genoa–Bastia | sev. times weekly | Corsica Line |
| Livorno–Bastia | sev. times weekly | Corsica Line |
| Livorno–Bastia | 3 times weekly | TTE |
| Piombino–Bastia | daily | Navarma |

| SERVICE | FREQUENCY | COMPANY |
|---|---|---|
| **Corsica from Sardinia** | | |
| Santa Teresa Gallura–Bonifacio | daily | Tirrenia |
| **Crete from Greece** | | |
| Piraeus–Iráklion | daily | Minoan Lines |
| **Crete from Italy** | | |
| Ancona–Patras–Iráklion | weekly | DFDS |
| **Crete from Egypt** | | |
| Alexandria–Iráklion | weekly | DFDS |
| **Cyprus from Greece** | | |
| Piraeus–Larnaca | twice monthly | Black Sea Steamships |
| Piraeus–Rhodes–Limassol | weekly | Sol Maritime Lines |
| Piraeus–Rhodes–Limassol | weekly (June 15–Sept. 26) | Hellenic Med Lines |
| Piraeus–Rhodes–Limassol | weekly | Lesvos Maritime Co. |
| **Elba** | | |
| Piombino–Portoferraio | daily | Navarma |
| Piombino–Portoferraio | daily | Toremar |
| **Greek Islands** | | |
| Piraeus–Chios–Mytilini (Lesbos) | daily | Lesvos Maritime Co. |
| Piraeus–Sámos | 3 times weekly | Shipping and Tour Co. |
| Ancona–Katakolon–Piraeus–Mykonos | weekly | Med Sun Lines |
| Brindisi–Corfu–Ithaca–Kefallinia–Patras (also in reverse direction) | 3 times weekly (June 2–Sept. 26) | Ionian Lines |
| Patmos–Iraklion–Corfu–Ancona | weekly | Med Sun Lines |
| Rhodes–Iráklion–Santorin–Piraeus–Ancona | weekly | Med Sun Lines |
| Piraeus–Mykonos | weekly | Med Sun Lines |

There are also many local ferry services between the Greek mainland and the islands and from island to island. The most important of these services are run daily, some of them at very frequent intervals during the day. Among services carrying both local and tourist traffic are the following: Perama–Salamis, Arkitsa–Loutra Aidipsou, Oropos–Eretria, Glyfa–Aghiokambos, Patras–Sami, Patras–Sami–Ithaca, Patras–Paxi, Patras–Corfu, Corfu–Paxi, Kyllini–Zákynthos, Kavala–Thásos, Keramoti–Thásos and Alexandroupolis–Samothrace.

| SERVICE | FREQUENCY | COMPANY |
|---|---|---|
| **Malta from Italy** | | |
| Naples–Valletta | weekly | Tirrenia |
| Catania–Syracuse–Valletta | 3 times weekly | Tirrenia |
| **Pantelleria** | | |
| Trapani–Pantelleria | sev. times weekly | |
| **Pontine and Lipari Islands** | | |
| Naples–Capri–Ischia–Ponza | sev. times daily | Caremar |
| Naples–Lipari Islands (incl. Stromboli, Panarea and Lipari) | twice weekly | Siremar |

There are also local ferry services between Porto Santo Stefano/Argentario and the island of Giglio, between Terracina and Formia and the island of Ponza, between Formia and the island of Ventotene and between Trapani and the island of Favignana.

| SERVICE | FREQUENCY | COMPANY |
|---|---|---|
| **Rhodes from Greece** | | |
| Piraeus–Rhodes | weekly | Sol Maritime Lines |
| Piraeus–Rhodes | weekly (June 15–Sept. 26) | Hellenic Med Lines |
| Piraeus–Rhodes | weekly | Lesvos Maritime Co. |
| Piraeus–Rhodes | weekly | Adriatica |
| | | |
| **Rhodes from Italy** | | |
| Venice–Piraeus–Rhodes | weekly | Adriatica |
| Venice–Piraeus–Rhodes | weekly (June 15–Sept. 26) | Hellenic Med Lines |
| | | |
| **Sardinia from Italy** | | |
| Genoa–Porto Torres | daily | Tirrenia |
| Genoa–Olbia/Arbatax | sev. times weekly | Tirrenia |
| Genoa–Porto Torres | 3 times weekly | Canguro |
| Livorno–Olbia | daily | TTE |
| Civitavecchia–Golfo Aranci | daily | Italian State Rwys |
| Civitavecchia–Olbia | daily | Tirrenia |
| Civitavecchia–Porto Torres | 3 times weekly | Tirrenia |
| Civitavecchia–Cágliari | daily | Tirrenia |
| Naples–Cágliari | twice weekly | Tirrenia |
| | | |
| **Sardinia from Sicily** | | |
| Palermo–Cágliari | weekly | Tirrenia |
| Trapani–Cágliari | 3 times weekly | Tirrenia |
| | | |
| **Sardinia from France** | | |
| Toulon–Porto Torres | twice weekly (season) | SNCM |
| | | |
| **Sardinia from Corsica** | | |
| Bonifacio–Santa Teresa Gallura | daily | Tirrenia |
| | | |
| **Sicily from Italy** | | |
| Genoa–Palermo | 3 times weekly | Grandi Traghetti |
| Genoa–Palermo | weekly | Tirrenia |
| Livorno–Palermo | 3 times weekly | Grandi Traghetti |
| Naples–Catania/Syracuse | weekly | Tirrenia |
| Naples–Palermo | daily | Tirrenia |
| Naples/Reggio Calabria–Catania/Syracuse | 3 times weekly | Tirrenia |
| Reggio Calabria–Messina | daily | Italian State Rwys |
| Villa San Giovanni–Messina | daily | Italian State Rwys |
| | | |
| **Sicily from Sardinia** | | |
| Cágliari–Palermo | weekly | Tirrenia |
| Cágliari–Trapani | 3 times weekly | Tirrenia |
| | | |
| **Tunisia from France** | | |
| Marseilles–Tunis | sev. times weekly | Cie Tunisienne |
| Marseilles–Tunis | twice weekly | SNCM |
| | | |
| **Tunisia from Italy** | | |
| Genoa–Tunis | weekly | Cie Tunisienne |
| Genoa–Tunis | weekly | DFDS |
| Naples–Tunis | weekly | Tirrenia |
| Trapani–Tunis | weekly | Tirrenia |
| Palermo–Tunis | weekly | Tirrenia |

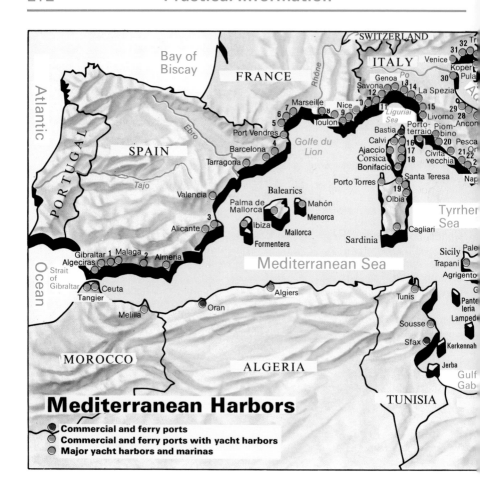

**Mediterranean Harbors**

- ● Commercial and ferry ports
- ◐ Commercial and ferry ports with yacht harbors
- ○ Major yacht harbors and marinas

## Yugoslavia from Italy

| | | |
|---|---|---|
| Ancona–Split | twice monthly | Turkish Maritime |
| Ancona–Zadar | weekly | Adriatica |
| Ancona–Zadar | daily | Jadrolinija |
| Pescara–Split | daily | Adriatica |
| Bari–Dubrovnik | weekly | Adriatica |
| Bari–Dubrovnik | weekly | Jadrolinija |

## Yugoslavia from Greece

| | | |
|---|---|---|
| Igoumenitsa–Corfu–Bar | weekly | Jadrolinija |

## Yugoslavia–Dalmatian Coast

| | | |
|---|---|---|
| Rijeka–Rab–Zadar–Split–Hvar–
Korčula–Dubrovnik–Bar | 4 times weekly | Jadrolinija |
| Rijeka–Dubrovnik–Bar | weekly | Jadrolinija |

There are also many small local ferries serving the numerous islands off the Dalmatian coast: Rijeka–Porozine (Cres), Brestova–Porozine, Crisnjeva–Voz (Krk), Crikvenica–Voz, Senj–Lopar (Rab), Jablanac–Stara Novalja (Pag), Karlobag–Pag, Zadar–Preko (Ugljan), Biograd–Tkon (Pašman), Split–Rogač (Šolta), Split–Vis (not for foreigners), Split–Supetar (Brač), Makarska–Sumartin, Split–Vira (Hvar), Split–Starigrad, Drvenik–Sućuraj, Ploče–Trpanj (Pelješac), Drvenik–Trpanj, Orebić–Domincé (Korčula), Split–Vela Luka, Split–Lastovo (not for foreigners), Mišnjak (Rab)–Stara Novalja (Pag).

> Owners of **caravans** (trailers) and **motor caravans** should check the maximum permissible dimensions – which may vary from ferry to ferry – with the company concerned or a travel agent.

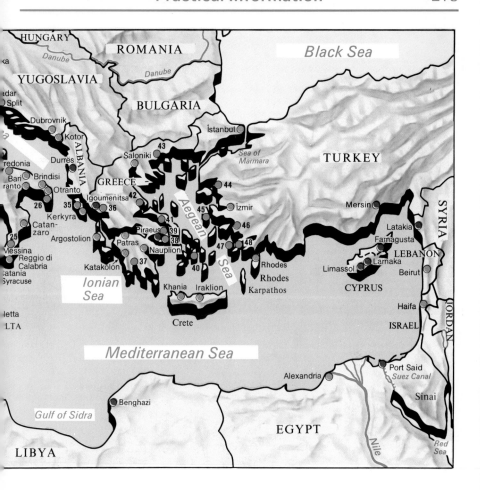

## Yacht Harbors and Marinas

1 Estepona
   **Marbella** (Marina José Banus)

2 Puerto de Motril

3 Jávea

4 Palamós

5 Port Leucate
   Port-la-Nouvelle

6 Cap d'Agde

7 La Grande-Motte

8 Sanary-sur-Mer

9 Cogolin
   St-Tropez
   Cannes

10 Beaulieu-sur-Mer
   Menton

11 San Remo

12 Imperia
   Alassio

13 Portofino
   Santa Margherita Ligure
   Rapallo

14 Chiavari
   Lavagna

15 Marina di Carrara
   Viareggio

16 Macinaggio

17 Campoloro

18 Porto Vecchio

19 Porto Cervo

20 Punta Ala
   Port' Ercole

21 Anzio

22 Gaeta

23 Pozzuoli

24 Amalfi

25 Scilla

26 Gallipoli

27 Molfetta

28 Pésaro

29 Cesenatico

30 Chioggia

31 Caorle

32 Monfalcone

33 Mali Lošinj

34 Punat
   (Krk)

35 Gouvia
   (Corfu)

36 Preveza

37 Kalamata

38 Zea
   Mounykhia

39 Vouliagmeni

40 Ermoupolis
   (Syros)

41 Khalkis

42 Volos

43 Kavala

44 Çeşme

45 Chios

46 Kuşadasi

47 Lakki
   (Leros)

48 Bodrum

A caique, the characteristic Aegean craft

## Information and Bookings

**Adriatica**
*Sealink UK Ltd,*
162/203 Eversholt Street,
**London** NW1 1BG;
tel. (01) 387 1234.

**Black Sea Shipping Co.**
*CTC Lines,*
1–3 Lower Regent Street,
**London** SW1Y 4NN;
tel. (01) 980 5833.

**Caremar**
Mole Beverello,
I-80133 **Naples**, Italy;
tel. (081) 31 53 84.

**Compagnie Nationale
Algérienne de Navigation**
2 Quai No. 9, Nouvelle Gare
Maritime,
**Algiers**;
tel. 61 14 78.

**Compagnie Tunisienne de
Navigation**
5 Avenue Dag Hammerskjoeld,
**Tunis**;
tel. 24 29 99.

**Corsica Line**
5 bis rue Chanoine-Leschi,
F-20294 **Bastia**, Corsica;
tel. (95) 31 18 09.

**DFDS Seaways**
*DFDS (UK) Ltd,*
Latham House, 16 Minories,
**London** EC3N 1AD;
tel. (01) 481 3211.

**Epirus Line**
*Windward Shipping (London)
Ltd,*
Northumbrian House,
14 Devonshire Square,
**London** EC2M 4TL;
tel. (01) 247 9856.

**Fragoudakis Line**
*Stelp and Leighton Agencies Ltd,*
238 City Road,
**London** EC1V 2PR;
tel. (01) 251 3389.

**Grandi Traghetti SpA di
Navigazione**
*Associated Oceanic Agencies
(UK) Ltd,*
Eagle House,
109–110 Jermyn Street,
**London** SW1;
tel. (01) 930 9534/7499.

**Hellenic Mediterranean Lines**
18 Hanover Street,
**London** W1R 9HG;
tel. (01) 499 0076.

**Ionian Lines**
4 Marni Street,
**Athens**, Greece;
tel. (01) 8 23 60 12–13.

**Italian State Railways**
10 Charles II Street,
**London** SW1;
tel. (01) 930 6722.

**Jadrolinija**
*Yugotours Ltd,*
Chesham House,
150 Regent Street,
**London** W1R 5FA;
tel. (01) 734 7321.

**Karageorgis Lines**
*M.A. Karageorgis Lines (UK) Ltd,*
36 King Street,
**London** WC2E 8JS;
tel. (01) 836 8216.

**Lesvos Maritime Company**
*Louis Tourist Agency Ltd,*
429 Green Lanes, Haringey,
**London** N4 1HA;
tel. (01) 348 1834.

**Libra Maritime**
*Lion International Travel Services
Ltd,*
71 Braeside Avenue,
**Brighton** BN1 8RN;
tel. (0273) 555403.

**Med Sun Lines**
*Cosmopolitan Holdings Ltd,*
91 York Street,
**London** W1H 1DU;
tel. (01) 402 4255.

**Minoan Lines**
P.O. Box 120,
**Iráklion**, Crete;
tel. 24 12 05–09.

**Navarma**
Via A. de Gasperi 55,
I-80133 **Naples**, Italy;
tel. (081) 32 08 08, 31 07 82.

**R Line**
*CIT,*
10 Charles II Street,
**London** SW1;
tel. (01) 930 6722.

**Shipping and Tour Company
of Samos and Ikaria**
Metaxas Building (4th floor),
16–18 Aristidou Street,
**Piraeus**, Greece;
tel. 4 17 73 50.

**Siremar**
Via Francesco Crispi 120,
**Palermo**, Italy.

**SNCM** (*Société Nationale
Maritime Corse Méditerranée*)
*P & O Normandy Ferries,*
Arundel Towers,
Portland Terrace,
**Southampton** SO9 4AE;
tel. (0703) 32131, 34141.

**Tirrenia Line**
*Sealink UK Ltd,*
Victoria Station,
P.O. Box 29,
**London** SW1V 1JX;
tel. (01) 834 8122.

**Toremar**
Scali del Corso 5,
**Livorno**, Italy;
tel. (0586) 2 27 72.

**Trasmediterránea**
*Melia Travel,*
12 Dover Street,
**London** W1X 4NS;
tel. (01) 499 6731.

**Turkish Maritime Lines**
*Walford Lines Ltd,*
Europa Trading Estate,
Fraser Road,
**Erith**, Kent DA8 1QN;
tel. (03224) 41177.

# Language

On the islands in the European part of the Mediterranean it is an advantage for visitors to have at least a smattering of the local language; but in the main tourist areas the staffs of hotels, restaurants and shops are likely to have some knowledge of English and other European languages. In Malta and Cyprus English is widely spoken; in Tunisia (Jerba) French is likely to be more useful, though here again hotel staff will have some English; while a knowledge of German may be helpful in the countries which send "guest workers" to Western Germany (Yugoslavia, Greece and certain parts of Italy, particularly in the south).

# Accommodation

In the European part of the Mediterranean the hotels in the higher categories are usually of international standard, and even middle-grade establishments normally provide an acceptable level of comfort and amenity. This is true also of the tourist hotels in other areas, for example on Jerba (Tunisia).

The classification of hotels into categories and the standards of quality applied differ from country to country: hotels in a particular category in one country will not, therefore, necessarily offer the same amenities as hotels in the same category in another country.

For the sake of simplicity a standard method of classification is applied to all hotels listed in this Guide. Luxury hotels are designated by the letter L, while other hotels are graded in four classes, from I to IV.

**NB:** In Italy hotel and restaurant checks (bills) should be carefully preserved and provided to Government tax investigators on request.

Breakers at Akko (Acre), on the Israeli coast

# Bathing Beaches
(A Selection)

## Pollution
Tourists should be aware that pollution of the sea water at European coastal resorts, particularly on the shores of the Mediterranean, represents a severe health hazard. Not many popular resorts wish to admit to this, but many now realize the dangers and erect signs, albeit small ones, forbidding bathing. These signs would read as follows:

|  | **French** |
|---|---|
| No bathing | *Défense de se baigner* |
| Bathing prohibited | *Il est défendu de se baigner* |

|  | **Italian** |
|---|---|
| No bathing | *Vietato bagnàrsi* |
| Bathing prohibited | *È vietato bagnàrsi* |

|  | **Spanish** |
|---|---|
| No bathing | *Prohibido bañarse* |
| Bathing prohibited | *Se prohibe bañarse* |

**Argo-Saronic Islands**
Aegina
Moni
Hydra
Spetsai

**Balearics**
See under Majorca, Minorca, Ibiza and Formentera

**Capri**
Marina Grande
Marina Piccola

**Corfu**
Sidarion
Roda
Akra
Kassiopi
Kouloura
Nisaki
Pyrgi
Benitses
Moraitika
Mesoyi
Lefkimmi
Kavos
Aryirades
Sinarades
Pelekas
Palaiokastritsa

**Corsica**
Bastia Plage
   Plage de Toga
St-Florent
Moriani Plage
Solenzara
Porto-Vecchio
   Plage de St-Cyprien
   Plage de Palombaggia
Bonifacio
   Calalonga Plage
   Tonnara Plage
Propriano
Ajaccio
   Plage St-François

Cargèse
   Plage de Pero
   Plage de Chiuni
Porto
Calvi
Ile-Rousse

**Crete**
Khania
Rethymnon
Iráklion
Amnissos
Sitia
Ermoupolis
Aghios Nikolaos/Elounda
Ierapetra

Elounda, Crete

**Cyclades**
Andros
Tínos
Mykonos
Syros
   Posidonia
   Ermoupolis
Náxos
Ios
Santorin/Thera
Melos
Sifnos

**Cyprus (S and W)**
Larnaca
Limassol
Paphos

**Cyprus (N and E)**
Kyrenia/Girne
Famagusta/Maǧusa

Kyrenia/Girne, Cyprus

**Suha Punta beach on the Yugoslav island of Rab**

**Elba**
Portoferraio
Marciana Marina
Marina di Campo
Porto Azzurro

**Euboea**
Likhas
Loutra Aidipsou
Limni
Amarynthos
Nea Styra
Karystos
Paralia Kymis
Aghia Anna

**Formentera**
Playa d'es Pujols

**Ibiza**
Ibiza Town
San Antonio Abad
Portinatx
Cala San Vicente
Santa Eulalia del Río

**Ionian Islands**
Lefkas
Kefallinia
  Argostoli
  Vlakhata
Zákynthos
  Alyka
  Laganas
  Vasiliko

**Ischia**
Casamicciola Terme
Lacco Ameno
Forio
Barano

Cala Pí, Majorca

Paguera
Camp de Mar
San Telmo
Puerto de Sóller
Cala San Vicente
Puerto de Pollensa
Puerto de Alcudia
Ca'n Picafort
Cala Ratjada
Cala Bona
Porto Cristo
Calas de Mallorca
Porto Colom
Cala d'Or
Cala Santanyi/Cala Figuera
Colonia de Sant Jordí
Cala Pí

**Malta**
Sliema
St Julian's
St Paul's Bay
Mellieha
Marfa

**Minorca**
Mahón
Cala'n Porter
Playa de Son Bou
Santo Tomás
Cala de Santa Galdana
Ciudadela
Arenal d'en Castell

**Northern and Eastern Aegean Islands**
Thásos
Samothrace
Lemnos
Lesbos
Chios

**Rhodes**
Trianda
Rhodes Town
Faliraki
Afandou
Kharaki
Lindos
Plimiri
Apolakkia

Zarzis, Tunisia

**Jerba**
Houmt Souk
Zarzis

**Lipari Islands**
Canneto/Lipari
Vulcano
Stromboli

**Majorca**
El Arenal
Cala Mayor
Illetas
Palma Nova/Magalluf
Santa Ponsa

Sardinia – E Coast
Arbatax
La Caletta
Costa Smeralda
  Porto Cervo
  Capriccioli
  Porto Rotondo
Palau/Baia Sardinia

Sardinia – W and NW Coasts
Costa Paradiso
Santa Teresa di Gallura
Platamona Lido
Alghero
Bosa Marina
Costa Verde

Sicily – N and E Coasts
Capo Calavà
Cefalù
Lido Mortelle
Taormina
Aci Reale

Sicily – S and W Coasts
Città del Mare
Trapani
Marinella/Selinunte

Eraclea Minoa
Marina di Ragusa
Portopalo

Sporades, Northern
Skiathos
Skopelos
Skyros

Sporades, Southern
Sámos
Kalymnos
Kos

Tremiti Islands
San Domino

Yugoslav Islands
Krk
Cres
Lošinj
Rab
Pag
Murter
Brač
Hvar
Korčula
Lopud

# Information

## Cyprus

### Republic of Cyprus

**Cyprus Tourism Organisation,**
213 Regent Street,
**London** W1R 8DA;
tel. (01) 734 9822.

**Cyprus Trade Center,**
13 East 40th Street,
**New York,** NY 10016;
tel. (212) 686 6016.

**Cyprus Tourism Organization,**
18 Th. Theodotou Street,
**Nicosia;**
tel. (021) 4 33 74.

**Tourist Information Bureau,**
5 Princess de Tyras Street,
**Nicosia;**
tel. (021) 4 42 64.

**Tourist Information Bureau,**
15 Spyrou Araouzou Street,
**Limassol;**
tel. (051) 6 27 56.

**Tourist Information Bureau,**
Democratias Square,
**Larnaca;**
tel. (041) 5 43 22.

**Tourist Information Bureau,**
International Airport,
**Larnaca;**
tel. (041) 5 43 89.

**Tourist Information Bureau,**
3 Gladstone Street,
**Paphos;**
tel. (061) 3 28 41.

**Tourist Information Bureau,**
**Ayia Napa;**
tel. (046) 2 17 96.

**Tourist Information Bureau,**
**Platres;**
tel. (054) 2 13 16.

### Diplomatic missions

**British High Commission,**
Alexander Pallis Street,
P.O. Box 1978,
**Nicosia;**
tel. (021) 7 31 31–37, 4 87 41, 4 87 03, 4 83 78.

**United States Embassy,**
Therissos Street and Dositheos Street,
**Nicosia,**
tel. (021) 6 51 51–55.

**Cyprus High Commission,**
93 Park Street,
**London** W1Y 4ET;
tel. (01) 629 5350.

**Cyprus Embassy,**
2211 R Street NW,
**Washington,** DC;
tel. (202) 462 5772.

### Airlines

### Republic of Cyprus

**Cyprus Airways,**
Euston Centre,
29–31 Hampstead Road,
**London** NW1
tel. (01) 388 5411.

**Cyprus Airways,**
c/o British Airways,
100 New Street,
**Birmingham;**
tel. (021) 236 7000.

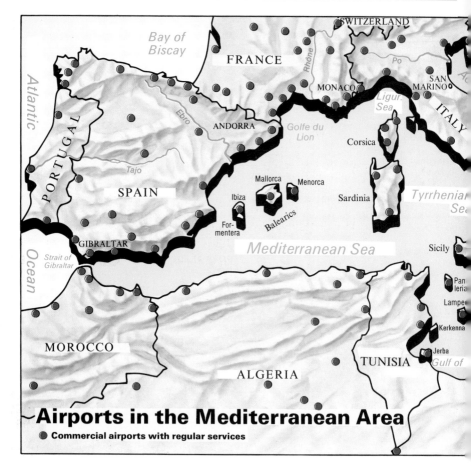

# Airports in the Mediterranean Area

● Commercial airports with regular services

**Cyprus Airways,**
c/o British Airways,
19–21 St Mary's Gate, Market Street,
**Manchester;**
tel. (061) 228 6311.

**Cyprus Airways,**
21 Athanasiou Dhiakou Street,
**Nicosia;**
tel. (021) 4 30 54.

## Turkish-occupied Cyprus

**Cyprus Turkish Airlines,**
28 Cockspur Street,
**London** SW1Y 5BN;
tel. (01) 930 4851).

## France

**French Government Tourist Office,**
178 Piccadilly,
**London** W1V 0AL;
tel. (01) 491 7622

**French Government Tourist Office,**
610 Fifth Avenue,
**New York,** NY 10021;
tel. (212) 757 1125.

**French Government Tourist Office,**
Suite 430, 645 N. Michigan Avenue,
**Chicago,** IL 60601;
tel. (312) 337 6301.

**French Government Tourist Office,**
360 Post Street,
**San Francisco,** CA 94012;
tel. (415) 986 4161.

**French Government Tourist Office,**
20 Queen Street W,
**Toronto;**
tel. (416) 593 4717.

**French Government Tourist Office,**
1840 Sherbrooke Street W,
**Montreal;**
tel. (514) 931 3855.

**Secrétariat d'Etat au Tourisme,**
8 Avenue de l'Opéra,
F-75041 **Paris;**
tel. (1) 7 66 51 35.

Within France tourist information can be obtained from *Comités régionaux de tourisme* and *Comités départementaux de tourisme* and from the **Offices de Tourisme** and *Syndicats d'Initiative* to be found in almost every town.

**Touring-Club de France** (*TCF*),
6–8 Rue Firmin-Gillot
F-75737 **Paris Cedex 15**
tel. (1) 532 2215
The TCF has branch offices in the larger French towns.

**Automobile-Club de France,**
6–8 Rue Firmin-Gillot
F-75737 **Paris Cedex 15**
tel. (1) 532 2215

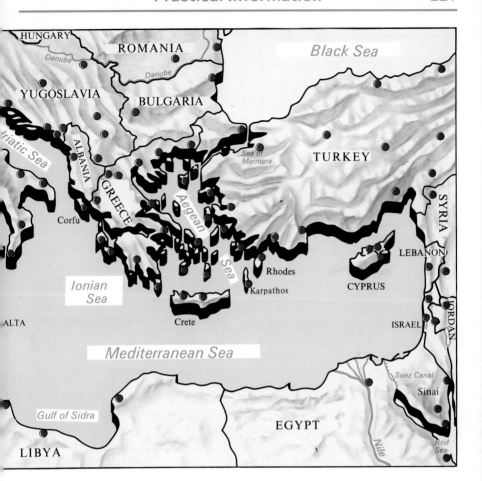

**Air France,**
158 New Bond Street,
**London** W1Y 0AY;
tel. (01) 499 9511.

**Air France,**
666 Fifth Avenue,
**New York**, NY 10019;
tel. (212) 841 7301,
reservations and information 247 0100.

**Air France,**
151 Bloor Street W,
**Toronto**;
tel. (416) 364 0101.

**Air France,**
979 de Maisonneuve Street W,
**Montreal**;
tel. (514) 284 2825.

**Air France,**
1 Square Max-Hymans,
F-75741 **Paris**;
tel. (1) 2 73 41 41.

**Air Inter,**
12 rue de Castiglione,
F-75001 **Paris**;
tel. (1) 2 61 82 84.

## Greece

**National Tourist Organization of Greece**
195–197 Regent Street,
**London** W1R 8DL;
tel. (01) 734 5997.

Olympic Tower,
645 Fifth Avenue,
**New York**, NY 10022;
tel. (212) 421 5777.

611 W. Sixth Street,
**Los Angeles**, CA 90017;
tel. (213) 626 6696.

168 N. Michigan Avenue,
**Chicago**, IL 60601;
tel. (312) 782 1084.

Suite 67, 2 Place Ville Marie,
**Montreal**;
tel. (514) 871 1535.

**Ellinikós Organismós Tourismoú** (*EOT*),
Amerikis 2,
**Athens**;
tel. (01) 3 22 31 11.

There are tourist information offices in the larger Greek towns. In smaller places information can be obtained from the **Tourist Police** (*Astynomia allodapon*), who are responsible for helping foreign visitors in Greece.

**Automobile and Touring Club of Greece**
(*ELPA*),
Mesoyion 2,
**Athens**;
tel. (01) 7 79 16 15–19.

Branch offices in the larger Greek towns, including Kerkyra (Corfu) and Iráklion and Khania in Crete.

**Greek Touring Club,**
Polytekhniou 12,
**Athens**;
tel. (01) 5 24 86 01.

**Olympic Airways,**
141 New Bond Street,
**London** W1;
tel. (01) 493 7262.

**Olympic Airways,**
649 Fifth Avenue,
**New York**, NY 10022;
tel. (212) 750 7933.

**Olympic Airways,**
Leoforos Syngrou 96,
**Athens**;
tel. (01) 92 92/1.

## Italy

**Italian State Tourist Office**
(*Ente Nazionale Italiano per il Turismo*, ENIT)
1 Princes Street,
**London** W1R 8YA;
tel. (01) 408 1254

Suite 1565, 630 Fifth Avenue,
**New York**, NY 10111;
tel. (212) 245 4822-4.

500 N. Michigan Avenue,
**Chicago**, IL 60611;
tel. (312) 644 0990-1.

Suite 801, 360 Post Street,
**San Francisco**, CA 94109;
tel. (415) 392 6206-7.

Store 56, Plaza,
3 Place Ville Marie,
**Montreal**;
tel. (514) 866 7667.

Via Marghera 2,
I-00185 **Rome**;
tel. (06) 4 95 27 51.

There are ENIT offices at the main frontier crossings into Italy and in the ports of Genoa, Livorno and Naples. Within Italy tourist information is provided by regional tourist offices (*Assessorati Regionali per il Turismo*) in regional capitals, provincial tourist offices (*Ente Provinciali per il Turismo*), spa administrations (*Aziende Autonome di Cura*) and local tourist offices (*Aziende Autonome di Soggiorno e Turismo*).

**Touring Club Italiano** (*TCI*),
Corso Italia 10,
I-20100 **Milan**;
tel. (02) 8526-1.

Branch offices in Bari, Rome and Turin.

**Automobile Club d'Italia** (*ACI*),
Via Marsala 8,
I-00185 **Rome**;
tel. (06) 49 98.

Branch offices in all provincial capitals, in major tourist centers and at the main frontier crossings.

**Alitalia,**
251–259 Regent Street,
**London** W1;
tel. (01) 734 4040.

**Alitalia,**
666 Fifth Avenue,
**New York**, NY 10111;
tel. (212) 582 8900.

**Alitalia,**
Palazzo Alitalia
Piazza Giulio Pastore
00144 **Rome**;
tel. (06) 54441

Desks at all Italian airports.

## Malta

**Malta Government Tourist Office,**
16 Kensington Square,
**London** W8 5HH;
tel. (01) 938 1712

**Malta National Tourist Organization,**
Harper Lane,
**Floriana**, Malta;
tel. 2 44 44.

**Malta Tourist Information,**
1 Citygate Arcade,
**Valletta**, Malta;
tel. 2 77 47.

**Air Malta,**
23–24 Pall Mall,
**London** SW1Y 5LP;
tel. (01) 839 5782–4, 930 2612–7.

Also at London Heathrow and Manchester Airports.

**Air Malta,**
285 Republic Street,
**Valletta**, Malta;
tel. 2 12 07, 2 68 19.

**Maltese Embassy,**
2017 Connecticut Avenue W,
**Washington**, DC;
tel. (202) 462 3611.

## Spain

**Spanish National Tourist Office**
57–58 St James's Street,
**London** SW1A 1LD;
tel. (01) 499 0901–6.

665 Fifth Avenue,
**New York**, NY 10022;
tel. (212) 759 8822.

180 N. Michigan Avenue,
**Chicago**, IL 60601;
tel. (312) 641 1842.

Suite 710, 209 Post Street,
**San Francisco**, CA 94108;
tel. (415) 986 2125.

Suite 201, 60 Bloor Street W,
**Toronto**;
tel. (416) 961 3131.

Within Spain tourist information can be obtained from *Delegaciones Provinciales de Turismo* in the provincial capitals and *Oficinas de Información de Turismo* in the larger towns.

**Real Automóvil Club de España** (*RACE*),
3 José Abascal 10
**Madrid**;
tel. (91) 4 47 32 00.

Branch offices in the larger towns.

**Autoclub Turístico Español** (*ATE*),
Calle del Marqués de Riscal 11,
**Madrid**;
tel. (91) 2 07 07 02.

**Iberia Air Lines of Spain**
Venture House (4th floor),
29 Glasshouse Street,
**London** W1R 5RG;
tel. (01) 437 9822.

565 Fifth Avenue,
**New York**;
tel. (212) 793 500, reservations and information
793 3300.

1002 Bloor Street W,
**Toronto**;
tel. (416) 964 6645, reservations and information
964 6625.

1242 Peel Street,
**Montreal**;
tel. (514) 861 7211, reservations and information
861 9531.

Calle Velázquez 130,
**Madrid**;
tel. (91) 2 61 91 00.

Desks at all Spanish airports.

## Tunisia

**Tunisian National Tourist Office**,
7A Stafford Street,
**London** W1X 4EQ;
tel. (01) 499 2234.

**Office National du Tourisme Tunisien**,
Avenue Mohammed-V,
**Tunis**;
tel. 25 91 33.

**Tunis Air**,
24 Sackville Street,
**London** W1X 1DE;
tel. (01) 734 7644–5.

**Tunis Air**,
113 Avenue de la Liberté
**Tunis**;
tel. 28 81 00.

**National Automobile Club de Tunisie**,
28 Avenue Habib-Bourguiba,
**Tunis**;
tel. 24 39 21.

**Tunisian Embassy**,
29 Princes Gate,
**London** SW7 1QG;
tel. (01) 584 8117.

**Tunisian Embassy**,
2408 Massachusetts Avenue NW,
**Washington** DC 20008;
tel. (202) 234 6644.

**Tunisian Embassy**,
515 O'Connor Street,
**Ottawa**;
tel. (613) 237 0330.

## Yugoslavia

**Yugoslav National Tourist Office**
(*Turistički Savez Jugoslavije*)
143 Regent Street,
**London** W1R 8AE;
tel. (01) 734 5243 and 439 0399.

Suite 210, Rockefeller Center,
630 Fifth Avenue,
**New York**, NY 10020;
tel. (212) 757 2801.

Dragoslava Jovanovicá 1
YU-11000 **Belgrade**;
tel. (011) 33 25 91

Within Yugoslavia information can be obtained from local **Tourist Offices** (some of which can also arrange for accommodation in private houses).

There are also a number of **travel agencies** in Yugoslavia which can make arrangements for accommodation, excursions, etc.

**Yugoslav Automobile Association**
(*Auto-Moto Savez Jugoslavije*),
Ruzveltova 18,
YU-11000 **Belgrade**;
tel. (011) 40 16 99

Branch offices in larger towns.

**Yugoslav Airlines** (*JAT*)
201 Regent Street,
**London** W1R 8AE;
tel. (01) 734 0320.

630 Fifth Avenue,
**New York**, NY 10020;
tel. (212) 1 800 223 1365 (toll-free).

20 Queen Street W,
**Toronto**;
tel. (416) 593 1600, reservations and information
593 1500.

**Shipping lines: see p. 214**

**Airports: see map on pp. 220–221**

To facilitate identification, each place-name is followed by the international distinguishing sign (as used on motor vehicles) for the country. Ancient and other historical names are assigned to the country within which the place now lies.

CY = Cyprus  
E  = Spain  
F  = France  

GR = Greece  
I  = Italy  
M  = Malta  

TN = Tunisia  
TR = Turkey  
YU = Yugoslavia